OUR FIRST REVOLUTION

OUR FIRST REVOLUTION

The Remarkable British Upheaval That Inspired

America's Founding Fathers

MICHAEL BARONE

THREE RIVERS PRESS
NEW YORK

Published in the United States by Three Rivers Press, an imprint of the
Crown Publishing Group, a division of Random House, Inc., New York.
www.crownpublishing.com

Three Rivers Press and the Tugboat design are registered trademarks
of Random House, Inc.

Originally published in hardcover in the United States by Crown Publishers,
an imprint of the Crown Publishing Group, a division of Random House, Inc.,
New York, in 2007.

Library of Congress Cataloging-in-Publication Data
Barone, Michael.
Our first revolution: the remarkable British upheaval that inspired
America's founding fathers / Michael Barone.
Includes bibliographical references and index.
1. Great Britain—History—Revolution of 1688.   2. Great Britain—
History—Revolution of 1688—Influence.   3. Great Britain—History—
1660–1714.   I. Title.
DA452.B37 2007
941.06'7—dc22   2006037007

ISBN 978-1-4000-9793-7

Printed in the United States of America

Design by Lauren Dong
Maps by David Cain

10 9 8 7 6 5 4 3 2

First Paperback Edition

Contents

Author's Note

During the seventeenth century, England and some parts of the Netherlands used the Old Style calendar, while almost all of Europe used the New Style calendar. That meant that dates were ten days earlier in England than on the Continent. Here dates of events in the British Isles are given in Old Style, those of events on the Continent in New Style. Where it may be helpful to avoid confusion, both dates are given.

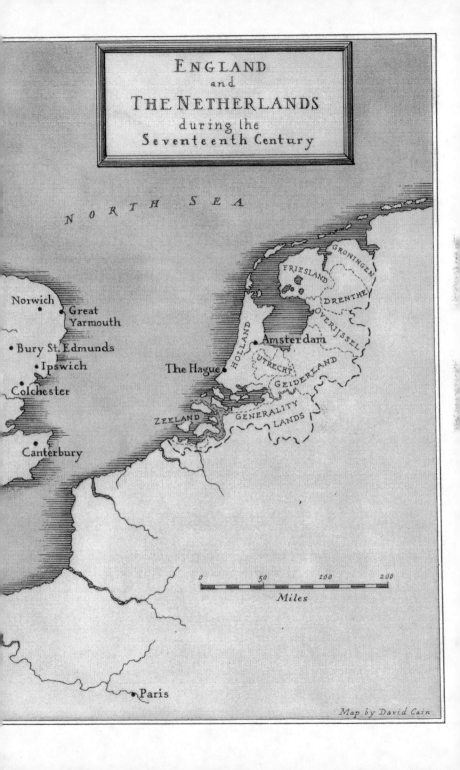

Chapter 1

THE IMPROBABLE REVOLUTION

THE FIRST REVOLUTION: what is generally known as the Glorious Revolution. In recent years Americans have been devouring books on our nation's Founding Fathers—Benjamin Franklin, George Washington, John Adams, Thomas Jefferson, Alexander Hamilton—some written by academic historians, others by gifted professional writers. As these writers help us understand, the Founders did not spring from a historical vacuum. Before the break with the Crown, they regarded themselves as Englishmen, as inheritors of the system of government and the traditional liberties of England. As they moved daringly into a revolutionary and republican future, they looked back on a heritage that was shaped by many historical events. Not least among them was what most Englishmen referred to as the Glorious Revolution of 1688–89. This term referred to the series of events that resulted in the ouster of King James II and the installation of King William III and Queen Mary II, and in changes in English law, governance, and politics that turned out to be major advances for representative government, guaranteeing liberties, global capitalism, and a foreign policy of opposing hegemonic powers on the European continent and in the world beyond.

The First Revolution, as it will be called here, was a reference point, an example, indeed a glowing example, for the American

Founders. The Founding Fathers began their rebellion not by reject-ing the achievements of the Glorious Revolution, but by arguing that Parliament and King George III were denying them their rights as Englishmen that were gained in that Revolution and the revolutionary settlement — the laws passed in 1689 and the 1690s. It is true that as the Founding Fathers created their own revolution and formed their republic, they did not fully accept the Revolutionary settlement — the set of laws and customs established during and immediately following the Glorious Revolution. The new nation would have no monarchy or titled nobility, no religious tests for public office, and no national es-tablished church. But the founders also self-consciously copied some features of the Revolutionary settlement, from yearly sessions of Con-gress to the establishment of a national bank and a funded debt to the Second Amendment right to bear arms.

The Glorious Revolution has long been recognized in Britain as a founding event that has shaped the character of the nation ever since. But this First Revolution has gotten much less attention in the United States. For much of the second half of the twentieth century, aca-demic historians in this country as well as in Britain have devoted much more attention to the events of 1641–60, events that brought to the fore radicals who could be seen as ancestors of the Marxist revolu-tionaries of the twentieth century. The Glorious Revolution was seen, in contrast, as something in the nature of a coup d'état brought off by royals and nobles, a shuffling of power between dead white males (never mind that important parts were played by Princesses Mary and Anne, Queen Mary Beatrice, and Sarah Churchill). But there is a strong argument that the events of 1641–60 were less than consequential in shaping the English polity and what would become the American in-heritance than was the Revolution of 1688–89 and the Revolutionary settlement that was worked out in the 1690s. Those changes proved to be far more enduring.

The Revolution of 1688–89 was the first change of government in England that was at the time called a revolution. Twentieth-century historians often refer to the events of 1641–60 as the English Revolu-tion,[1] but this complicated series of events — described by recent his-torians as three separate civil wars and a republican interregnum — was not called a revolution in the seventeenth century.[2] In contrast, the events of 1688–89 were the first to be widely, almost universally, labeled a revolution by contemporaries.[3]

The First Revolution was a tremendously consequential event and a tremendously improbable one. "I cannot forbear remarking," wrote the Cumberland landowner and regional political magnate Sir John Lowther in his *Memoirs of the Reign of James II,* "how wonderfullie this thing succeeded in opposition to so many visible and apparent accidents, anie one of which whereof they had happened, the whole design must certainly have miscarried."[4] It was, writes historian J. G. A. Pocock, an "amazing and unpredicted transaction,"[5] or, as the historian Paul Rahe writes, it "was by no means inevitable. It more nearly resembled a freak accident."[6] William of Orange, stadholder of the Netherlands, assembled an army variously estimated at 15,000 to 20,000 men and a flotilla of five hundred ships, crossed the English Channel in the usually wind-tossed month of November, then pushed James II to order his army to retreat without a battle. Princess Mary, William's wife, and Princess Anne cooperated in the ouster of their father, James II. It was, as Pocock continues, "a spectacular display of reason of state rising above the restraints of common morality; daughters dethroned their father, even the sanitized version of *King Lear* was hard to perform for many years, and what William of Orange and John Churchill severally did is still enough to take your breath away if you think about it."[7] Or, as the Calvinist and usually humorless William said to the Anglican clergyman Gilbert Burnet after his troops successfully landed in England, "Well, Doctor, what do you think of predestination now?"[8]

The First Revolution happened in an England and a Europe very different from today's. This mostly bloodless revolution occurred after more than a century of religious wars. In England, Henry VIII broke with the Catholic Church when denied a divorce, and in 1532 was declared the Supreme Head of the Church of England. Under Henry and his young successor Edward VI, the Church of England adopted many Protestant doctrines: the king was the Supreme Head of the Church, monasteries were closed, English translations of the Bible and an English Prayer Book were introduced.[9] Edward died at 16 and was succeeded in 1553 by his older sister Mary I, who returned England to Catholicism and executed some 300 Protestants. She died in 1558 and her Protestant sister Elizabeth I reestablished the Church of England.

Despite the established Church of England, many forms of belief persisted under Elizabeth and her successor James I (1603–25). There were Puritans, a loosely defined group who wanted to simplify Church ritual and belief, and Presbyterians, who believed that the Church should be governed by elders selected by congregations rather than by bishops selected by the king. There were, living secretly and also in the open, Catholics who remained loyal to the Church of Rome. Religious differences played an important role in the Civil War that broke out between Charles I and Parliament in 1642 and that resulted in the execution of the king in 1649. The parliamentary governments led by Oliver Cromwell and others banned Church of England clergy from preaching, ordered Catholic priests out of the kingdom, and stripped churches of ornament and paintings and broke stained-glass windows. When Charles II was restored to the throne in 1660, the Church of England was again established. But in the years since Charles I was executed, there had grown up Dissenting Protestant sects that would in time be known as Presbyterians, Congregationalists, Baptists, and Quakers. The treatment of these Dissenting Protestants and of Catholics became lively political issues in Charles II's reign and that of his brother James II (1685–88). [10]

These religious struggles in England went on simultaneously but not in close connection with the struggles between Protestantism and Catholicism in continental Europe. Martin Luther nailed his 95 Theses to the door of the church at Wittenberg in 1517 and defended his doctrines at the Diet of Worms, summoned by the young Emperor Charles V in 1521. Lutheranism and other forms of Protestantism spread in what is now Germany, Scandinavia, France, the Netherlands, Switzerland, the Czech Republic, Poland, and Hungary through much of the sixteenth century. The Peace of Augsburg of 1555 was based on the principle of *cuius regio eius religio:* the ruler of each state would determine its religion. Protestantism seemed to prevail over about half of Christian Europe.

The Catholic Church responded to this Reformation with a Counter-Reformation. The Council of Trent, concluded in 1563, reaffirmed traditional Catholic doctrine and ordered internal reforms of the Church. Counter Reformation Catholicism was characterized by a rigorous faith, elaborate ceremony with incense and inspiring music, beautifully decorated baroque churches to inspire awe and to make the Mass an emotionally moving experience. The baroque churches still found today from Rome to France and Germany, Bohemia and Poland, Spain and the Spanish and Portuguese colonies of Latin America are concrete evidence of the confidence and verve of the Counter-Reformation Catholic Church.

In different countries Catholics went on the offensive. In France, leading Protestant Huguenots were murdered in the St. Bartholomew's Day Massacre in 1572; after the Huguenot Henri IV became king in 1589, he faced civil war and converted to Catholicism, concluding, "Paris is worth a Mass." In what is now Germany, the Catholic Hapsburg Holy Roman Emperors went on the offensive in the Thirty Years' War (1618–48), and Protestantism was extirpated in what are now the Czech Republic, Slovakia, Hungary, Poland, and large parts of Germany. The treaties of Westphalia ended this conflict in 1648, recognizing the independence of states, including those within the Holy Roman Empire, and the right of their rulers to determine their religion. The United Provinces of the Netherlands, which had been fighting their Catholic Spanish overlords since 1568, were recognized as an independent Protestant nation, outside the empire. But the overall result of these religious wars was that by the late seventeenth century about two-thirds of the people of Christian Europe lived in Catholic domains and "between 1590 and 1690 the geographical reach of Protestantism shrank from one-half to one-fifth of the land area of the continent."[11] "Every observer of the contemporary scene knew that effectively the principle of *cuius regio eius religio* operated," writes the historian K. H. D. Haley. "No Catholic king ruled over a Protestant people."[12]

England and the United Provinces, the two states intimately involved in the First Revolution, were thus small Protestant outliers on the northwest fringes of a mostly Catholic continent. They were also exceptions to the trend in Europe toward stability imposed by abso-lutist governments.[13] "In 1590," writes Reformation historian Diarmaid MacCulloch, "around half of the European land-mass was under the control of Protestant governments and/or Protestant cul-ture: in 1690 the figure was only around a fifth."[14] Christian Europe, that is Europe excluding the Ottoman Empire, which came up to the gates of Vienna in 1683, had about 100 million people at the time of the Glorious Revolution. England had about 5 million,[15] its sister king-doms Scotland and Ireland about 1 and 2 million respectively. Britain's North American colonies had about 250,000. London was the one huge city in the British Isles, with 375,000 people around 1650 and 490,000 around 1700, about 10 percent of England's population. The next largest town, Norwich, had only 30,000, and there were about 60 towns with populations between 2,500 and 11,000.[16] The United Provinces of the Netherlands had 2 million people. In contrast, France was a demographic monster, with 20 million people, and there were about 18 million in the many states that now make up Germany. Spain, sapped by constant warfare and colonial overextension, had about 7.5 million and the Spanish Netherlands, approximately today's Belgium, another 1.5 million; Spain's Latin American colonies had ap-proximately 10 million, while the English North American colonies had only 280,000.[17]

France was not only the most populous nation in Europe, but by many measures the richest. Amsterdam and London had trade ties to large parts of the world, and the United Provinces and England had large navies; France could not only afford a large navy, but fielded huge armies besides. Its rich farmlands produced every nontropical crop, and its state-protected industries produced unmatched luxury goods. In the 1650s France had been preoccupied by the civil war known as the Fronde. But that was over by 1661, when Cardinal Mazarin died and the 23-year-old Louis XIV began 54 years of personal rule. Louis soon embarked on military campaigns to expand his kingdom. He started major wars in each decade. His forces were led by able generals and by the King himself on occasion; his military engineers and fortifi-cations were the best in Europe. The French army invaded the United Provinces in 1672 with 130,000 men, outnumbering the Dutch forces by four to one.[18]

Louis also sought to expand the realm of Catholicism. "Louis spurred on the Duke of Savoy," writes MacCulloch, "in his murderous campaign against his Protestant subjects: Louis overturned his grandfather's religious settlement for France by revoking the Edict of Nantes in 1685. Louis conquered largely Protestant lands of the Empire in Alsace, finally making a Catholic Strasbourg out of Martin Bucer's proud Strassburg, which long before had been the prime candidate to lead the Protestant world."[19]

Louis XIV's France, with its commitment to Catholicism and its trend toward absolutist government, seemed the wave of the future in the 1670s and 1680s. It was the largest nation-state and militarily the mightiest. Its king consolidated his power by setting aside institutions that traditionally limited royal power, like the Estates General, which did not meet from 1614 to 1789, and consigned the formerly powerful regional nobles to the ritualized court life of first the Louvre and then Versailles. Other rulers followed his example. In Bavaria and Brandenburg forceful rulers broke the power of the estates, as did the rulers of the Rhenish Palatinate and Baden. A similar process occurred in the domains of the Austrian Hapsburgs. Denmark and, a quarter-century later, Sweden developed absolutist government, while in Spain and Portugal the power of the legislative assemblies, the Cortes, was sharply curtailed.[20] Many in the smaller German states feared the trend would prevail there.[21] Republicanism was on the wane, alive in the bustling Netherlands and backward Switzerland, ailing in a declining Venice and extinct in most of the rest of Italy (with the conspicuous exception of the small city of Lucca), defunct after the Restoration in England. The forces resisting absolutism were those asserting ancient, arguably feudal, rights, and local particularity: the vestiges of the past. Absolutism, seemingly modern and efficient, seemed the way of the future.[22]

Yet in the long run absolutism did not prevail. Out of one corner of Europe, in the British Isles, an alternative emerged, constitutional monarchy with limits on government, guaranteed rights, relatively benign religious toleration, and free market global capitalism. After the Glorious Revolution the merchant class as well as the nobility successful cabined in the power of king and prince. The nobility did not totally dominate the life of society, and merchants and entrepreneurs were left free to trade and innovate.[23] And here the key event was the First Revolution, in which the Protestant stadholder of the Netherlands supplanted the Catholic king of England, Scotland, and Ireland, and ensured that those countries would continue on a course very different from that of France and its continental imitators. This First Revolution was thus a long step forward toward the kind of society we take for granted now. It provided the backdrop for the amazing growth, prosperity, and military success of eighteenth- and nineteenth-century Britain — and for the American Revolution and the even more amazing growth, prosperity, and military success of the United States.

Here is the improbable story of how it happened.

Chapter 2

THE CATHOLIC DUKE

THE KING'S CHAPEL at Whitehall Palace, London, Easter Sunday, March 30, 1673. Whitehall was then the largest palace in Europe and the center of the monarch's power from 1530 until it burned in 1698. Its nucleus was built on the Thames by Cardinal Wolsey and seized by Henry VIII and added onto; the result was a mixture of Italian, French, and even Middle Eastern motifs, decorated with fantastic beasts, acanthus sprigs and checkerboard squares, and pinnacles adorned with heraldic beasts. It ran from the Thames across King Street (now called simply Whitehall), and included a tennis court, a bowling green, and a pit for cockfighting.[1] Whitehall Palace had somewhere between 1,500 and 2,000 rooms. During the reign of Charles II, the most prominent rooms were assigned to the king and queen and the king's brother, James, Duke of York, with many others assigned to courtiers and several of the king's mistresses.

The atmosphere was far from grand: a Dutch visitor noted that the carpets were faded and stained "but would be valuable if they were clean" and that when dishes were set before the king he first "cut off heads from hares and partridges or cut off legs from fowls for [his dogs] as the readiest food, and stuck a morsel in the open jaws of every beast who then took it up with him on to a chair to gnaw."[2] "It was the unbuttoned ease, the air of summer relaxation that he brought to the monarchy, rather than his sexual license," writes the historian J. H. Plumb of Charles II, "that undermined the awe and respect of his courtiers, servants, and supporters and provided so much grist to his enemies and to those who wished to belittle the monarchy."[3]

In the king's apartments at the north end along the river was his chapel, where Charles II, his brother the Duke of York, and the court attended services.[4] There they were on display in this "teeming village of more than 1,000 inhabitants,"[5] and anything out of the ordinary that happened in services would quickly be news in this village of Whitehall and beyond. And so it became quickly known when in April 1673 the Duke of York did not take communion at Easter services.[6] This was a clear signal that he was no longer a member of the Church of England and an indication that he was a Roman Catholic.

THIS WAS A matter of the greatest moment. In a time when wars were fought over religion, when rulers routinely imposed their religious preferences on their people, the prospect of a Roman Catholic king was profoundly disturbing to the political order in all three of Charles's kingdoms, England, Scotland and Ireland.

Charles II surely knew that. He sat not very securely on the throne: his father had been beheaded in Whitehall, the very same palace from which he ruled as king, and he had spent more than a decade in exile and poverty. When Charles learned that James had converted to Catholicism, he promptly removed James's two daughters, Mary and Anne, from his care and forbade him to announce his conversion publicly.[7] Then he begged James to take the sacrament of the Established Church.

Charles was tall and dark, charming and courteous, interested in scientific experiments, the mechanics of plays and the latest performances in the reopened theaters, and active athletically into his fifties. He was also a pragmatic, cynical, tolerant man, unencumbered by any strong religious beliefs, who did not want to face an avoidable crisis.[8] As he said in a letter to a courtier, "I would have everyone live under his own vine and fig-tree. Give me my just prerogative and I will never ask for more."[9]

But James, "poor, stupid, brave James," as the historian Ronald Hutton called him,[10] was made of different stuff. He was indefatigable and forthright, he loved the military camp and reveled in risking the dangers of battle. He saw issues in simple terms — black and white, good and evil.[11] He was utterly self-confident, but often showed bad judgment, "with the easy courage of the limited mind," as the historian J. P. Kenyon put it.[12] One historian even compared him with the rigid and pious King Philip II of Spain.[13] Raised as an Anglican, and as given to womanizing as his older brother, he nonetheless took religious doctrine seriously, if only because he saw it as a mainstay of the established order.

And he and Charles had every reason to know what could happen when that order was overturned, as it had been in England in the 1640s. Charles, born in May 1630, James, born in October 1633, and their sisters lived for most of the 1630s in Richmond Palace, a dozen miles up the Thames from London and Westminster. It seems to have been an idyllic existence; certainly that is the impression given by Van Dyck's paintings of the royal children. But the idyll ended abruptly. In 1640 their father, King Charles I, faced a rebellion in Scotland; in 1642 he found himself leading an army against the army of Parliament; this was the beginning of the English Civil War. From the comforts of a peaceful palace in the countryside the two young princes and the queen were set on the move. Their mother, Queen Henrietta Maria, was sent in 1642 to The Hague, the seat of the United Provinces of the Netherlands, to join her daughter Mary, married at the age of 9 to the 14-year-old William of Orange, heir to the stadholder Frederick Henry.[14] Charles stayed by his father's side in his military headquarters in Oxford and in battle. James was sent by his father to visit the governor of Hull, where the weapons that had been used in the Scottish rebellion were stored; the governor, switching sides as so many did in those days, took the 8-year-old Duke of York prisoner for several days. Then Charles and James were nearly captured at the Battle of Edgehill in 1642.

In 1645 the 15-year-old Charles was named nominal commander of the king's forces in the West Country; when they were conclusively beaten in March 1646 he fled with his council to the Scilly Isles, in the

Atlantic Ocean southwest of England. A month later the entourage sailed to Jersey, the largest of the Channel Islands just off the French coast, then two months later traveled to a palace outside Paris where his mother had moved from the Netherlands.

In April 1646, King Charles I fled Oxford for Scotland, hoping he might get better treatment there than he could get from the English Parliament, leaving his son James behind at Oxford. In June the royal court at Oxford surrendered and James was sent back to London to live under Parliament's control. James was allowed to meet with his father after the Scots turned him over to the English. Charles I feared that Parliament, to undermine his authority, would declare James king and urged him not to accept the crown. James was determined to escape Parliament's grip; in April 1648 he crawled out of a window from St. James's Palace, rendezvoused with a royal officer in St. James's Park, and was transported, disguised as a girl, to a Thames riverboat and then to a Dutch ship that brought him to the Netherlands — quite an adventure for a 14-year-old.[15] In July 1648 his brother Charles moved to The Hague as well. They were there when they heard the news that the parliamentary army had expelled most members of Parliament in Pride's Purge in December 1648 and the new Rump Parliament ordered the king's execution in January 1649.

The two teenaged Stuart princes were now exiles in Europe. Their father was dead and their future was uncertain. They had little money; the Stuarts were not a great landowning family. Even after the restoration of Charles II it was calculated that the earls of Essex, Sunderland, and Halifax owned more land that the King.[16] The Stuarts still had supporters in England, Scotland, and Ireland, but Parliament had an army and in Oliver Cromwell a military leader who never lost a battle. Their mother, Henrietta Maria, had refuge and a small allowance from her relatives in France, but her sons mistrusted her political judgment and resented her bossiness. They relied more on their sister Mary and her husband William II, who by then had succeeded his father as stadholder and who helped to finance Charles's attempts to return to power. In July 1649 Charles went to France and in September to Jersey, hoping to sail for Ireland, but Cromwell and his army were too strong there.[17] He returned to the Netherlands to negotiate with Scottish leaders who wanted him to take the Presbyterian Covenant, a Calvinist doctrine very different from that of the Church of England—something his father had refused to do—and promised to support him as king of Scotland in return. After promising to take the Covenant if he became king, Charles arrived in Scotland in June 1650, but Cromwell marched toward Edinburgh in July and destroyed a Scottish army at Dunbar. Charles was crowned king in January 1651 and took the Covenant—an acceptance of Calvinism urged on him by his Catholic mother and one that presaged the support his Catholic brother would give Dissenters in 1687 and 1688.[18]

But Charles got into political disputes with the fractious Scots. Armies led by Cromwell and General George Monck controlled Edinburgh and Glasgow, and in desperation Charles in August 1651 marched south to England. There his outnumbered and under-supplied force was destroyed by Cromwell at Worcester in September 1651. Charles fled on foot, disguised himself as a laborer, was sheltered by Catholic gentry, and was hidden at one point in an oak tree, "an experience which he never forgot and was ready to recount in detail at the slightest encouragement in after life."[19] After five weeks he managed to get to a ship that took him to France. These experiences left a mark: ever after he was sympathetic to Catholics and antipathetic to Scots. More than once, despite Parliament's disapproval, he issued declarations of indulgence in 1662 and 1672 tolerating Catholics as well as Dissenting Protestants, although Parliament forced him to disown them.[20] And he never set foot in Scotland again.[21]

※✿※

CROMWELL'S ARMY CONTROLLED England from 1649, Scotland from 1651, and, after a brutal three-year campaign, Ireland from 1652. Stadholder William died of smallpox in November 1650, leaving power in the hands of Amsterdam merchants and Dutch politicians unsympathetic to the Stuarts and desirous of good relations with England. Cardinal Mazarin, the effective ruler of France during the childhood of Louis XIV, did not wish to antagonize Cromwell either while France remained at war with Spain, which it did until 1659, or during the Fronde rebellion of 1649–53. Neither did the Spanish, who had given up their claim to the United Provinces irrevocably in 1648 and were eager to hold on to the Spanish Netherlands. The Stuarts were not a family with ancestral lands, and much of the royal land was sold off under the Commonwealth;[22] their wealth came mainly from the Crown, and it was dissipated by confiscation of royal lands and the selling off of Charles I's art collection, "the tragic dispersal of the greatest single assemblage of Western works of art the world has ever seen," in Joseph Alsop's words.[23]

With no other viable options, the princes resorted to arms. Charles, who assumed the title of king after his father's death, lived mostly off the proceeds of privateers he sanctioned — a common way for monarchs and pretenders to make money in the seventeenth century. James fought in the French army from 1652 to 1655 under the great general Turenne (then a Protestant, who converted to Catholicism in 1668); when France made an alliance with Cromwell's regime, he went to fight with the Spanish forces in the Netherlands until 1659.[24] Charles also fought in the Spanish army in 1657 and 1658.

In the meantime the Commonwealth government established by the Rump Parliament quickly became unpopular because of the dismissal of the bishops and the old forms of worship in the Church of England, the maintenance of a standing army and high taxes to support it, and the encouragement of increasingly radical religious sects. These were popular causes with two generations of radical historians in the twentieth century, but not with the mass of the English people in the seventeenth. The Rump was replaced in December 1653 by a Protectorate, with the parliamentary forces' most successful general, Oliver Cromwell, as Lord Protector. "Oliver Cromwell's government had closed theatres, taken down maypoles and ordered shopkeepers to stay open on the superstitious feast of Christmas Day," writes Diarmaid MacCulloch. "Fatally in the late 1650s, a small number of enthusiastic army officers had been created 'Major-Generals' with charge of designated areas of the country to enforce such measures as well as to raise taxes for the army, and they were cordially loathed by most of the population."[25] Cromwell's strength and determination kept the government together, but he died in September 1658. His mild-mannered son Richard succeeded him as Lord Protector, but was forced out by the army in May 1659. The army recalled the Rump in July 1659, ousted it in October, and then restored it in December. There had been seven governments in less than twelve months.[26]

This was chaos — intolerable. "During the time men live without a common Power to keep them all in awe, they are in that condition which is called Warre; and such a warre, as is of every man, against every man," wrote Thomas Hobbes in *Leviathan*. And a bloody war it was: recent estimates are that in England 190,000 people died, 3.7 percent of its population, a higher proportion than in World War I or World War II; that in Scotland 60,000 died, 6 percent of the population, and in Ireland 660,000, an astonishing 41 percent of the population.[27] "In such condition, there is no place for Industry; because the fruit thereof is uncertain: and consequently no Culture of the Earth; no Navigation, nor use of the commodities that may be imported by Sea; no commodious Building; no Instruments of moving, and removing such things as require much force; no Knowledge of the face of the Earth; no account of Time; no Arts; no Letters; no Society; and which is worst of all, continuall feare, and danger of violent death; And the life of man, solitary, poore, nasty, brutish, and short."[28] Hobbes was not alone in taking such a dark view; the evidence suggests that most Englishmen were heartily sick of parliamentary government and were eager for the order they had come to believe could only be established by the restoration of the King.

Seizing the moment to switch sides, General Monck led his army south from Scotland to England. In January 1660, Monck arrived in London, and in February he dissolved the Rump Parliament and called for elections for a Convention (the term for a Parliament not called into being by the king). In Breda in the United Provinces, Charles in April issued a declaration promising a "free and general pardon" to those who showed "the loyalty and obedience of good subjects (except such person as shall hereafter be excepted by Parliament)," "liberty to tender consciences" and security of property as established by Parliament. "No man shall be disquieted or called into question for differences of opinion in matter of religion which do not disturb the peace of the kingdom."[29] In April the Convention met, complete with the House of Lords, and in May it voted to restore the king. On May 28,

Charles II landed in Dover and was greeted with cheers and bonfires; the next day, his 30th birthday, he was similarly greeted in London.[30] "Ordinary people flocked the streets as far as Rochester, so that the procession was seven hours in passing through the city," ran one report; there were "an infinite number of Bonfires . . . almost as many fires in the streets as houses, throughout London and Westminster," ran another.[31] There seems to be little doubt that this Restoration was generally popular.[32]

For Charles and James, the Restoration came as a piece of incredible good luck, resulting in almost no part from their own efforts. After nearly two decades of flight, exile, and impoverishment, they were now installed as King of England and Duke of York, to general popular acclaim. They seem to have taken their good fortune in different ways. Charles, almost always cheerful, seems to have been at heart a pessimist. Things could go horribly wrong, he knew from experience, and he wanted to hold on to his throne—"did not wish to go on my travels again"— more than anything else. "The King and his courtiers," writes the historian J. H. Plumb, "were haunted by the thought that they might be back in Brussels, Cologne, Paris, or Strasbourg."[33] His skepticism and his temperament led him to support broad tolerance of different religions and divergent opinions, so long as his own position was not threatened. In his Breda declaration and in the two declarations of indulgence he later issued, he expressed an inclination to religious tolerance. But he retreated from each of them at the insistence of Parliaments determined to uphold the authority of the Church of England. His foreign policy followed no steady course—he fought the Dutch in 1664–67, made an alliance with them in 1668, then allied with the French against them in 1672–73. In the 1660s he weathered one disaster after another: the London plague of 1665, the London fire of 1666, the destruction of much of the fleet at the Medway by the Dutch in 1667. He understood that his own popularity was contingent; as the crowds cheered him from Dover to London in May 1660 he remarked "that it could be nobody's fault but his own that he had stayed abroad so long when all mankind wished him so heartily at home."[34] The one cause for which he proved himself willing to take grave risks was his loyalty to family; he refused to consider divorce from his childless queen, or to push aside his brother as his successor. Primogeniture was the only reason he was king, and he would not abandon that cause.

James, in contrast, seems to have emerged into the Restoration period as an optimist. God had given his family back the throne, and He surely would help them achieve other goals. If Charles simply wanted to keep the throne, James in time became determined to advance what he had come to consider the true religion: he wanted to make England safe for Catholicism. He was willing to take grave political risks and go to a great deal of trouble to achieve his goal. But like his brother he believed in family loyalty. So long as Charles was king, James obeyed him, even when he thought his policies were grievously wrong and even when Charles sent him into exile at a time when his own succession was at risk. When he became king himself, he expected others to obey him similarly, most especially his daughters Mary and Anne. When frustrated by Parliament, he did not accede as Charles often had, but set off against great opposition on an ambitious project to produce a pliable Parliament, and his optimism prevented him from recognizing the opposition his steps were provoking at home and in the Netherlands. Charles, skeptical and aware that so much had gone wrong, was wary of risk. James, fervent in his beliefs and pleased that so much had gone right, was eager to take risks that ultimately brought him down.

In 1660 the Restoration resulted in the dissolution of the army and the reestablishment of the Church of England. Parliament restored the king's powers as they had existed in 1641: he could choose his ministers and all officers of state, command the militia, direct foreign policy, veto legislation passed by Parliament, and dispense individuals from obeying Parliamentary statutes. He was granted a revenue from taxation of some £1,200,000, which was considered generous, though it turned out to be insufficient to meet the expenses of government and court for most of the next 20 years.[35] James, at 26, was installed as Lord High Admiral of the fleet, a position he took seriously. He was also in charge of the post office and Lord Warden of the Cinque Ports, a position that gave him control of several seats in the House of Commons.[36]

The Cavalier Parliament elected in 1661, which remained in office until 1679, provided for less toleration of Presbyterians and Dissenting Protestants than Charles had promised in his declarations. The Corporation Act of 1661 limited local office to those who had taken communion in the Church of England within the past year, and Quakers were penalized in an act of 1662 for meeting in services with more than five people.[37] The Act of Uniformity of 1662 required all clergymen of the Church of England to adhere to the Thirty-nine Articles and the Book of Common Prayer, which effectively excluded Presbyterians (who disagreed with some of its doctrines and wanted the Church ruled by congregations rather than bishops) from its ranks; it also required Anglican clergymen to "declare and believe that it is not lawful upon any pretence whatsoever to take arms against the King": passive obedience. The Act of Uniformity effectively excluded Presbyterians and Dissenters from the Church of England, and Parliament in addition passed new penal laws to discourage them from maintaining their separate religious identities.[38] Under the penal laws passed during the reign of Elizabeth I, English men and women were required to attend Church of England services once a week and to take communion three times a year, with penalties including a fine of £20 a month or one-third of the income of one's estate. In addition, the Conventicle Act of 1664 fined those who attended any unofficial church service £5 for the first offense, £10 for the second, and £100 for the third. A second Conventicle Act in 1669 levied heavier fines on those who allowed their premises to be used for illegal services. The Five Mile Act of 1665 forbade any minister ejected from his church under this act from living within five miles of his former church or in any town.[39]

The hope of the framers of these laws was that they would squeeze out Nonconformity, which had been such a source of rebellion and disorder in the 1640s and 1650s, and pressure all Protestants to come within the state-sustaining enclosure of the Church of England, whose preachings of passive obedience would preserve the public order.[40] The established Church provided a means for the regime to communicate directly with the people. To complete the state monopoly of the sources of information, Parliament in 1662 passed the Licensing Act, requiring that state censors approve material before it could be printed.[41] But the penal laws were spottily enforced and failed to snuff out Presbyterianism and Dissent,[42] while the Licensing Act was unsuccessful in limiting the printing of inflammatory material.

JAMES AND CHARLES were both unmarried in 1660, and thoroughly promiscuous; Charles's first illegitimate child, James, Duke of Monmouth, had been born in 1649 when Charles was not yet 20. But in love as in politics, the brothers differed. James married impulsively and against political interest; Charles obtained a bride after careful consideration and to apparent political advantage. He married Catherine of Braganza, a Portuguese princess, in 1662, after lengthy negotiations; she brought with her in her dowry the territories of Tangier, in northern Morocco near the Straits of Gibraltar, and Bombay in India, plus trading privileges in Portuguese colonies in Brazil and the East Indies and £330,000. "A match made for money," writes the historian Mark Kishlansky.[43] Charles fathered 14 illegitimate children and maintained royal mistresses in splendor[44]—"God would not make a man miserable only for taking a little pleasure out of the way," he once said[45]—but he produced no legitimate heir; Catherine's three pregnancies ended in miscarriages.[46]

James had married earlier. In 1656, while in exile, he met Anne Hyde, daughter of Lawrence Hyde, an adviser to Charles since 1645[47] and later, as Earl of Clarendon, his chief minister from 1660 until 1667. In 1659 James promised to marry Anne; in spring 1660 she became pregnant; they were married secretly in September 1660. Charles had resisted the marriage, and James's mother, Henrietta Maria, was strongly opposed to her second son's marriage to a commoner. After a son was born, James tried to abjure the marriage, but Charles would have none of that, and in December 1660 James publicly acknowledged the marriage. Despite James's frequent infidelities the marriage proved successful, and Anne, intelligent and shrewd, managed James's finances and influenced his political activities to the point that Samuel Pepys, Clerk of Acts in the Navy Board, wrote in his secret diary, "The Duke of York, in all things but his codpiece, is led by the nose by his wife." Anne produced seven children in 11 years, of whom two,

Princesses Mary and Anne, survived early childhood: each would become Queen of England, Scotland, and Ireland.[48] But Anne Hyde would not: she grew grotesquely fat and died of breast cancer in March 1671 at 34.[49]

Charles was indolent and pacific; James was active and bellicose. Neither came to power with any firm ideas about foreign policy. In exile they had been bit players in the drama of conflict between what turned out to be a declining Spain and a rising France; both were aware that England's chief commercial and naval rivals were the Dutch. In 1659 France and Spain finally made peace after long hostilities, and Charles, aware of his good luck in having gained the throne without much effort on his own part, went not in search of battle. James was made of different stuff. As his father-in-law Clarendon later wrote, "Having been even from his childhood in the command of armies and in his nature inclined to the most difficult and dangerous enterprises, he was already weary of having so little to do and too impatiently longed for any war, in which he knew he could not but have the chief command."[50] Nor was James's vision limited to the fields of battle he knew firsthand in England, France, and the Netherlands. Always partial to France, he was hostile to the republican Netherlands and jealous of its worldwide trade.

James kept a close eye on England's North American and Caribbean colonies, and in the early 1660s he and others prepared plans to seize Dutch settlements on the Atlantic Ocean and to establish an English slave trade to North America. English sailors seized Dutch slave trading posts in the Cape Verde Islands and on the Guinea coast. In March 1664, Charles signed a charter assigning a vast stretch of North America to James — in contravention of the charter he had issued to Governor John Winthrop of Connecticut in 1660. In April 1664, James sent Richard Nicolls, a soldier who had been in exile with him, with four ships and 450 men to take over the Dutch West India Company settlement of Nieuw Amsterdam. The local commander, Peter Stuyvesant, wanted to resist, but the townsmen were happy to surrender, particularly because Nicolls promised religious tolerance to the heterogeneous settlers. Nieuw Amsterdam surrendered, and the town and the colony were named for James — New York: America's greatest city was named for the 30-year-old duke.[51] The Dutch wanted it back, but in the treaty after the war they agreed to leave New York to England in return for the formerly British island of Run in the East Indies, the world's major source of nutmeg.[52] James had connected England's New England and Chesapeake Bay colonies and established New York as an English city—achievements essential to the establishment of the United States as we know it.

Not surprisingly, a general war with the Dutch followed in 1665. James took personal command of the fleet and, showing great bravery, won a major victory in the North Sea off Lowestoft. But his wife, brother, and mother persuaded him not to risk his life in battle again. His interest in the war faded; in 1667, against his advice, the fleet was kept in the Thames Estuary and the Dutch fleet broke the chain across the river at Chatham and captured the *Royal Charles* and set fire to many other ships at Medway. Charles sued for peace and dismissed Clarendon from office.[53] The dismissal of his father-in-law undermined James's position, and over the next three years some of Charles's courtiers argued that he should either divorce the queen in order to remarry and produce a legitimate heir, or declare the Duke of Monmouth legitimate. Both would have the effect of removing James from his position as heir to the throne. Charles, then and later, proved obdurately unwilling to abandon his wife or his brother.

It was during this period, evidently by early 1669, that James decided to become a Catholic.[54] One reason it may not have seemed as unusual a choice to him as it did to most Englishmen was that James was surrounded by Catholics: his mother, Queen Henrietta Maria, was Catholic, as were Charles's Queen Catherine of Braganza and two of Charles's mistresses, Barbara Palmer, Duchess of Cleveland, and Louise de Kerouaille, Duchess of Portsmouth.[55] In early 1669, James's wife, Anne, became a Catholic also, even though her father, Clarendon, was a staunch upholder of the Church of England.[56] James's conversion was evidently a matter of conviction. Unlike Charles, he took religion seriously, and had been very much a High Anglican, tutored by an acolyte of William Laud, Charles I's Archbishop of Canterbury, who had been beheaded in the Civil War. High Anglicans called services Mass and regarded their creed as much like Catholicism. A more direct and less cynical man than his brother, he thought through the theological arguments and decided that there was no justification for the Reformation. He noted that the Church of England claimed authority because of the apostolic succession transmitted through generations of bishops. But that raised a question. "How, he wondered, could the Church of England condemn the [Protestant non-Anglican] sects for denying its authority and separating from it when it had itself separated from the Catholic Church?"[57] Catholicism was the one and true Christian faith, he decided, and so he would embrace it.

Another Catholic in the Stuart family was Charles's favorite sister, Henriette-Anne, whom he called Minette. She was the wife of Louis XIV's brother, the Duke of Orleans.[58] In May 1670, Minette sailed across the English Channel to Dover, where she and a French party of more than 200 met with Charles, James, and Charles's entire court.[59] The occasion was to celebrate the king's 40th birthday—and the 10th anniversary of the day he arrived in Dover to be restored to the throne—but there was also serious business. There Charles, James, and four of the king's ministers settled with the French ambassadors the terms of a treaty they had been negotiating for months with Louis XIV, Charles and James's first cousin (Henrietta Maria was the sister of Louis XIII and the daughter of Henry IV).

Charles and Louis had met in 1646, when Charles was a strapping, tall 16-year-old refugee from the English Civil War and Louis was the diminutive 8-year-old King of France. Now, in Dover, Charles agreed to join Louis in a war on the Dutch Republic by sending 40 ships and 4,000 troops. In return, Louis would pay Charles an annual subsidy of £230,000. Also, for reasons that have never been understood, Charles agreed that he and James would publicly convert to Catholicism when it was expedient; at that point Louis would pay another £150,000. The treaty did not say whether the war or the conversion should come first, and Minette was unable to pin Charles down on the timing of the conversion. The terms of the treaty were kept secret and, astonishingly, remained unknown to the public until 1830.[60] To Charles's sorrow, Minette died, apparently of peritonitis (there were rumors she was poisoned), three weeks after their happy meeting in Dover.[61] The Treaty of Dover marked a sharp shift in Charles's foreign policy, one that is hard to explain by geopolitical interest—except for England's commercial and naval rivalry with the Dutch—and may have been more an act of family solidarity.

Pursuant to the Treaty of Dover, England joined France in its war on the Dutch in March 1672. That war produced near disaster for the Dutch, as the French army swept through German lands and occupied most of the land of the Dutch Republic. The Dutch responded by appointing the 21-year-old William of Orange, Charles and James's nephew, as commander of the army; he promised to "die in the last ditch" and ordered the opening of the dikes; the flooding kept the French out of Amsterdam and The Hague. England was not successful at sea. In July, James led the fleet in search of the Dutch fleet, but it refused battle and the ships returned to port in August.[62]

When Parliament met in February 1673, for the first time in nearly two years, the House of Commons refused to provide funds needed for the fleet to sail unless Charles revoked the Declaration of Indulgence he had issued in March 1672; this declaration suspended penal laws against those worshiping outside the Church of England and allowed those in prison to be released after paying fees, allowed Dissenting Protestants to worship in churches and required that they be licensed, and allowed Catholics to pray in private houses.[63] The king needed money from Parliament for the fleet. Both the Commons and the Lords were opposed to allowing the king to suspend a penal law, and in the year the indulgence was in force, some 1,500 Dissenting ministers and chapels were licensed—a source of alarm to backers of the established Church.[64] Charles soon capitulated, and tore the seal from the declaration and broke it.[65]

In March 1673, Parliament also passed the Test Act, requiring public officials to take communion in the Church of England and swear an oath of allegiance denouncing the Catholic doctrine of transubstantiation, which holds that the blood and body of Christ are literally taken in the Eucharist. This would disqualify James and other Catholics from public office. There were signs that Charles supported the measure, and no sign that he thought it would lead to a regime crisis: perhaps he thought that James would take the oath in order to retain office. Or perhaps he needed the money for war so badly and hoped that military success would overcome any problems.[66] Or perhaps he thought he could command James to take the oath; as Antonia Fraser writes, "Charles respected his brother but he did not fear him. He had been the senior partner all their lives."[67] But the Test Act, and James's response to it, would precipitate a political crisis that lasted for the next 15 years and was only resolved by the Revolution of 1688–89.

THE 1673 SESSION of Parliament ended on Easter Saturday, and the following day John Evelyn heard the sermon at the king's chapel and "staied to see whether, according to custom, the Duke of York received the communion with the King; but he did not, to the amazement of every body." Coming immediately after the Test Act, this "gave exceeding grief and scandal to the whole nation, that the heir of it, and the son of a martyr for the Protestant religion, should apostatize. What the consequence of this will be, God only knows, and wise men dread."[68] In June, just before the deadline set by the Test Act, James resigned the offices he held, including his cherished position as Lord High Admiral (though he retained that position in the empire outside England).[69] As one gentleman wrote another, "Great is the talk of the town on these sudden alterations, especially of his royal highness's laying down. . . . The generality of people being so bold as to say he must not think to have the favour of England if he professes openly a Roman Catholic; nay, further, that his majesty must not make him commander of his forces, which is of great moment, etc., with many other such rude and barbarous talk."[70]

Then in September James married again—just before Parliament, which might have forbidden the marriage, was to meet in October. His first impulse after Anne Hyde died was to marry for love, but the practical Charles would have none of that: James must have a European bride who would bring a dowry and political advantages. Negotiations were begun for the hand of an Austrian archduchess; this would improve relations with the Austrian and Spanish Habsburgs. Then, in 1673, Holy Roman Emperor Leopold I's wife died, and he announced he would marry the archduchess himself. With no French princesses available, James's agents shopped around for a match with a French ally who could bring a dowry from Louis; James insisted on a beautiful wife, though Charles said one could get used to any face in a week. In July, Louis XIV offered two princesses of Modena, and James chose the 15-year-old Mary Beatrice, who had wanted to enter a convent. The marriage was performed by proxy in September, and Mary Beatrice set off for England. The needed dispensations from the pope—a political enemy of Louis XIV, who wanted to control the Catholic Church in France—were not obtained until 1676.[71] But by September 1673, James's open Catholicism and his second marriage raised the gravest questions. He was the heir to the throne and, with a 15-year-old wife, might very well produce a male heir who would take precedence over his two Protestant daughters. England seemed likely to have a Catholic king and a Catholic dynasty for the foreseeable future.

The issue of James's Catholicism and his marriage to a Catholic princess dominated English politics for the next 15 years, though James never seemed to understand the problem. As his biographer John Miller observes, "To James the transition from Anglicanism to Catholicism had been so easy and natural that he could not understand why others should not find it easy and natural."[72] But most Englishmen did not find it easy or natural at all. Their hostility to Catholicism at that time can hardly be overstated.[73] "Popery is such a thing as cannot, but for want of a word to express it, be called a religion," wrote Andrew Marvell, poet and member of Parliament, "nor is it to be mentioned with that civility which is otherwise decent to be used in speaking about the differences of human opinion about divine matters."[74] The memory of the persecution and execution of nearly 300 Protestants during the reign of Mary I (1553–58) was kept alive by John Foxe's *Actes and Monuments of these Latter Days,* known popularly as *Foxe's Martyrs,* a perennial best seller second only to the Bible.

Well known also were Catholic attempts to kill the monarch: the Ridolfi Plot of 1571, the Throckmorton and Babington assassination attempts in the 1580s, the Gunpowder Plot of 1605, in which Guy Fawkes and other conspirators came close to blowing up the Houses of Parliament and which was remembered every year (as it still is) on

November 5, Guy Fawkes Day. English Protestants were horrified when the "Winter King" of Bohemia, Frederick the Elector Palatine, and his wife, James I's daughter Elizabeth, were driven into exile by the forces of the Catholic emperor Ferdinand II in 1619; there were demands that England go to war to restore them.[75] The fear of Catholics did not abate over the years. It was also widely believed that the London fire of 1666 was set by Catholics. A stone erected at 25 Pudding Lane, just north of London Bridge, where the fire was thought to have broken out, read: "Here by ye permission of Heaven, Hell broke loose upon this Protestant city from the malicious hearts of barbarous Papists, by ye hand of their agent Hubert, who confessed, and on ye ruines of this place declared the fact, for which he was hanged (vizt) that here began that dredful fire, which is described and perpetuated on and by the neighbouring pillar." The monument nearby blamed the fire on "the treachery and malice of the Popish Faction . . . in order to the carrying on their horrid plot for extirpating the Protestant religion and old English liberty and introducing Popery and slavery." [76]

There were also continued suspicions about the true religion of the royal family. Charles I and Charles II both married Catholics, and their queens maintained Catholic priests and attendants in Whitehall Palace. In the early 1640s there had been fears that Charles I in his struggle with Parliament would make common cause with Irish Catholics. Charles II spent much of his exile at Catholic courts in Paris and Brussels, and both he and James fought with Catholic armies. The fears of Catholic domination were great enough that the Restoration Parliament felt it advisable to pass a law making it a serious offense to "publish or affirm the King to be an heretic or papist, or that he endeavours to introduce popery."[77] Catholics apparently made up only 2 percent of the population, but they were more heavily concentrated among the households of the nobility and gentry; the second Test Act of 1678 may have excluded 20 percent of the peers from taking their seats in the House of Lords.[78]

There were harsh laws against Catholics. The penal laws passed during the reign of Elizabeth I made it high treason to convert someone to Catholicism and a felony to be a convert oneself or to attend mass. Catholic priests were subject to the death penalty. The oaths of allegiance and supremacy, dating from 1559 and 1606, required central and local officeholders to acknowledge the monarch as head of the Church of England and to deny the pope's right to depose kings (Pope Pius V issued a papal bull in 1570 deposing Elizabeth I and absolving her subjects of allegiance; it has never been repealed).[79]

Still some Englishmen remained Catholics, and the anti-Catholic laws were mostly not enforced. Local justices of the peace and sheriffs were reluctant to enforce the laws against friends and neighbors. Only the exclusion of Catholics from local public office was effectively, though not always, enforced.[80] In everyday life Catholicism did not seem a vibrant threat to most Englishmen. Yet they had little doubt that Catholics would, if they could, trample on English liberties. Catholic Spain attempted to invade England in 1588; Catholics attempted to blow up Parliament in 1605; Catholic France was now the greatest power in Europe, looming just over the Channel. Englishmen could observe that in most of Europe the principle of *cuius regio eius religio* operated: the religion of the monarch became the religion of the people.

The prospect of the Duke of York's accession to the throne may have seemed distant: in March 1673, Charles was just 42 and in apparently excellent health—more robust, it seemed, than his younger brother; James might never be king at all. But Charles had no legitimate children, death often came suddenly in the seventeenth century, and James was younger (and would outlive his brother by 16 years).

On Guy Fawkes Day in November, John Evelyn wrote in his diary, "This night the youths of the City burnt the Pope in effigy, after they had made procession with it in great triumph, they being displeased at the Duke for altering his religion, and marrying an Italian lady."[81] Most Englishmen may have been willing to tolerate Catholic neighbors, but many were not ready to tolerate a Catholic king.

Chapter 3

※

YOUNG
REVOLUTIONARIES

THE BINNENHOF, THE Hague, April 19, 1678. The Binnenhof, "a peculiar jumble of medieval remains, Renaissance invention and contemporary improvisation,"[1] was the center of government of the United Provinces of the Netherlands, located in the small city of The Hague, some 30 miles south of Amsterdam, north of the northernmost branch of the Rhine River and just inland from the sand dunes on the North Sea. Unlike Amsterdam, the great metropolis, The Hague was always a seat of government, the homes of the counts Holland, the States General, and the elected stadholders of the United Provinces. It turned its back to the sand dunes and the sea; the canals were less prominent than the Vijver, in whose still waters visitors could see a serene reflection of the Binnenhof, its Gothic spires just rising over the newer outbuildings. Here, in the Gothic hall built by Count William of Holland in 1249,[2] had met since 1583 the States General, the representative assembly of the seven states — Holland, Zeeland, Utrecht, Gelderland, Overijssel, Friesland, Groningen — that made up the United Provinces.[3] At the center of the Binnenhof was the Gothic Ridderzaal, with its cobblestone courtyard flanked by wings and outbuildings with pierced arches. On one side is the Vijver, a small lake whose waters flowed into defensive ditches, a vestige of the moat that had once surrounded the castle.

Here were the offices of Prince William of Orange, stadholder of the Netherlands for the previous six years and therefore captain-general of the army and admiral-general of the navy. And here on April 19 he met with John Churchill, a representative of King Charles II and his brother, James, to discuss the terms on which England would join the United Provinces in their war against France.[4] Ten years later Prince William and Churchill, two brave and daring men, would play critical parts in the Revolution of 1688–89. But in 1678, these two 27-year-old men were meeting to discuss matters of war and peace at the Binnenhof.

The Hague and the Binnenhof, like London and Whitehall Palace, had a far from serene history. It was here that the States General abjured the allegiance to Philip II of Spain in 1581, here that the 72-year-old Advocate Johan van Oldebarneveldt was executed in 1619 on the order of the States General at the behest of the stadholder Maurits of Orange, here that six regents from the state of Holland who wanted to reduce the standing army were arrested by stadholder William II in July 1650.[5]

The United Provinces was a country unlike any other, the richest part of Europe by some measures, unusually tolerant of different religions and beliefs,[6] a republic governed under an elaborate and often disputed set of rules. Dutch traders, building on their near monopoly of the trade in North Sea herring—the Great Fishery—dominated the Baltic trade in lumber, naval stores, and grain; the trade in Spanish wool and dyestuff exports; the Italian and Levant "rich trades," the trade in spices with the Dutch East Indies and Ceylon, the limited trade with Japan (only Dutch traders were allowed there after 1641); and the slave trade between Africa and the Spanish, Portuguese, Dutch, and British colonies in the Americas. In 1650 three-fourths of the seagoing trade of Europe was carried by Dutch ships.[7] In 1670, Dutch ships carried more cargo than those of Spanish, Portuguese, French, English, Scottish, and German ships put together, and 10 percent of the United Provinces's adult males were sailors.[8] Amsterdam had commercial control over key raw materials including Spanish wool, Turkish mohair, Spanish-American dyestuffs, Dalmatian mercury, Caribbean sugar, and East Indian pepper and cinnamon.[9] The

Dutch also produced exports marketed by their merchants—high-quality silks, cottons and linens, Delftware, tile, paper, tobacco, sail canvas, pipes.[10] They imported marble from Italy; it was in Amsterdam that Louis XIV bought the marble for his palace in Versailles.[11]

Around the beginning of the seventeenth century the Dutch established the Bank of Amsterdam—modeled on the central banks that made Venice and Florence continental powers—the Amsterdam Bourse, commodities markets, a market in maritime insurance, and a low-interest national debt. All these made Amsterdam the world's premier finance center.[12] The Dutch Republic developed a national debt, and after 1655 it could borrow at only 4 percent—far lower interest than other governments had to pay.[13] In contrast, the English government had to borrow at much higher interest, and London as yet had no central bank, no insurance exchange, no established stock market or commodities markets.

By 1672 the United Provinces had 2 million people, with 200,000 in Amsterdam, 72,000 in Leiden, 50,000 in Haarlem, 45,000 in Rotterdam, and 30,000 in The Hague: the most urbanized country in Europe.[14] But all this success and this concentration were precarious. "There was something special about the Dutch situation—its fortune and its predicament—that did set it apart from other states and nations in baroque Europe," Simon Schama writes. "That something was its precocity. It had become a world empire in two generations; the most formidable economic power stretched across the globe from Van Diemen's Land [Tasmania] to Novaya Zemlya [in the Russian Arctic Sea]. But the Dutch were claustrophobic circumnavigators. All that power and stupendous wealth was, in the end, sucked into the cramped space between the Scheldt and the Ems: the swarming *bijenkorf* (beehive) of two million. The prodigious quality of their success went to their heads, but it also made them a bit queasy. Even their most uninhibited documents of self-congratulation are haunted by the threat of *overvloed,* the surfeit that rose like a cresting flood—a word heavy with warning as well as euphoria."[15]

The government of the United Provinces was a combination of a representative republic and a federal state, "an intricate cross between confederacy and federal state in which one province, Holland, presided over the others,"[16] in the words of the historian Jonathan

Israel. It was formed on a makeshift basis in the years after the United Provinces rebelled against the rule of Spain in 1567. Its founding document was the Union of Utrecht, set out in 1579 as a temporary expedient, which established the States General that met daily from 1593.[17] Members of the States General were selected by members of the assemblies (confusingly also called states) of the seven provinces, who were in turn selected by representative assemblies from the various towns. Public office in the towns, the seven states, and the States General was held by members of the regent class—a few nobles, but mostly rich merchants and professionals, those who had made fortunes and those who inherited them.

The state of Holland, which included Amsterdam, Leiden, Haarlem, Rotterdam, and The Hague, had almost half the United Provinces' population[18] and produced even a larger share of its income and wealth.[19] As a practical matter, the United Provinces needed the support of Holland and of Amsterdam to pay for its navy and army.[20] And yet Holland was only one of the seven states represented in the States General, and was by no means always dominant. Members of the States General were supposed to support only measures that had been approved by the assemblies of the seven states, which were selected by the local officials of the various towns, under a bewildering variety of rules. Writes William III's biographer Stephen Baxter, "The Republic, like Poland, had a *liberum veto;* any town could block a decision of one province, any one province that of the States General. Like Poland, it would pay a terrible price for its liberty."[21]

The representatives of each state often returned home for instructions, and in each state representatives often went back to their towns, all of which made decision-making difficult and time-consuming.[22] The seven states did not even agree on the calendar: Holland and Zeeland adopted the New Style Gregorian calendar in 1582; the other states did not follow suit until 1700, so in Amsterdam the date was ten days later than in Groningen.[23] "It was certainly not the most efficient of constitutions," the historian K. H. D. Haley writes. "Although in many other respects the Dutch found imitators, there was never any possibility that anyone would wish to copy their political institutions."[24]

The stadholder was thus the chief executive of the Dutch Republic, appointed for life, but still subject to the orders of the States General. "The office of stadholder was in no way comparable with that of the royal dynasties of baroque Europe, justified by divine unction and armed with absolute power."[25] And each state could also appoint a stadholder, with power over its local military forces. Often, but not always, the stadholder of the Republic was a member of the House of Orange, princes of the independent town of Orange on the Rhone River just north of Avignon. The most famous prince of Orange, William the Silent, had led the Dutch revolt against the Spanish in the 1570s and 1580s. But in Friesland, the northeast corner of the United Provinces, the stadholdership became hereditary in the House of Orange-Nassau, cousins of the Oranges. And each state and town also elected an administrative official, the pensionary. Through most of the seventeenth century, there were persistent tensions between the States General and the State of Holland, between the Amsterdam merchants and adherents of the House of Orange. The States General and the Orangists tended to favor a strict form of Calvinism, with a ban, seldom enforced, on public Catholic worship; Amsterdam and Holland tended to favor a less stringent form of Calvinism, and tolerance of Catholics and even Jews.[26]

The Orangists and the States General, more fearful of threats to Protestantism and their territory, tended to favor military preparedness and military action against Spain until the 1650s and against France thereafter; Amersterdam and Holland from the 1640s, more eager to see trade flourished unhampered by war, tended to favor lower military spending and more emphasis on seeking peace through diplomacy.[27] The Orangists argued that sovereignty lay with the United Provinces as a whole; Amsterdam insisted that it lay with each of the seven states, which in practice would usually mean with Amsterdam.[28]

Although places in government could be held only by members of the state Calvinist Church, other religions were tolerated, to the point that the United Provinces was a "land of religious minorities," with many Catholics, who were a majority in the Generality lands of North Brabant (which were not part of any of the seven states), many Protestants of all stripes, and among Europe's largest number of Jews.[29] As the English ambassador William Temple wrote in 1672, "It is hardly to be imagined, how all the violence and sharpness, which accompanies the differences of religion in other countries, seems to be appeased or softened here, by the general freedom which all men enjoy, either by allowance or contrivance."[30] Religious and political differences were aired in *coranto* newsletters and in pamphlets that were widely distributed; there was little censorship and a lively adversarial media.[31] At a time when printing presses were carefully controlled by governments in most countries, the Dutch Republic had the biggest concentration of printing presses in Europe, almost entirely unrestricted; Dutch *corantos* circulated from 1618; more than 10,000 pamphlets are known to have been published between 1579 and 1713.[32] Thanks to their type foundry and papermaking industries, the Dutch could print large quantities — 10,000 or more — of broadsides, pamphlets, and books, not only in Dutch, but also in French, English, German, Czech, Hebrew, and Armenian.[33] The United Provinces were the center of free intellectual thought in Europe, the place where philosophers like Descartes and Pascal and Spinoza lived and wrote: the center of new media for the entire continent. Dutch tolerance and freedom were not so much the product of philosophers as they were of a practical accommodation necessary to holding together a small nation often threatened by the greatest powers of Europe — and to leave its people free to make money. British and American freedoms have their roots mainly in English law and tradition, but in the late seventeenth century they were also nourished by the example and assistance of the Dutch.

THE WILLIAM OF Orange who met John Churchill in The Hague in 1678 was a posthumous child; his father William II died suddenly of smallpox a few days before William III's birth in November 1650. From that time until the French invasion of the United Provinces in April 1672, there was no stadholder; the Dutch were not about to elect an infant or a child as their captain-general and admiral-general. In those years the States General and the Amsterdam merchants tended to prevail, and the guiding force in government was Johan de Witt,

Grand Pensionary of Holland from 1653. De Witt was willing to fight naval wars with the English in 1652–55 and 1665–67 in protest of the Navigation Acts that closed English home and colonial markets; he recognized as well that the most dangerous enemy of the Dutch on land was no longer Spain, which had recognized the independence of the United Provinces in 1648, but the much larger and richer France. In 1668, de Witt got the United Provinces to sign a treaty with England as a protection against France. This antagonized the young French king Louis XIV, but the Dutch failed to build up the military forces needed to repel a French invasion.

William III was heir to considerable lands and to a tradition of Dutch leadership. The Orange family owned the city of Orange (until Louis XIV seized it)[34] and extensive lands in France, Burgundy, the Spanish Netherlands, and the United Provinces.[35] But William's grandmother's demand that he be elected stadholder was a non-starter.[36] William's mother, Mary, and his grandmother and uncle, Amalia of Solms-Braunfels and Frederik Willem of Friesland, tried to advance his interests but quarreled among themselves and none had good political instincts. The state of Holland, partly to please Cromwell's government in England after the first Dutch war, passed a law permanently excluding William's appointment as stadholder and another opposing his appointment as captain-general of the United Provinces if he were appointed stadholder of another state. In 1662 the States of Holland and Zeeland prohibited the appointment of William to any office for six years, and in 1667 they passed a Perpetual Edict abolishing the office of stadholder of Holland and declaring that no captain-general of the United Provinces could be appointed stadholder of any state.[37] The Perpetual Edict seemed to preclude William's election at least until he turned twenty-two, the time when the edict stated that he could be appointed captain-general.

William was raised by Orange family servants, led by Frederik van Nassau-Zuylestein, an illegitimate son of William's grandfather. His education included some English tutors until his mother's death in 1660, and he was steeped in his family heritage and trained for a military career.[38] As a result, wrote one amateur historian, "the boy, isolated, unhappy, strictly trained, cherishing a bitter sense of wrong, showed remarkable signs of intellectual precocity, which impressed all who met him, and an extraordinary firmness of character, which raised very high the expectations of his numerous adherents."[39] That firmness of character seems to have exhibited itself as haughtiness and taciturnity to some, as cautious reticence and careful self-control to others.[40]

Just as he must have become aware of his family's great heritage, he must have realized that it made him a target of its enemies and critics, and he evidently became careful not to betray his own feelings and goals. "The Prince was almost never to show his personal feelings," wrote Stephen Baxter. "He had a bad temper and could lose it in private. In public, however, he kept his temper better than most of the men of his day. Sometimes, on large matters, he remembered grievances and took his revenge at the appropriate time. Often he simply forgot them."[41] To many, William seemed cold and reserved, with "forbidding lethargic manners"[42] and a "sullen, misanthropic temperament."[43] He was short and unattractive, hunchbacked and hooknosed, with a rasping cough,[44] and poorly dressed.[45] He was evidently not given to small talk, and was impatient with court socializing.[46] He was on frank and intimate terms throughout his lifetime with only a few men, most of whom he had known from boyhood—Zuylestein; Willem van Bentinck, son of a military officer from Overijssel who had been a page to William and had accompanied him on his first trips to England in 1670 and 1677; Henrijk Tracejectinus, Count von Solms-Braunfels, his uncle and captain of his personal guard; Everaard van Weede von Dijkvelt, from the landowning class of Utrecht, a supporter of the de Witt regime who came to William's side in the war of 1672–78; and Gaspar Fagel, Grand Pensionary of the state of Holland, who after 1672 became one of William's chief allies until his death in December 1688.[47]

In 1666 Johan de Witt removed the 15-year-old William's servants and began to supervise the young man's upbringing himself. He tried to indoctrinate him in republican principles, but he also tutored him in political negotiations, setting daily exercises in solving problems of political negotiation—a fine training for dealing with the complexities of Dutch politics.[48] In the same years William became the effective head of the Orangist party. In 1668, two months before he turned 18, he accepted the old family position as First Noble of Zeeland; since he owned two of the six towns with a vote in the assembly of Zeeland and as first noble had a vote himself, he had effective control of one of the seven states.[49] In May 1670, under a provision of the Perpetual Edict, he got a seat on the Council of State with the traditional family prerogative of casting the final vote. He also kept an eye on events in England, where he stood fourth in line to the throne, behind James, Duke of York, and James's two daughters. He made a visit to London from November 1670 to February 1671, trying to collect a debt from Charles II and meeting his future wife, Mary, who was then eight years old.

By the middle of 1671 it was apparent that the French and English were preparing to wage war on the United Provinces. There was a widespread demand that William be appointed captain-general, though the Perpetual Edict barred such an appointment until he turned 22, in November 1672. In December 1671 six of the states were prepared to offer William the traditional Orange position of captain-general for life, but Holland would agree only to an appointment for one year, with many limitations. William refused in January, but, after further negotiations, agreed in February and was named captain-general and admiral-general for one year. Holland then voted to extend the appointment to life when he turned 22.[50]

In April 1672 France and England, covetous of the riches of the Netherlands, declared war on the Dutch Republic; they were soon joined by the prince-bishop of Münster and the archbishop-elector of Cologne, who ruled territories just east of the United Provinces (the archbishop was one of the several electors who, on the death of the Holy Roman Emperor, chose his successor).[51] The Dutch navy was strong, but the army, after 24 years of peace on land, was small and poorly equipped, and its captain-general lacked military experience and was hamstrung by limits on his power. The United Provinces' only ally was the Spanish Netherlands, which could provide little in the way of military forces or money. On June 1 the French and their allies advanced rapidly from the east. Louis XIV swept across the Rhine and the territory of the bishop of Münster into Overijssel, Groningen and

Friesland in the north. By June 15 William retreated from the Ijssel River line to Utrecht, where town leaders would not admit them inside the walls and refused to let them demolish the suburbs to protect the town; the retreat continued west on June 17 to the state of Holland.

Five of the seven states were occupied by the French; only Holland and Zeeland were still in the hands of the Dutch. They were protected not so much by land fortifications and fortresses as by water — the waters of the North Sea to the west, where the Dutch hoped their navy would protect them from the English, and to the east by the Water Line created by the opening of the sluices and cutting of the dikes ordered by de Witt and William. Peasants tried to rebuild the dikes, but at the cost of flooding farms and villages, William persisted and the Water Line prevented the French from advancing.

De Witt's government sent envoys to seek peace terms from Louis XIV, but faced angry voices of disapproval from the clergy and the city mobs; de Witt was attacked and wounded by would-be assassins on June 21 in The Hague. On June 29 William, brought to Dordrecht by the local regents to restore order, was surrounded by a mob of citizens who forced the regents to sign a demand offering him the office of stadholder; regents in Rotterdam and Gouda were forced by mobs to sign similar statements. On July 4 all the 19 representatives in the state of Holland voted to name William stadholder; on the same day they rejected the harsh terms brought back from the French by de Witt's envoy.[52]

Later that month the Duke of Buckingham, Charles's envoy, sought out William and offered him a princely state in part of the Netherlands under the sovereignty of France and England; William brusquely turned it down. As the contemporary historian Gilbert Burnet told the story, "The Duke, at parting, pressed him much to put himself in the King's hands. The Prince cut him short; he said that his country had trusted him and that he would never deceive or betray them for any base ends of his own. The Duke answered that he was not to think any more of his country, for it no longer existed ... and he repeated the words often, 'Do you not see that it is lost?' The Prince said, he saw it was indeed in great danger, but there was a sure way never to see it lost, and that was to die in the last ditch."[53] On August 15 William arranged for the printing of a letter in which Charles offered him a principality of his own and blamed the war on the folly of the States General party.[54] The letter's contents further highlighted William's staunch refusal to accept Charles's offer, and his determination to save the Republic.

This was the first instance of William using propaganda — through the new media of the printing press and the pamphlet — at a critical moment to move opinion his way. More than any other European ruler, William, with his exposure to the politics of the Netherlands, where the views and feelings of a large and literate public counted for much, understood the importance of shaping public opinion and developed the capacity to do so through widely distributed pamphlets. Five days after publication of Charles's letter, on August 20, de Witt and his brother Cornelis were murdered by a mob in The Hague, at the gates of Gevangenenpoort prison, catty-corner from the Binnenhof and facing the Vijver; local officers did not intervene as the de Witts were disemboweled and their bodies hung upside down. William ousted many local government officials and installed his own choices, demonstrating at an early age a mastery of the intricacies of Dutch politics.[55]

William was now, at 21, at the head of affairs in the United Provinces. But, as his biographer Stephen Baxter puts it, "He inherited the Water Line, a defeated army, a country half occupied and more than half beaten."[56] He gained the authority to replace officials in some towns, and used it deftly. Militarily, the Dutch were imperiled in the winter of 1672–73 as the Water Line turned to ice. But Dutch lines mostly held, and Louis was forced to send some of his troops away to fight the forces of the Holy Roman Emperor and the Elector of Brandenburg. William learned lessons that he never forgot, that Louis XIV's France was a mortal threat and that the survival of the Netherlands depended on having foreign allies, even (as in the case of the emperor) Catholic ones.

He also appreciated the value of the printing press not only at home but abroad. When the French invasion seemed to be overwhelming the United Provinces, William deployed his propaganda in

England. Secretly he saw to the dissemination in England of Orangist propaganda, identifying French power with that of the Catholic Church, by his agent Peter du Moulin; the pamphlet *England's Appeal from the Private Cabal at Whitehall to the Great Council of the Nation* had great impact in March 1673.[57] The Dutch Republic's printing presses were worth 40,000 men, du Moulin boasted.[58] This pamphlet appeared as Parliament was pressing Charles to revoke his Declaration of Indulgence suspending the penal laws and approve the Test Act requiring officeholders to be members of the Church of England in return for money for the navy. He got the money, but it proved unavailing as the Dutch navy whipped the English navy in 1673 and disrupted English trade so much that Charles sued for peace. The mighty 41-year-old English king was thus frustrated by his 22-year-old Dutch nephew, who, only months before, had seemed likely to be forced to fulfill his promise to die in the last ditch.

Things continued to go better for William and the Dutch. In August 1673 Spain and thus the Spanish Netherlands entered the war on the Dutch side, and William won two victories against the French. In February 1674 the English made peace with the United Provinces. By June 1674 the Dutch had forced the French off all of their land except for two frontier fortresses.[59] The war with France continued, but the Dutch Republic had averted ruin and William was now firmly established. He had more than enough income from his landholdings and investments to support himself and his court in time of peace,[60] and he could tap the wealth of Amsterdam in time of war. "King James once remarked wryly that William was richer than the King of England, and it was true," writes John Carswell. "But the nature of William's wealth was even more important than its amount. The fact that it was private gave William an independence and a freedom to pursue his own ends that James lacked."[61] As captain-general he had the use of the Anglo-Dutch brigade of English and Scottish soldiers stationed in the Dutch Republic since the sixteenth century and generally subject to the stadholder's command, as well as the Blue Guards, commanded by Solms, and paid for out of his personal income.[62] William had to deal with the complicated Dutch political system and had "long practice in the art of bending representative assemblies to do his bidding. . . . [H]e was a prince who perfectly understood the value, wherever large resources and revenues were needed, of close collaboration with parliaments."[63] In April 1675 he came down with smallpox, but unlike his father, mother, and wife, he survived; he was tended by Bentinck, who slept in bed with him to catch the disease, which was thought to decrease its virulence.[64]

All the while he took care to maintain his position in England. William was pleased by Charles's appointment in 1674 as chief minister of the Earl of Danby, who favored an anti-French, pro-Dutch foreign policy and strong support of the Church of England at home.[65] Danby helped produce the peace with France in 1674, and in 1677, when William, after an exploratory trip by Bentinck,[66] traveled to England to seek marriage with his cousin Princess Mary, Danby supported him.[67] This was not a love match: William's biographer Stephen Baxter writes that William had expected to inherit the English throne since childhood and for years supposed that Princesses Mary and Anne were disqualified by their mother's commoner status, as they would have been in many continental monarchies; but when he discovered that their claims were regarded as stronger, the natural move was to marry the older of the two.[68] William took care to ask Charles first for her hand, and only spoke to James after Charles had approved, to James's displeasure. The 15-year-old Mary cried inconsolably for a day and a half when told that she was to be married to the ungainly William, who was 12 years older and four inches shorter than she.[69] The marriage took place in her bedchamber at Whitehall Palace on November 4, 1677. "The ceremony was performed by Bishop Compton, who had been entrusted with the care of Mary's religious education. 'The King, who gave her away, was very pleasant all the while.'"[70] Also present at the ceremony were members of James's household, including John Churchill.[71] Now William was married to the young woman who was second in line to the English throne.

✣

SO IN APRIL 1678 William and Churchill were not strangers, "They must have met frequently in 1677–78, not only on business, but in society," was the judgment of Churchill's great biographer and descendant, Winston Churchill.[72] But they were not of the same temperament. If William was ungainly and taciturn, Churchill was handsome and prepossessing, endowed with courtly skills: "[H]is affability and seeming openness, unfailing patience, persuasiveness and readiness to listen, his control and concealment of anger and indignation that he often felt but reserved for his private correspondence, and above all his ability to establish a personal rapport even with strangers."[73]

That difference reflected a sharp difference in backgrounds. William had lived all his life as the representative of a royal house with a heritage of public responsibility. Churchill had risen to his present position from obscurity. Churchill was the son of Winston Churchill, a country gentleman from the West Country with an estate worth £160 a year, who backed Charles I against the parliamentary forces in the Civil War of the 1640s; he was wounded in 1645, was fined £480 in 1651, and lived in his pro-Parliament mother-in-law's house throughout the 1650s.[74] John Churchill was born in 1650, a year after his sister Arabella. In his biography of his ancestor, Winston Churchill advances interesting surmises about the effects on John Churchill of growing up in the politically divided house of his father's mother-in-law. "The two prevailing impressions which such experiences must arouse in the mind of a child would be, first, a hatred of poverty and dependence, and, secondly, the need of hiding thoughts and feelings from those to whom their expression would be repugnant. To have one set of opinions for one part of the family, and to use a different language to the other, may have been inculcated from John's earliest years. To win freedom from material subservience by the sure agency of money must have been planted in his heart's desire. To these was added a third: the importance of having friends and connexions on both sides of a public quarrel. Modern opinion assigns increasing importance to the influences of early years on the formation of character. Certainly the whole of John Churchill's life bore the imprint of his youth. That impenetrable reserve under graceful and courteous manners; those unceasing contacts and correspondences with opponents; that iron parsimony and personal frugality, never relaxed in the blaze of fortune and abundance; that hatred of waste and improvidence in all their forms — all these could find their roots in the bleak years in Ashe."

When Charles II was restored to the throne in May 1660,

Winston Churchill's prospects naturally improved. He set up his own household again and was elected to Parliament in 1661; in 1665 he got an appointment in the administration of the Irish land settlement. [75] He also obtained places in the household of the Duke of York first for his daughter Arabella and then for his son John. Arabella became James's mistress sometime in 1667 — the story goes that he was smitten with her when he saw her fall off a horse — and was the mother of four of his children, including her son James Fitz-James, who, as the Duke of Berwick, fought with great skill on James's side during the Revolution of 1688–89 and for France, and therefore against his uncle, in the War of Spanish Succession in 1701–13. [76]

In September 1667, when he was 17, John Churchill was commissioned as an ensign in the King's Own Company in the First (later Grenadier) Guards. In 1668 he was sent to Tangier in Morocco, which was an English possession as part of the dowry of Queen Catherine of Braganza. There he met many of the "Tangerines" who served under him later and many veterans who had served in posts in colonies as far away as Barbados and Virginia. For five months in 1670 he served with the Mediterranean fleet.[77]

Churchill rose because of his proximity to the great and the powerful and because he possessed great courtly skills. As his contemporary Bishop Burnet recorded, "He was a man of noble and graceful appearance, bred up in the court with no literature: but he had a solid and clear understanding, with a constant presence of mind. He knew the arts of living in court beyond any man in it. He caressed all people with a soft and obliging deportment, and was always ready to do good offices. He had no fortune to set up on: this put him on all the methods of acquiring one."[78] In September 1670 he returned to London and, at 20, became the lover of 30-year-old Barbara Castelmaine, one of the many mistresses of Charles II, who made her Duchess of Cleveland.

In 1672, when England went to war against the Dutch and various German states as an ally of Louis XIV's France, Churchill sailed with James on his flagship when it was attacked by the Dutch. For his bravery Churchill was promoted to captain and sent to lead British troops in the French army. He fought at the siege of Maastricht in June 1673, where he saved the life of his commander, the Duke of Monmouth, Charles's oldest illegitimate son, and was personally praised by Louis XIV. He served in Westphalia in late 1673 under the great French marshal Turenne, who called him *"Quel homme. Quel fortu homme."* He continued in the French army after Charles concluded a peace treaty with the Dutch in February 1674, and took part in a forced march across the Vosges mountains in wintertime and in the French victory at Turckheim in January 1675. There, writes the historian Stephen Webb, "the old marshal taught the young captain that psychological superiority over the enemy could be achieved by startling mobility and constant aggression; that advantages of position could be consolidated by carefully sited, skillfully served, fully supplied artillery; and that a clear eye for the ultimate opportunities in battle was preserved by coolness and calmness."

Tired of fighting, he decided to return to England and on his way had an audience with Louis at Versailles. In London he was promoted to lieutenant colonel of James's Marine regiment and given the positions of gentleman of the bedchamber and master of the robes in James's household. He was able to pay the fees required for these offices because the Duchess of Cleveland at some point made him a gift of £5,000; he evidently used £4,500 of that to buy a £500 annuity from the Marquis of Halifax—the foundation of what became one of England's greatest fortunes.[79] He was one of the officers who organized the military expedition to Virginia after Bacon's rebellion of 1676, an expedition that installed new officials by restructuring local charters through *quo warranto* proceedings—the method Charles and James would use against their English political adversaries in the 1680s.[80]

In 1675 Churchill met 14-year-old Sarah Jennings, daughter of a member of the House of Commons from St. Albans and a member of James's household. Sarah was strong-willed, self-possessed, self-confident, and Churchill seems to have been immediately taken with her. His parents wished him to marry a richer woman, Catherine Sedley, also of the Duke of York's household and later one of his mistresses. But he wanted Sarah Jennings. She would have nothing to do with him short of marriage. In 1677 she came into a small inheritance after her brother died in a fire, and Churchill asked the Duchess of York for her hand. Some time in the winter of 1677–78 they were married, perhaps at the Duchess's apartments in Whitehall, perhaps at a Jennings family house in Hertfordshire.[81] As one of Sarah's recent biographers writes, "The wedding has sometimes been described as 'secret,' but it was not an elopement: it was only unofficially announced so that Sarah could keep her place as a virginal Maid of Honour. However, neither Sarah nor any other witness has left a description of it." This marriage was to be one of the sources of Churchill's power, for Sarah Churchill soon became, and remained until 1709, the trusted confidante and close adviser of Princess Anne, the younger daughter of James, and queen from 1702 to 1714.

On April 5, 1678, immediately after they were married, John was sent to Brussels.[82] This was Churchill's first stop on his trip to The Hague, under instructions from James and Charles to negotiate the terms and conditions under which England would enter the war with France on the Dutch side. It was a mission with a cynical purpose. Charles had signed a treaty with the Netherlands in January offering to support the peace terms proposed by William and reinforcing Charles's adherence to a military alliance if those terms were rejected by Louis XIV.[83] Louis was heartily sick of the war and had offered the United Provinces a peace recognizing its independence and offering more-favorable terms of trade in 1672. The Amsterdam merchants wanted to accept, but William was holding up the peace talks to seek better terms.[84] It is unclear whether Charles actually intended to join the Dutch in war against France; more likely he was employing Churchill to give William and his allies leverage in the negotiations, and many in England suspected that he was building up an army not to fight France in Europe, but to maintain his regime at home.[85] Churchill conducted successful negotiations first with the Duke of Villa Hermosa in Brussels and then with William in The Hague. The allies got favorable terms in the Treaty of Nijmegen, signed in July. [86]

❧

BUT WHAT ELSE did these two young men talk about? Their first meeting lasted three hours. Churchill evidently impressed William "as the coolest head and warmest heart" he had ever met.[87] Winston Churchill, who immersed himself in the documents of the period, speculates tantalizingly on what the two young men said. John Churchill "got on extremely well with William of Orange. No doubt he set himself to do so. They were exactly the same age. If the conversation turned on religion, they were agreed. If the aggrandizement of France became the topic, was this not the campaign in prospect? If talk ran upon the art of war, here was the profession of their lives. All the actions of the still continuing war in which they had fought, though in different theatres and on opposite sides, furnished an inexhaustible theme. Their talks may have ranged very far. We can in imagination see them poring over the map of Europe with eyes that understood so much about it. William, who was not hostile to young men, must have greatly liked to talk with his agreeable contemporary, who seemed to have the ear of every one at the English Court and had such grounding in the secrets of politics and power as was usually the privilege of princes."[88] There is conflicting evidence on William's opinion of Churchill. William's biographer says he had rejected Churchill as English ambassador.[89] One of Churchill's biographers says he sought Churchill's services in his army continuously over the next ten years.[90] Evidently William respected his military skills, which helped him gain promotion the next month at age 28 to brigadier general,[91] but distrusted him as a servant of his father-in-law and feared he would not be a reliable conduit to the king.[92]

Of William's purposes Churchill can have had little doubt. William's determination to fight the French in 1672 and his spurning of the offers of Charles and James left no question about what was clearly the central purpose of his life. As an admiring writer puts it, "He and he alone did not stand for merely personal ambition or personal glory, but some absolute idea, which he describes again and again as *la cause commune* and for which he was prepared to make endless sacrifices. . . . *La cause commune* was the unification of Europe against the power of France."[93] To that cause he obviously wished to attach England: his marriage brought him closer to his uncles and gave him the potential of directing policy should Mary become queen.

William presumably did not know the terms of the secret Treaty of Dover. But he may have suspected that Charles was receiving subsidies from Louis, and could not rule out the possibility he might do so again. He was certainly not naïve enough to count on England as a permanent ally. He knew that James had agreed to his marriage with visible reluctance; he had, after all, sought permission from the king and not from the princess's father. He surely knew that Churchill was James's creature, with no other visible source of influence. He knew that James was Catholic, and that in the past he had been inclined to a friendly policy toward France and Louis XIV. He knew that James had supported Charles's decision to fight with France against the United Provinces in 1672–74 and that Churchill had been fighting in the French army even after that. He could expect that Churchill understood his policy. But he could not have trusted him very far. If Churchill had suggested that he shared his opposition to Louis and his Protestant faith, he could not very well have counted on such assurances. He could hardly have been confident in 1678 that Churchill would carry on *la cause commune* from 1702 to 1711.

These men were operating in a world where power was ephemeral and where great changes could occur quickly. Twenty-first-century readers may look over lists of kings and suppose that their succession was automatic and that they held untrammeled power. William and Churchill, like Charles and James, knew from bitter personal experience that that was very far from being the case. Had Oliver Cromwell, who died at 58, lived on into the 1660s and 1670s, Charles and James might have remained exiles all their lives. Had Louis not invaded the United Provinces in 1672, William might have remained no more than a military official of a republic controlled by his political adversaries. Had Churchill and his sister not attracted James's attention, he might have been nothing more than an impecunious and obscure country gentleman. The fates of Charles I and Johan de Witt reminded everyone that the penalty for political failure was harsh. The fate of William's father, dead of smallpox while still in his twenties, reminded them that life could be short and that political gains could vanish suddenly.

Both of these men were for the moment staking much on James, Duke of York. Churchill's whole career depended on him. William depended on him for support as an ally in the short run and for preserving the succession of Mary in the longer term. For both men James's Catholicism was a problem. For Churchill it meant that his patron might have difficulty gaining and holding the crown. For William, it meant that his father-in-law might not be a reliable supporter of his policy of opposing France. Neither had any choice but to depend on him for the time being. But when James became king, he embarked on a course that persuaded both of them to collude in the acts that became known as the Glorious Revolution.

Chapter 4

EXCLUSION POLITICS

LONDON, JANUARY 1, 1679. Dawn came late in the English winter, and the morning light was typically dim. Then suddenly, late in the morning, the skies went quickly dark. John Evelyn, faithful member of the Church of England, was atttending church services, "when so strange a Clowd of darknesse came over, and especially, the Citty of London, that they were faine to give-over the publique service for some time, being about 11 in the forenoone, which affrited many, who consider'd not the cause, (it being a greate Snow, and very sharp weather,) which was an huge cloud of Snow, supposed to be frozen together, and descending lower than ordinary, the Eastern wind, driving it forwards."[1] Evelyn was a member of the new Royal Society, commissioned by Charles II, and inclined to scientific explanations of natural phenomena. But many Englishmen were more inclined to see unusual occurrences as omens or as evidence of plots. Just as the Great Plague of 1665 and the enormous London fire of 1666 were widely seen as the products of Catholic conspiracies, in January 1679 the talk of London was of a Catholic plot to kill the king and, as Andrew Marvell put it, "to Convert the Established Protestant Religion into down-right Popery."[2]

This Popish Plot was alleged most prominently by Titus Oates. Oates was a disgraced clergyman of the Church of England who in

March 1677 declared himself a Catholic. He persuaded the English Provincial of the Society of Jesus to send him to study first in Valladolid, Spain, and then at the Jesuits' English college in St. Omers, France, from which he was expelled. He returned to London in June 1678 and contacted Israel Tonge, an elderly Church of England minister with an obsessive belief in Catholic conspiracies. Oates gave Tonge a document with 43 articles alleging a Jesuit conspiracy to kill Charles II and the Duke of York. Through an acquaintance who had conducted scientific experiments with Charles, he was able to get an audience with the king in Whitehall Palace on August 13. Charles, impatient as ever with detail, asked for a précis and handed the matter over to his chief minister, the Earl of Danby, while he went off to Windsor. On September 6, Oates presented his sworn statement, with more accusations, to Middlesex County Justice Edmund Berry Godfrey. Oates went before the King's Council on September 28 with similar charges, notably against the queen's physician, Sir George Wakeman, and then again before the Council with Charles present the next day, and arrests were made.

As John Evelyn, a Kent landowner who seems to have known everyone in London, noted in his diary entry for October 1,

I went with my Wife to Lond: The Parliament now being alarmed with the whole Nation, about a conspiracy of some eminent Papists, for the destruction of the King, & introducing Popery; discovered by one Oates and Dr. Tongue, which last, I knew, being the Translator of the Jesuites Morals: I went to see & converse with him, now beng at White-hall, with Mr. Oates, one that was lately an Apostate to the Church of Rome, & now return'd againe with this discovery: he seem'd to be a bold man, & in my thoughts furiously indis-creete; but everybody believed what he said: & it quite chang'd the genius & motions of the Parliament, growing now corrupt & intrested with long sitting, & Court practices; but with all this Poperie would not go downe: This discovery turn'd them all as one man against it, & nothing was don but in order to finding out the depth of this &c: Oates was encourag'd, & every thing he affirm'd [taken] for Gospel: The truth is, The Roman

Chath: were Exceeding bold, & busy every where, since the D[uke
of York]: forbore to go any longer to the Chapell &c:"[3]

That so urbane and sophisticated an observer as Evelyn should
take Oates's charges so seriously shows the strength of anti-Catholic
feeling and of the fear of Catholic subversion that permeated the
society.

One accusation hit its target: Edward Coleman, secretary to the
Duchess of York and former secretary to the duke, had written letters
in the 1670s to Louis XIV's confessor, promising vaguely to promote
Catholicism in England and seeking and accepting bribes. These letters were found when Coleman's effects were searched, but no other
incriminating documents were discovered among the Jesuit's papers.
All these were secret proceedings, but rumor spread the charges, or
something like them, around London and England.

On October 12, Justice Godfrey left his house in London and was
last seen that day in St. Martin's Lane; on October 17 his body was
found, strangled and run through with his sword, on Primrose Hill
near Hampstead, several miles away. This caused a furor when Parliament convened on October 21. Evelyn's diary entry for that day reads,
"The barbarous murder of Sir Edmund Bery-Godfry, found strangled
about this time, as was manifest by the Papists, (he being a Justice of
the Peace, and one who knew much of their practices, as conversant
with Coleman, a Servant of the . . . now accus'd) put the whole nation
in a new fermentation against them."[4] Charles II mentioned the plot,
"of which I shall forebear any opinion, lest I seem to say too much or
too little: but I will leave the matter to the law."

Both the Lords and the Commons began investigating; the Commons summoned Oates, who now implicated several Catholic lords,
and five of them were arrested. Tonge appeared to charge that there
was a new gunpowder plot to blow up Parliament, and the cellars of
Westminster Palace were searched. Both houses questioned Coleman
and demanded that all Catholics be removed from London, to which
Charles agreed; chains were placed across the streets. On November 1
the Commons passed a resolution "that there hath been and still is a
damnable and hellish plot, contrived and carried on by popish recu-

sants for the assassinating and murdering the King, and for subverting the government, and rooting out and destroying the Protestant religion."[5]

Oates's charges, detailed and delivered confidently with convincing circumstantial detail, were entirely false, though they led to the discovery of Coleman's incriminating letters. He seems to have been a compulsive liar, bent on fame and fortune, which he did achieve for a while. Charles, who, after his alliance with France and because of his brother's conversion, could not afford to be seen as sympathetic to Catholicism, felt obliged to investigate his charges, even though he seems to have regarded Oates as a liar.[6] Interestingly, Oates steered clear of implicating James, who stood to become king if anyone murdered Charles.[7] Letters, purportedly by Jesuits, sent to James's Jesuit confessor on August 31, were obviously forged; these alerted James to the charges in September, and their swift discrediting made him feel secure against further accusations.[8]

Coleman's letters were more damaging; in one, James was said to have associated himself with Coleman and pledged to support France's interests, and in another Coleman said Charles was "odious to all the nation and the world." To the papal internuncio he wrote that he had told Louis's confessor, "We have here a mighty work upon our hands; no less than the conversion of three kingdoms [England, Scotland, and Ireland], and by that perhaps the subduing of a pestilent heresy which has domineered over the greater part of this northern world a long time. There were never such hopes of success since the death of Queen Mary [1558], as now in our days."[9] Oates told the Lords on October 30 that the Jesuits had forged James's signature and seal, but the Earl of Shaftesbury, a minister of the king from 1661 to 1673 and thereafter a leader of parliamentary opposition to the Court, moved on November 2 that James be removed from Charles's presence, and on November 3 Charles decided that James should stop attending the Privy Council and "all places where any affairs of the nation were agitated."

This was a severe blow to James, who, despite being ineligible for public office in England since 1673, had continued to be influential at Court and, in the absence of his brother, or because of Charles's indolence, the guiding spirit.[10] He was especially active in colonial affairs. He procured the appointment of his protégé, Sir Edmund Andros, as governor of New York when it was restored to England, and he supported Andros's improvement of New York's defenses and harbors, which made it "the dynamic center of the English empire on the American continent."[11] He "directed the Virginia operations of the crown" from August to November 1676 in response to Bacon's rebellion in Virginia, replacing the proprietarial government with a royal charter and installing a military commander directly responsible, over the governor's head, to the Crown. Virginia was the largest of the North American English colonies, and James set the terms that would in time be applied to others: the Crown would appoint the governor and provincial council; a lower house, the House of Burgesses in Virginia, would be elected, but the king's appointees would introduce most important acts and the government in London would have to approve them. At the same time, no strenuous efforts were to be made in Virginia or other colonies to bolster the privileged position of the Church of England. James, far more than Charles or any one of the king's ministers, interested himself in and shaped the governance of the North American colonies, in which "American colonies thus became English provinces."[12]

To maintain his own power, Charles was prepared to sacrifice James's. On November 9, Charles addressed both houses and offered to accept any laws limiting the powers of a Catholic king, "to make you safe in the reign of my successor, so as they tend not to impeach the right of succession, nor the descent of the Crown in its true line, and so as they restrain not my power, nor the just rights of any Protestant successor." The Lords continued to consider a bill to bar all Catholics from serving in Parliament or appearing at Court. On November 20, James asked that he be exempted from its terms, and the next day the Lords agreed. In the Commons this aroused anger. "Coleman's letters! Coleman's letters!" James's opponents shouted. But one member argued that exempting James didn't matter: "If the Duke remains in the Lords' house he cannot singly and solely, on his own vote, stop any business." Another said, "If this prince should go into another place, it must cost you a standing army to bring him home again"—in other words, it would mean another civil war. As the historian J. G. A. Pocock has written, "We can never overestimate the impact on the English of all classes of the Civil Wars, the regicide, and the deep uncertainties of the 1650s, a set of experiences which they had not desired, hated as they have hated nothing else in their history and found incredibly difficult to explain to themselves."[13] Others raised the specter that would be raised again and again in the next three years of another civil war. The Commons accepted the provision exempting James by a vote of 158–156.[14] Coleman was speedily tried before more details of the letters could come out, and was executed on December 3: the only one accused who might have implicated James in genuine offenses.[15] But an account of his trial, including three of the letters, was published in December, giving further publicity and credibility to Oates.

Meanwhile, other witnesses came forward to corroborate Oates's charges or to add charges of their own and explain Godfrey's death — William Bedloe, a highwayman and confidence man from Bristol (he charged that the Catholics planned to depose Charles and put him in a convent); Miles Prance, a Catholic silversmith in Covent Garden; Stephen Dugdale, a Catholic and former land steward to the Catholic Lord Aston, a Staffordshire landowner. The streets of the city of London were patrolled by 2,500 men-at-arms every night; the Lords, Commons, and justices of the peace were busy sifting evidence; beyond London there were rumors of priests disembarking from ships and arms being delivered to plotters and night riders on nefarious errands. There were demands that the King raise the militia and dismiss the army that was raised to fight in the Netherlands but had never seen combat. Charles vetoed a bill requiring him to call up the militia, but approved the new Test Act, which barred all Catholics but James from Parliament. On November 20, Charles issued a proclamation requiring the immediate seizure of all priests and Jesuits in England "in order to their trial." Rumors swirled, as the accusations were not made publicly. Lurid sermons were preached against Papists and reproduced in pamphlets distributed by the thousands; bonfires were lit with images of the pope and the alleged plotters; houses were searched for priests.

Charles was angered when Oates accused the queen of being part of the plot to murder him, and remained entirely unconvinced after examining Oates personally; he told the clergyman and historian Gilbert Burnet that Catherine "was a weak woman, and has some disagreeable humours, but was not capable of a wicked thing; and considering his faultiness toward her in other things he thought it a horrid thing to abandon her." Oates accused the queen before the Commons, which voted on December 1 to request that she be banished; the next day the Lords refused to agree.[16] This caused some to doubt Oates's veracity, for almost everyone correctly considered the charges against the queen preposterous. John Evelyn notes in his diary for November 24, "Oates on this grew so presumptuous as to accuse the Queene for intending to Poyson the King; which certainly that pious & vertuous Lady abhorred the thought of, & Oates His circumstances, made it utterly unlikely in my opinion: 'Tis likely he thought to gratifie some, who would have ben glad his Majestie had married a more fruitfull Lady: but the King was too kind a husband to let any of these make impression on him."[17]

Another controversy arose in December 1678. Thomas Osborne, Earl of Danby, had been Charles's Lord Treasurer since 1674. He was a firm backer of the Established Church and thus in line with the general trend of opinion in the Commons in the Cavalier Parliament. He also was a pioneer in using government appointments to secure majorities for the king in the Commons. The previous Cabal ministry (so called from its leading members Clifford, Arlington, Buckingham, Ashley Cooper, and Lauderdale) had backed the Third Dutch War in 1672 and 1673; Danby came to power as Charles was signing a peace treaty with the United Provinces, and he followed a consistent policy of opposing Louis XIV. He played a major role in gaining permission for the marriage in 1677 of James's daughter Mary to William of Orange, Louis's most persistent and dedicated opponent in continental Europe. But Danby's adroit management of the Court interest in the Commons had led many members to oppose it in what they called the Country interest. Danby sought to cooperate deftly with the prosecution of the Popish Plot, but was still widely distrusted. Then, on December 19, Ralph Montagu, who had been dismissed as ambassador to France after pursuing one of the king's illegitimate daughters,[18] produced letters in Parliament from Danby ordering him to seek French subsidies. Danby was impeached by the Commons on December 21, but defended himself vigorously in the Lords on December 23, showing the king's signature on his file copies of the letters, and the Lords declined to imprison him. Charles, wishing to keep Danby's services and keep him out of the Tower of London, prorogued Parliament December 30, abruptly ending the session.[19]

AND SO AS the new year began with a cloud enveloping London, a cloud hung over the government and over James. Trials were held in January and February of Catholics accused by Oates, Bedloe, Prance, and Dugdale, and despite the weakness of much of the evidence, guilty verdicts and death sentences were voted by juries, and executions were carried out. On January 24, 1679, Charles dissolved Parliament, and elections were held for all Commons seats for the first time since 1661, with the new Parliament to meet in March. Such an interval was not uncommon in seventeenth-century England: Charles I dissolved Parliament in 1629 and ruled without a Parliament until 1640, and the Long Parliament elected in November 1640 continued in office, with vacancies filled in by-elections and its membership pared by purges, until it was dissolved in March 1660. A Convention Parliament (so called because elections were not called by order of the king, then still in exile) was elected in April 1660; candidates who had not supported the Commonwealth government were not eligible to run. The Convention Parliament was dissolved by Charles II in December 1660, and elections were held in April 1661. This Cavalier Parliament was dominated by members who had been loyal to Charles I during the Civil War — hence the label Cavalier Parliament — and who were adherents of the Church of England.

The House of Commons in 1660 consisted of 507 members returned from 52 counties and 215 parliamentary boroughs. The 39 English counties, from huge Yorkshire to tiny Rutland, elected 2 members each and the 12 Welsh counties 1. The 12 Welsh boroughs and 5 English boroughs elected 1 member each; the city of London and the linked boroughs of Weymouth and Melcombe elected 4 each; the 190 other English boroughs elected 2 each.

Very many Englishmen had the right to vote in these elections. In each county, votes could be cast by all "forty-shilling freeholders," men who owned property with a rental value of 40 shillings or £2 a year. In boroughs the franchise varied. In some the right to vote was attached to the ownership of certain pieces of property; in some it was limited to the officers of the borough corporation; in many, all freemen, that is adult males not bound to service, could vote. Yet at this time voting was still a new concept. In the late sixteenth and early seventeenth centuries there were seldom contests in any county or borough. Rather, service in Parliament was seen as a privilege or a duty, devolving on those who were due recognition as leaders in their communities. "Electoral contests," writes the historian Mark Kishlansky of this period, "were truly exceptional events, events that violated anticipated patterns of behavior rather than fulfilled them, events that were aberrant rather than normative."[20] He goes on, "Personal attributes, prestige, standing, godliness — were all implicit in officeholding. Their presence qualified individuals for place, their absence disqualified them. Individuals represented communities by virtue of the possession of these qualities, not by reflecting the special interests or ideals of particular groups of constituents. In all but a handful of instances, most of which are exceptionally well documented, before 1640 ideology was absent from the process of parliamentary selection."[21]

This began to change with the coming of the Civil War and the Restoration. Political issues were clear, and choices between rival candidates were made for political reasons, as were informal determinations of which two candidates were to stand unopposed.[22] The king's ministers began to try to influence by-elections in the long period between 1661 and 1679 when the Cavalier Parliament was in office. During this time "a pent-up demand for seats . . . allowed for the kind of planning on the part of candidates and government officials that had never before been possible."[23]

Then, after the first election of 1679, there emerged a binary issue, whether James, Duke of York, should be excluded from the throne. That produced a sudden flowering of what amounted to a national two-party politics that played itself out in the field of battle set by the ancient and widely varied rules and customs attached to the election of members of the House of Commons from the counties and boroughs.

This two-party politics was the initiative not so much of the voters as of elite politicians. But the voters were not entirely passive,[24] and they were numerous. Hundreds of 40-shilling freeholders could vote in small counties, thousands in large counties; and price inflation brought even more men into the 40-shilling category. There were contests in about one-third of the county elections from 1660 to 1689 and in more than 40 percent in the two elections of 1679.[25] In the boroughs, the size of the electorates varied widely. In some burgage boroughs, where the vote was limited to owners of certain properties, elections were manipulated though not without contest. "Old Sarum, deserted since the 16th century, had already become an electoral joke. In 1660, all the burgages had fallen into the hands of five owners. It was seemingly the practice to create faggot votes," cast by cooperative locals. In contrast, "Yorkshire was the largest constituency [in area] in England, and this made election contests so expensive that there was a marked reluctance on the part of candidates to go to the poll," and there was only one election between 1660 and 1689 in which there were more than two candidates for an electorate of 8,000 to decide.[26]

In both counties and boroughs, large landowners and local officials including lord lieutenants (who could deploy the militia) exerted great influence over elections.[27] The king made little direct effort to affect elections, but the Duke of York as Lord Warden of the Cinque Ports recommended members for their seats, and the Duke of Monmouth, by virtue of his various offices, had influence in several.[28] Votes were cast in public in one location, determined by county sheriffs who were generally responsive to local landowners and were inclined to set conditions favored by them with an eye to affecting the result. There were increasingly arguments about and changes in election rules and procedures.[29]

We tend to suppose that political power in England was in the hands of only a few people in the late seventeenth century. That was true in the sense that the landed gentry had influence far out of proportion to their numbers. But it was also true that a large percentage of the adult male population was entitled to vote in contested elections.

As the century went on, an increasing number of elections were contested, and even where they were not, the opinions of potential voters
played a role in determining who would stand as a candidate and who
would not. The county electorates during this period totaled about
140,000[30] — not an inconsiderable number, approaching 10 percent of
the adult male population. Adding in those entitled to vote in the boroughs, the total electorate may have been more than 300,000, more
than 20 percent of adult males.[31]

It may be objected that the lack of contests in many counties and
boroughs effectively disenfranchised those entitled to vote, but population was also concentrated: about 10 percent of the population lived
in greater London (covered by the boroughs of the City of London,
Westminster, and Southwark, and the counties of Middlesex and Sur-
rey). And there were frequent contests, especially in February 1679,
when some 22 seats were contested in 17 counties, and 103 borough
seats were contested in 84 boroughs.[32] The boundaries of the counties,
the incorporation of the boroughs, and the franchise qualifications
there were the result of ancient practice, dating from the fourteenth
century in England and the sixteenth century in Wales. "The old representative system," writes the historian Linda Colley, "had grown up
in response to the demands of particular communities and private interests, and its franchise provisions reflected a bewildering variety of
local customs. It was a patchwork and emphatically not a seamless gar-
ment."[33] Yet they pointed at least vaguely in the direction of modern
representative democracy.

In France and other continental countries where monarchs were
reaching for absolute power, the old forms were being set aside and
rendered otiose: the French Estates General had not met since 1614
and would not meet again until 1789. In England something similar
might have happened: Charles I governed without Parliament from
1629 to 1640, and in the 30 years after the Restoration, Parliament was
out of session longer than it was in.[34] But in England the political issues thrown up during the reign of Charles II, particularly the issue of
exclusion — whether the Duke of York should be excluded from the
throne — produced an electoral politics, and a party politics, with re-
semblances to the party electoral politics that emerged in the United

States in the 1790s and again in the 1830s and in Britain in the 1850s and 1860s.

꩜

So this parliamentary system had within it the seeds of representative government. And this vestigial electoral system had within it the seeds of party politics[35]— seeds that burst into sudden flower in the two elections held in 1679. "Competition among the gentry for social distinction, for patronage, and for influence at court mixed with the emerging ideological divisions over politics and religion. The combination was potent. . . . More than any other factor—though many were at work—it was competing candidates that created the electorate."[36] The public Catholicism of James, Duke of York; the widespread unpopularity of fighting alongside Catholic France against the Protestant United Provinces; the fears triggered by the Popish Plot: all these raised political issues that were addressed in the parliamentary elections that Charles had felt forced to call.

This was certainly not the king's desire; his decision to dissolve Parliament was evidently prompted by his desire to save Danby and by his recognition that Danby could no longer secure majorities for funding the disbanding of the army, which Charles desperately needed. He hoped that the new Commons would be disposed to vote the money and not to demand the impeachment of Danby. Danby, worried about preserving his position, persuaded Charles on February 28, while elections were still being held, to order James to leave England. James obeyed his older brother and sailed to the Netherlands on March 3. He visited William and Mary in The Hague, and then in April settled in Brussels in the Spanish Netherlands, where John Churchill joined him.[37] Before he left, James did get Charles to support his right to inherit the throne by once again swearing that his only marriage had been to the queen, reaffirming the bastardy of his son the Duke of Monmouth, now a spirited 28-year-old soldier and for some Protestants the candidate of choice to succeed his father. But James feared that Charles would renege on his frequent avowals that he would not accept exclusion.

The elections held in February 1679, in the shadow of the Popish

Plot, produced a House of Commons even less inclined to defer to the king. It was no longer a Cavalier Parliament. As the historian J. R. Jones writes:

> The country Opposition had always claimed a monopoly of anti-Papist zeal, and in the continued excitement caused by the Plot this was an electoral asset of some value in places with a wide franchise. For many years by-elections had shown that opinion had changed considerably since 1661, and that the balance of local interests had often altered. Many of those elected in the early years of the Cavalier Parliament had since lost their local standing, quarrelled with their neighbors or patrons, or become too poor to seek reelection. Others had neglected their interest or slighted the voters, assuming that the Parliament would be eternal. Those who had accepted pensions and places of profit often found themselves under intense attack, since lists had been published of those alleged to have sold their honor and their country to Danby and abetted his infamous designs.[38]

But Danby was a manipulator of already elected members, not an election organizer, and the Crown did not enjoy the patronage interests it would use to elect candidates in the eighteenth century; few of the lords inclined to support the king had influence over more than a few seats in the Commons.[39] "Attempts were made to control" the House of Commons, J. H. Plumb writes, "through managed elections—Charles I and Oliver Cromwell both tried that, but to no avail—or through exploitation of loyalty, well warmed with pension and place, and kept steady by a patriotic foreign policy. . . . Danby, who saw the possibilities of this approach more realistically than any other seventeenth-century politician, also failed. The Popish Plot and the Exclusion Crisis blew his party to smithereens, and like so many others he finished in the Tower."[40]

We can know what the election results meant, because they were interpreted by one of the shrewdest and most knowledgeable political figures of the age, Anthony Ashley Cooper, the Earl of Shaftesbury.[41] Shaftesbury compiled a list of the incoming members of the House of

Commons, and next to the name of each appended one or more letters describing his political leanings — *w.* for worthy or *H.* for honest, indicating those who opposed the Court, and *v.* for vile or *B.* for bad, indicating those who supported the Court.[42]

Shaftesbury's position as a longtime political player gave him a clear vantage point from which to judge the incoming members of Parliament. He was a rich man, with large landholdings in Dorset and the West Country, and as an active investor and proprietor of the Carolina colony he was familiar with the leading financiers and lawyers in the City.[43] Only five feet tall, he was a man of energy and boldness and was involved actively in politics, in the most unsettled of times, almost all his adult life and even before (he was elected to the House of Commons in 1640 at age 18).

When he was Lord Chancellor he supported the Test Act and urged Charles to divorce and remarry in order to produce a Protestant heir. Charles dismissed him from office in September 1673. Shaftesbury responded not by retiring quietly but by leading opposition to the king's ministers in the House of Lords in 1674, becoming "the great popular leader against all the measures of the court," and rather than retire to the country he remained in the capital. In February 1677 he moved in the House of Lords to declare that Parliament was defunct because it had not been called into session for more than a year; that motion failed and he was held in the Tower of London until February 1678. He made a statement of contrition and was released, receiving a message "that his Majesty thought it were much better he were at home in the country."[44] But he replied that he had become so accustomed to the Tower that he would prefer to return there rather than leave London.[45] When news of the Popish Plot spread, Shaftesbury encouraged Oates and the other informers. Consistently throughout his career, Shaftesbury supported toleration of Presbyterians and Dissenting Protestants, but not of Catholics. He was willing to invoke harsh measures — he caviled not at all at the execution of the alleged plotters and urged that one of them be threatened with the rack — and, unlike the king and Danby, he showed utter disregard of the possibility that the charges were untrue.[46] For those who search through history to find champions of our own values,

Shaftesbury is a problem: he was a supporter of habeas corpus and of religious toleration for many, yet he was an unscrupulous prosecutor of baseless charges against others. He was also the patron of John Locke, whom he met when Locke was studying medicine at Oxford and who advised him to have surgery for an abscess, which saved his life.[47] Locke lived in Shaftesbury's London household from 1667;[48] he wrote a constitution for the Carolina colony of which Shaftesbury was a proprietor, and was closely involved in all of Shaftesbury's political dealings.

Shaftesbury's vote count showed that his forces had almost a two-to-one majority in the new House of Commons, with similar proportions among old members and the many new ones.[49] As his biographer K. H. D. Haley writes, "153 members were marked 'ow,' that is, 'old' (members of the previous Parliament) and 'worthy,' and 149 were 'nH,' 'new' and 'honest.' 98 were 'ov,' 'old' and 'vile,' and 60 were 'nB,' 'new' and 'bad' and 36, all newly elected members, were marked as doubtful."[50] So Shaftesbury entered the new Parliament in a position of great strength, but with many new members who would need careful management. Charles's attempts to conciliate the Commons did not work. As Parliament opened in March he declared a pardon for Danby; the Commons rejected that and, despite Shaftesbury's preference that Danby be ordered to go into exile (as Charles's first Lord Treasurer, the Earl of Clarendon, had done in 1667), the Lords voted for attainder in April and accordingly Danby was sent to the Tower of London, where he stayed for five years.[51] Charles then was persuaded by Sir William Temple, the pro-Dutch former ambassador to the Netherlands, to appoint to the privy council many of his leading opponents, including Shaftesbury, whom he made Lord President.[52]

The Commons responded by unanimously supporting a resolution stating "that the Duke of Yorke's being a papist, and the hopes of his coming into the Crown, has given the greatest Countenance and Encouragement to the present Conspiracies and Designs of the Papists against the King and the Protestant Religion."[53] Charles responded, as he had before, by saying that he would support limitations on the powers of a Catholic king. Parliament was adjourned for five days, and supporters of exclusion pondered the alternatives to James: Should

Princess Mary be queen, in which case the guiding hand would be that of William of Orange, or should the impetuous Duke of Monmouth be recognized as the rightful heir? "I do not know three of a mind," wrote the pro-exclusion Algernon Sidney, "and . . . a spirit of giddiness reigns amongst us, far beyond any I have ever observed in my life."[54] A bill of exclusion, excluding Catholics from the throne, was introduced May 11 and passed five days later by a vote of 207–128: Shaftesbury's vote count was spot on. Anti-Catholic sentiment was strong: on no other bill in Charles's reign had either side mustered two hundred votes. The Commons also voted a habeas corpus bill, a measure forestalled by Charles's previous prorogations and adjournments. The Lords, preoccupied with the question of whether the bishops—sure votes for the Court—could sit on the capital charges against Danby and, with the pending trial of five Catholic lords on Popish Plot charges, passed its own version of the habeas corpus bill. On May 26 the Commons agreed to the Lords' terms, and just in time. On May 27, Charles prorogued Parliament until August 14, and also signed rather than vetoed the habeas corpus bill—the one enduring legislative accomplishment of the exclusion Parliaments.[55]

⚘

As DEBATE RAGED in the Commons and the Lords in May 1679, something else happened, quietly, that would have noisy consequences: the Licensing Act of 1662 expired. The printing press, controlled by royal prerogative until 1640, had been a potent means of disseminating ideas in the heady days of the Civil War and Cromwellian rule. Charles II got first the House of Lords and then the Commons to limit it by the Licensing Act of 1662,[56] but it extended only until the end of the Cavalier Parliament, and even before that it was never entirely effective.[57]

William of Orange, familiar with the free press of the Netherlands and the need to influence public opinion in a country with representative government, tried to influence English opinion against the Third Dutch War in 1672 and 1673, and achieved considerable success with his agent Peter du Moulin's *England's Appeal from the Private Cabal at Whitehall to the Great Council of the Nation*.[58] In 1677 Shaftesbury's agents were able to distribute pamphlets, *Some Considerations upon the Question whether the Parliament is dissolved* and *The Grand Question concerning the prorogation of this Parliament.* The official in charge of suppressing unlicensed pamphlets, Sir Roger L'Estrange, unable to suppress them, was careful to make sure that *A Pacquet of Advices and Animadversions sent from London to the Men of Shaftesbury,* sponsored by the government, could circulate unmolested.[59] "Printed vindication or rejoinder, rather than censorship," writes historian Mark Knights, "was recognized as the best means of countering an opposing viewpoint — a recognition that the mind could not be forced in politics any more than in religion."[60] *"O Printing!"* wrote Andrew Marvell, poet and member of Parliament. "How thou hast disturbed the Peace of Mankind! That Lead, when moulded into Bullets, is not so mortal as when founded into Letters."[61] The political pamphlet, which would be such a powerful instrument in the making of the American Revolution, was a similarly powerful instrument in England a hundred years before.

England was too free and footloose a society for any government to impose conformity or suppress disagreement,[62] and London, where perhaps 70 percent of adult males were literate,[63] was too concentrated and too open to prevent people from congregating and talking. It was a giant city for its time, with nearly 500,000 people in a country of 5 million, and was probably already the largest city in Europe.[64] But all these people were packed into a small area, along the Thames from a point just east of the Tower west through the burgeoning West End north of St. James's Park, and south to Whitehall Palace and Westminster.[65] In this small area it was easy for people to bump into each other. "The diaries of Pepys, Evelyn, Reresby and Hooke reveal the constant visits, the bumping into people at court and on the [Royal] Exchange, in the park or at a theater, the shared meals and coach journeys, the meeting and the mingling and the endless talk."[66] They could meet members of the Lords and Commons in the law courts of Westminster Hall and at the nearby stalls where refreshments were sold.[67] They met in taverns and increasingly at a new venue, the coffeehouse.[68] "A total of 29 different Whig clubs have been found in London alone during the Exclusion crisis," writes the historian Tim

Harris. "Along with the Green Ribbon Club [which met at the King's Head Tavern in Chancery Lane], they included clubs held by Shaftesbury at the Swan in Fish Street, the Angel Tavern, near the Old Exchange, the Queen's Arms and the Nag's Head, and a club held at the Salutation Tavern in Lombard Street by the Duke of Bucking-ham."[69] Then there were the coffeehouses. The first coffeehouse had been opened in Holborn in 1650; by 1663 there were 82 in London[70] and, by 1700, 2,000.[71] London "was the metropolis of the nation: it was the linchpin of the networks through which information, ideas, and culture were disseminated. London was the great talking shop of Restoration England, and it was in the buzz of the coffeehouses that deals were done, information exchanged, gossip spread and subversive thoughts unleashed."[72] Typically they contained the *London Gazette,* the twice-weekly government publication, but other journals as well, including the *Amsterdam Gazette* even while Britain was at war with the United Provinces,[73] and letters from soldiers and sailors telling of the course of battle.[74]

Coffeehouses were licensed after 1673, but this did not enable the government to control the printed material they disseminated; efforts by Danby in 1675 and 1676 to persuade coffeehouse proprietors to sup-press antigovernment pamplets failed.[75] As one supporter of the king wrote during the controversies of 1679–81, "[W]e have the Coffee-House Tables continually spread with the noisome Excrements of dis-eased and laxative Scribblers."[76] In response the government began printing publications of its own.[77] The coffeehouses in time became places where men did business — stockbrokers were removed from the Royal Exchange in 1697 and stockbrokers traded shares at coffee-houses, while Edward Lloyd started underwriting insurance at his coffeehouse in 1700[78] — but in the late 1670s and early 1680s the coffee-houses were more important as political meeting places and as a form of mass media. So knowledge of the charges made in the Popish Plot, theoretically limited to the king, his ministers, and members of Parliament, now spread through the coffeehouses to London and from there out in the countryside. And with the expiration of the Licensing Act, there were even fewer limits on the printed word. As the historian John Kenyon writes, after 1679 the government "never felt strong enough to prohibit any publication that did not libel the King or his immediate family, and only the most daring of those."[79]

The issue raised by the Catholicism of James in 1673 and inflamed by the Popish Plot in 1678 remained open in the long days of early summer 1679. Shaftesbury evidently thought that he could get Charles to give in on exclusion as he had on other issues before. Facing a hostile House of Commons, Charles had given in and revoked the Declarations of Indulgence he had issued in 1662 and 1672, had given his approval to the Test Act in 1673, and had abandoned his mentor (and James's father-in-law) Clarendon in 1667.[80] There was obviously a majority against exclusion in the Lords, which seldom voted against the Court. But Shaftesbury probably thought that now that he was one of the king's leading ministers, he could bring pressure on the peers and bishops and that the king would be feel himself compelled to yield so long as the Commons remained solidly committed. Shaftesbury seemed confident he could succeed; he said he was convinced that "things must be worse before they could be better."[81] In exclusion he had a polarizing binary issue, one you must be either for or against, impossible to compromise on so long as parliamentarians remained unconvinced that it was impossible to rely on limitations on a Catholic king. As the historian K. H. D. Haley writes, "On the question whether James should succeed or not, it was difficult to escape the responsibility of making up one's mind, and afterwards it was even more difficult (though not impossible) to change it."[82]

But Charles proved more stubborn than Shaftesbury expected. Shaftesbury counted on the king's needing Parliament to vote him money, unaware that Danby's fiscal tightening had made Charles less needy and more able to live on his income and existing taxes. Charles also remained loyal to members of his immediate family, a family whose only major economic asset was, as his poverty in exile made clear, the Crown. For all his talents — he was an intelligent and shrewd man, with wide-ranging interests in everything from sport to science — it was obvious that Charles would have cut little figure in the world but for the fact that he was the oldest son of a king. He could recall his father's insistence that his brother James not usurp his own hereditary right of inheritance, and he knew that James, even when his views differed, always respected his primacy and obeyed him. He respected and perhaps had real affection for Queen Catherine, who never caused him trouble despite his flagrant infidelities, and resisted all attempts to force him to divorce her. He was evidently perplexed in 1672 that his nephew William refused his offer of a royal title (subordinated of course to Charles and Louis XIV), when that seemed so convenient to the rest of the family. He was led into the secret Treaty of Dover — disclosure of which could have proved ruinous in England — at least in part out of loyalty and affection for his sister Minette. Look at Van Dyck's glossy portraits of Charles and his siblings in their serene days of security and safety in the 1630s: this seems to have been a happy family that remained loyal to their father as long as he lived, remained loyal to the new head of the family as long as he did, and would remain loyal to each other, including the next rightful heir — and brave the consequences.[83]

Shaftesbury's determination and Charles's stubbornness combined to produce the first political parties in English history, the Whigs and the Tories.[84] Both names were insults. *Whig* was a Scottish term used for horse thieves and applied to Presbyterians. *Tory* was an Irish term used for outlaws and applied to Catholics.[85] Whigs tended to favor toleration of Dissenters as well as the exclusion of James from the throne; Tories strongly favored the primacy of the Church of England and advocated passive obedience to the king. The creation of a Whig political party organization began as Charles prorogued Parliament on May 27, 1679, and accelerated as he dissolved Parliament on July 12 and called for new elections in August. A revolt of Covenanters broke out in Scotland in early June, and Charles appointed his bastard son the Duke of Monmouth commander of the army there. Everyone remembered that a Scottish rebellion in 1638 had led to the Civil War and the downfall of Charles I, but this time Monmouth won a decisive victory at Bothwell Bridge on June 22. That reduced pressure on the King, but at the same time gained prestige for Monmouth, who seemed to some to be an alternative to the Duke of York as the heir to the throne.[86] There turned out to be fewer contested elections in August 1679 than there had been in February, largely because supporters of exclusion who had won their seats in earlier contests were not challenged this time.[87]

These have been judged to be the first two-party elections in English history: the sudden emergence of two-party national politics within a system that had previously provided for a very different kind of politics. "Local interests and family connections still formed the basis of most candidatures and contests, but many elections were now fought in addition on national issues. . . . Moreover, the Press, which in the previous election had been of little influence, contributed greatly to the systematic political character of the contests."[88] Even a historian skeptical of the central importance of the exclusion issue writes, "If party politics first emerged between 1679 and 1681 it was because the constitutional conflict added a new layer of polarity over, and to a large extent overlapping with, the religious one and because anti-popery both drew men into political controversy and to some extent justified their expressions of discontent."[89] This led in time to an acceptance of the legitimacy of policy differences and party loyalties, and a decline in "the expectations of uniformity that had been current in the early Stuart period and that the Restoration regime attempted to resurrect."[90] The Court influence was exerted in favor of the Tories who opposed exclusion. But the Court influence, though more organized than it was in February, was nowhere near as organized and pervasive as it would become in the eighteenth century.[91]

Shaftesbury, nominally at least one of the king's chief ministers, was very much in favor of exclusion. With his intimate knowledge of men and constituencies, Shaftesbury seems to have been something of a campaign manager for the early Whig party. Pamphlets were circulated, as widely as they had been in the 1640s and 1650s,[92] urging the rejection of "favourers of Popery" and the election of "men of good conscience and courage, thoroughly principled in the Protestant religion." Their titles included *Unanimous Club of Voters* (which listed those said to have taken pensions from Danby's government),[93] *England's Great Interest in the Choice of a New Parliament,* and *Sober and Serious Queries, humbly offered to all good Protestants in England, in order to a choice of the New Parliament.*[94] Voters were urged to vote against candidates supported by local landowners and for those who supported sound principles, i.e., exclusion. "Rather take a Stranger if recommended by an unquestionable Hand, than a Neighbour ill affected to your interest. 'Tis not pleasing a Neighbour, because rich and powerful, but saving England that you are to eye."[95] Such partisan electioneering did not succeed everywhere: some counties and boroughs elected both supporters and opponents of exclusion.[96] But it certainly was a far stronger factor than it had been since the Restoration of Charles II. Elections, once mostly uncontested, now became structured events, with nomination, speeches, campaign rallies; candidates appeared at polling sites and addressed electors, nominated tellers of the vote, and kept tallies of the vote themselves.[97]

There was often tumult. In Norfolk, a county with 6,000 voters, the Tory landowner Lord Yarmouth's son grabbed the writ of election and tried to postpone it to the disadvantage of the Whigs, and the sheriff tried to get voters to take an oath that they had attended Church services, but the crowds resisted this; one Tory candidate fled and two Whigs were elected.[98] In Norfolk some three thousand voted over three days; leaders on both sides entered the county town leading processions of two hundred mounted men.[99] The Whigs won both seats despite the efforts of the second Duke of Albemarle, son of General George Monck, who himself had been elected to the Commons in the county of Devon at age 13.[100] In Buckinghamshire the Tory sheriff switched the election from Aylesbury to the Tory town of Buckingham; a caravan of Whigs spent the night in a village outside and then stormed early into town, led by the mercurial Duke of Buckingham, and won both seats.[101]

The City of London, with 6,000 voters, had returned four Whigs in February; the Tory sheriff delayed the election till the end of the election period, to minimize its effect on elections elsewhere, but amid a crowd of 5,000 liverymen the Court candidates could win no more than 500 votes and the election was over in an hour.[102] In the city of Westminster, with an electorate of 25,000, the largest in England, the poll went on for eight days, and one Whig was defeated only after the king's servants were brought in from Windsor to vote; the result was one of many challenged in the Commons and was overturned by a party-line vote.[103]

THE POSITION OF the Whigs was weakened in the summer of 1679 by two unexpected events. One was the acquittal on July 18 of the queen's physician, George Wakeman, on charges by Titus Oates that he was plotting the death of the king. The presiding judge, Lord Justice Scroggs, who had given great credence to Oates's evidence in his jury charges in a previous trial, in this one cast grave doubt on it.[104] The chief accuser of the Popish Plot now stood at least partly discredited. John Evelyn, who attended the trial, wrote, "I do looke on Oates as a vaine, insolent man, puff'd up, with the favour of the Commons, for having discovered something realy true; as more especially detecting the dangerous intrigue of Coleman, proved out of his owne letters; & of a general designe, which the Jesuited party of the Papists, ever had, & still have to ruine the Church of England; buyt that he was trusted with those great secrets he pretended, or had any solid ground for what he accused divers noble men of, I have many reasons to induce my contrary beliefe."[105]

The other unexpected event was the sudden illness of King Charles on August 21. For the next few days he seemed to be in danger of dying. Several lords who opposed exclusion—the soldier Lord Feversham, the Marquis of Halifax, the Earl of Essex—sent word to James.[106] They feared that the king would die and that Monmouth, on the scene and in command of an army, would move to succeed him. John Churchill sped to Brussels and brought back James, "dressed like a French officer in his scarf," across the Channel and on a breakneck horseback ride to Whitehall, where they found that the king had recovered.[107] Still, the king's sudden illness seems to have affected everyone's thinking. Before, he had been a vigorous and healthy man of 49; now it seemed possible he could die suddenly at any time. That meant that James's succession—or a revolt against it—could happen at any time. The Commons had voted to exclude him from the throne; would the Duke of Monmouth, in command of an army, try to achieve that result? It would matter very much who was in place to take command.

With that in mind, Halifax and Essex, who joined with

Shaftesbury in opposing the Court from 1673 to 1678 but who opposed exclusion, then persuaded the king that James had to depart again and that Monmouth had to leave, too.[108] James returned to Brussels, and Monmouth, removed from the captaincy general of the army and from the command of the Life Guards in favor respectively of the King and the second Duke of Albemarle,[109] went to Utrecht in the United Provinces. In October Charles permitted James to travel to Scotland, and by land through England. On October 14 the king dismissed Shaftesbury from the Privy Council and his position as Lord President. The next day he prorogued the new Parliament, moving its opening day from October 30, 1679, to January 26, 1680.[110] The battle was joined.

Shaftesbury proceeded to mount what amounted to a political campaign, designed to get Charles to agree to the exclusion of James. On November 5, Guy Fawkes Day, and November 17, Queen Elizabeth I's birthday, there were giant demonstrations, complete with burnings of effigies of the pope and the College of Cardinals at Temple Bar, the boundary between the City of London and Westminster. These were well organized and elaborate affairs; the pope's effigy cost £100 and the burning was witnessed by 150,000 to 200,000 people in London.[111] On November 27, Monmouth, without permission from his father, returned from exile and stayed at Shaftesbury's house in the City of London. The Guards lit bonfires in the streets outside Whitehall in honor of their former commander: John Evelyn noted "The Bells & Bone-fires of the Citty at this arival of D: M: publishing their joy to the no small regret of some at Court; This Duke (whom for distinction they cal'd the Protestant Duke, though the sonn of an abandoned woman) the people made their Idol of."[112] Shaftesbury never committed himself to supporting Monmouth as heir, though many thought he did. He still held out the possibility that Charles could be persuaded to divorce the queen, remarry, and produce a new heir — one who would likely be a minor when Charles died, in which case the government might well be guided by whoever could command a majority in the Commons. By leaving this possibility open, Shaftesbury helped guarantee that William of Orange would not support exclusion. William might hope that his wife Mary might be made monarch in place of James, in which case he would rule. But either Monmouth or a new son of Charles would establish a new hereditary line.[113]

The Whigs circulated petitions urging the king to disregard the advice of his evil ministers to allow James to return and to prorogue Parliament. These were effectively a substitute for pamphlets, which during this prorogation were effectively prohibited by a proclamation against the press.[114] The first petition drive was organized in November in London and Westminster. It was followed by dozens of petition drives throughout the country. The signatures not just of those entitled to vote but of ordinary Englishmen were sought.[115] This was not the first time petition drives had been organized; there was one in the 1640s during the period of civil war. But this drive had support from leading lords and landowners and reached deeper into the population. "House-to-house canvassers collected signatures. Tables, pens, ink and forms were placed in taverns and at the Royal Exchange. . . . Agents were sent into the counties with printed forms for subscription; many of these men had previously been active during elections. They, together with local men, went from parish to parish collecting signatures, and leaders were appointed to present the completed petitions."[116] A proclamation was issued prohibiting petitioning, but it could not be enforced. Tories, opponents of exclusion, responded by circulating petitions of their own, many of them labeled "abhorrences," abhorring exclusion and upholding the position of the Established Church against Dissenters,[117] but they had many fewer organizers and obtained many fewer signatures.

The constant petitioning, and the continued charges of a Popish plot, amounted to a Whig campaign against the king. In response Charles purged local officials from office who were not qualified under the Corporation Act, which authorized local government. The Court used *quo warranto* proceedings to eject Whiggish local officials and to put Tories in their places. Shaftesbury contined to demand a session of Parliament and called on independent members of the Privy Council to resign in protest, and several did.[118] Charles continued to prorogue Parliament, setting the date of the session back from January 26 to April 15, May 17, July 1, July 22, and August 23; ultimately Parliament did not convene until October 21, 1680.[119]

In the elections for the sheriffs of London that July, the Court was unable to prevent Whigs from winning by margins of greater than two to one; these sheriffs took into their hands the selection of London juries. Shaftesbury sought to indict James as a Catholic recusant and the Duchess of Portsmouth, one of the King's mistresses, as a common nuisance, but the indictments were suppressed by judges.[120] Meanwhile the Duke of Monmouth refused to obey Charles's order that he leave the country in January 1680; he refused to take his former offices in return for exiling himself from the country for a year, and he made a triumphal tour of the West Country that summer.[121]

From all these commotions William of Orange kept a careful distance. The Earl of Sunderland, one of Charles's ministers, urged William to come to England, but William refused.[122] He entertained Monmouth cordially in The Hague, but disclaimed responsibility when he returned to England without the king's permission. William maintained a cordial correspondence with Charles and also with others in the various factions in England;[123] his main interest was getting Charles and Parliament to agree to an alliance against France.[124] Sunderland, whose changes of position over the years make for a dizzying narrative, in June tried to tempt the Whigs to support an anti-French alliance and limitations on a Catholic king rather than exclusion, agreeing with Charles that exclusion was "an unlawful and unjust thing."[125] Then in the fall he promised them to get the king to agree to exclusion.[126]

When the Commons finally came into session in October, more than a year after the elections, the Whigs quickly moved an exclusion bill forward. Aggressive leadership came from Sir William Jones, a City lawyer and enemy of Shaftesbury.[127] Tories, more organized than before, said any bill must name the heir; the Whigs, divided over that, refused. Several prominent members who had opposed exclusion in the last Parliament supported it this time. The bill received its third reading and was passed on November 11.[128] But Charles, despite Sunderland's maneuvering, remained obdurate. As the House of Lords considered the bill, he stood by the fire and watched as an unlikely defender of his policy outdebated his former ally Shaftesbury.

This was Sir George Savile, Viscount (later Earl and Marquis) of Halifax. Halifax came from fine Cavalier stock; his uncle the Earl of

Strafford had been impeached by Parliament and beheaded in 1641; he was also a nephew of the Earl of Shaftesbury, and his first wife was the sister of the Earl of Sunderland. Temperamentally he was a contrarian, a course he could indulge because he was financially independent, a Nottinghamshire and Yorkshire landlord with an income of £10,000 a year who exhibited a certain diffidence about politics. After serving one year in the House of Commons he had not bothered to be elected to the Cavalier Parliament in 1661, but served on the public accounts commission after the fall of the Earl of Clarendon as the king's chief minister in 1667, and was rewarded with a baronetcy in 1668.[129] Clarendon had denied him a peerage on the grounds that he "was looked on as void of all sense of religion even to the doubting, if not denying, that there is a God."[130] Long leery of the growing power of Louis XIV's France,[131] he was brought into government in 1672 to off-set feeling against Charles II's alliance with France against the United Provinces. But he opposed Charles II's declaration of indulgence and voted for the Test Act of 1673 and went into opposition generally; he was rated "thrice worthy" by Shaftesbury in 1677.[132]

Halifax styled himself a "trimmer," one who modulated the course of opposing factions; he opposed the Test Act of 1678 in a form that would have excluded James, Duke of York, from the House of Lords, but supported a resolution that the duke be removed "from the King's presence and counsel."[133] On exclusion he was obdurate. He supported Charles's proposals for limitations on the power of a Catholic monarch, but over the course of two years he vociferously opposed exclusion. He was not unwilling to oppose the king: after Charles had named the impeached Earl of Danby a marquis, Halifax maintained that the report must be a "flamm," that it was impossible to believe the king could be so ungrateful to his people, but that if he had, it was "not to be borne." "My God," said Charles, "and I must bear it and say nothing."[134] But on November 18, 1680, after Lord William Russell grabbed the exclusion bill from the table in the Commons and rushed it over to the Lords, Charles must have been pleased to watch Halifax best Shaftesbury in seven hours of debate. Halifax evidently argued—only fragmentary accounts of the debate remain—that exclusion would lead to civil war, a civil war in which James might well have Ireland, Scotland, and France on his side.[135]

The debate was quickly followed by a vote on the first reading. The Lords had a solid majority of peers and bishops for Court measures during Danby's ministry, and the same majority continued to oppose exclusion.[136] How much Halifax's eloquence mattered is unclear; the Court, with the votes of appointees and bishops in hand, would surely have prevailed in any case. But the margin of 63 to 30 effectively extinguished the possibility that Parliament would exclude James from the throne.[137] The Whigs launched vicious attacks on Halifax and demanded his removal from office. In debates on other issues, the Whigs continued to denounce James and demand exclusion, but under the rules the bill could not be brought up again. The Whigs supported an Act of Association that would have made those who proclaimed James the rightful successor traitors and would have resulted in a purging of Tory lord lieutenants, deputies, justices, and military officers.[138] In the 1640s Parliament had led an armed rebellion against Charles I. In 1680 it seemed to be leading legal rebellion against Charles II.

❧

ON JANUARY 10, 1681, Charles prorogued Parliament once again. Before Parliament was suspended, the Whigs quickly passed bills to declare Catholics responsible for the fire of 1666, to decry the persecution of Dissenting Protestants, and to declare that Monmouth should be restored to his offices.[139] But these expired when, on January 18, Charles dissolved the Parliament, called for new elections, and decreed that the new Parliament would meet in March not in London but in Oxford. The bitterness of the political atmosphere led a few Whigs to change their views or not run again.[140] During the session, the Whigs had published the votes of the House of Commons and printed the statements of accusers of the Popish Plot.[141] Now the Whigs, as they had in 1679, distributed their pamphlets and the Tories, more organized than before, responded in kind.[142] "Liberty was in danger" was the message of one Whig pamphlet, "for the constitution — the best in the world — was threatened. Already abroad, in France and Spain, and nearer home in Scotland, parliaments had become disused through the 'cunning and address' of princes, the 'servility and folly' of the nobility and gentry, the 'suppleness, treachery and fawning' of the clergy, and the 'ignorance and stupidity' of the common people. Its enemies were to be found both at home and abroad, the Papist party in England and Louis XIV who, it was said, 'shakes his fasces over us.' "[143] Tories summoned up memories of the 1640s and 1650s and argued that the Whigs were bent on tolerating Dissenting Protestantism, which was as much of a threat to the Church of England as was Catholicism. As one Tory wrote, "The Papists would destroy our Church and State; so would the Common-Wealthsmen; the Papists would set up Popery and absolute Monarchy; the other an Amsterdam Religion, and Arbitrary Government in the hands of many."[144]

The Whigs won speedy victories in London, where local officials contrived to hold the election early. In Westminster, where the voting before had taken eight days, the incumbent Whigs were reelected in three and a half hours.[145] In the counties, contests tended to follow the same lines as in the second election of 1679. In Norfolk the two exclusionist members were reelected. In Essex, where the Duke of Albemarle's efforts had failed tumultuously in August 1679, the two Whig members were reelected unopposed.[146] Similarly, Buckinghamshire, where a change in the site of the election in August 1679 led to a spirited contest, the Whig magnate Thomas Wharton was reelected, and Richard Hampden, grandson of one of the parliamentary heroes in the 1640s, won the other seat, both without opposition.[147]

Tories organized opposition, but were unable to defeat Whigs in Worcestershire or Yorkshire; they could field no candidates in Kent.[148] Whigs blamed their defeats in some constituencies — Cambridgeshire, Bristol, Southwark — on hostile sheriffs and returning officers. But they won in other constituencies when they sent in Whig lords to rally the voters.[149] During the campaign period Shaftesbury and John Locke drafted instructions to new members, versions of which were sent out as "up addresses" from the people, urging members to vote no money to the Crown until exclusion was passed, investigate the Popish Plot, and make habeas corpus more effective.[150] The Tories presented addresses as well, also urging prosecution of the Popish Plot, but also calling on members to "cheerfully" vote money to the king and to honor the king's prerogatives.[151]

The king arrived in Oxford after taking in the spring races at Burford in the Cotswolds, and his supporters settled into quarters at Merton, Christ Church, and Corpus Christi Colleges; the Whigs occupied Balliol, and many of them arrived "armed to the teeth."[152] It was, John Evelyn wrote, "An extraordinary sharp, cold Spring, not yet a leafe on the trees, frost & snow lying: whilst the whole nation was in a great ferment."[153] The king brought 500 troops, and some of the Whigs had their own armed retainers. In his opening statement on March 21, Charles held himself once again amenable "to remove all reasonable fears that may arise from the possibility of a Popish successor's coming to the Crown" and to "hearken to any expedient, by which the religion might be preserved, and the monarchy not destroyed." The Commons, perhaps hoping for compromise, delayed action on exclusion until March 26. The Whigs pressed for an exclusion bill, with no successor specified. Tories advanced a bill for a regency, with James still king but banished from the kingdom.[154] The Whigs continued to emphasize the dangers supposedly shown by the Popish Plot, while the Tories started exploiting fears that the exclusion of James would lead to another civil war.

The debate continued as the Commons met in the Sheldonian Theater and the Lords in the Hall of Christ Church, where Charles watched their deliberations. The king proceeded to send for the House of Commons, and the official known as Black Rod went to the Sheldonian and commanded their presence. They entered the hall through a narrow stairway and saw the king in his robes and crown, which had been smuggled into the building and which he was required to wear when he dissolved Parliament. Which he promptly did: the tall robed king must have been an imposing sight in a hall full of men who took care to arrive at Oxford armed. "All the world may see to what a point we are come, that we are not like to have a good end when the divisions at the beginning are such."[155]

The Whigs prepared for new elections and published pamphlets; the Tories issued "loyal addresses" that thanked the King for his declaration justifying dissolution. Intellectual support for the Tory position came from Robert Filmer's book *Patriarcha,* written in the 1620s but published only in 1680, proclaiming a divine right of kings and the duty of subjects to give passive obedience to his commands. "To Majestie or Sovereignty belongeth an Absolute Power not to be subject to any law," Filmer wrote. Echoing that, a Tory in the House of Commons proclaimed, "I am of opinion that Kings of England have their right from God alone, and that no Power on Earth can deprive them of it."[156] But others argued that the king was bound by the laws, including those that established the Church of England: "Active obedience [is] to be yielded to the King as Supream, in *omnibus licitis,* in all things lawful."[157] And Filmer, who had written in a much earlier and quite different time, seemed hardly likely to provide a convincing philosophical basis for monarchical authority; "how extraordinarily dingy," writes J. H. Plumb, "to have to fall back on the antiquated Filmer."[158]

Charles did not claim to rule except within the law, but after the Exclusion Crisis he was determined to rule without Parliament. In January 1681, Louis XIV had approached Charles through his ambassador Barillon and offered him a payment of 1,500,000 livres a year for three years—about £110,000—in return for Charles withdrawing from his alliance with Spain and making no alliance against France. Charles held out for more, and just before the Oxford Parliament met, Louis offered 2,000,000 livres; Charles accepted. With Louis's subsidy, and with the economies of his most recent ministers, Charles had an income sufficient to maintain the government in peacetime, and no longer needed, as he had during most of his reign, to have Parliament vote new taxes to raise more money.[159] William of Orange journeyed to London in July 1681, but found the Whigs still insisting on exclusion and Charles opposed to that and to any action against Louis XIV. To Laurence Hyde, James's brother-in-law and chief advocate in Charles's government, William denied that he backed exclusion.[160] According to Burnet—a partisan witness, to be sure—Charles in a private meeting in Windsor said that "whenever the Duke of York should come to reign, he would be so restless and violent that he could not hold it four years to an end," and told William to pay attention only to those of his letters that were closed with a particular seal.[161] A wink and a nod, perhaps, and a hint that William would have the throne soon enough if he would let James alone for a few years.

Charles proceeded to shore up his powers through legal process. Shaftesbury, whose agents had been stirring up accusers in a bogus Irish Popish plot, was arrested in July and sent to the Tower of London to await trial by the House of Lords, which seemed sure to order him executed. But first there had to be a true bill issued by a grand jury, whose members were chosen by the Whig Lord Mayor and sheriffs of London. Shaftesbury had close ties to the merchant community of London, and the jurors chosen were merchants "worth a million of money," including John Houblon and Michael Godfrey, who in 1694 would become respectively the first governor and deputy governor of the Bank of England.[162] The jury met in November, and the jurors closely questioned and discredited the witnesses and returned a verdict of *ignoramus*—we know of no reason he should be charged—and he was released, to the cheers of the Whigs.[163]

Meanwhile, Charles was acting to reduce the powers of the Whigs in the City, which had become "virtually a republic, an Amsterdam on the Thames," as one historian put it.[164] He prevented a Whig from becoming leader of its Artillery Company, and purged Whigs from the lord lieutenancy. The government brought *quo warranto* proceedings to deprive the City of its existing charter, and maneuvered to elect a Tory as lord mayor in 1681. Tory clubs were formed, and a mob of Tory law students smashed the windows of the King's Head Tavern in Chancery Lane, where the Whiggish Green Ribbon Club met. Elections to the Common Council had shown a shift from the Whigs to the Tories,[165] and in 1682 the Tories, with irregular tactics and amid a furious pamphlet war, elected the two sheriffs and another lord mayor.[166]

Shaftesbury left his house in Aldersgate Street when the new sheriffs took office and soon fled to Amsterdam, whose power he had in 1672 said must be destroyed; he died there in January 1683. Monmouth conducted a triumphal tour in Chester and the northwest, but was arrested on his return home. He was removed as chancellor of Cambridge University, and his portrait was burned.[167] The Court continued its campaign of seeking the surrender of municipal charters, followed by the filling of all local offices with Tories.[168] The Crown brought *quo warranto* proceedings against fifty-six boroughs, and between April 1682 and February 1685 they surrendered their charters and were awarded new ones that allowed the king to nominate mayors, aldermen, and burgesses.[169]

The intended and effective result was that boroughs that had elected Whig MPs were now in the hands of Tories, to the point that "the Crown, in fact, could now pack Parliament" in any future election.[170] Even in boroughs without representation in Parliament, charters were changed and offices filled with men who would enforce the laws against those who attended religious services outside the Church of England.[171] Dissenting Protestants as well as Catholics were widely prosecuted. In June 1683 an obscure tradesman revealed details of a plan to assassinate Charles and James at Rye House in Hertfordshire. Amid a swirl of charges and countercharges, many of them possibly false, trials were held and Lord William Russell, one of the Whig leaders in the Commons, and the republican Algernon Sidney were executed, while the Earl of Essex committeed suicide in the Tower.[172]

It was some time in the years before these events that John Locke, who fled to the Netherlands in September 1683,[173] composed his *Two Treatises on Government,* to refute Filmer and to justify the overthrow of Charles's rule; it was not published until November 1689, and then anonymously; although it was widely taken, in England from the 1690s and in America in our own Revolutionary period, as a justification of the Glorious Revolution, it actually was written as a justification for exclusion or for the armed rebellion that was planned by Shaftesbury and that resulted in the Rye House Plot[174] and "transform[ed] Hobbses's teaching into a doctrine of anticipation, resistance, and revolution."[175] Monmouth was involved in the plot — evidently he was expected to lead an army in rebellion in Scotland[176] and to take the throne himself. He was forgiven by the king, but when he would not confess publicly, Charles banished him from the kingdom.[177] William of Orange sent his trusted aide Willem van Bentinck to London to assure the king of his loyalty and to gather any news he could.[178]

In June 1683 another event of some moment took place: the marriage of Princess Anne, James's younger daughter, to Prince George of Denmark. Anne's religious education had been conducted by Henry Compton, Bishop of London, and she was a staunch Anglican; George was a Lutheran Protestant. But he was also a Dane, and his brother King Christian V was at that time an ally of Louis XIV. Prince George turned out to have no political leanings of any consequence, or any great influence; as Charles said of him, "I've tried him drunk, and I've tried him sober, and there's nothing in him."[179] Anne was guided in her political views not so much by her husband as by her friend from childhood, Sarah Churchill; John Churchill escorted Prince George from Denmark to England, and after the wedding Anne got the king to name Sarah as one of her ladies of the bedchamber.[180] This marriage did, however, alarm William of Orange, who noted that Anne received a more generous settlement than his wife had. He could not be sure if his worries that George would be an agent for a pro-France policy or that Anne would prove susceptible to her father's Catholicism would turn out to be unjustified.[181]

The years after 1681 have generally been labeled the Tory Reaction, and there does seem to have been some shift of opinion, visible in some election results as in London. But it was also, Tim Harris argues, a change in "mobilization": "In the late 1670s the Whigs were very successful at mobilizing the masses against the government of Charles II and the Catholic succession by playing on people's fears of popery and arbitrary government in both the future and the present, but in doing so they were able to exploit genuine dissatisfaction that already existed at the grass-roots level in many places across the three kingdoms." If the Whigs had been emboldened to mobilize by the Popish Plot and the Tories had been intimidated, the balance worked the other way after the dissolution and especially after the exposure of the Rye House Plot, and the Tories managed to "rally those who were not natural Whigs but who had temporarily become convinced that something must be wrong because of all the noise that the Whigs were generating. Now the Tories were making a lot of noise themselves — they were rhyming noise with noise, as L'Estrange put it in his own inimitable way."[182]

Once the Tory propaganda campaign seemed to be working, the government urged the Stationers' Company of London to enforce its by-laws regulating the publishing trade, and many newspapers — Tory as well as Whig — were shut down. "What we see, in other words, is a government which realized that it had been unable to contain the public sphere, which recognized that it temporarily needed to engage with it, and which, after having successfully done so, then sought to contain it once again."[183]

And to contain it militarily. From Scotland, and while in London when Parliament was not in session from February to October 1680, James adroitly placed loyalists, including John Churchill and George Legge, in key military positions, in the garrisons near London and at Hull, Portsmouth, and Chester, and in the "plantations" as well — Tangier (until it was abandoned in 1683), Virginia, Jamaica, Barbados, New York, and Pennsylvania. Perhaps he was anticipating another civil war — or was threatening civil war should Parliament vote to exclude him from the throne.[184] In Scotland he continued Monmouth's lenient treatment of the Dissenters, whose rebellion had been broken in June 1679, but took steps against those in political rebellion. In 1681 he got the Scottish Parliament to agree to additional taxes and a Test Act requiring adherence to Protestantism, allegiance to the monarchy, and an oath not to make any alteration of church and state. The Scottish Parliament also passed a law guaranteeing James's succession to the Scottish crown: a step that could result in war if England should reject him.[185]

His conduct was seen, at least by English Tories, as evidence that he would as king support the Church of England — and that, should he be excluded in England, he would have Scotland behind him. Through Churchill, he urged Charles to govern without Parliament, cooperate with Louis XIV, and allow him to return to England.[186] Churchill tried without success to persuade James to go back to the Church of England; as he wrote to George Legge, "You will find that nothing is done in that which was so much desired, soe that sooner or laiter we must all be undone."[187] In February 1682, Charles, prompted by the minister who was keeping tight rein on his finances, Laurence Hyde (later the Earl of Rochester), James's brother-in-law, allowed James to return to England. He was received enthusiastically in Yarmouth and Norwich and joined Charles at the races in Newmarket, then returned to London with him. When he returned to Scotland to bring his wife to England, his ship sank and 150 people drowned. But with

Churchill's help, James made it to safety in a lifeboat, and returned with his still-young wife to England.[188] James named Churchill a Scottish baron in return for his rescue.[189]

※❧

THE REST OF Charles's reign seemed peaceful. The strong popular feeling for exclusion and the Whigs seemed to abate; a countervailing popular feeling for the Crown and the Church of England seemed to grow stronger.[190] These were the peak years of prosecution for absence from Church of England services, rising from 310 in 1681 to 718 in 1684, and there were 3,800 arrests in London for violation of the penal laws; more than at any other time since the Restoration, the Church of England had something in the nature of a religious monopoly.[191] After the discovery of the Rye House Plot, Charles restored James to the cabinet council in June 1683, and in May 1684 James was restored to the Privy Council. James persuaded Charles to pardon Catholic recusants who had served Charles I in the Civil War, and to make Rochester the lord lieutenant of Ireland.[192] And he successfully urged the granting of a charter to the Quaker William Penn, his ally in urging religious tolerance, for the colony of Pennsylvania in 1682. But James was frustrated in his desire to eliminate colonial assemblies in Virginia and Jamaica by Halifax, whose advice was accepted by the king.[193] James accepted an assembly in New York, but installed the Catholic Thomas Dongan as governor and insisted on toleration of Catholics and Dissenters as well.[194] And he prevailed in December 1684 in the creation of the Dominion of New England, which dismissed the assemblies of Masschusetts, New Hampshire, Rhode Island, and Connecticut, and replaced them with rule by the governor, Sir Edmund Andros, who had earlier been driven out of New York.[195] James's project of eliminating the colonial assemblies, had it not been reversed after the Revolution of 1688–89, would have vastly altered American politics, by preventing the colonists from gaining political experience and eliminating the forums where much of the protest against the British government in the 1760s and 1770s was voiced.

In England the government continued to alter the borough charters and to install reliable lord lieutenants, sheriffs, and justices of the peace, to maintain order locally, and to produce favorable outcomes in the next parliamentary elections, although Charles continued governing without one.[196] The great controversies that had produced civil war, the Commonwealth and Protectorate, the Restoration, and the Exclusion Crisis seemed to be over.

Chapter 5

KING JAMES

WHITEHALL PALACE, FEBRUARY 1685, the apartments of the king. On Monday, February 2, Charles suffered a stroke while shaving. He was given the customary enemas and bleeding, and weakened over several days. He refused to take the sacrament from the Anglican bishops and bid James bring in a priest, who, after the room was cleared of all Protestants, received him into the Catholic Church. Perhaps, after all, his promise to Louis in 1670 to convert had been made out of religious conviction. Charles died February 6, at age 54, nearly 25 years after the Restoration.[1] "The History of his reigne," John Evelyn wrote in his diary, "will certainly be the most wonderfull for the variety of matter & accidents above any extant in former ages: The [sad tragical] death of his father, his banishment, & hardships, his miraculous restauration, conjurations against him; Parliaments, Warrs, Plagues, Fires, Comets; revolutions abroad happning in his time with a thousand other particulars."[2]

Charles II left a seemingly tranquil inheritance to his brother James II, who immediately summoned his council and asserted his succession. Charles had ruled without a Parliament for nearly four years and seemed content to continue on that course indefinitely. Yet England was only momentarily tranquil. It was a kingdom in which power was held largely by bluff. The king had no large standing army at his command, as Louis XIV had in France; he had just 8,865 soldiers in England, 2,199 in Scotland, and 7,500 in Ireland, plus six regiments of the Anglo-Dutch brigade stationed in the Netherlands—not huge military forces in kingdoms with 5 million, 1 million, and 2 million inhabitants.[3] The six troops of the Royal Dragoons, made up of soldiers withdrawn from Tangier, were called to London on the king's death, but their numbers were in the hundreds.[4]

James faced a potential pretender, the Duke of Monmouth, Charles's oldest natural child, who had successfully quelled a rebellion in Scotland and was, at Charles's death, a welcome guest at William of Orange's court in The Hague.[5] England was a kingdom with an Established Church, but one in which many people were Dissenting Protestants and a few were Catholics. It had a ferocious criminal code, but the law was by no means always enforced. It was a country where most people felt that a monarchy was needed to hold society together and regretted the republican experiment of the 1650s, and it was a country with a horror for the disorder of civil war. In the last years of his reign, Charles had seemed more powerful than ever before.

Yet in many ways his government was weak: England was a nation lightly governed, with an unsteady order that had been overturned more than once in living memory, a regime that in the ordinary course of things exerted only a gentle Lockeian control but where the menace of Hobbesian disorder lurked and threatened to spring into life. Lightly governed: as historian Tim Harris writes, "To make its rule effective, the crown depended on the cooperation and unpaid assistance of a wide range of people at the local level—not just the lord lieutenants and their deputies, and the gentry JPs who ran the counties, and the merchants and businessmen who ran the [borough] corporations, but also the more humble types who played a crucial role in governance and law enforcement in their capacities as trial jurors, parish constables, nightwatchmen, militiamen and even informers."[6]

JAMES IMMEDIATELY ASSURED the Privy Council that despite his own faith he would govern as a supporter of the Established Church. "I shall make it my endeavour to preserve this government both in church and state as it is by law established. I know the principles of the Church of England are for monarchy and the members of it have shown themselves good and loyal subjects; therefore I shall always take care to defend and support it. I know too that the laws of England are sufficient to make the king as great a monarch as I can wish; and as I shall never depart from the rights and prerogatives of the crown, so I shall never invade any man's property." Well-chosen words: a promise to govern as his brother had since 1681, in support of an Established Church that in turn counseled passive obedience to the monarch.[7]

James made few changes in personnel, although he did elevate John Churchill by granting him the stewardship of the borough of St. Albans, the home of Sarah's family, by naming him to his own post as governor of the Hudson's Bay Company (Churchill paid £400 for his stock and sold it in 1692 for nearly £5,000), by naming him an English baron (thus putting him in the House of Lords), and by sending him as a special envoy to Louis XIV to seek new subsidies.[8] He appointed his brother-in-law, the Earl of Rochester, as lord treasurer and Rochester's older brother, the Earl of Clarendon, as lord privy seal. He worked diligently at his desk and paid down Charles's debts. He insisted on raising the revenues authorized for Charles, though legal authority lapsed on his death; he evidently calculated that this would pressure Parliament to grant him the same revenues.[9] He insisted on decorum and had little time for the rollicking courtiers whose company Charles delighted in; while Charles received foreign envoys in his bedchamber with his hat in his hands, James received them in a special room, "with his hat firmly on his head."[10] He declared that anyone who came to court drunk would be expelled, and that husbands should be faithful to their wives (though he was not), and that sons should obey their fathers. He drank little and ate his meat and fish with a "universal sauce" made of parsley and dry toast.[11]

He also commissioned the architect Christopher Wren to build a Catholic chapel in Whitehall Palace, with statues and carving from Grinling Gibbons and Arnold Quellin and frescoes from Verrio.[12] This was not a universally popular move; John Evelyn noted on March 5, "To my griefe I saw the new pulpet set up in the popish oratory at W-hall, for the Lent preaching, Masse being publiqly saied, & the

Romanists swarming at Court with greater confidence than had ever ben scene in England since the Reformation, so as every body grew Jealous to what this would trend."[13] As his conversion and adherence to the Catholic faith showed, James had poor political judgment and was obstinate in his determination to stick with a course of action once he had made up his mind. His biographer John Miller writes matter-of-factly of "his basic lack of intelligence" and "his inability to appreciate what was, or was not, politically feasible." He goes on, "His obstinacy was that of a slow and unintelligent man who was always fearful that abler men would get the better of him."[14] James's goal, as he often said, was to "reestablish" Catholicism in England, not by forcible conversion or by having it declared the Established Church, but by putting Catholics on the same footing as members of the Church of England. He thought that many would then choose to become Catholic, as he had done. "Did others enquire into the religion as I have done, without prejudice or prepossession or partial affection, they would be of the same mind in point of religion as I am."[15] In order to do this, he tried to get Parliament to repeal the penal laws against Catholics and the Test Acts of 1673 and 1678.

But the Parliament he called for on February 16 was not of the same mind. Elections were held in March and April. They resulted in a vast turnover in membership since the elections held during the Exclusion Crisis in 1679 and 1681. The remodeling of the borough charters and the appointment of local officials sympathetic to the Court in the last four years of Charles's reign meant that the Court exerted more influence on elections than ever before; the results also reflected a genuine revulsion against the Whigs after the Exclusion Crisis and the Rye House Plot.[16] Only eight of the 33 surviving members from the counties were returned to office; five were defeated at the polls, and 28 for one reason or another chose not to stand.[17] A majority, 52 percent, of House of Commons members had been elected for the first time, the highest percentage in any Parliament between 1660 and 1690, even though only four years had passed since the last election, while there were 18 years between the elections of 1661 and 1679.[18]

Tories prevailed in most elections in the counties and boroughs. The City of London, its charter remodeled, returned four Tories in place of four Whigs. In Westminster the incumbent Whigs did not stand, and two Tories were returned.[19] In Norfolk the two Tories rejected in 1681 were elected with more than 3,400 votes each, compared with 672 and 494 respectively for their Whig opponents; the Tory vote was of the same magnitude as in the two 1679 elections, while the Whig vote was only a small fraction of what it had been then.[20] In Essex the Whig incumbent was running again, but was outmaneuvered by the Tories, led once again by the Duke of Albemarle; the election, expected to take two or three days, was over by lunchtime on the first day.[21] But in Buckinghamshire, though the Tory sheriff switched the election from Aylesbury to tiny Newport Pagnell, Thomas Wharton's Whigs once again camped out and prevailed by a wide margin. [22]

Overall the result was a House of Commons with a large Tory majority. Only a small number of former members like Wharton were able to hang on. More even than the Cavalier Parliament, James's Parliament was heavily Anglican and inclined to support the king and the Church of England. In the three exclusion Houses of Commons, 48 percent of members were Anglicans and 24 percent "probable Anglicans"; in James's Parliament, 78 percent were Anglicans and 16 percent "probable Anglicans"—again, the highest percentages in any Parliament between 1660 and 1690.[23]

Parliament met on May 19 and seven days later the Commons voted James for life the same revenues as had been voted for Charles in 1660. These had been inadequate during most of Charles's reign, but as trade increased, the yields became higher. Charles's revenues did not reach the expected £1,200,000 during much of his reign, but with the increase of trade in the 1680s they reached £1,300,000 in 1684 and rose to £1,600,000 by 1687.[24] So in the absence of war James would not find himself obliged to summon a Parliament to get money. Parliament also voted additional revenues to pay off Charles's debts, which James dutifully did, and to refurbish the fleet, one of his favorite projects.[25]

This was a Parliament inclined to passive obedience, at least so long as the king seemed inclined to stay within the law. But this was not a Parliament that was entirely of the same mind as the new king.

On May 27 a committee of some 330 members petitioned James to en-force all the laws against religious nonconformity, as they had been enforced during the last four years of Charles's reign.[26] The king protested and the Commons laid the measure aside. James's goal was repeal of the penal laws and the Test Acts, to allow Catholics freedom of worship and the right to hold public office. The petition to enforce the penal laws should have been a clear indication to him that this An-glican Parliament would never agree.

❧

IN MAY AND June, James faced armed rebellions, by the Duke of Ar-gyll in Scotland and the Duke of Monmouth in England. In January Monmouth had been entertained grandly by William of Orange and his wife (they were all first cousins, grandchildren of Charles I and Henrietta Maria) at their court in The Hague; William claimed, probably disingenuously, that he believed Monmouth still enjoyed Charles's favor. But he could have had no doubt that he did not enjoy James's, and on the news of Charles's death, Monmouth was promptly advised to leave The Hague.[27] Nor did William consider Monmouth's interest his own. Mary was now the heir to the English throne, and as queen she would undoubtedly let herself be guided, as in politics she always did, by William. William did fear that James might disinherit his older daughter, but he knew that if Monmouth should seize the throne, he would never get near it. Early in May the Duke of Argyll sailed from Holland to Scotland with three ships laden with arms; late that month Monmouth sailed from Holland to England with four ships laden with arms. The ships had gotten away because they were at the Texel, fifty miles north of Amsterdam and outside its jurisdiction; its officials needed to get the approval of the States General to assem-ble a force to stop them, and failed to do so in time.[28] William proba-bly did have information about Argyll's trip, from his Scottish secret agent William Carstares, who was in touch with James Stewart, the drafter of Argyll's manifesto; and he probably had some information about Monmouth's expedition as well.[29] In any case he promptly of-fered to send to Scotland in James's service the three Scottish regi-ments serving in the United Provinces, and to England the three

English regiments there as well, and to lead them himself; they were sent over, under the superintendence of Willem van Bentinck, but arrived too late for the fighting.[30]

Argyll landed in the Scottish Highlands and was easily defeated, then beheaded a few days later.[31] In the meantime the Scottish Parliament granted James generous revenues, declared that kings of Scotland had "sacred, supreme, absolute power and authority," and passed an act declaring it a capital crime to attend a Presbyterian field conventicle, a service held outside the Established Church.[32] It took longer to dispatch Monmouth. On June 11 he landed with only 150 men in southwest England, in Lyme Regis, a borough represented in the Commons by Sir Winston Churchill, the father of John Churchill; together they brought the report of the landing to the king. Baron Churchill was sent as a brigadier general with cavalry to stop him, but found that the militia had fled and many had gone over to Monmouth. The militia in England since Anglo-Saxon times consisted of able-bodied men obliged to keep arms and subject to being called up for military service; since 1573 it was the practice to form small groups called trained bands, all of which together comprised some 90,000 men in the seventeenth century. But their service was limited by custom, often to their home counties.[33]

Monmouth raised a force from the ordinary folk of the West Country, which at one point reached 7,000 men, including members of the local militia who had deserted.[34] He marched north to Taunton, where he proclaimed himself king June 18. James made Louis Feversham, a French Protestant and the nephew of Marshal Turenne, commander; this raised the ire of the Duke of Albemarle, who refused to serve under him, and of Churchill, who did serve anyway, but grumbled, "I see plainly that I am to have the trouble, and that the honour will be another's."[35] Churchill led the troops harassing Monmouth's forces as they marched to Bridgwater, Glastonbury, with the ruins of its ancient abbey, and to Wells, with its splendid cathedral, then across the steep Mendip Hills to Kenynsham, just east of Bristol on the River Avon, on June 25. Monmouth faced Feversham's 200 cavalrymen in Bristol and, to the west, Churchill's cavalry and Feversham's larger royal army to the west near the spa town of Bath. Monmouth marched south and managed to avoid outright defeat, but saw his forces continually harrassed and melting away.

He was back in Wells by July 1 and Bridgwater by July 3. He prepared to march north again, but, noting that the royal army three miles away in Sedgemoor was not properly entrenched, decided on a night attack July 5, in what turned out to be the last battle fought on English soil.[36] It was a daring gamble and one that failed. Churchill rallied the army in the middle of the night; Monmouth's cavalry made missteps in the dark; at dawn the rebel forces were being raked by cannon fire, and Monmouth and about 50 men fled, hoping to reach a port and seize a ship. He was discovered in a ditch, disguised as a shepherd, on the morning of July 8. Taken to London, he begged for mercy at James's feet and promised to become a Catholic; he was executed July 15.[37] Soldiers in the rebel army were hanged, and Lord Chief Justice Jeffreys convened what has been known ever since as the Bloody Assizes, sessions of court in which more than 300 alleged Monmouth supporters were sentenced to death and 1,200 ordered to be sold as slaves in Barbados.[38] The bodies of the executed were hung up in the countryside and left to rot as a grisly caution on the perils of rebellion.

By the time of the Battle of Sedgemoor, the English army had been increased to 15,710 men; by the end of 1685 it numbered 19,778. The army had no recognized existence under English law. "Under Charles and James," writes John Childs, "it occupied an extra-constitutional position and can be regarded as a department of the royal household totally under the authority and patronage of the king and his nominees."[39] James argued that the militia that Albemarle and others were supposed to have raised had proven unreliable in suppressing Monmouth's rebellion, and that a standing army was required; since Parliament had given him an income large enough to finance this, the decision was his.[40] But ever since the rule of the parliamentary armies in the 1650s, many Englishmen feared the existence of a standing army. It did not help that James had commissioned many Catholic officers when the army was enlarged to meet the Monmouth rebellion, claiming that he had a dispensing power and could dispense with the Test Act.[41] This followed his decision in Scotland, which did not have a Test Act, to appoint the Catholic Earl of Dumbarton commander of his troops there and put the Catholic Duke of Gordon in charge of the Highland forces in May 1685.[42]

✳✳✳

THE PARLIAMENTARY SESSION was adjourned July 2, before Sedgemoor, and Parliament did not meet again until November 9. In between came news from France that shook England. Louis XIV's grandfather, Henri IV, inherited the throne in 1589 when he was a Protestant Huguenot. After some years of civil war he became a Catholic, famously saying, "Paris is worth a Mass." But he evidently had some tenderness for his former fellow Protestants, or perhaps simply wanted an end to religious warfare, and in 1598 he issued the Edict of Nantes, guaranteeing Protestants certain limited religious toleration — in areas where Calvinism was already established — and allowing them to hold public office.[43]

This ran contrary to Louis XIV's desire to end ancient particularism of all kinds and put all his subjects on an equal footing below him, and beginning in the 1660s he started to reduce the Huguenots' privileges and freedoms. This course was reinforced after 1679 by the influence of his mistress and later his second wife, Madame de Maintenon, a former Huguenot and now a pious Catholic.[44] In 1679 began the *dragonnades,* armed attacks by dragoons against the Huguenots and the quartering of troops on their land and homes. Louis ordered Protestants excluded from the professions and their schools, while colleges, chapels, and hospitals were closed or turned over to Catholics. On October 8, 1685 (September 28 in England), Louis formally revoked the Edict of Nantes. The Huguenots, many of them rich merchants and highly skilled craftsmen, fled the country in large numbers — perhaps 100,000 — and flocked especially to Amsterdam and the United Provinces, to London and England, and to Berlin and Brandenburg.[45] Trying to prevent the outflow of Huguenots, Louis ordered that only those who were English or Dutch citizens could leave; even their French wives and children must stay behind.

News of these developments stirred fear in England. John Evelyn's diary entry for November 3 noted

The French persecution of the Protestants, raging with uttmost barbarity, exceeding what the very heathens used: Innumberable persons of the greatest birth, & riches, leaving all their earthly substance & hardly escaping with their lives, dispers'd thro' all the Countries of Europe: The Fr: Tyrant, abrogating the Edicts of Nants &c in favour of them, & without any Cause on the suddaine, demolishing all their Churches, banishing, Imprisoning, sending to the Gallies all the Ministers: plundring the common people, & exposing them to all sorts of barbarous usage, by souldiers sent to ruine & prey upon them; taking away their children; forcing people to the Masse, & then executing them as Relapsers: They burnt the libraries, pillag'd their goods, eate up their filds & sustenance, banish'd or sent to the Gallies the people, & seiz'd on their Estates.[46]

James deplored the revocation of the Edict and ordered a collection to aid the refugees — but only those who followed the liturgy of the Church of England. But he also agreed to suppress a book by one refugee, and allowed French officials to search for fugitives in English ships in French ports.[47] And he encouraged the Lord Chancellor of Scotland, the Earl of Perth, to convert to Catholicism in the autumn of 1685.[48] All this alarmed a people raised on the Book of Common Prayer and *Foxe's Martyrs*. Protestants were being persecuted by a Catholic king in France. What would a Catholic king do in England?[49]

When Parliament met on November 9, James's speech increased those fears. He demanded money for the enlarged army. "There is nothing but a good force of well-disciplined troops in constant pay that can defend us from such as, either at home or abroad, are disposed to disturb us." He decried "how weak and insignificant the militia was" in suppressing Monmouth's rebellion.[50] He knew the Catholic officers well, and insisted on keeping them. "I will neither expose them to disgrace, nor myself to the want of them, if there be another rebellion to make them necessary to me." The Commons seemed prepared to vote money for the army, but, on November 13, by a 183–182 vote, resolved to decide on the issue of Catholic officers before voting supply. Court appointees, including the paymaster of the army, voted against the Court. The next day the Commons voted an address declaring the commissioning of Catholic officers illegal but indemnifying the officers against prosecution. James told them he had expected no such response. John Coke, treasurer of the Queen Dowager's Household, exclaimed, "We are all Englishmen and are not to be frighted out of our duty by a few high words." He was promptly sent to the Tower of London. The House voted James £700,000 for an army, but on terms that authorized only £30,000 for the first few years. On November 19 the Lords debated the Catholic officers as James stood and watched disapprovingly. The next day James prorogued Parliament. It would not sit again during his reign.[51]

CHARLES II HAD gained his fullest powers after the Exclusion Crisis and the dissolution of the Oxford Parliament by allying himself with Anglicans whose first goal was the supremacy of the Church of England. On their behalf he had engaged in his last four years in more vigorous prosecution of Catholics and Dissenters than he had in the preceding 21. If his natural tendency, expressed in the Declaration of Breda in 1660 and the declarations of indulgence in 1662 and 1672, was for religious toleration, he evidently considered religious persecution not too great a price to pay for the support he had gotten from Tory Anglicans during the Exclusion Crisis and afterward. Charles's installations of Tories in local government ensured that when James II succeeded him, he would get a Parliament that was heavily Anglican and inclined to passive obedience.

But James did not keep his half of Charles's unspoken bargain — persecution of Catholics and Dissenters. On the contrary, tolerance of Catholics was his primary goal. If he could not get it one way, he would try to get it another. By the end of 1685 he seemed set on a strategy. Having been given an adequate income, he would rule without Parliament. Unlike Louis XIV, he was not bent on wars of conquest: he would not need to go to Parliament for money to pay for them. He would promote toleration not only for Catholics but also, beginning in 1687, for Dissenters by administrative action. James's admirers over the years have portrayed him as a genuinely tolerant man, prepared to give others the same liberty that, as king, he gave himself. And there is not much evidence that he was bent on persecution; however bad his political judgment, he knew that he could not persecute all Protestants in Protestant England. But James's policy was not seen in such a kindly light by very many of his subjects. They saw Protestantism on the defensive in Europe, they saw Protestants persecuted in France, they heard the tales of the Huguenots who fled to London. They feared that absolutist government was the wave of the future, in Catholic countries especially, and they considered Catholicism and absolutism two sides of the same coin.[52]

They saw that in Scotland, Ireland, and the American colonies, James was amassing royal power and extending toleration to Catholics — and more. In Scotland, James's Lord Chancellor the Earl of Perth and his brother, Secretary of State the Earl of Melfort, had converted to Catholicism, and by the end of 1685 were encouraging open celebration of the mass in Edinburgh and installation of a Catholic chapel in Holyrood Palace. Attendance at mass had been a high crime in Scotland since 1560, but Perth assured James that was not a problem: "Scotland is not as England. Measures need not be too nicely kept with this people, nor are wee to be suffered to imagine that your Majesty is not so far above our laws as that you cannot dispence with them."[53] In February 1686, James replaced his chief minister in Scotland, the Protestant Duke of Queensberry, with the Catholic Perth.[54]

In Ireland moves were quickly taken to disarm the Protestant milita.[55] James undermined the Anglican lord lieutenant, the Earl of Clarendon, by appointing Richard Talbot, Earl of Tyrconnel, commander of the army in Ireland. Tyrconnel, a Catholic (married to Sarah Churchill's sister Frances), purged Protestant officers and appointed many Catholics in their places, until the officer corps was 40 percent and the rank and file was two-thirds Catholic, and Catholics were installed in most local civilian offices by September 1686.[56] Protestants who had benefited from the confiscation of Catholic-owned lands in the Cromwell period began to fear for their property, and many sent their movable possessions over to England.

In the American colonies James had already put in place a new royal government in Virginia in 1683 and had consolidated Puritan Massachusetts and Plymouth and the more heterodox New Hampshire and part of Rhode Island into a single Dominion of New England. Their representative assemblies were abolished, and his governor Sir Edmund Andros levied taxes, banned town meetings, challenged land titles, and displaced Puritan Congregationalism from its position as an established church and declared a policy of religious toleration in its place. Opponents were summarily fined and imprisoned. Over the next two years the Dominion's boundaries were extended to include the rest of Rhode Island as well as Connecticut, New York, and New Jersey. In the colonies farther south, James made less change: his ally the Quaker William Penn was proprietor of Pennsylvania; Maryland was ruled by its Catholic proprietor Lord Baltimore; and Virginia was in the grip of a royal governor.[57] James made New York (of which James was the proprietor), not Jamestown or Boston, the center of gravity in the colonies, and established the alliance with the Iroquois Indians against the French, one condition of which was the prevention of white settlement in the Iroquois lands of upstate New York and the Appalachian barrier running to the south.[58] James's abolition of colonial assemblies was resented and soon would be reversed. But his policy of discouraging settlements west of the Appalachians stayed in place until the 1770s and was one of the colonists' grievances against the British government.

James was embarking on a course that would prove his ruin — and that led directly to the Revolution of 1688–89. In this course he was assisted and encouraged by one of the most remarkable characters of the period, Robert Spencer, the Earl of Sutherland. Spencer gained that title in 1643, when he was two years old and his father was killed in battle while serving in King Charles I's personal troop. The Spencers were an obscure family who had made their money as large-scale sheep farmers in Northamptonshire, but they became connected to several of England's most notable noble families. His mother was the daughter of the Earl of Leicester and was a member of the Sidney family that included the famous Elizabethan courtier and poet Philip Sidney; Algernon Sidney, the republican theorist executed after discovery of the Rye House Plot in 1683, was his mother's brother. In 1656,

Sunderland's sister married Sir George Savile, later the Marquis of Halifax; the same year his aunt became the third wife of Anthony Ashley Cooper, later the Earl of Shaftesbury. In 1700, Spencer's son Charles would marry the daughter of John Churchill, then Earl of Marlborough; their sons, thanks to an act of Parliament that allowed the title to pass through female heirs, became dukes of Marlborough. Another son became Earl Spencer. And so Sunderland as well as the first Duke of Marlborough are ancestors of Winston Churchill and the current Earl Spencer and his late sister, Diana, Princess of Wales.

Sunderland was brought up as an Anglican during the years of Cromwell's rule. In May 1661 he took his seat in the House of Lords at age 19. In 1663 he disappeared the night before he was to marry Lady Anne Digby, the daughter of the Earl of Bristol, and later went off to Europe, where he spent time with his uncle Henry Sidney, Halifax's brother Henry Savile, William Penn, the admiral's son who was not yet a Quaker, Sidney Godolphin, and Henry Compton, the future Bishop of London. In 1665 he returned to England and married Lady Anne.[59]

Sunderland is described by his biographer J. P. Kenyon as "over-sensitive, irritable and highly-intelligent"[60] and "a proud man, passionate, ill-tempered and wilful."[61] He was capable of being charming, but often was angry and bullying, and he was, as his conduct to Lady Anne Digby shows, capable of changing his mind and changing it again. At Althorp, his house in Northamptonshire, the Sunderlands in the 1660s entertained such future political enemies as the Duke of York and the Duke of Monmouth, the Marquis of Halifax and Henry Sidney. He spent lavishly on paintings and furniture, gambled for large sums, and rebuilt Althorp, where the park was designed by Louis XIV's landscape architect André Lenôtre. In November 1670, not yet 30, he was appointed envoy to Spain at the behest of the Earl of Arlington, and in March 1671 he was appointed ambassador to France. Sunderland spent lavishly and pleaded with Arlington for more money; he was recalled in March 1673, when Charles II was faced with a hostile Parliament. When he returned to London, his patron Arlington was out of office and his relatives Shaftesbury and Halifax were in opposition to the new chief minister, the Earl of Danby. But

Sunderland, in need of funds, stayed with the Court. He became close to the king's mistress Louise de Kerouaille, Duchess of Portsmouth, and worked out the details of her son's becoming the Duke of Richmond, and through Portsmouth gained influence with Danby and the king.[62]

In February 1679, Charles appointed Sunderland as one of his two secretaries of state. He remained as Danby fell and was sent to the Tower, as Charles came out for a bill limiting the powers of a Catholic king, and as Shaftesbury led the move to exclude James from the throne. In July, Sunderland urged Charles to dissolve Parliament, which he did July 10 over the fierce protests of Shaftesbury. After Shaftesbury was dismissed from office, Sunderland was effectively one of the king's three chief ministers, with Laurence Hyde, James's brother-in-law, and Sidney Godolphin. But the tide turned when Sunderland voted for exclusion in 1680 under the misguided illusion that the king would accept exclusion if Parliament voted him money for war.

In January 1681, Charles dismissed Sunderland from office and took the unusual steps of ordering him to vacate his apartments in Whitehall Palace and of denying him the payment usually made by the next appointee — a payment the always financially embarrassed Sunderland badly needed.[63] But Sunderland was not kept out of power for long. "Alone in his generation," Kenyon writes, "Sunderland had set out to acquire through experience and reflection on experience an exact knowledge which could be applied to any scheme of foreign policy at will."[64] Sunderland approached James through Laurence Hyde and asked to be forgiven, and persuaded the Duchess of Portsmouth to ask Charles to return him to office, which Charles did in July 1682. Now Sunderland pursued not the Protestant alliance he had tried to construct in 1680 and 1681, but the pro-French policy Charles had decided on. He encouraged the marriage in July 1683 of Princess Anne to Prince George of Denmark, whose brother the king was an ally of Louis XIV (she had been spurned by Prince George of Hanover, who ultimately became King George I).[65]

James had hopes — and William had fears[66] — that Anne could be converted to a pro-French policy and Catholicism, and there was talk that her sister Mary might be passed over to make her James's heir. But working against that were Anne's Protestant faith and her friendship with Sarah Churchill, who had known Anne since they played as children in St. James's, and whom Anne had Charles appoint as one of her ladies of the bedchamber after her marriage.[67] When Anne's First Lady of the Bedchamber, Lady Clarendon, left when her husband was appointed lord lieutenant of Ireland, Sarah was named to the place. Anne was desperate for Sarah's friendship and insisted that she eschew formality; at her suggestion Sarah addressed her as Mrs. Morley, and she called Sarah Mrs. Freeman.[68] Sarah encouraged Anne to restrict pressure from James and his queen to convert to Catholicism. Instead, Anne became fervently Anglican, perhaps the strongest Anglican ever to sit on the throne.[69] She adored but also dominated her husband, who was regarded by everyone else as an amiable lightweight and was persuaded to name as his military and naval aides John Churchill's brothers Charles and George.[70]

When Charles died, James felt he needed to retain Sunderland for his ability to manage the parliamentary elections and to maintain good relations with Louis XIV. But James elevated his brother-in-law Laurence Hyde, by now the Earl of Rochester, to be his chief minister, and followed Rochester's policy of renewing a treaty with the Dutch rather than Sunderland's pro-French policy. Sunderland avoided being made lord lieutenant in Ireland by suggesting Hyde's brother, the Earl of Clarendon, for the post. In October 1685, Sunderland's rival Halifax was dismissed from office when he refused to promise James to support repeal of the Test and habeas corpus acts: the man who had led the fight against exclusion was out and a man who had voted for exclusion was in. In December, Sunderland was given the office of lord president as well as secretary of state; at the same time Sunderland was negotiating a pension of £7,000 a year with the French ambassador. After the king prorogued Parliament in November, Rochester wanted it to meet again in February, while Sunderland argued that James could do without it. James, loyal to his brother-in-law, kept Rochester in office until January 1687, but disregarded his advice on almost every issue.[71]

Why did James elevate a man who had voted to exclude him from the throne? He evidently took the same view of him as did his biographer Kenyon: Sunderland needed office for the money it would bring, and he had learned from his dismissal in 1681 never to oppose a king. As Kenyon writes, "Only a man essentially straightforward in character could have neatly reversed his political thinking once in a lifetime: Sunderland did it twice. From 1682 to 1688 he carried with him a bitter memory of the fate that overtakes those who try to anticipate the needs not the wishes of their kings, who consult their welfare and not their desires. Henceforth no policy, provided it carried the stamp of royal approval, would be too outrageous for his acceptance; and whenever he ventured to lead his master it would be from behind. As he remarked [according to Burnet]: 'He wondered that anybody would be so silly as to dispute with kings; for if they would not take good advice there was no way of dealing with them, but by running into measures till they had ruined themselves.' "[72] James's biographer John Miller tends to agree. "Unencumbered by principles of his own, Sunderland committed himself to and tried to anticipate the wishes of the king."[73]

And who can resist quoting Winston Churchill's summary of the career of his ancestor?

He seemed to be born into the very heart and centre of social and political England, and he was connected with both parties by ties of blood. He never made speeches; but he had a vast familiarity with leading figures in every camp and throughout the aristocracy. He knew better than any other man the politics and inclination of the different noble families; and he had access to all. Hence his knowledge and opinions were invaluable to a succession of sovereigns. He had voted for the exclusion bill, but was soon back in Charles's Cabinet, and acquired the highest favour under James. He had ousted the Hydes by outbidding them in favouring James's autocratic and Papist designs. To ingratiate the King he had become a Papist. He was now virtually Prime Minister. He had encouraged the King on the course which led to his ruin. We find him later, only two years after the Revolution, taking his place as the trusted confidant of William III, and during practically the whole of William's reign he was the power behind the making of

Cabinets. An astounding record, outstripping the fiercest hatreds and mounting upon every form of error, treachery and disaster![74]

✦✦✦

IF JAMES COULD not get Parliament to repeal the penal laws against Catholics or the Test Acts — and if it was not obvious in June 1685, it was certainly obvious by November 1685 that he could never get this Parliament to do so — then he would use what he considered his dispensing and suspending powers to make them a nullity. Early on he suspended the penal laws, limiting the prosecution of any who had supported his father in the Civil War; that included most Catholics but few if any Dissenting Protestants.[75] He dispensed with the Test Acts by appointing Catholic officers in the army assembled to quell Monmouth's rebellion. He set up an unofficial council of Catholics to advise him on religious matters, and after November 1685 he allowed Sunderland to attend its meetings; Sunderland in turn cultivated the queen, James's favorite among the Jesuits, Edward Petre, and the French ambassador Barillon.[76] In March 1686 he granted amnesty to those imprisoned under the penal laws, mainly Quakers — a clearly legal exercise of executive clemency — and granted many commissions to Catholics in the army.[77] In April 1686 he asked the Scottish Parliament to repeal the penal laws against Catholics, but was unable to get a satisfactory measure through the ordinarily pliable Lords of the Articles, the committee that steered legislation through the single house.[78] Catholic establishments were set up in London — a Franciscan headquarters in Lincoln's Inn Fields, a Carmelite convent in the City, Benedictines ensconced in St. James's Palace, a Jesuit church and school in Savoy House on the Strand.[79] When legal questions were raised about whether James could dispense with the Test Act in appointing military officers, James dismissed six judges and arranged a collusive lawsuit, *Godden v. Hales,* in which the court ruled in June 1686 that " 'tis an indispensable prerogative of the kings of England to dispense with penal laws in particular cases and upon particular necessary reasons," of which each king was the sole judge.[80]

James was not bothered by the anomaly that, though a Catholic, he was head of the Church of England. He ordered the Anglican bishops to ban anti-Catholic sermons and, when they continued anyway, in February 1686 required them to reissue a 1662 Directions to Preachers, which banned controversial sermons and "abstruse and speculative notions." In May 1686 he took on Henry Compton, Bishop of London, who had superintended the religious instruction of Princess Anne and who had won great visibility for organizing hospitality and charity for the Huguenot refugees who streamed in from France after the revocation of the Edict of Nantes.[81] He ordered Compton to suspend the rector of St. Giles in the Fields for preaching an anti-Catholic sermon. Compton, scion of a landed family who was a soldier in the Life Guards until age 30,[82] was made of stern stuff and refused. So, in July, James created an Eccelesiastical Commission to discipline the clergy, including those in the universities.[83]

James proceeded to use his dispensing power to appoint Catholics to many military, government, church, and university offices. He insisted that all his advisers share his views and urged the Protestants among them to become Catholics. Sunderland ultimately did convert, though he kept the king and others unclear about his intentions until he finally announced his conversion in June 1688.[84] In late 1686 the Earl of Rochester postponed his dismissal by convincing the king that he was seriously considering conversion.[85] Admiral Arthur Herbert, a libertine who owed his promotions to James, refused to consider it; when James said "that he had not been so regular a liver as to make the Test a case of conscience," Herbert replied, "Every man has his failing."[86] Another officer, Piercy Kirke, parried the King's demand for conversion by replying, "Your Majesty knows that I was concerned at Tangier, and being oftentimes with the Emperour of Morocco about the late King's affairs, he oft desired the same thing of me, and I passed my word to him that if I ever changed my religion I would turn Mohometan."[87] In July 1686, James appointed five Catholics to the Privy Council. He confirmed in place the Anglican curate of Putney, who had become a Catholic.[88] He tried to get Charterhouse School to admit a Catholic; the trustees, including the Earl of Danby, Bishop Compton, and the Archbishop of Canterbury, William Sancroft, refused, and James dismissed Sancroft from exercising his authority.

James once again prorogued Parliament in October 1686 and set about remodeling local government by ousting Anglican justices of the peace and other local officials and replacing them with those amenable to him, mostly Catholics. To the English army he added more Catholic officers and Irish recruits, and this enlarged army of 13,000 was assembled at a camp in Hounslow Heath, 12 miles west of London, each summer starting in 1686.[89] Catholics were appointed to head the garrisons in the ports of Hull and Dover, and James's natural son (by Arabella Churchill) the Duke of Berwick was appointed governor of the key naval port of Portsmouth.

In March 1687 he issued a Declaration of Indulgence in Scotland, setting aside all laws against Catholics and Presbyterians and promising, probably unconvincingly, that lands formerly owned by Catholic abbeys and churches would not be seized from their current owners — a preview of the Declaration of Indulgence he would issue in England in April.[90] These actions antagonized the supporters of the bishops of the Church of Scotland who had supported him during his sojourn there from 1679 to 1682.[91] The Indulgence was mostly accepted by the Presbyterians, but they continued to denounce the Catholics for whose sake James had acted.[92] It also prompted Gilbert Burnet, a Scottish minister of the Church of England in exile in the Netherlands, to write a pamphlet titled *Some Letters: containing an account of what seemed most remarkable in Switzerland, Italy, etc.,* in which he argued "that popery and poverty go together, because popery goes with tyranny and tyranny is econocidal." In chapter after chapter, Burnet compared the relative prosperity and freedom from unreasonable burdens enjoyed by Protestant-ruled states even when, like the Dutch or the Protestant Swiss, their lands were inherently poor, with the miseries that afflicted the populations of Counter-Reformation absolutisms.[93]

What was James's goal in all this? To "establish" Catholicism in England, as he put it in private — not actually to make it the state religion, but to allow Catholics to practice their faith on equal terms with other Christians and to qualify for public office. He evidently overestimated the number of existing Catholics in England and had confidence, almost surely misplaced, that Catholicism would spread if the Anglican Church lost its preferments. He wanted tolerance of

Catholicism to be strong enough to survive the reigns of his Protestant daughters. And he may have hoped for a Catholic succession if his daughters Mary and Anne should die childless (as both in time did) and were to be succeeded by the next heir, his sister Minette's daughter Anna Maria, a Catholic and the wife of Duke Vittorio Amadeo of Savoy, or her heirs.[94] In that case, rather than his reign being a brief Catholic interlude, his daughters' reign would have been a somewhat longer Protestant interlude. "It is this possibility," argues the historian J. R. Jones, "which in James' mind would obviously serve God's purposes by facilitating a long-term return of the English nation to the True Church, that provides the context for his two central policies with which he was to persist right up to the eve of the Revolution, the establishment of universal tolerance, and the preparation of a Parliament pre-engaged to legislate according to his directives."[95]

At some point in late 1686, apparently at the suggestion of the ever-flexible Sunderland, James decided to ally himself to Dissenting Protestants as well as Catholics: if the Anglicans would not back him, he would back their adversaries. It was a daring reversal of alliances in a kingdom where Catholics were a small minority and Dissenters were a minority of unknown size; James was seeking the support of Dissenters whom he had long distrusted and whose persecution he had readily supported.[96] Winston Churchill took a dim view of this strategy some three centuries later. "Here, then, was the King of England breaking down the natural pillars of his throne and seeking to shore it up with novel, ill-assorted, inadequate props."[97] In March 1687, James, discouraged that so many of his officials had preferred to lose their jobs rather than support repeal of the Test Acts and penal laws,[98] issued a declaration of liberty of conscience: neither Catholics nor Dissenters would be prosecuted under the penal acts. In April he issued a Declaration of Indulgence to the same effect.[99] This was probably drafted in consultation with William Penn, the Quaker whom Charles II had made proprietor of the colony of Pennsylvania in 1681.[100] James, not unreasonably, had hopes that the Dissenters and Quakers would be grateful after having passed through a period of heavy prosecution and suppression from 1681 to 1685.[101] But at the same time the Anglican establishment could not have been happy with an act that ended their spiritual monopoly;[102] attendance at Church of England services sharply declined after the Declaration.[103]

※❀※

IN THE MEANTIME James's relations with his son-in-law, William of Orange, were deteriorating. William had staunchly supported James during the Duke of Monmouth's rebellion, and had sent the English and Scottish regiments to England to quell it. Even before the rebellion was crushed, William sent his trusted aide Bentinck to London to soothe James.[104] But James was unhappy that William refused to expel English exiles, including Gilbert Burnet, clergyman and historian, who strongly opposed James.[105] James was encouraged by Sunderland to believe that William had backed the opposition in the November 1685 Parliament.[106] On his side, William was furious in early 1686 that James had not done more to get Louis XIV to renounce his annexation the year before of the principality of Orange, a possession that not only gave William income, but was responsible for his enjoying the status of a royal sovereign.[107] William feared that Louis would attack the United Provinces again, and that James would be his ally as Charles had been in 1672. He was alarmed that James had signed a treaty with France in May 1686, and did not believe that it was limited, as it was, to their possessions in North America.[108]

At the same time, James was displeased that William seemed to be arranging an anti-French alliance with the League of Augsburg, formed in July 1686 by the Emperor Leopold I, various German states, Sweden, and Spain.[109] In spring 1686, when the English and Scottish regiments were back in the Netherlands and in the pay of the United Provinces, William turned down James's choices of commanders, and in May James said he would name no more. But in July 1686 he appointed the Earl of Carlingford, an Irish Catholic, to command one regiment; William said that the appointment of a Catholic would arouse great controversy, and refused.[110] "There was now," writes Stephen Baxter, "a complete failure of communication between the English and the Dutch governments. Each imputed the worst motives to the other's conduct."[111] In September 1686, Viscount Mordaunt visited William and urged him to invade England. William, according to

Burnet, "only promised in general, that he should have an eye on the affairs of England; and should endeavour to put the affairs of Holland in so good a posture, as to be ready to act when it should be necessary: and he assured him, that, if the King should go about either to change the established religion, or to wrong the Princess in her right, or to raise forged plots to destroy his friends, that he would try what he could possibly do."[112] He reacted less positively when the Quaker William Penn, on a trip to the United Provinces in November 1686, tried to persuade him that James was sincere in tolerating all religions.[113] William replied that he supported repeal of the penal laws, but that he opposed the repeal of the Test Act, which he considered "as such a real security, and indeed the only one, where the King was of another religion" than the Church of England, as both he and James were.[114]

William proceeded to keep a close eye on affairs in England. His ambassador in London was poorly informed, partly because he did not understand French,[115] already firmly established as the language of diplomacy, and the English ambassadors to the United Provinces, Bevil Skelton and then his successor the Marquis of Albeville, were both fiercely hostile to William. So, in February 1687, William sent a trusted envoy, Everaard van Weede, Heer van Dijkvelt, to London purportedly to seek a reconciliation with James and more discreetly to "sound out the leaders of all parties and to encourage them to stand firm against the King's romanizing policies."[116] Dijkvelt's first mission failed. He managed to get audiences with James in March and May, but Dijkvelt was, in the words of Stephen Baxter, "an arrogant and spiteful man, who created enemies wherever he went."[117] The king bristled at his suggestion that he intended to disinherit his daughter Mary, and Dijkvelt rejected James's pleas that William and Mary support the repeal of the Test Act and the penal laws.[118] After his meetings with James, Dijkvelt, furnished with a list of all members of the House of Lords annotated with their views on James's policy of indulgence, conducted rounds of meetings and dinners with political figures of all stripes and issued reports to William as well as to the Grand Pensionary of Holland Gaspar Fagel, and Willem van Bentinck.[119] When Dijkvelt returned to the United Provinces in June, he brought back messages, some verbal and some written, from Sunderland, Clarendon, Rochester, Halifax, the Earl of Nottingham, the Earl of Danby, and the Earl of Shrewsbury.[120]

Also, Dijkvelt made inquiry about whether Anne could be persuaded to convert to Catholicism — in which case James might declare her rather than Mary as his successor. He brought back with him a letter of March 1687 from John Churchill assuring William that Anne "was resolved, by the assistance of God, to suffer all extremities, even to death itself, rather than be brought to change her religion."[121] Churchill added that he was of the same view and would place his Protestant faith above his loyalty to the king. "My places and the King's favour I set at nought, in comparison to being true to my religion. In all things but this the King can command me; and I call God to witness, that even with joy should I expose my life for his service, so sensible am I of his favours. I know the troubling you, sir, with thus much of myself, I being of so little use to your highness, is very impertinent, but I think it may be a great ease to your highness and the princess to be satisfied that the Princess of Denmark is safe in the trusting of me; I being resolved, although I cannot live the life of a saint, if ever there be occasion for it, to show the resolution of a martyr."[122] Anne vouched for Churchill in her own letter to her sister Mary. "Nay, if it should come to such extremities, I will chuse to live on alms rather than change [religion]. . . . So I have desired Lord Churchill (who is one that I can trust, and I am sure is a very honest man and a good Protestant) to speak to Mr. Dykvelt for me, to know what it is he has to say to me, and by the next opportunity I will answer it, for one dares not write anything by post."[123] Backing these up was a letter dated April 1687 from Lady Sunderland, a devout Anglican, urging William not to support James's program.[124]

THE UNIVERSITIES OF Oxford and Cambridge were strongholds of the Established Church; all students and fellows had to take the oaths of allegiance and supremacy. But in 1686 James began suspending that requirement, and in April 1687 he ordered the fellows of Magdalen College, Oxford, to elect his candidate as their new president. They refused and elected their own candidate. James's Ecclesiastical Commission declared their action void and James ordered the election of a third candidate. The fellows refused again, and James came to Oxford in September and berated them. "Go home and show yourselves good members of the Church of England. Get you gone, know I am your king. I will be obeyed and I command you to be gone. Go and admit the Bishop of Oxford head, principal, what do you call it of the college, I mean president of the college. Let them that refuse it look to it; they shall feel the weight of their sovereign's displeasure." The commission threw the 25 fellows out of Magdalen and declared them ineligible for any office in the Church of England. This was opposed by the chancellor of the university, the Duke of Ormonde, who for many years during Charles's reign had been lord lieutenant of Ireland, and it convinced many Anglicans that James was out to destroy their church.[125]

James dissolved the Parliament in July 1687 and began preparations for elections to a new Parliament that he hoped would repeal the penal laws and Test Acts.[126] This was a major undertaking. No previous monarch or minister had attempted to influence elections so thoroughly, with the possible exception of Charles II after the Exclusion Crisis; the other closest precedents were the exclusionists' own electioneering in the second 1679 and the 1681 elections.[127] The historian J. R. Jones argues that "the campaign to pack Parliament was easily the most important [factor] in provoking the Revolution," because it "threatened to produce a subservient Parliament that would make the crown financially independent, with the result that Parliament itself might follow many European Estates into misuse." This was an attempt to move England toward "some form of absolutism," which was "realistic in the context of the general development and extensions of systems of absolutist power and government, principally in France, but also in Sweden, Denmark, and many German states."[128]

But parliamentary elections could not be affected without first changing the local officials — the lord lieutenants of the counties, the justices of the peace, the various officials of the borough, the aldermen and members of livery companies in London — who conducted and effectively controlled the elections, and without changing the franchise in many boroughs. Between 1681 and 1685, Charles II's officials had remodeled the counties and boroughs by making sure that reliable Tories—opponents of exclusion, supporters of the Church of England—had effective control. Those officials had indeed produced a Tory Parliament for James II in the elections in 1685. But now that James wanted a Parliament that would repeal the Test Acts and penal laws, he needed to put new personnel in place. James's chief agent was Robert Brent, a Catholic lawyer specializing in transferring money and bequests to overseas Catholics, and who was given responsibility for delivering secret service money and for issuing pardons.[129]

This, Jones writes, "meant an invasion of the life and autonomy of local communities throughout the country by professional agents of the central administration."[130] English government could not operate effectively without the active engagement of many men in the localities, but personnel could be and often were changed for various reasons. Now changes were made for political reasons.[131] Lord lieutenants and London aldermen were removed and more than one thousand members of London's livery companies were ousted.[132]

In May 1687 lord lieutenants were reminded that the "militia within your lieutenancies . . . be not mustered" unless and until the king so ordered.[133] James ordered the county militias to seize the weapons owned by those not entitled to keep or bear arms under the restrictive Game Act of 1671, but this seems to have gone largely unenforced.[134] In October 1687 lord lieutenants of the counties were commanded by Sunderland to put three questions to justices of the peace and other local officials: Would they support repeal of the Test Acts of 1673 and 1678 and penal laws; would they support parliamentary candidates who did; and would they live peaceably with men of all religions? In December it was announced that all lists of JPs and deputy lieutenants would be revised, and in the first three months of 1688 thousands of county and borough officials who gave unsatisfactory answers were dismissed.[135] James received detailed and by no means overly optimistic reports of the responses.[136] The responses to the three questions had only begun to be reported, followed by dismissals of those who gave unsatisfactory answers. The landowning class in the counties—mainly Anglican, used to exercising local influence—

responded negatively to the three questions; the response was more positive in the boroughs and especially among those dependent on royal favor in the towns.[137] Starting in late September there was a purge of those who gave unsatisfactory answers from the City of London livery companies. That was followed by purges of officials in the counties and provincial boroughs in November.[138] Lamented John Evelyn, "Popish Justices of the Peace established in all Counties of the meanest of the people: Judges ignorant of the Law, and perverting it: so furiously does the Jesuite drive, & even compell Princes to violent courses, & distruction of an excellent Government both in Church & State."[139]

James increasingly surrounded himself with Catholics. His court consisted mostly of Catholics, in whose numbers Sunderland apparently could now be counted (he professed himself inclined to convert, but delayed a public declaration until June 1688).[140] The remaining Protestant advisers were those with military titles, like Baron Churchill, Lord Feversham, and Lord Dartmouth (his longtime aide George Legge, now a leading officer in the navy), and largely apolitical civil servants like Sidney Godolphin and Samuel Pepys. Leading Protestant peers with large regional followings remained out of London and in their country seats, including Rochester and Clarendon, the Duke of Beaufort in the southern marches of Wales, the Earl of Bath in the southwest, and the Earl of Danby in Yorkshire.

The sparsity of attendance at court contrasted with the stream of English nobles to William's court in The Hague in the summer of 1687.[141] Others corresponded with William. The Earl of Nottingham told him that "the government would have difficulty in overcoming the Dissenters' fears of Roman oppression or Anglican vengeance, and that the King's advisers were hopelessly divided on this and on other points." In a letter, Halifax promised William that there was no likelihood of an early election.[142] Halifax, who had opposed both exclusion and repeal of the Test Acts and penal laws, strove to ensure there would be no early election by publishing anonymously a pamphlet called *Letter to a Dissenter,* warning that Catholicism was by its nature incapable of toleration. "This alliance between Liberty and Infallibility is bringing together the two most contrary things in the world. The

Church of Rome doth not only dislike the allowing liberty, but by its principles cannot do it." After arguing that toleration was as forbidden to Catholics as wine to Muslims, Halifax concluded, "You are therefore to be hugged now only that you may be the better squeezed at another time."[143]

Halifax's argument was in line with the Anglican view that James's toleration was only part of a policy of weakening the Church of England, and that toleration of Dissent would in time be abandoned. Anglicans, on the defensive, now looked more favorably on comprehension, that is the inclusion of Presbyterians and other Dissenters within the Church. By the spring of 1688 the Church was supporting toleration of Dissenters — a vivid contrast with its support of prosecutions of non-Anglicans from 1681 to 1686.[144] James's lurch toward the Dissenters had set in motion a virtuous circle, in which the Church competed with the king to show toleration to those who so recently, and with the support of both, had been persecuted.

Always stubborn and determined, James persevered. He made a royal progress in the West Country in September and was heartened by the response there, though Sunderland was less impressed. At court, surrounded by Catholics, he was eager to move ahead with his policies, despite the entreaties of Sunderland, who urged him to go slow. He could see that James enjoyed less than total support from the Dissenters — the Presbyterians, who had hoped for a broader Church of England that would include them, were particularly dubious — and that Catholics were not a large enough constituency to produce a pliable Parliament.[145]

James had more success in Scotland, where his appointee Perth seemed in control of the usually pliable one-house Parliament. And James had even more success in Ireland, where a majority of the population was Catholic, though most landowners were Protestant. In January 1687, James removed Clarendon as lord lieutenant and appointed as lord deputy Tyrconnel, who had already been appointing French-trained Catholic officers in the army.[146] Tyrconnel sought to overturn the Restoration land settlement that favored Protestant landowners, a step that James resisted, but he replaced Protestants with Catholics throughout the government,[147] and negotiated with the French Intendant General of Marine about making Ireland a French base.[148] By September 1687 he seemed in effective control of James's third kingdom.[149]

By October, William of Orange had concluded that Tyrconnel was trying to transform Ireland into a potentially independent, pro-French Catholic state, one that could be a refuge for James if he was expelled from England, or, in the event of James's death, might recognize as monarch James's illegitimate son the Duke of Berwick rather than his wife Mary.[150] It apparently was Tyrconnel's idea that "the Irish would be fools or madmen if after his [James's] death they should submit to be governed by the Prince of Orange," he was reported to have said in 1686, "or be longer slaves to England, but rather set up a king of their own and put themselves under the protection of France."[151]

On his progress through the West Country in September, James ventured as far north as Chester, the port for Ireland, where he met with Tyrconnel, who got him to agree to a change in the Irish land settlement and to consider that Ireland should be formally separated from England in the event of a Protestant succession.[152] During his stay in Chester he journeyed a short distance to make his devotions at the shrine of St. Winifred's Well at Holywell, near Flint, where Catherine of Aragon had prayed for an heir, then rejoined the queen, who had been taking the waters at Bath.[153]

ON OCTOBER 24 the French ambassador Barillon heard a rumor that Queen Mary Beatrice was pregnant. By November 3 that "was the talk of the court," and on November 14 the pregnancy was officially announced.[154] Mary Beatrice had in 1675 given birth to a son who died in infancy,[155] and five other children had died in infancy;[156] other pregnancies had ended in miscarriages. Her pregnancy came as a surprise to the Court, and was seen by some Catholics as divine intervention. They seemed confident that this pregnancy would produce a son — so confident that some Protestants suspected the pregnancy was a sham.[157]

If a son was born, he would replace Princess Mary as the heir to the throne, and his succession would likely mean a string of Catholic monarchs stretching far into the future. James was already 54, the age his brother was when he died, and the general expectation had been that he would be succeeded in reasonably good time by the Protestant Mary, who would be governed by her husband William. Now it seemed possible that James would be succeeded by an infant or child, with the staunchly Catholic Queen Mary Beatrice as regent, presumably with the compliant Sunderland as her chief minister.[158] England still dreaded the prospect of civil war. They had welcomed Charles II back in 1660; they had abandoned the cause of exclusion when the Tories claimed the Whigs raised the specter of '41, the year when the revolt broke out against Charles I; they had not rallied to the Duke of Monmouth. But now the situation was moving toward revolution.

Chapter 6

Dutch Invasion

VERSAILLES, JANUARY 1688. Louis XIV had moved in 1682 from the Louvre in Paris to what had once been a hunting lodge in Versailles, and now the two main wings of the palace were completed; the Orangerie was under construction, and the porcelain Trianon had been demolished to be replaced by one built of marble. The Hall of Mirrors was complete, but the chapel was not yet built. The palace was overcrowded with nobles whose presence the king commanded, and with the king's ministers, who had working quarters; the halls were full of refuse and the stench was unbearable.[1] "The French nobility, invited or summoned from their estates," writes Winston Churchill, "were housed in one teeming hotbed of subservience, scandal, and intrigue in the royal palace."[2] The king had brought his court from Paris to Versailles because he disliked the city, from which he had been forced to flee as a child during the Fronde revolt, and loved the fresh air, forests, and footpaths of the country. Louis was a hard-working king who insisted on punctuality and ceremony. He was attended by his doctors and designated lords when he woke each morning and put on his clothes and his wig; he attended mass and then tended to business in his study and then lunched, usually alone; then came more work in his study, a change of clothes, and hunting or a long walk. Then more time in the study, a visit to the chambers of his seccond wife, Madame de Maintenon, a formal supper, time in the study with his legitimate and illegitimate children, then he dressed for bed, fed his dogs, and gave a final audience to those with business for him.[3]

Louis, his unadmiring courtier Saint-Simon tells us, had "a passion for detail. He was interested in everything that touched on his troops: uniforms, arms, maneuvers, training, discipline, in a word, all sorts of vulgar details. He was just as interested in his construction projects, his households and his kitchens." And in public and private affairs, he "took great pains to inform himself on what was happening everywhere, in public places, private homes, and even on the international scene. He also wanted to know about family secrets and private relationships. Spies and informers of all kind were numberless."[4] At the end of 1687, Louis was 49; he had been king for 44 years and, after the death of Cardinal Mazarin, had assumed personal control of government—"l'etat c'est moi"—twenty-six years before. Louis was the greatest monarch in Europe, with the largest treasury and army and, with able ambassadors and agents in every capital, probably the best-informed man in Europe. Yet in the seventeenth century, communications, even for the Sun King, moved slowly, and decisions had to be made with imperfect information and carried out with incomplete supervision.

Throughout his active reign Louis had been on the offensive. Through war and diplomacy he expanded France's boundaries, but he did not achieve all his goals. He overran most of the Netherlands in 1672, but was forced to retreat and failed to destroy the United Provinces. In the following years he alienated erstwhile allies—Sweden, Denmark, Brandenburg, Bavaria. His secret payments to Charles II gained him an ally, but only for a time. He made peace with the United Provinces and its allies in 1678, but made an enduring enemy of William of Orange. In 1684 he signed a 20-year truce with the Habsburg power, Spain, and the Holy Roman Emperor Leopold I.

But Louis was still eager to expand France's boundaries to the east and to assert a claim to the Spanish throne on the death of the sickly, childless King Charles II, who was expected to die anytime. (He lived on until 1700.) He continued to make aggressive moves. In 1684 he ordered his fleet to bombard Genoa for the offense of building ships for Spain. In 1685 he revoked the Edict of Nantes, and in 1686 he sent French troops into Savoy to massacre Protestant Waldensians. In 1687 he refused to renounce the diplomatic immunity for a large swath of Rome around the French embassy. Pope Innocent XI refused to receive the French ambassador and to approve Louis's choice of French bishops, and excommunicated Louis himself.[5] In 1687, in anticipation of the death of his ally the elderly archbishop Max Heinrich Wittelsbach of Cologne — one of the seven electors entitled to choose new Holy Roman Emperors[6] — Louis procured the election of his client Cardinal Bishop Wilhelm Egon von Fürstenberg of Strasbourg, as coadjutor of Cologne.[7] Among Archbishop Wittelsbach's lands were the bishoprics of Hildesheim, Münster, and Liège, which included territory just south of Hanover, directly east of the United Provinces and along the Maas River in present-day Belgium: almost a necklace around the Dutch Republic.[8]

Opposition to this aggressiveness was growing. Elector Frederick William of Brandenburg had long been an ally of Louis's. Since 1640, when he became Margrave, he had expanded his domains from his capital in Berlin, eastward to Pomerania and Prussia, westward to the duchies of Cleve on the lower Rhine, Mark in what now is the Ruhr, and Ravensberg and Minden to the northeast; the population of his territories increased from 200,000 to nearly 1 million. Frederick William's was a military state, which hired out soldiers to others but tried to avoid war itself; it was also a tolerant state, which welcomed Dutch Protestants from the Spanish Netherlands and Jews and Huguenots from France. In May 1685, Frederick William sent an envoy to William of Orange; the result was a Dutch subsidy to Brandenburg and a defensive alliance of 15 years.[9] In January 1686, Frederick William agreed to provide 8,000 troops for Leopold on the Rhine, and in March 1686 they signed a secret mutual defense agreement.[10] In 1685 he publicly criticized Louis for revoking the Edict of Nantes.[11] France had lost a major and growing ally, for Brandenburg, renamed the Kingdom of Prussia, was to become a great power in the eighteenth century and the nucleus of the German Empire in the nineteenth.

Louis lost another ally in 1685 with the death of Charles, Elector Palatine of the Rhine, whose domains extended from both sides of the Rhine south of Mainz. Charles, like Frederick William, had followed domestic policies of tolerance of Christians of most stripes and of Jews, and of appeasing Louis abroad.[12] His successor, the Duke of Neuberg, although a Catholic, continued to support tolerance, but he was the father-in-law of Emperor Leopold I, an enemy of France, and opposed Louis; the Neuberg family also controlled the Duchy of Jülich-Berg, just east of the United Provinces.[13] Duke Ernest August of Hanover, eager for the office of elector, secretly sent the emperor 2 million crowns to support the struggle against the Turks.[14] In July 1686 came the formation of the League of Augsburg, led by Leopold and including Bavaria and the Palatinate, as well as Sweden and Spain (which owned lands within the Holy Roman Empire's boundaries). A few days later in July, William of Orange, attended by Willem van Bentinck and Henry Sidney, crossed the Dutch border to the Brandenburg duchy of Cleves and met with the elector Frederick William for nine days, after which they reviewed the Dutch army across the border in Mook, just south of Nijmegen, in an apparent show of strength and sympathy for the League.[15]

In 1687 there came a great reversal in the east. Four years earlier, in 1683, Pope Innocent XI and many European powers, with the conspicuous exception of France, had rallied to defend Leopold I when the Turks were at the gates of Vienna. The Turks were beaten by an army led by King John Sobieski of Poland, and the Turks retreated rapidly. In 1687 Leopold's armies drove them out of Hungary and occupied Budapest and threatened Belgrade. Those successes meant that new forces were available to oppose Louis in the west.[16]

From Versailles, Louis XIV watched these developments with close attention. At the beginning of 1688 he evidently calculated that France could intimidate and split the Germans and deter the Turks from making peace, that commercial pressure would keep the Dutch States General passive, and that James's position would remain strong in England.[17] The news of Queen Mary Beatrice's pregnancy must have strengthened this last assumption, on the theory that the birth of a male heir would convince James's countrymen that his regime would continue for many years, under him or under his widow as regent, and that it would be dangerous to oppose it. So Louis continued to act "as if he alone had the initiative, as if the rulers of Europe still waited for him to act before coming to their decisions. . . . He relied on tactics which had worked on an earlier occasion, apparently without appreciating the point that now his opponents and potential victims were forewarned and would discount his professions of peace because they had heard them before."[18]

＊

To WILLIAM THE pregnancy was obviously an ominous development. He had been a close observer of English politics since his childhood, when he assumed he would some day be king. In 1672 and 1673, when the Dutch Republic faced annihilation by Louis, his propagandists skillfully influenced English opinion. But he had been careful about intervening when the situation was less dire. As the historian J. R. Western notes, "Various important men in England — Arlington around 1670, Danby in the later seventies, Sunderland around 1680, Monmouth in his last years — tried to use William's influence to aid them in the struggle for power. Occasionally this brought results. In 1677 there was William's marriage and Charles's brief intervention at the end of William's first great war against France. In 1680, England nearly joined in a new anti-French coalition. But Charles's relations with his parliaments and William's relations with the Dutch republicans were so bad that neither could even appear to be an effective ally for the other, or for anyone else."[19] William had been careful to appear neutral during the exclusion debate, and he actively supported James against Monmouth's rebellion. Even as his relationship with James deteriorated, he hesitated to oppose him visibly. "According to every scrap of surviving evidence, Englishmen and Scots of all parties were pressing William to intervene in England in 1686 and 1687. They wished to force his hand. And again, according to all the evidence we have, the Prince listened to each group politely enough but refused to take the advice."[20] William's prime goal was to oppose the power of France, and it was obviously in his interest to maintain his standing as an heir to the English throne. But he had no reason to believe that any

of the competing political figures in England (with the possible exception of Halifax) shared his prime goal, and he seems never to have
trusted any of them to put his interests above theirs.

Nevertheless, William did take care to keep in touch with leaders
of all political complexions in England, by correspondence with figures as varied as James II, Halifax, Sunderland, Danby, and Rochester,
and through the visits of his trusted aides Everaard van Weede
Dijkvelt in the first months of 1687 and Count Zuylestein in August
1687.[21] The latter initiated a clandestine correspondence, complete
with invisible ink and secret couriers, to avoid surveillance by James's
agents—the same method used to send quantities of propaganda
pamphlets—which continued until the invasion of England in November 1688.[22] One longtime agent, the Scotsman James Johnston,
settled in England in October 1687 and maintained a steady secret correspondence with Bentinck, passing along information from sources
as diverse as one of Queen Mary Beatrice's bedchamber women, the
Marquis of Halifax, and William Penn, and organizing the distribution of Williamite propaganda.[23] Of the value of the written word he
had no doubt; in a letter to William's confidant Bentinck, in invisible
ink, he wrote, "If you intend to keep the nation in humour, you must
entertain it by papers. The Spirit of a People is like that of particular
persons, often to be entertained by trifles; particularly that of the English, who, like all islanders, seems to ebb and flow like the neighbouring sea. In the late fermentation about the Exclusion, the Excluders
never lost ground till they lost the press."[24]

Rumors about Mary Beatrice's pregnancy started flying on November 3 in London (November 13 in The Hague). At just about the
same time, probably a day or so earlier, the Grand Pensionary of Holland, Gaspar Fagel, William's close ally, sent a letter to James Stewart,
a former Scottish refugee in the United Provinces, who had been seeking William's endorsement of repeal of the Test Act. Stewart, the author of the manifesto for Argyll's unsuccessful rebellion in 1685,
returned to England in March 1687 apparently under the protection of
William Penn, but continued corresponding with William's Scottish
secret agent William Carstares.[25] Starting in June 1687, Stewart wrote
several times to Carstares urging him to get William to support repeal
of the Test Acts.[26] William, apprised of this correspondence, wrote to

Bentinck on September 21 saying that he approved a response to Stewart from Fagel and "that when Fagel shall have drafted the answer it would not be a bad idea to communicate it to Dr. Burnet. . . . Nobody would be more suitable to translate it into English, print it, and publish it."[27]

On November 15, in London, Stewart received Fagel's carefully drafted and translated letter dated November 4 (October 25 in England). Fagel wrote that William and Mary were personally in favor of toleration — not only for Dissenting Protestants but for Catholics — but that they opposed repeal of the Test Acts.[28] "No Christian ought to be persecuted for his conscience . . . yet all Politick bodies had ever made laws to secure the established Religion, and their own safety, by excluding the enemies thereof from all public employments, and the Test being of that nature declared that they could not consent to have it abrogated."[29] Stewart forwarded the letter to Sunderland and the king, who both insisted that the penal laws and the Test Acts must rise or fall together. Within days the printing presses of the Dutch Republic were busy, and something of the magnitude of 30,000 to 50,000 copies of *Their Highness The Prince and Princess of Orange's Opinion about a General Liberty of Conscience,* followed by excerpts from Stewart's letters, were circulating in England by the first days of January 1688.[30] William was promising Anglicans there would be no repeal of the Test Acts, but was also promising Catholics and Dissenters that they would not be persecuted in the next reign. He saw to it that Fagel's letter was available also in Dutch, French, and Latin, so as to reassure his Catholic allies that he would not respond to James's promotion of Catholicism with a persecution of Catholics.[31] Fagel's letter was in effect a campaign document, a platform of opposition to James's proposal to repeal the Test Acts, probably prompted by the fear that James's attempt to pack Parliament would be successful. As Willem van Bentinck was informed on December 8, " 'Tis certainly believed by all our wise men except Mylord Halifax, that we shall have a Parliament, and they say more certain, that it will be a packed one, chose only by those that return it, and that the prince should take his measures what he will do in that case, for that we must never expect to see a free parliament here under the present state of affairs."[32]

Through all this, William, like Louis, kept his eyes on all of

Europe. His goal all his adult life was to limit the power of France and preserve the Netherlands, whose tolerance he cherished, and the Protestantism that he believed in from destruction by the Sun King. As Halifax wrote after the Revolution, William "hath such a mind to France, that it would incline one to think, hee tooke England onely in his way."[33] William saw Louis's aggressive moves during James II's reign as a prelude to another general European war, and he feared— excessively, but not unreasonably—that James would place England in the service of France. Before November 1687 it seemed that England would come into his hands in a few years, perhaps sooner: James would die, William's wife Mary would be queen, and she had already agreed that in that event he must be King Regnant, not King Consort. Mary Beatrice's pregnancy threatened this inheritance. His biographer Stephen Baxter provides a convincing conjecture of his thinking: "But by the end of 1687 the problem was far more serious than it had been in 1672 or in 1680. The English political situation was completely out of hand. In Dublin Tyrconnel was obviously building a Festung Ireland, which would be a Catholic refuge in case of disaster and which might well be turned over to France in case of need. To such an extent James was clearly dismembering the inheritance to which the Prince felt himself entitled. William also felt, and to all appearances he felt sincerely, that James would join with Louis XIV for a war on Holland as soon as he felt strong enough. . . . Even if the Queen were truly pregnant, however, it seemed clear that the Jesuits would not allow her to have anything other than a healthy son."[34] The time to act was near. He could not risk armed intervention in England if a general war broke out in Europe that threatened the United Provinces—and one seemed likely to break out by an event that could happen any day, the death of the ancient Archbishop of Cologne. Yet he was better positioned to intervene in England than he had been before 1688. Louis's revocation of the Edict of Nantes in 1685 and his reimposition of high tariffs against Dutch goods in August and September 1687 led the hitherto peace-minded Amsterdam merchants to fear that the French were preparing to attack as they had in 1672, and led them to urge a retaliatory ban on French imports and, more important, made them inclined to support military action by William.[35]

UNLIKE WILLIAM AND Louis, James was not preoccupied with Europe. Instead was concentrating on his plan to secure a pliable Parliament by recasting local government.[36] In January 1688 agents were sent into the constituencies to lay the groundwork for a successful election.[37] Going to war on Louis's side would be an impediment to his plans, because it would require more money than his current revenues, and he would have to subordinate his goal of repeal of the Test Acts and penal laws to the necessity of securing more revenue.[38] Going to war on William's side was unthinkable, because he mistrusted William and had good reason to fear the might of France. James was also at a disadvantage because of the incompetence of his envoys in Paris and The Hague; he had to depend on information from French sources, which he knew might be self-serving; hence he ignored information from French sources that William was planning an invasion.[39] He was also dependent on Sunderland, who had a deeper knowledge than his other advisers both of foreign relations and of the difficulties of packing Parliament and governing the localities without a larger army, which could not be raised.[40] In this James was following the usual Stuart foreign policy, pursued with occasional exceptions by James I, Charles I, and Charles II, of largely ignoring the Continent and concentrating on holding power, with limited revenues and only small military forces, in England, Scotland, and Ireland. But what was happening on the Continent would have much to do with his fate.

Baron Churchill was watching events and working behind the scenes. He remained a member of James's court. "Meanwhile master and servant dwelt in all their old familiarity, and Churchill was constantly at the King's side in his bedroom, at his toilet, behind his chair at meals, and on horseback beside his carriage, just as he had been since he was a page."[41] He remained James's most talented general, though he had reason to believe that, just as he had been passed over for the highest command in favor of Feversham during the Monmouth rebellion, he might be passed over again in any future conflict by James's illegitimate son (and his own nephew) the Duke of Berwick, a Catholic who still in his teens had shown talent fighting in the Holy

Roman Emperor's army against the Turks.[42] In November 1687, Churchill tried to get James to appoint him head of the English regiments in the United Provinces and opposed Sunderland's moves to put them in the service of France.[43] But unlike Sunderland, Churchill heartily rebuffed any attempt to get him to convert to Catholicism. There is a story, told by an anonymous contemporary author, that on James's progress through the West Country in September 1687, Churchill told James that (as Winston Churchill paraphrases), "I humbly beseech your Majesty to believe that no subject in your three kingdoms would venture further than I would to purchase your favour and good liking; but I have been bred a Protestant, and intend to live and die in that communion; above nine parts in ten of the whole people are of the same persuasion, and I fear (which excess of duty makes me say) from the genius of the English nation, and their natural aversion to the Roman Catholic worship, some consequences which I dare not so much as name, and which it creates in me a horror to think of."[44] Churchill's influence was also apparent when he encouraged Princess Anne's husband, Prince George of Denmark, to refuse to dismiss his first gentleman-in-waiting, the Earl of Scarsdale, after he was dismissed as lord lieutenant of Derbyshire for refusing to carry out James's campaign instructions.[45] Churchill's communications with William, beginning with Dijkvelt's visit in early 1687, and his wife's intimacy with Anne were in the nature of insurance policies: while he continued at James's side, he had also enlisted in the ranks of the two daughters who were in line to succeed him to the throne.

Churchill was also in a position to conspire with others in the army to betray James in case of invasion. Winston Churchill, writing in the 1930s, takes it for granted that his ancestor did this, though documentation was lacking.[46] So does J. R. Jones, writing in the 1990s:

> Churchill proved to be easily the most important and influential person in the underground network of army officers who pledged their aid in bringing about a change of royal policy and the elimination of evil ministers. This change he termed a "change of government," a phrase which did not by any means imply James's deposition. He was uniquely placed to link the various conspirato-

rial military groups. Anne's household served as the centre during the preparatory phase, before the crisis developed. . . . Churchill had the advantage of renewing his extensive personal and professional connections within the army during the summer camps that assembled [in Hounslow Heath] under his command in 1687 and 1688. The regiments which he then inspected and exercised were the units that mattered since they would form any field army sent to oppose an invasion, and they were elite units. . . . Churchill also had long-standing connections with most of the leading military activists who met at the so-called "Treason Club" at the Rose Tavern in Russell Street: they were a combination of officers and ex-officers, many of the latter being Whigs and friends of Monmouth. Among them were many Tangerines [men who had served in Tangiers], several of whom had campaigned with him in 1685.[47]

The historian John Childs, in his book on the army in the Revolution, is similarly inconclusive. His own exhaustive research produced a "shortage of evidence" about the beginning and progress of the conspiracy, and he speculates that it began in unofficial gatherings at the Earl of Shrewsbury's house in London in the summer of 1687 and was advanced in the letter Dijkvelt carried back to William in June. But in his view the conspiracy "was probably little more than an intelligence-gathering organization and a debating club" until the Immortal Sevens' letter of June 30, 1688.[48] "The army conspiracy," he concludes, "was effectively founded during the summer camp on Hounslow Heath in 1688 and flourished in those formations which were in constant attendance on the court or were regularly stationed in or close to London: the regiments of horse and foot guards."[49]

Stephen Saunders Webb writes that Churchill "moved from mere consultations about securing the legitimate succession to actually planning a Protestant putsch" in April 1687, but aside from quoting Churchill's assurances to Anne, William, and James that he would put his Protestant faith above his loyalty to his patron the king, he presents no specific evidence that Churchill engaged in overt acts in this conspiracy before April 1688.[50] But Webb makes it clear that Churchill had unparalleled connections he could exploit in the army and navy, including the veterans from Tangier, the Duke of Grafton (the illegitimate son of Charles II and Churchill's onetime mistress the Duchess of Cleveland) who had fought at Sedgemoor, and in Princess Anne's household.[51] John Churchill does not seem to have been in the habit of telling anyone everything he knew, much less putting everything down on paper. Certainly he would not have put on paper evidence of an extensive conspiracy of army officers to betray the King.

In the first months of 1688, James's men were busy putting the three questions — would they support repeal of the Test Acts and penal laws? would they support candidates for Parliament who supported repeal? would they live in peace with their neighbors regardless of religion? — to officials and gentlemen in the counties and boroughs, and to army officers as well.[52] In January, James, angered by the mass distribution of Fagel's letter, ordered the two British regiments stationed in the Netherlands, and paid by the States General, to return to England. The States General replied that it was under no obligation to order them back and would not do so, though individual soldiers could leave voluntarily. William was evidently legally correct in saying that the decision should be left to the States General and that it was under no obligation to send them back. But William obviously preferred to have these forces at his disposal, and so now did the States General and the leaders of Amsterdam. In 1686 they had opposed enlarging the army, but by June 1687 they were sufficiently alarmed by the aggressive moves of Louis XIV to agree to financial reforms that enabled William to build and man 30 new ships. Now they were reluctant to see the British regiments removed.[53] In March, James ordered the individual soldiers to return to England, but few did.[54]

On March 14, Anne wrote to her sister Mary that she suspected that Queen Mary Beatrice's "great belly is a little suspicious. It is true that she is very big, but she looks better than she ever did, which is not usual. Her being so positive it will be a son, and the principles of that religion being such that they will stick at nothing, be it never so wicked, if it will promote their interest, give some cause to fear there may be foul play indeed."[55] Also in March the Earl of Danby was moved to take action. Danby, Charles II's leading minister from 1673 to 1678 and then a prisoner in the Tower of London until 1684,[56] was now ensconced far north of London in his extensive lands in Yorkshire, where he was confident he could raise troops, and he was aroused by James's campaign to pack Parliament. He wrote William that James's agents' "examination of the minds of the nobility and gentry has made such an union for the defense" of Protestantism and that "I verily believe they begin to despair of supplanting it by violent means, and it is certain they can do it in no other way." He added that Fagel's letter had added "courage to that union . . . and there wants only an opportunity to the greatest part of the nation to show their zeal for your services."[57]

Communicating such thoughts in writing was obviously dangerous, and it appears that Danby's letter was not delivered to William until late April, when two English naval officers traveled to the Netherlands. They were Admiral Edward Russell and Captain Arthur Herbert. Russell was a grandson of the fourth Earl of Bedford and part of a family that also produced the nineteenth-century prime minister Lord John Russell and the twentieth-century philosopher Bertrand Russell. He left his last naval command in 1682 and was part of the circle of the Earl of Shrewsbury, in whose London house Dijkvelt and Zuylestein had met with several of James's chief opponents in 1687.[58] Arthur Herbert was a courageous officer, but unpopular with his men, who entered the Duke of York's household and was Master of the Robes for James II. He surprised James by refusing to agree to repeal of the Test Acts and penal laws, "that he could not do it either in honour or conscience," but perhaps out of jealousy of George Legge, Lord Dartmouth, whom James made commander of the fleet.[59]

In England, Russell and Herbert had been part of the circle that met, often in the London house of the Earl of Shrewsbury, with Henry Sidney, of the family famed in Elizabethan times and uncle of the Earl of Sunderland. Sidney had served in the British regiments in the Netherlands from 1667 to 1679, and had been an envoy to the Netherlands from 1679 to 1681, and "of all Englishmen the man closest to William and most in his confidence."[60] William had wanted to make him commander of the British regiments in the Netherlands, but Charles II vetoed that. In 1688 he was, in Burnet's words, "the man in whose hands the conduct of the whole design was chiefly deposited by the prince's own orders."[61] Shrewsbury, from one of the oldest noble families in England, was raised a Catholic and became the 12th Earl in 1668, at age eight, after his father was killed in a duel with the Duke of Buckingham. In 1679 he became a member of the Church of England and hosted Dijkvelt and Zuylestein on their visits to London in 1687. Through Dijkvelt he sent William an assurance that he would be of his service; after Zuylestein's visit in August he went to The Hague with Halifax's recommendation that "he is, without any competition, the most considerable man of quality that is growing up amongst us."[62] Russell and Herbert were thus representatives of a wider group of nobles opposed to James's policies and to varying degrees friendly to William's cause, men with whom William, primarily through Sidney, had maintained an extensive correspondence since spring 1687. William also maintained an intelligence network in Scotland through two Scots exiles in the Netherlands, William Carstares and Sir James Dalrymple of Stair, who sent over agents to gather news and distribute propaganda.[63]

Russell and Herbert met with William at his palace at Het Loo, just outside the town of Appeldoorn at the edge of one of the Netherlands' largest forests, where William was entertaining the Elector of Saxony. They urged William to assemble a large naval force and a small army and land in England to intervene against James's campaign to pack Parliament. They assured him that he would have widespread popular support and that they spoke on behalf of "many of great power and interest." "Russell warned that the present moment was too good to miss. Even those indifferent in religion had no desire to turn papist, but 'men of fortune, if they saw no visible prospect, would be governed by their present interest.' The army was as yet too protestant to be a really reliable instrument for James but this too might alter."[64] In other words, a rebellion must come soon, or the government and army would be taken over by Catholics.

Or, if the rebellion did come and succeed without William's assistance, they hinted, they would go ahead anyway. William, as his biographer puts it, "had to capture control of a conspiracy. Otherwise, as he himself put it, the English would set up a republic. This would obviously deprive both the Prince and the Princess of their right. Also, and more important, it would be fatal to the Dutch. Of all conceivable forms of English political structure, that of a republic would be worst for Dutch interests. A republic would concentrate on colonial expansion and commercial enterprise. The Dutch knew this from bitter experience. They remembered Cromwell. Their trade had never recovered from the Navigation Acts of 1650 and 1651," which barred England and English colonies to Dutch merchants. "Charles II had re-enacted the Navigation Laws, but he had not been able to enforce them. . . . But a second English republic could be expected to enforce and even to extend the policy of the Navigation Acts. When, therefore, Russell threatened that if William did not join the conspirators they would go on without him, the Prince was obliged to acquiesce. By doing so he could direct the course of a revolution which was going to take place anyway."[65]

This was the time for decision. William, well informed of developments in England, probably expected that Russell and Herbert would propose something on this order. And presumably he had thought through what his reply would be. It was, as Lord Macaulay quotes him as saying to Dijkvelt, "now or never."[66] William's "single recurring nightmare" was an attack on the Dutch Republic and other Protestant states by Louis XIV, and his consolation for many years was that he might sometime soon, when his wife inherited the throne, be able to bring England in against Louis. But now, with the prospect of the birth of a Catholic Prince of Wales, with William's chance to succeed to the English throne becoming ever more slender, with James constructing a Catholic army and a Parliament willing to collaborate in the Catholicizing of the government, William had to act or to face a situation in which all his hopes were shattered.[67]

Burnet, the closest thing we have to an eyewitness, described the crucial interchange. "So Russel [*sic*] put the Prince to explain himself what he intended to do. The Prince answered, that, if he was invited by some men of the best interest, and the most valued in the nation, who should both in their own name, and in the name of others who trusted them, invite him to come and rescue the nation and the religion, he believed he could be ready by the end of September to come over."[68] This was not quite a promise that he would definitely act, but it was a promise that he might very well do so if his condition was met; and the mention of a specific month, September, generally considered the latest month in which it was feasible to launch naval operations in the English Channel, suggested a considered determination. Herbert and Russell left on or before April 29 (April 19 in England), when William mentioned their departure in a letter. They met in The Hague with Burnet, who told them that there were other contingencies that must be met. "The main confidence we had was in the Electoral Prince of Brandenburg, for the old Elector was then dying. And I told Russell in parting that, unless he died, there would be great difficulties, not easily mastered, in the design of the Prince's expedition to England." The elector Frederick William had for many years been an ally of France and had sent troops to fight the Turks in Hungary; William had deflected him from the French alliance in 1685 and signed a mutual defense pact with him, but he had refused to join the anti-Louis League of Augsburg.[69] Now William wanted to hire German troops, of which martial Brandenburg was a major supplier, to protect the United Provinces against French attack. At Het Loo, as Herbert and Russell were meeting with Burnet, William was also trying to hire some from the Elector of Saxony.[70] The train of events that resulted in the Revolution had been set in deliberate motion. It was to be given further impetus by King James's actions in England a few days later.

By April, James's campaign to elect a Parliament that would repeal the Test Acts and penal laws reached a new stage. His organizers had already probed opinion in the counties and boroughs, and now preparations were under way to push aside those who opposed his program and to install in decisive positions those who would support it.[71] On April 27 (May 7 on the Continent) James issued a second Declaration of Indulgence, promising religious toleration to all his subjects. In it he promised to call a new Parliament to meet by November at the latest, and said his goal was "the peace and greatness of our country."[72] On May 4/14 he ordered the Anglican clergy to read the proclamation in their churches on two successive Sundays; one effective medium of communication between the king and the people was the pulpit. Henry Compton, though suspended from his duties as Bishop of London, canvassed opinion among London clergy, as did Archbishop of Canterbury William Sancroft; Compton and some other bishops, according to William's agent James Johnston, were aware of William's tentative agreement to lead an invasion. On May 17/27, Sancroft and six other bishops went down the Thames from Lambeth to Whitehall Palace and delivered a petition arguing that the dispensing power — the power of the king to dispense with enforcement of the laws, in this case the Test Acts — was illegal by declaration of Parliament in 1663 and 1673 (when Charles II had been obliged to revoke his narrower declarations of indulgence). The bishops refused to order the clergy to read the proclamation; it was too great a challenge to the primacy of the Church of England. Passive obedience had been transformed, by great provocation, into passive resistance.[73]

James was furious. "This is a standard of rebellion," he said the next day. "Is this what I have deserved who have supported the Church of England and will support it? . . . God hath given me this dispensing power and I will maintain it. I tell you there are seven thousand men, and of the Church of England too, that have not bowed the knee to Baal."[74] Copies of Sancroft's petition were quickly printed and soon distributed throughout London, and only a handful of London clergymen read the petition.[75] To James's surprise and dismay, prominent Dissenting Protestant leaders supported the bishops' refusal to order the reading of the letter. William kept a close eye on the controversy; he noted in a letter to Bentinck (in the rough and ready French that William used to correspond with even his Dutch intimates) that *"cette affaire des évêques pourroit porter les affaires promptement à des extremités"* (this affair of bishops could carry matters promptly to extremes).[76]

Sunderland advised that James ignore the bishops' refusal. But James believed that his father had been doomed by showing weakness in crisis, and he was taken aback at the bishops' attack on his suspending power. On June 1 he brought a legal action for "scandalous libel" against the seven bishops. When asked to give bail June 7, they refused and the next day were marched off to the Tower, and received cheers from the London crowds.[77] "Wonderfull was the concern of the people for them," Evelyn wrote, "infinite crowds of people on their knees, begging their blessing & praying for them as they passed out of the

Barge; along the Tower wharfe &c."[78] The garrison at the Tower drank to the bishops' health and refused to drink to their colonel's or the king's.[79] The same Englishmen who were ready to believe Titus Oates's falsehoods about a Popish plot were ready, a decade later, to see a policy of alleged tolerance as an attempt to impose Popish tyranny. Several days later the bishops were set free on bail, put up by the Marquis of Halifax, the Earl of Danby, the Earl of Nottingham, and the Earl of Carlisle.[80]

JUST DAYS AFTER James issued his Declaration of Indulgence, two deaths in Europe changed the prospects for war there. On April 29/May 9, Elector Frederick William of Brandenburg died. Within days William was writing to the new elector, Frederick III, who was heir to William's Orange estates and so had a motive for supporting him on what might be a fatal invasion of England.[81] Suddenly it seemed that the Dutch might be able to hire soldiers from Brandenburg. Then Archbishop Max Heinrich of Cologne died on May 24/June 3. This meant that Louis XIV would try to install his candidate for the archbishopric, Cardinal Wilhelm Egon von Fürstenberg, over the opposition of the emperor and Pope Innocent XI.[82] That would likely mean a general European war.

In England, James seems to have taken little note of these developments, but to William in The Hague and Louis in Versailles they were matters of the highest import. Louis would have to decide whether to send his forces in the Rhineland to assert his claims in Cologne. In the meantime, on May 28/June 7, in response to the strengthening of William's navy, he offered James to send 15 French ships from the Mediterranean to Brest, to be at the disposal of the English. But James and Sunderland, wishing to avoid a French alliance, which would antagonize William and would undermine their program to secure a pliable Parliament, turned down the offer on June 4/14.[83] They did not know that William had already made something in the nature of commitments to intervene in England and that with these two propitious deaths he could see the way open to a situation, with Louis committed to the Rhineland, where he would face strong opposition, which would allow him to launch an invasion of England without endangering the Netherlands.

On June 10/20, Queen Mary Beatrice went into labor. She believed she had conceived in early September, when she met the king at Bath after his western progress; her doctors said conception came in early October, but she was right. Lords of the council were admitted to her bedchamber at nine in the morning and stood at her bedside, opposite the midwives, with the king at the foot. As J. P. Kenyon tells the story, "About a quarter to ten, just when the atmosphere in the room was approaching the intolerable, even by seventeenth-century standards, the child's first cry was heard. It was shown first to Lady Sunderland, who gave the King a prearranged signal that it was a boy. Within the hour the guns of the Tower were booming in honour of a Catholic heir, and messengers were thudding away down the shires with letters from Sunderland announcing the birth of James Francis Edward, Prince of Wales."[84] Bonfires were lit in London that evening, but the crowds were not enthusiastic.

The news was not met with celebration in all quarters. "*A young Prince* borne, which will cause disputes," reads the entry in John Evelyn's diary. "This was very surprizing, it having been universally given out that her Majesty did not look till the next moneth."[85] Most of the witnesses to the birth were Catholic—Sunderland announced his conversion a few days later—and some Protestants, like the minister Sidney Godolphin, took care to stand where they could not see what was happening. John Churchill and Sarah Churchill were not available; Sarah's sister Frances Tyrconnel, a Catholic, was there. Many believed the infant was suppositious, smuggled into the bedchamber in a warming pan, it was said. Princess Mary in The Hague had for months doubted that Mary Beatrice was really pregnant. Absent also, taking the waters at Bath, was Princess Anne, two of whose children had died of smallpox in 1687 and who had suffered an apparent miscarriage in April 1688. She was decidedly of the opinion that the baby was suppositious. After she returned to London, she wrote Mary on June 18/28, " '[T]is possible it may be her child; but where one believes it, a thousand do not. For my part, except they do give very plain demonstrations, *which is almost impossible now,* I shall ever be of the number of unbelievers."[86] William's agent James Johnston wrote a pamphlet casting doubt on the birth and calling for an inquiry by the Parliament James had promised.[87]

Sunderland proposed that James take the occasion of the prince's birth to pardon the seven bishops; James instead raised the charge from scandalous libel to seditious libel. He was evidently confident of a guilty verdict, and in seventeenth-century trials, judges routinely browbeat defendants and witnesses hostile to the government, expatiated on the evils of defendants' deeds, and otherwise ungently guided jurors toward guilty verdicts. James had another advantage. The trial was set for June 29, and the army was due to assemble in those long hours of midsummer daylight on June 27 at Hounslow Heath, 12 miles — less than a day's march — from Whitehall Palace, west of Kew Gardens and north of Hampton Court Palace and closer to London than Heathrow Airport is today. There Baron Churchill hosted James for dinner on the first night.[88]

The panel of jurors for the bishops' trial was chosen by the sheriff of London and included Dissenters and employees of the navy and revenue administration. But when court opened on June 29, it soon became clear that two of the four judges were hostile to the prosecution and to the dispensing power. "If this be once allowed of," said one judge, "there will need no Parliament; all the legislature will be in the King." By upholding the dispensing power, said another, "not only the laws of the Reformation but all the laws for the preservation of the Christian religion are suspended." The crowd was even more hostile to the Crown. When Sunderland arrived in a sedan chair to testify, the crowd greeted him with cries of "popish dog"; in the courtroom he was hissed so loudly that his testimony could hardly be heard, and he left the courtroom by a back way. Unusually, the judges left to the jury not only the question of whether the bishops had published a document, but also whether or not it was libelous, a decision usually reserved by the judges for themselves. No one doubted that the bishops had made a statement, and ordinarily the judges would have ruled it a libel, thus virtually ensuring a guilty verdict. The decision was left open overnight, and the jury came in the next morning with a verdict of not guilty.[89]

Spectators in the courtroom cheered for half an hour. Church bells rang. After dark there were bonfires all over London, more than for the prince's birth 10 days before, and a crowd burned an effigy of the pope outside St. James's Palace. "There was a lane of people," reported Evelyn, "from the Kings Bench to the water-side, upon their knees as the Bishops passed & repassed to beg their blessing: Bon fires made that night, & bells ringing, which was taken very ill at Court and appearance of neere 60 Earles & Lords &c upon the bench in honor of the Bishops, & which did not a little comfort them; but indeede they were all along full of Courage & cheerfull."[90] Soldiers assembled just three days before at Hounslow Heath gave a great shout when they heard the verdict.[91] As Winston Churchill tells the story, "'What is that clamour?' asked the King. 'Sire, it is nothing; the soldiers are glad that the Bishops are acquitted.' 'Do you call that nothing?' said James."[92]

In the days afterwards, James ordered the Ecclesiastical Commission to ascertain why clergymen had failed to read the proclamation and to punish those who had, but nothing was done; attempts by judges to prosecute those who lit bonfires were followed by juries voting acquittal.[93] As the historian J. P. Kenyon writes, "The government was quite powerless to halt the wave of rejoicing that spread out from London to the whole of England, sweeping most of the Dissenters with it. The birth of a Prince had given them the prospect of a Catholic dynasty in perpetuity: the trial of the seven bishops was a gratuitous demonstration of how a Catholic monarch treated Protestants who had always regarded him with the most devoted loyalty: their acquittal substituted contempt for fear. An incompetent despotism is a contradiction in terms."[94] The historian John Miller has a similar conclusion: "The foundation of popular acceptance, so necessary for a stable regime in early modern England, had been dangerously eroded."[95] Royal authority was theoretically absolute, but in practice in England — in teeming London — it rested on a subtle tissue of deference, and that subtle tissue was now fatally pierced.

On the day of the bishops' acquittal, June 30, seven of the leaders of the movement against James met in the Earl of Shrewsbury's house in London. Since Herbert and Russell had returned in May from their

meeting with William, Sidney and Russell had worked to get prominent men to sign a letter asking William to come over to England. In
June, William sent Zuylestein to London, purportedly to congratulate
James on the birth of the prince — a dazzlingly cynical pretext. His real
mission was to determine who was willing to call on William to invade,
and on what terms. Not shadowed by agents of the naïve James, he
met with Sidney, Russell, Danby, and Shrewsbury.[96] On June 30 the
Immortal Seven, as they came to be known by admirers of the Glorious Revolution, signed the letter, calling on William to intervene and
pledging to support and act in his aid, whenever it should come. They
left no doubt they hoped it would come quickly. "We have great reason to believe, we shall be every day in a worse condition than we are,
and less able to defend ourselves, and therefore we do earnestly wish
we might be so happy as to find a remedy before it is too late for us to
contribute to our own deliverance." They said that nineteen out of
twenty in the nation were dissatisfied with James, and that many officers in the army were actively discontented.[97]

The Seven were not necessarily the seven most prominent men in
England.[98] The Marquis of Halifax and the Earl of Nottingham were
canvassed, but refused to sign.[99] The Earl of Danby was probably the
most prominent, a former high minister of Charles II identified with
the Anglican party (though when the Tory party was formed to oppose
exclusion, he was in the Tower), capable of raising men-at-arms in
Yorkshire and the North Country. Another, much less prominent,
signer, Lord Lumley, a landowner in County Durham and a former
Catholic who had been stripped of his commission in the army, could
help in this. The Earl of Devonshire, with great estates in Derbyshire,
could do the same in the North Midlands; he also had a grievance, having been fined £30,000 for striking a courtier and former governor of
Virginia named Culpeper in Whitehall Palace in 1685.[100] The Earl of
Shrewsbury mortgaged his estates for £40,000 and sailed to the
Netherlands. Henry Sidney and Admiral Edward Russell also crossed
to the Netherlands to assist in preparing the invasion. The seventh
signer, Bishop of London Henry Compton, the first Anglican bishop
to find himself at odds with James, had supervised the education and
fortified the Anglicanism of Princess Anne; his role would be to see

her safely to the side of William when he came to England. In the meantime he traveled north, purportedly to visit his sister. Admiral Arthur Herbert, disguised as a common sailor, but destined to be the commander of the fleet in the invasion, sped the letter to The Hague by July 6/16.[101]

❧

EVEN AS JAMES was attempting to produce a favorable Parliament, he was relying for his security on the army he had inherited and increased in size in response to the Monmouth rebellion in summer 1685. He allowed the county militias, so closely tied to local landowners and notables, to wither away.[102] As the historian J. R. Jones writes, "James' army was intended, like the New Model in the 1650s, primarily as a police force, almost as an army of occupation."[103]

But how loyal was that army and, most especially, its officers, connected as so many of them were to nobles and gentry who were opposed to James and his program? One locus of disloyalty was the Treason Club, which met at the Rose Tavern on Russell Street in Covent Garden (a property developed by the Earl of Bedford,[104] a relative of Admiral Edward Russell and the executed Lord William Russell) and which "grew almost organically from the fashionable young gentlemen and who mixed with the Restoration wits, dramatists, and rakes in their lairs at the Rose Tavern and Will's Coffee House."[105] This group included officers with Whig, Monmouth, or Dutch connections, including Charles Godfrey, who was married to John Churchill's sister Arabella. "Although there is no evidence," writes John Childs, "it seems likely that the plans for the defection of parts of the English army were arranged through the club's auspices."[106]

Then there were the Tangerines, those veteran officers who had served together in Tangiers, of which the most prominent were Colonels Charles Trelawney and Percy Kirke and Baron John Churchill; they also included the Duke of Grafton and Lord Cornbury, son and heir of the second Earl of Clarendon, and thus second cousin to Princesses Mary and Anne. Grafton, whose mother the Duchess of Cleveland had been Churchill's mistress and benefactor, had served with distinction next to Churchill at Sedgmoor and had been passed over for promotion by James.[107] Most of the Tangerines had served under foreign flags—Churchill with the French army, for example—and "were well acquainted with foreign practices; as a result they were [not] squeamish about changing sides and did not suffer from scruples of allegiance." The Tangerines also had many fellow veterans in various units.[108] Once the army was assembled at Hounslow Heath, and James tried to assess the number of officers who were in favor of repeal of the Test Acts and penal laws, Thomas Langston, a member of both the Treason Club and the Tangerines, started an Association of Protestant Officers and spread rumors that James wanted to replace all Protestant officers with Catholics, as had in fact been done by Tyrconnel in Ireland.

Communication with William of Orange was evidently maintained by ships sailing to and from the United Provinces, based at ports on the east coast of England and Scotland not closely watched by the government.[109] Childs concludes, "The number of active military conspirators was very small, probably no more than twenty or thirty, but they formed a tightly-knit group bound together by ties of blood, marriage, political allegiance, and a common concern for their future careers. This exclusive club was responsible for organizing and executing the trickle of defections which wrecked James's confidence in his armed forces and removed the one obstacle which stood between the Prince of Orange and the throne of England."[110]

In this they played on fears, widespread in the army, that James intended to replace more Protestant officers with Catholics and to introduce Irish soldiers—the great majority of them Catholics, thanks to Tyrconnel's efforts—into England. Evidence of those fears came on September 6, when the Duke of Berwick, in command of the garrison in the naval port of Portsmouth, ordered captains to accept Irish Catholics in their companies; six Protestant captains refused and were dismissed.[111] The threat that the army would be remodeled—that is, staffed largely with Catholics—over the winter of 1688–89, as so many boroughs had been remodeled by James's agents, was, in the view of J. R. Jones, the second most important factor, after the security of the United Provinces, convincing William that he must invade.[112]

In the conspiracy in the army, Churchill seems to have played an important and quite possibly a central role.[113] Exactly what he did, we do not know. But on August 4 he wrote a letter to William of Orange that leaves no doubt he was in touch with William's agent Henry Sidney and in accord with his plans. "Mr. Sidney will lett you know how I intend to be have my selfe; I think itt is what I owe to God and my Country; my honor I take leave to put into your Royalle Hinesses hands, in which I think itt safe, if you think there is anny thing else that I ought to doe, you have but to command me and I shall pay an entier obedience to itt, being resolved to dye in that religion, that it has pleased God to give you, both the will and power to protect; I am with all respect, your Royalle Hinesses obedient sarvant, Churchill."[114] As Winston Churchill notes, "Such a letter written by a serving officer, at a time when conspiracy was rife and invasion imminent, was a deadly guarantee. Its capture or betrayal would justly involve the forfeit of his life at the hands of either a civil or a military tribunal. The invitation of the seven notables had been sent in the precautions of cipher. But Churchill's letter, which survives to this day, is in his own handwriting, signed with his name. He seems to have wished to share in a special degree the risks which his friends the signatories had incurred."[115]

As WELL-PLACED officers in the army and a few in the navy plotted to rise against James if William invaded, James continued to concentrate on his plans to pack Parliament. His chief manager, the Catholic lawyer Robert Brent, had hired agents who canvassed voters and potential voters and reported on the minutiae of local politics. They concentrated not on counties, which had large electorates heavily influenced by independent local landowners, but on the boroughs, whose charters and franchises could be changed by legal proceedings.[116] In June, July, and August, Brent's agents were busy purging county and borough officials, instituting legal proceedings against the charters of recalcitrant borough corporations and issuing new charters revising their franchises, canvassing local voters, distributing propaganda pamphlets, and finally compiling a list of 106 royally approved candidates.[117]

James's methods struck many as illegitimate, but they were not unprecedented. No previous king had had his appointees intervene in the election process (Charles II had remodeled corporations after 1681, but had never risked an election during the rest of his reign), but James was using methods similar to those employed by the Earl of Shaftesbury and the Whigs in elections in 1679 and 1681. Indeed he was using some of the same operatives, who earlier had recoiled at the prospect of a Catholic king, but were now allied with the Dissenters who were supporting James against the Church of England.[118] And in the boroughs they were successfully winning over Whig and Dissenting local property owners, "usually men of restricted ambitions and limited mental horizons . . . [who] were absorbed in the little worlds of their own communities, and many [of whom] stood to gain financially from possession of municipal office," and most of whom "would gain personally from religious toleration and equality of civil rights."[119] If Shaftesbury had effectively invented political parties, political platforms, and campaign organizations, James, seemingly effectively, imitated the man who would have deprived him of the throne and whom he and his brother had forced to flee for his life.

On August 24 orders in council were made for writs of election, to be issued for September 16, for the meeting of a new Parliament on November 27.[120] Some purges of borough governments continued, but most of that work had already been done, and now it was down to the removal of recalcitrant town clerks. New charters were issued — 28 in August and September 1688, as compared with only two in all of 1687 and two more in the first months of 1688; the new charters were concentrated in major towns with "well-established urban oligarchies, where the agents needed all the help they could get."[121] In September, Sunderland, who had previously remained remote from election management, wrote to thirty-three individuals directing them to run as candidates, and to lord lieutenants informing them of the names of approved royal candidates, in the counties.[122] This meant relying on regional powers like the Duke of Beaufort in the marchlands and Wales, and the Earl of Bath in the southwest.[123]

Most historians have followed the lead of Macaulay and have assumed that James's campaigning was bound to fail.[124] But J. R. Jones, who has studied the details most closely, reaches another conclusion, one that Bentinck's informants reached in December 1687. "The evidence does not support the old view that the campaign was a muddle and ended in confusion, and that it could not possibly have succeeded. Not only did James persist with the campaign, but his opponents feared that the chances of success were considerable."[125] One reason was his apparent success in London. In 1679 and 1681 the electorates in the City of London, Westminster, and Middlesex County had mostly rejected Court nominees; in 1679 the Court delayed elections in London until late in the process, for fear the results would stimulate opposition elsewhere, and the king called for the 1681 session of Parliament to sit in royalist Oxford rather than in turbulent London.[126] In 1683 the Court installed Tory sheriffs and aldermen, and Tories prevailed in 1685. But by 1688, James's agents had purged the livery companies and established control of the sheriff and aldermanic elections, and were proposing to reduce the "large, rapacious and turbulent" electorate of Westminster by 90 percent; their newly installed officials, "a mixture of Catholics, opportunists and Whigs" seemed likely to prevail.[127]

The final reports in the second week of September from Brent's agents in the field suggested that James was likely to win a majority in the House of Commons.[128] "To summarize: approximately 200 constituencies, returning 400 out of the 513 MPs, had been subjected to some kind of direct governmental intervention. A working majority must have seemed to be within reach."[129] On August 24, James obtained orders in council for writs for a new Parliament to be issued on September 16 and for the new Parliament to meet on November 27. The evidence indicates he hoped to have a majority in the House of Commons and he was prepared to create new peers if necessary to have a majority in the House of Lords.[130] If his efforts to pack the Commons and swamp the Lords had been successful, James, in W. A. Speck's words, "would have reduced the English parliament to the level of a French provincial estate. . . . James, therefore, did attempt to make royal authority in England absolute."[131] French-style absolutism might really have sprung to life in England in late 1688 or early 1689 — absent a Dutch invasion.

The amount of detailed work this campaign required helps to explain why a king like James, conscientious about attending to business and determined to achieve his goal, remained unaware of the dangers he faced from William and the conspirators with whom he was apparently in constant touch; in his diary entry for August 10, John Evelyn noted that "Dr. Tenison," the vicar of St. Martin-in-the-Fields, "now told me there would suddainly be some greate things discovered, which happened to be the P: of O: intended coming."[132] Nor does James seem to have troubled himself much with events in Europe; only Sunderland among his ministers had much knowledge or interest in foreign relations.[133] James and Sunderland evidently did not see that Louis was contemplating a European war to shore up and expand France's eastern frontiers, and that William was contemplating an invasion of England to protect his dynastic interest and to yoke Britain in with the Netherlands as an enemy of Louis.[134]

FOR LOUIS, TIME was of the essence. Some of Emperor Leopold's forces, under Max Emanuel of Bavaria, were tied down in the siege of Belgrade in the summer of 1688, but it appeared that the emperor would soon complete the conquest of the Hungarian and Transylvanian basin—and free up all his forces for action in the west.[135] By the end of the summer it was becoming clear that Pope Innocent XI would not accept the election of von Fürstenberg as Archbishop of Cologne and would not recognize the right of the Duchess of Orleans to a share of the inheritance of the Rhenish Palatinate. At some point in the summer Louis decided that he would go to war—a quick war, he expected, that would be over by January 1689.[136]

On August 22, at a council of war, Louis ordered a preemptive strike at the fortress of Philippsburg, which spanned the Rhine just north of Alsace—and far south of the Netherlands.[137] Louis was preparing to send troops into the middle Rhine, even though he had plenty of information indicating that William was preparing an invasion of England, which he never would have done if he had learned that French troops had headed north into the Netherlands.[138] It was a calculated risk, and not necessarily a reckless one. As his biographer John Wolf writes, "Louis hoped that French intervention in the Rhineland would keep the Turks from making peace; it would also allow William to embark for England and thereby open a civil war, which Louis believed would last a long time and effectively tie up both England and the Netherlands. Civil war in England and the Holy War in Hungary would leave the German princes at the mercy of France."[139] Not an irrational analysis for an aggressive and optimistic king.

William of Orange spent the summer of 1688 preparing for an invasion, while keeping his options open. The letter sent by the Immortal Seven was written on June 30, which was July 10 in the Netherlands, and William evidently acted quickly when he received it. Prayers at Princess Mary's chapel for the newborn Prince of Wales were canceled, and William and Mary and Dutch officials failed to attend a celebration of his birth given by the English ambassador. Bentinck was called into conference, and on July 24 he left on a secret mission to German princes.[140] The business of assembling two armies, one to invade England and the other to protect the United Provinces, and a navy as large as any the Dutch had ever assembled, was demanding, and William relied heavily on the capable Bentinck.[141]

On or about July 20, William initiated a secret dialogue involving Bentinck, Dijkvelt, Fagel, and three of the four burgomasters of Amsterdam.[142] Though long reluctant to support a war, the Amsterdammers were alarmed by the French bans and higher import fees on Dutch imports imposed in 1687, and feared this French *guerre de commerce* might lead to a real *guerre,* and supported a buildup of the army and the invasion armada, which continued through the summer.[143] William also took care to secure able military leadership; on July 22 he urged the veteran soldier General Armand Schomberg, who had quit Louis XIV's army after the revocation of the Edict of Nantes and was now in the service of the Elector of Brandenburg, not to volunteer for a campaign in Hungary and to prepare for war in the west.[144] The Amsterdam council collaborated with the military buildup, but, hoping for removal of the French import restrictions, declined to vote to ban French commodities in the state of Holland, but also warned the French d'Avaux ambassador that a continuation of the import restrictions would mean war.

In September, William traveled to Germany and in Minden met

with the new Elector Frederick III of Brandenburg; he reported to Amsterdam on September 6 that he had secured promises of sufficient troops from Frederick and the dukes of Hanover and Celle to protect the United Provinces. D'Avaux, on Louis's order and perhaps against his own sensitive understanding of the predilections of the Dutch, warned the States General on September 9 that a Dutch invasion of England would oblige Louis "not only to come to James's assistance, but to regard the first hostile act committed by your troops, or your ships, against His Britannic Majesty as an open infraction of the peace and act of war against his own crown."[145] The Amsterdam council still declined to ban the import of French products, but it was clear to all close observers in the city that a vast flotilla of ships was being assembled and provisioned.[146]

D'Avaux reported this to Louis, who regally declined to change his plans. The English ambassador, who was not in the United Provinces for most of August, provided less information to James and Sunderland, and they tended to discount the reports from French sources of a military buildup, fearing that the French were trying to involve them in a quarrel that was not their own; and they probably felt, plausibly, that autumn was too late in the season for a naval attack.[147] James did order the fitting out of 35 new ships on August 21/31, but did nothing to increase the size of his army; the French ambassador told him it was too late in the season to bring any French ships from the Mediterranean to Brest.[148]

The French army was now massed on the frontiers, but it was not clear to William or James whether it would move against the United Provinces, into the lands of the electorate of Cologne, or, farther south, to the middle Rhine facing Alsace. Much of the Dutch army was encamped at Nijmegen, within reach of the lower Rhine and in position to defend the republic, but also within easy range of the ports from which William's fleet could sail; ammunition boats went up the river to the camps, but were not unloaded.[149] On August 31/September 10, French troops entered the lands of the electorate of Cologne, at Bonn, on the Rhine; in opposition, Brandenburg troops seized the garrison at Cologne. On September 5/15, Louis's envoy at Rome read a denunciation of Innocent XI and French troops entered the papal enclave of Avignon. On September 7/17 the fall of Belgrade eleven days earlier was announced in Rome and the teenaged Prince of Bavaria, Joseph Clement von Wittelsbach, was confirmed as Archbishop of Cologne.[150]

William and Grand Pensionary Fagel met in secret session with the States of Holland and got them to agree to full mobilization of Dutch troops and, on September 12/22, to approve the German troop agreement; Holland's agreement was vital, since it provided so much of the money needed to pay the Germans.[151] On September 14/24, the states of Gelderland and Overijssel approved the Prince's plans.[152] On the same day Louis made his decisive move and sent French troops to lay siege to the fortress of Philippsburg that spanned the Rhine and prepared to occupy the adjacent Palatinate.[153] Three days later, on September 17/27, the news of the siege of Philippsburg reached William, to whom it was readily apparent that Louis's troops would be tied down in the middle Rhine for the rest of the fighting season and that the United Provinces would be safe from attack. For the first time he could be sure he was free to invade England. The Amsterdam stock market rose 10 percent on hearing the news.[154] Amsterdam, long dubious about banning French goods, decided to do so after Louis ordered the seizure of all Dutch ships in French ports.[155]

On September 19/29, a secret session of the States General was convened at The Hague, where Fagel laid out William's full plans. The French trade measures had grievously damaged the Dutch economy and made war with France inevitable. If the Dutch remained passive, James might overcome his domestic opposition by packing Parliament and then join France against the United Provinces: 1672 all over again. The peril facing the Dutch Republic could be overcome only if William invaded England and procured the election of a free Parliament, which would not be under Catholic and French influence—and which might in time join the Dutch against France. The States General unanimously agreed to support William's invasion; the States of Holland even authorized the burgomasters to requisition ships by force if necessary. As historian Jonathan Israel summarizes the agreement, "The essential purpose of the Dutch invasion of Britain was quite specific and was spelt out clearly: it was to make the English

Crown and nation 'useful to their friends and allies, and especially to this state,' as it was expressed in the secret resolution of 29 September of the States of Holland, and, as the Haarlem deputies put it in their report home, 'make this state secure against all external danger.' Safeguarding the Protestant religion, and securing the dynastic interests of the Prince and Princess of Orange in England were, admittedly, tagged on as additional reasons; but both of these were given far less emphasis than the strategic factor."[156] From the point of view of the Dutch, the invasion they sanctioned, and which only they were in a position to finance and authorize, was essential to their national interest, which is to say in their economic interest as well; their interest in supporting Prototestanism was secondary, and their interest in the governance of England ranked even behind that. But in the circumstances they were all bound up together, and the purpose was "to crush late Stuart absolutism thoroughly, turn England into a parliamentary monarchy, and, by so doing, transform Britain into an effective counter-weight to the then overmighty power of France."[157]

This promise to aid William's invasion did not mean that the United Provinces were declaring war on England. Rather, under the accepted legal theories of the day, William was acting in his capacity as a sovereign prince (though he was prince of a principality, Orange, that he had never seen and that had been effectively annexed by France) who was entitled to assert his dynastic rights against another prince (James II); the United Provinces was only promising to aid him in what was legally, for all that it did to advance representative government and guaranteed liberties, a royal enterprise.[158]

On the same day that William learned of the siege of Philippsburg, September 17/27, James received a letter from his ambassador saying that William's fleet would embark in a week's time; this was evidently the first time the king took the threat of invasion seriously, or so the perceptive French ambassador Barillon reported.[159] James evidently still hoped that the Dutch could be blocked by the English fleet, and was doubtful that William would risk a sea crossing so late in the year.[160] But he withdrew his standing army from Scotland into England, which left Presbyterians and others opposing him relatively free to organize.[161] "I went to Lond:," reads John Evelyn's diary entry for

September 18, "where I found the Court in the uttmost consternation upon report of the Pr: of Oranges landing, which put White-hall into so panic a feare, that I could hardly believe it possible to find such a change."[162]

On September 21/October 1, James published a declaration that there would be elections for a Parliament to meet November 27, but he conceded that only Protestants could be seated and that any bill for religious toleration would also confirm the Acts of Uniformity of the Church of England.[163] James did this on the advice of Sunderland, who feared an invasion would cost him his head and, in the words of his biographer J. P. Kenyon, "surrendered himself entirely to the dictates of blind panic"[164] in which he evidently concluded that the king could not depend on Catholics and Dissenters against William's forces, but must regain the support of Anglicans.[165] To one obdurate Anglican whose support he very much needed, his military commander John Churchill, James gave a suit of the king's armor as he rode out to the army on September 25.[166] Then, on September 28/October 8, James withdrew the writs for parliamentary elections and issued a proclamation announcing the imminence of an invasion—an attempted conquest by a foreign power, it said, "although some false Pretences relating to Liberty, Property and Religion, contrived or worded with Art and Subtlety may be given out."[167]

ART AND SUBTLETY—and also great force. These were what William of Orange brought to his invasion of England, to make what came to be called the Glorious Revolution. He brought with him a force of at least 15,000 men and 500 ships, the largest fleet ever assembled in the English Channel—four times the size of the Spanish Armada of 100 years before.[168] "By every measure," writes the historian Dale Hoak, "this was the largest military maneuver of its kind since the end of the Roman Empire and, before the advent of the battleship, certainly the greatest such operation ever launched in northern European waters."[169] He also employed skillful propaganda, as he had before, in 1672 and 1673, when he sought to persuade the English that they should leave their alliance with Louis XIV and stop fighting the

Dutch, and as he had when he had caused to be printed and distributed Fagel's letter promising religious toleration and retention of the
Test Acts. The most persuasive mass medium of the day was the pamphlet, and the Dutch were the masters of the pamphlet. They had the
freest press in Europe, and the most printing presses, capable of printing in English, French, Czech, Hebrew, and Armenian, as well as
Dutch; the most type foundries and paper factories; and, as a small and
prosperous nation, they had a fine appreciation of the power of ideas
to shape men's acts.[170]

On September 30/October 10, William published his *Declaration*—
full title, *The Declaration of his highness William Henry, prince of Orange, of
the reasons inducing him to appear in armes in the kingdom of England*—"one
of the greatest and most decisive propaganda coups of early modern
times."[171] Some 60,000 copies were printed in English in secrecy in
The Hague, Amsterdam, and Rotterdam—a huge number at a time
when printings of 2,000 were considered high—and on October
24/November 3 were sent off from Amsterdam into England.[172]
William and his friend Bentinck controlled the circulation of the *Declaration* and its smuggling into England. As Jonathan Israel writes,
"When all dimensions are considered—military, naval, financial, lo-
gistical, diplomatic, domestic—together with the clever propaganda
campaign masterminded by Bentinck, which had an important effect
in England, it was arguably one of the most impressive feats of organization any early modern regime ever achieved."[173]

In the *Declaration,* William cited his invitation from the Seven,
and said his expedition had been "called by the English nation" and
was "intended for no other design, but to have a free and lawful parliament assembled as soon as possible." He was "appearing in arms" to
save the Church of England and the "ancient constitution" of England
and to oppose the "absolute power" of James's "evil Counsellors." He
also sought an "inquiry into the birth of the pretended Prince of
Wales . . . and to the right to succession." This was a set of reasons
barely overlapping with those he had used to justify the invasion to
the Dutch. He was careful to avoid Whig slogans and criticisms of
Charles II; the *Declaration* was framed to be acceptable and attractive
to Tories as well as Whigs. It focused instead on the suspension of the

Test Act and the suspending and dispensing powers in general, the creation of the Ecclesiastical Commission, and the suspension of the Bishop of London.[174] So widespread was its distribution and so attractive were its arguments that that James's government despaired of suppressing it and instead reprinted it with critical comments and refutations.[175] The States General published a statement on October 18/28 explaining why they had decided to "assist His Highness in crossing in person to England with ships and troops." This was aimed at a different audience and widely circulated in Europe, especially at courts with allies and potential allies in the coalition against Louis XIV.[176] Missing from this propaganda was mention of the primary reason that the Dutch States General supported the invasion: to prevent James II from bringing England into an alliance with France and to get England to join the military coalition of the Dutch.[177]

Missing also from the *Declaration* was any mention of the size of the forces William was amassing. The invitation from the Seven suggested that masses of English gentry, yeoman, and soldiers would spring to William's side when he came over. And at least one of the signers, Danby, clearly had the capacity to raise regional forces. But over the years William had learned to distrust the promises of English politicians. The Whigs might be for him; but he could remember that the founder of the organized Whig party, the Earl of Shaftesbury, had been an enthusiastic backer of the Dutch war in 1672 and that the theme of his speeches on the United Provinces was *Carthago delenda est*. He knew that the Tories had an allegiance to the Church of England, with its doctrine of nonresistance, and of course William himself was a Calvinist, no more an Anglican than James.[178] Israel argues, "Neither Prince nor States regarded the English opposition to James II as very reliable and both were determined to invade Britain with an army powerful enough to destroy James even without any military help from the English. The Dutch were intent on breaking James' authority and destroying his army — as far as possible by demoralizing it first — for it was from this that Parliament's supremacy and the turning of England round against France would follow."[179] Henry Sidney, in The Hague in July 1688, reports William as saying "he could not believe what they suggested concerning the king's army being disposed to come over to him, nor did he reckon, as much as they did, on the people of the country coming in to him; he said he could trust neither of those things. He could not undertake so great a design, the miscarriage of which would be the ruin of England and Holland, without such a force as he had reason to believe would be superior to the king's own, though his whole army would stick to him."[180]

It is generally held that William brought over an army of 15,000 or a little less, and that James had at his disposal 40,000 troops, with half in garrisons or (until he called them south) in Scotland, and another 20,000 available to face William's army.[181] Jonathan Israel, looking at the evidence from his perspective as a historian of the Dutch Republic, sees the matter differently:

> The army which the States General sent into Britain was actually a good deal larger and more powerful than Williamites subsequently cared to admit or than modern historians have generally realized. Nearly all modern accounts compute only the 14,352 regular infantry and cavalry which formed the core of the invading army and some accounts give a total figure as low as 11,212. But such figures are arrived at by omitting substantial sections of the army from the count. . . . If we include the Huguenots, the English, Dutch, and Scots volunteers, and the men of the (very substantial) Dutch artillery train in the reckoning, it emerges that the invasion army totalled at least 21,000 men and in my own view — because of the deliberate swelling of the Dutch regiments beyond their nominal strength — slightly more. Furthermore, the States General sent *only* their best regiments — all the crack regiments of the Dutch army — so that it was an army of exceptionally high quality and experience, for its size, as well as being massively supplied and equipped in a way that was unusual for seventeenth-century armies.[182]

It was also a reliable army. James's demand for the recall of the Anglo-Dutch Brigade in early 1688 had resulted in the exodus of only a few dozen officers, mostly loyal to James, while William took care to fill their places with Englishmen and Scots loyal to him, like the talented Thomas Talmash, a member of the Rose Tavern group, who came over in March, and John Cutts, a veteran of Monmouth's rebellion, who had fought at the siege of Buda in Hungary. He made sure to retain the services of Captain Hugh Mackay, commander of the three Scots regiments.[183]

James's withdrawal on September 28/October 8 of the writs for the parliamentary elections came before he could have read William's *Declaration* or ascertained the size of William's military forces. But the proclamation of invasion clearly anticipated William's propaganda campaign, and the reports from his ambassador in The Hague now tended to verify the earlier French reports of a massive military force that James had discounted. The abandonment of the parliamentary elections, claimed to be a concession to their unfeasibility in time of invasion, also raises the question again of how successful James's attempt to pack Parliament might have been. Most historians over the years have argued that it was bound to fail, but J. R. Jones more recently makes the case that it might have succeeded, that James's agents through the kind of legal hugger-mugger employed successfully by Charles and James up through the election of 1685 could have secured a working majority in the House of Commons. The fact is that we can never know how successful James's campaign would have been — and that manipulation of ancient legislative practices had succeeded in establishing absolutist government in other European countries in the era. But in any case on September 28/October 8 James abandoned this course, and turned back to the Anglicans for support.

To seek their support he asked the bishops to meet with him on October 3/13. They urged him to abolish the Eccelesiastical Commission, restore the old borough charters, and call for a free Parliament. To the dismay of his Catholic advisers, he complied speedily. On October 5/15 the Ecclesiastical Commission was abolished. On October 6/16 the old charter of the City of London — the most important corporate charter in the kingdom — was restored. On October 11/21, one day after William's fleet put out to sea, the Bishop of Winchester was authorized to restore the Fellows of Magdalen College, Oxford. On October 17/27 James annulled all proceedings against borough charters since 1679. Catholics were dismissed from the lord lieutenancies, and Tory justices of the peace were reinstated.[184] James's Catholic advisers stoutly opposed these measures; Sunderland, who underwent a "startling transformation in his demeanour in the course of three weeks — from boldness to timidity, from blind courage to wide-eyed terror,"[185] urged more-rapid and wider-ranging concessions to extricate the king from this crisis and to postpone gaining advantages for Catholics to the future. But although James wobbled irresolutely between his warring advisers, the actions he did take amounted to the abandonment of the campaign he had embarked on a year before to secure a pliable Parliament and a betrayal of the agents who had been energetically advancing his cause.

This was the second of James's great political betrayals; the first was the betrayal of the Anglican Tories who had supported him in the first year of his reign, and his new pledges of loyalty to them must have been met with some skepticism. To those historians who see James as a genuine believer in religious toleration, this second betrayal is hard to explain — an act of cowardice perhaps, but from a man who previously had shown bravery, even rash bravery, cowardice seems out of character. It is easier to explain if one sees as James's first goal, like that of Charles before him, the maintenance of the principle of hereditary succession. Charles had risked much for this in the Exclusion Crisis, and James, facing invasion from the husband of the daughter disinherited by the birth of his son, was taking what he evidently saw as the only means of preserving it once more. But his concessions left local government in limbo, unable to take measures like arresting those who seemed likely to rally to William.[186] And in Scotland, where James had withdrawn the army in September, William's proponents declared for a free Parliament in line with William's *Declaration,* and persuaded the Earl of Perth to resign and flee from Edinburgh.[187] James's concessions left many who had opposed his campaign unmollified; as Sir John Bramston said, "Some would think one kick of the breech enough for a gentleman."[188] William countered it by issuing a second *Declaration* dated October 14/24 arguing that "the imperfect redress that is now offered is a plain confession of those violations of the Government that we have set forth" and that the English still needed "a declaration of the rights of the subjects . . . not by any pretended acts of grace to which the extremity of their affairs has driven them."[189]

If William's preparations for an invasion were no longer a secret, neither was the presence of a conspiracy in the army. In his diary entry for October 6, John Evelyn wrote, "The apprehension was (& with reason) that his Majesties Forces, would neither at land or sea oppose them [William's army] with that viggour requisite to repell Invaders."[190] James, worried about the loyalty of his English officers, proposed to create a British general staff to surround them with more reliable Scottish and Irish officers. On October 16/26 Churchill blocked this proposal, and the next day at the army encampment near Salisbury he once again pleaded his loyalty to the King. James evidently believed him, and spurned the advice of his loyal generals Feversham and Ailesbury, who begged him "to clap up seven or eight of the heads" of the conspiracy, including "the Prince of Denmark, the Dukes of Ormond and Grafton, Lord Churchill, Mr. Kirkk, Mr. Trelawney &c but . . . fatally, the King could not resolve."[191]

Instead, James continued his concessions with a proclamation on October 17/27 ordering the restoration of all old charters and discarding the election agents who had worked for him in the campaign.[192] He was placing all his bets on the Anglican interest, and the loyal Anglican John Churchill. But William was also counting on the religious loyalties of Protestant officers. In his *Letter to the English Army,* dated October 18/28, he cited Tyrconnel's purge of Protestant officers in Ireland and argued that James would use his English officers and then discard them once absolutism was put in place and Protestantism ruined.[193] Admiral Arthur Herbert signed a *Letter to all Commanders of Ships and Sea-men* making the same case.[194] The navy had few Catholic officers; James had made the Catholic Sir Roger Strickland the chief admiral, but with the invasion looming he replaced him with his longtime Protestant aide George Legge, whom he had made Baron Dartmouth. Other naval officers, at the behest of Captain Edward Russell, canvassed captains to persuade them not to fight the Dutch flotilla, and several naval officers—Captain Matthew Aylmer, Captain George Churchill (John Churchill's brother), Lieutenant George Byng—were in contact with William's agents, but as it turned out the winds prevented the two fleets from meeting.[195]

ON OCTOBER 20/30, William's fleet set sail. The Dutch people seem to have regarded the expedition as "crucial to the Republic's survival as a major, independent European power," Jonathan Israel writes. "The passage of the States General's crack regiments from their garrisons to the places of embarkation produced scenes of intense emotion, crowds of Dutch men and women cheering, praying, and weeping as they went. Nor was it only the Reformed clergy who, at the bidding of the burgomasters, laid on rousing sermons and special services for the invasion of England but also, as at Haarlem, the Mennonite, Lutheran, and Remonstrant churches. . . . At Amsterdam, the Portuguese Jewish community—whose lay leaders were closely involved in helping to organize the expedition—also laid on special services and prayers to implore the Almighty to grant favourable winds and ensure the success of the States General's 'armada.'"[196] But favorable winds did not greet the armada. A strong storm came out of the west that evening, with high seas and lightning, and damaged the fleet and sent the ships back to port at Hellevoetsluys. Not until October 23/ November 2 was it clear that all the ships returned safely, and that only 400 horses were lost. But repairs had to be made, and for eight days no favorable wind appeared. These must have been agonizing days for William of Orange and for the men serving under him. "Sailing morale, naturally enough, had dropped very low," Baxter writes. So much depended on their expedition, yet this late in the season no favorable wind could be counted on.[197]

Yet one did finally arrive, the "Protestant wind" from the northeast, on November 1/11. The 500 Dutch ships set out into the waters of the North Sea and then changed course to the south and, with a fine wind behind them, by November 3/13 were sailing past Dover into the English Channel, with bands playing military music and guns saluting onlookers at Dover and Calais.[198] The English fleet was penned in by the tides or out of commission; George Churchill had sent his ship back to port, allegedly for provisioning.

William had set no destination for his fleet as he was planning his invasion. One possibility was to sail up the North Sea to land in the northeast of England, where the Earl of Danby had undertaken to raise troops in Yorkshire; that was where the fleet was headed when it was repelled by the storm of the evening of October 20/30. The other possibility was to sail southwest through the Channel, to land at one of the several ports west of Portsmouth and the Isle of Wight large enough to unload the ships but not garrisoned by English soldiers — Poole, Weymouth, Lyme Bay (where Monmouth had landed in 1685), Torbay, Dartmouth, Falmouth. Lord Dartmouth of course did not know William's destination and anchored the king's ships in the Gunfleet off Harwich, a position that protected them against the storms they might have faced if they had anchored off the Nore, by the Thames estuary. But an ebb tide and the northeast wind that propelled William's fleet down the Channel kept Dartmouth's ships penned in the Gunfleet. He got under way only on November 4/14, as William's fleet was passing the Isle of Wight, and then faced winds that had suddenly come from the west. Those same winds kept William's fleet from heading as far west as the narrow peninsula of Cornwall (where his troops might well have been confined for the winter) and sent it into Torbay. William landed on the propitious day of November 5/15, Guy Fawkes Day in England, the anniversary of the foiling of the Catholic plot to blow up Parliament.[199] The Revolution was on.

Chapter 7

THE CIVIL WAR THAT
DID NOT HAPPEN

TORBAY, DEVON, NOVEMBER 5/15, 1688. It was a dark time of year, with scarcely nine hours of dim sunlight and 15 hours of darkness, with fog and drizzle that morning. The northeast wind that wafted William's fleet down the Channel had changed to a west wind the night before—fortunately for William, since his pilots had overshot the Devon peninsula and the west wind brought them back to Torbay, with the Channel waters on the east and the small mountains of the Dartmoor to the west. Torbay today is one of Britain's Channel resorts, proud of the palm trees that can grow in its relatively warm and temperate climate, with steep hills rising behind a crescent-shaped bay and several miles of sandy beach. Count Solms, commander of William's Blue Guards, was the first on shore, followed by the Anglo-Dutch regiments and the cavalry. Men, materiel, and horses were unloaded without incident within 24 hours; Lord Dartmouth's fleet was driven by the west wind back into the sands of the Downs, east of Kent. William himself landed at the south end of the bay, near the village of Brixham. William had his secret agent, the Scot William Carstares, lead the troops in the 118th Psalm: "They came about me like bees, and are extinct even as the fire among the thorns; for in the name of the Lord I will destroy them." To the Church of England clergyman Burnet, the Calvinist and usually humorless William said, "Well, Doctor, what do you think of predestination now?"[1]

William's men camped out in villages and rural land around the bay, and ventured in heavy rain through the steep hills inland, avoiding the steep cliffs north of the bay and the wide mouth of the River Teign, reaching Kinaskerswell on November 7 and Chudleigh on November 8. They paid local farmers for their chickens and eggs, and encountered no resistance.[2] On November 9, with William mounted on a "milk white palfrey armed cap-à-pie, a plume of white feathers on his head,"[3] they entered Exeter, the county town of Devon, an ancient Roman trading town and a fuller and manufacturer of woolens since the time of Elizabeth I, and a port that accounted for more than one-quarter of England's cloth exports in the 1680s. Exeter had a twelfth- and thirteenth-century cathedral, with Norman transeptal towers and manuscripts of Saxon poetry; an Elizabethan Guildhall, with portraits of Devon native General Monck and Charles II's sister Minette; a Norman castle and narrow sixteenth-century streets. Along the River Exe was a canal, the first in England, built in 1676, connecting the city with the Channel.[4]

The borough of Exeter was in a state of political turmoil in James's reign. Sir Edward Seymour, elected to Parliament in 1685, was a veteran Devon politician, a Tory, and a supporter of the Church of England ("though it was said . . . he had not been inside one for seven years").[5] But he was against James's policy and was opposed, in turn, by his Devon rival, the Earl of Bath.[6] "I am of the opinion," Bath wrote Sunderland, "if his Majesty will have this mayor and chamber continue, Exeter must be made a garrison merely to defend them, and they cannot render him any service to countervail such expense." In November 1687 the Privy Council removed the mayor and 13 of the common council and installed a wealthy dyer of Presbyterian sympathies as mayor. The new corporation seemed poised to elect MPs favorable to James, but the cathedral and Church interest was great, and in October 1688 the Earl of Bath, who said the town was "miserably divided and distracted . . . to be domineered over by a packed chamber of Dissenters," persuaded Sunderland and the king to reinstall the Anglican corporation.[7]

When William arrived, the bishop fled (to be quickly appointed Archbishop of York by James) and the newly installed Anglican mayor and council were hostile, but ordinary citizens gave William a tumultuous welcome.[8] It is hardly surprising, though it cannot have been altogether pleasing to William, that the leading men of Exeter did not come to his side. They had been shunted into and out of office by James; they had seen how those who had supported Monmouth three years before had fared in the Bloody Assizes; they were undoubtedly wary of William's troops, most of them Dutch and German, and many Catholic. William nonetheless wrote on November 16/26 to his German general Waldeck, on duty in the United Provinces, that he was confident of success because he found the state of affairs in England as it had been represented to him before he sailed.[9] Which is another way of saying that he did not expect many Englishmen to come over to him immediately, but to warily avoid taking sides. Which is what happened: nine of ten English lords took no action to help either William or James.[10]

꧁

IF WILLIAM HAD less than perfect information as he ventured forth in a politically unstable nation, so also did James. On November 6, just before he heard the news of William's landing, he met with four bishops, including Sancroft and Compton, and asked them to condemn William's invasion. The bishops refused. Affairs of state were not their concern, they said, and Sancroft noted that some of them had "presented your majesty a petition of the most innocent nature, and in the most humble manner imaginable, yet we were so violently prosecuted, as it would have ended in our ruin, if God's goodness had not preserved us." "I will stand on my own legs and trust to myself and my own arms," James replied.[11] In and near London he had a large army assembled, with many more troops in garrison. But he had to leave those in place, to quell uprisings in strategic places like the ports of Hull, Portsmouth, and Plymouth, and transportation nodes like Carlisle, Berwick, and Chester. He had not known where the invasion would come, and he could not rely on uprisings not occurring elsewhere. In 1685, when he faced the risings of Argyll in Scotland and Monmouth in the west, he was widely popular among the people and had firm support from those who manned the posts of local government. Now his popularity was less and the loyalty of those in charge of local governments — many of them remodeled and remodeled again, as in Exeter — was in doubt. The militia — the body of armed local freemen — had been left in disuse as James maintained his standing army and refused to fight,[12] and common people of all ranks seemed unready to spring to his defense; from the garrison at Plymouth the Earl of Bath reported that "the common people are so prejudiced with the late regulations and so much corrupted that there can be no dependence at present on the militia but only upon his majesty's standing forces."[13]

His best informed minister, Sunderland, after switching from one policy to another, had lost his nerve and had been dismissed on October 28; he was busy winding up his financial affairs and making plans to flee to the United Provinces.[14] James's election agents had been cast away and left to fend for themselves. The loyalty of some of his most favored military leaders, notably John Churchill, had been cast into doubt by others, like the Earl of Feversham. William's *Declaration* and other Williamite propaganda was circulating through the kingdom, while the king's publicists scampered to counter it. If he kept his army near London, he risked losing large swaths of the country to William's forces and the Englishmen who might rise to take his side. If he took his troops out to face William's, he would face the difficult tasks of transporting them across inferior roads (the Dutch were surprised at the poor condition of English roads) and supplying them in winter.[15]

On November 17, James left London for Windsor, and on November 19 he and many of his troops reached Salisbury. William and most of his troops were still in and around Exeter, though some cavalry moved 15 miles east to Axminster. But James faced threats behind and ahead of him, while William faced opportunities. On November 12, James's troops had fired on rioters in London and killed several. On November 15 there was news, later found to be exaggerated, that three regiments had deserted.[16] But there were other desertions from James to William: on November 12, Captain Burrington of Crediton; on November 13, Lord Colchester, Thomas Wharton, and Charles Godfrey, all Whigs and the last the husband of John Churchill's sister (and

James's onetime mistress) Arabella. On November 16, from the Salisbury encampment, there came over Lieutenant-Colonel Langston with most of the St. Alban's regiment, long in communication with William, and Edward Hyde, Lord Cornbury. Cornbury brought few troops, though his co-conspirator Langston brought over enough cavalry to reduce James's advantage in horse. But his desertion was notable because he was James's nephew, the son and heir of his Anglican brother-in-law the Earl of Clarendon.[17]

Then, on November 17, Sir Edward Seymour came out for William. Earlier deserters to William had been Whigs; Seymour was a prominent Tory, elected from Devon seats in every election from 1661 to 1705 (except for 1681), Speaker of the House of Commons from 1673 to 1679. Seymour stoutly opposed exclusion, but since James came to office he had been an outsider. In 1685, Seymour spoke against granting James revenues for life, and when he attacked the conduct of the 1685 elections, he was hissed. He had opposed Catholic officers in the standing army ("For officers to be employed not taking the Tests, it is dispensing with all the laws at once"), and served on the committee calling for their removal — the issue on which James broke with the Commons. When he joined William's forces, he asked Burnet "why we had not an association signed by all that came to us, since, till we had that done, we were as a rope of sand: men might leave us when they pleased, and we should have them under no tie." So Burnet drew up the Association "to stick firm in this cause and to another until our religion, laws and liberties are so far secured to us in a free Parliament that we shall no longer be in danger of falling under Popery and slavery," and to protect the prince against "desperate and cursed attempts of Papists and other bloody men." The Association was signed by almost all of those who rose in all parts of the country.[18]

Seymour's example may have inspired his rival for West Country influence, the Earl of Bath, also a Tory. On November 19, Bath, perhaps remembering that James had removed him from his post as Groom of the Stole and stopped his £5,000 pension, pledged his support to William, and undertook to seize the garrison at Plymouth from its Catholic commanding officer and to rally the Cornish gentry. Six days later John Churchill's brother, Captain George Churchill, sailed his ship into Plymouth harbor and came out for William.

William would no longer have to fear opposition to his west.[19] William remained in Exeter until November 19 and, during that time, set up an organized revenue system, a council of English advisers, and an intelligence system. He sent his cavalry east to Chard and Honiton, some 40 miles from the forward units of James's army at Warminster, in order to prevent being cut off in the Devon-Somerset peninsula as Monmouth had been in 1685.[20]

November 19 was the day James reached Salisbury, where he found his troops demoralized by the recent desertions and his generals at odds over whether to move forward and attack William's force or to retreat and hold London. Petitions for a free Parliament were being circulated among the soldiers.[21] James said later that his original plan had been to send his cavalry to take Axminster, Chard, and Langport, in a line about 40 miles west of Salisbury, in an effort to confine William's army to Devon, Cornwall, and western Somerset. But the poor roads and hilly terrain made a cavalry advance impracticable, and faulty intelligence suggested that William was already moving into Axminster (in fact he was not to reach Crewkerne, just east of Chard, until November 26). And James could not count on the cavalry not to desert. News came that on November 15, Lord Delamere had led an uprising in Cheshire; this meant that Chester, the main port for Ireland, was unavailable to James and could not be used to unload soldiers from Tyrconnel's Irish army.[22] James exhorted Lord Dartmouth to fight the Dutch fleet, but bad winds in the Channel prevented him; Captain George Churchill reported that his ship was unseaworthy, then put into Plymouth and joined William's forces.[23]

Exhausted, torn by conflicting advice, the normally aggressive and healthy James was plagued by nosebleeds: an eyewitness wrote that he was "very ill in his health and bleeds upon every occasion at the nose and mouth and much purulent matter comes out."[24] For four days he tried to review his troops and held conferences with his officers, but the nosebleeds often kept him in his quarters. He held a council of war on November 22. The Earl of Feversham advised a march to London. Others agreed, but Baron Churchill and the Duke of Grafton urged that they move forward and attack, with the king advancing accompanied by Churchill and fellow Tangier veterans Kirke, Trelawney, and Charles Churchill.[25] But by this time James may have feared, as he later said, that Churchill would kidnap him and turn him over to William.[26] The atmosphere is suggested by an eyewitness quoted by John Miller. "I can never forget the confusion the court was in. . . . The King knew not whom to trust and the fight was so great that they were apt to believe an impossible report just then brought in that the Prince of Orange was come with twelve thousand horse between Warminster and Salisbury. . . . Everybody in this hurly-burly was thinking of himself and nobody minded the King, who came up to Dr. Radcliffe and asked him what was good for the bleeding of his nose."[27]

On the night of November 22, Baron Churchill, the Duke of Grafton, and Colonel Berkeley dined with the king until midnight. After dinner the three men had a long conference with Prince George of Denmark, Princess Anne's husband,[28] and then they rode off from James's camp with some 400 officers and troopers and headed west to join William's forces. William had arrived in Axminster on November 22. Churchill and his company galloped nearly 40 miles in the early hours of the 23rd over hilly land and the valley of the River Stour, and sometime on November 24 arrived in Crewkerne, a dozen miles from Axminster.[29]

Churchill left behind in Salisbury an extraordinary letter to James, acknowledging his indebtedness to the king. "Yet I hope the great advantage I enjoy under Your Majesty, which I own I can never expect in any other change of government, may reasonably convince Your Majesty and the world that I am actuated by a higher principle, when I offer that violence to my inclination and interest as to desert Your Majesty at a time when your affairs seem to challenge the strictest obedience from all your subjects, much more from one who lies under the greatest personal obligation to Your Majesty. This, sir, could proceed from nothing by the inviolable dictates of my conscience, and a necessary concern for religion (which no good man can oppose), and with which I am instructed nothing can come in competition."[30] Churchill's arrival was noted by William, who wrote to Bentinck on November 24, "A gentleman has just arrived to convey me Lord Bristol's respects, who said that in passing through Crochorn [Crewkerne], he found there Lord Churchill with about four hundred horses, all officers who are coming to join us."[31] He welcomed

Churchill at Axminster with formal ceremony. Soon behind him came half of the officers of the most professional royal regiments and most of James's general staff, and in a few days between 3,000 and 5,000 men.[32]

Churchill's desertion came just as news of other rebellions reached James. He already knew of Lord Delamere's rising in Cheshire—not terribly surprising, given that Delamere had moved toward starting a diversionary rising to aid the Duke of Monmouth in 1685. On November 21 the Earl of Devonshire, one of the Immortal Seven, seized Nottingham, down the Derwent River from his country house Chatsworth. On November 22 the Earl of Danby, though disappointed that William had not landed in the north of England, nevertheless came to his aid by seizing the Yorkshire County town of York. Soon he was investing the garrison at Hull, urging Protestant soldiers to be true to their religion. Danby's forces took Hull on December 3, which evidently startled James, and Lumley's forces took Durham on December 5. Within a few days other important towns were in the hands of William's allies—Northampton and Leicester and Derby in the Midlands, Carlisle and Newcastle in the north, Gloucester in the West Country, Norwich and King's Lynn in East Anglia.[33] Even with the slow communications of the day, a picture was being filled in with one detail after another, contributing to an overall impression: the nation was rising against James II, with not only William's foreign troops but English gentlemen and yeomen in the lead, with Whigs like Delamere and Devonshire making common cause with Tories like Danby and Bath and Seymour.[34]

Churchill's desertion was not the only contribution he made to William's cause. Another was made through the influence of his wife Sarah on Princess Anne and her household. Anne had been dubious about the queen's pregnancy, and told her sister Mary that she regarded the baby born on June 10 as suppositious, and she parried her uncle the Earl of Clarendon's efforts to get her to speak about the issue with the king.[35] On November 24, the morning after Churchill rode off to William's lines, James was urged to arrest Prince George's secretary, but refused. He dined that evening with Prince George and the Duke of Ormonde, long the lord lieutenant of Ireland, and after dinner George and Ormonde, like Churchill, Grafton, and Berkeley before them, rode off to join the Prince of Orange.[36] Stunned when he heard the news the next morning, James ordered that Sarah Churchill and Mrs. Berkeley, one of Anne's other attendants, be confined to St. James's Palace. But Sarah and Mrs. Berkeley remained with Anne at her quarters in the Cockpit, the southwest extension of Whitehall Palace near the entrance to today's Downing Street. Sarah, forewarned of the news of George's flight, went off to visit Bishop Compton in his house on Suffolk Street, just west of today's Trafalgar Square, to arrange for their escape. Anne persuaded the queen to delay the king's order to arrest Sarah until the next day.

On the evening of November 25, Anne retired to bed and ordered her bedchamber locked. Then she, Lady Churchill, and Mrs. Berkeley dressed again and went down a secret wooden staircase from Anne's apartments, which Sarah had constructed six months before for this purpose. At one o'clock in the morning on November 26 they were met by Bishop Compton, the former soldier, in jackboots and armor and wielding pistols, and the Earl of Dorset. They proceeded to Compton's house in Suffolk Street, wading through the mud of Pall Mall, where Anne lost a shoe, then were taken by a carriage to the bishop's residence in Aldersgate in the City of London. In the late November dawn they left London and were driven to Epping Forest, northeast of the city and east of the River Lea, to Copt Hall, Dorset's home in Hertfordshire. On November 27 they traveled overland, off the main roads, with Compton dressed in lay attire and armed with swords and pistols, northwest to Castle Ashby, the home of Compton's nephew the Earl of Northampton, just east of Northampton. On November 30, Anne and her party went to Leicester, and on December 1 they reached Nottingham, where she stayed under the protection of the Earl of Devonshire and other lords, who quickly brought in 5,000 troops as insurance against local Catholic lords. On her arrival there "the mayor and aldermen treated both her Highness and his Lordship ye Bishop with two noble banquetts, and all demonstrations of respect and joy were shewd, with which her Highness was very well pleased and seemed wonderful pleasant and cheerful."[37] Anne had done what she needed to do to preserve her succession to the throne.

JAMES LEFT SALISBURY for London, where he arrived on the afternoon of November 26. Now both his daughters had deserted him. His older daughter, still back in The Hague, was obviously supporting her husband's invasion, while his younger daughter had now slipped through his agents' fingers and joined his enemies, as had her husband. His best general, the man whose whole career he made, had deserted him, as well as many of his officers, including his nephews Cornbury and Grafton. James, like his brother Charles, throughout his career put great stock in family loyalty; the children of the affectionate Charles I, through all their troubles, never deserted each other, even as they dropped one political ally after another; they were willing to take grave political risks, as Charles II had in the Exclusion Crisis, to remain true to family.

To the Stuarts, primogeniture was a principle of paramount importance, the only basis for their entitlement to the throne. They were not a rich family, apart from their claims on the throne and on other royal titles; the exiled Charles and James had much smaller incomes than their nephew William of Orange, who with his wide landholdings in France, the Holy Roman Empire, and the Netherlands, was the richest man in the United Provinces even when he was a youth in the hands of his political enemies. They were not men endowed with the talents that brought Oliver Cromwell to the fore; nobody would have elevated them to power had they not been in line to the throne. Apparently James expected that his daughters would accept, out of family loyalty, their displacement out of the succession by the birth of Prince James Edward in June 1688. His behavior suggests this: his tardiness to believe that Mary's husband was preparing an invasion against him; his refusal to heed the advice of Feversham and others to arrest Anne's husband and Churchill, the guiding force in Anne's household, even in the face of evidence of conspiracy. He had accepted his brother's orders, even his orders to quit England, at great personal risk and despite his principled opposition to them; he had never questioned the authority of a brother who, after all, was only a few years older and with whose course he often strongly disagreed. He evidently found it hard to believe that his daughters would question his own authority.

Would he have acquiesced even if Charles had disinherited him by declaring Monmouth his legitimate successor, or if Charles had signed an exclusion bill? No one can be sure, but there is at least a possibility that James would have obeyed Charles in death as he always had in life; evidently James's enemies who encouraged Charles to legitimize Monmouth and who believed that Charles could be pressured to sign an exclusion bill must have thought so. Now James, who had always been faithful to his family, was deserted by his family, in the interest of a man whom he had addressed in a letter as recently as September 17 as "my sonne, the Prince of Orange." "God help me!" he cried when he returned to London. "Even my children have forsaken me."[38]

James's situation was not quite hopeless. He was still king, and still had troops willing to support him. But he could not expel William's army. His project of electing a Parliament that would repeal the Test Acts and the penal laws and would open the way to Catholic participation in government and proselytization — that project was lost beyond repair. He had abandoned his election agents and he had consented to the removal from public office of the Catholics and Dissenters who he had hoped would enable him to achieve his goals. He would have to summon a Parliament, and the best he could hope for was a Tory Anglican Commons. But the Tories clearly mistrusted him after he abandoned them, and were not propitiated by his reversal of policy in September and October; the Whigs had never trusted him, even when he had worked for toleration of Dissenters. A parliamentary committee could investigate the birth of the Prince of Wales, and declare him suppositious; it could command that his son be educated as a Protestant, as his daughters were; it could declare that some Protestant relation should serve as regent in place of Queen Mary Beatrice in the event of his death. James had originally hoped a policy of tolerance to Catholics would be well enough established during his reign that it could survive in the reign of his daughter. Now it was obvious that he would not be allowed to gain tolerance of Catholics in his own reign, much less affect the reigns to come.

On November 26, William was in Crewkerne, some 20 miles east of Axminster; on November 27 he reached Sherborne, 15 miles further east. The road to Salisbury was open before him; the chances of a battle with James's troops seemed near zero after the king's retreat to London. On November 27, James summoned the lords in London to a council at which about 40 appeared. Almost all said the king needed to negotiate with William and summon a Parliament. James promptly did call a Parliament for January 15 — despite his earlier claim that elections were impossible in time of invasion — and commissioned the Marquis of Halifax, the Earl of Nottingham, and Sidney Godolphin to negotiate with William.[39] John Evelyn, in his diary entry for December 2, records,

> Visited my L. Godolphin, then going with the Marquis of Halifax, & E: of Nottingham as Commissioner to the Prince of Orange: He told me, they had little power: Plymouth declared for the Prince & L: Bath: Yorke, Hull, Bristol, all the eminent nobility & persons of quality throut England declare for the Protestant Religion & Laws, & go to meete the Prince; who every day sets forth new declarations &c: against the Papists: The Greate favorits at Court, priest[s] & Jesuites, flie or abscond: Every thing (til now conceiled) flies abroad in publique print, & is Cryed about the streetes: Expectations of the Pr: coming to Oxon: Pr: of Wales & greate Treasure sent daily to Portsmouth, Earle of Dover Governor: Addresse from the Fleete not gratefull to his Majestie: The Popists in offices layd down their Commissions & flie: Universal consternation amongst them: it lookes like a Revolution.[40]

James could not have regarded his envoys as entirely loyal to him. Halifax, though generally in opposition to the Earl of Danby's government in the 1670s and always an enemy of a French alliance, had decisively opposed exclusion in the Lords and had served James as a minister in 1685. But he declined to support James's program of repealing the Test Acts and penal laws and was dismissed from government. His essay *The Character of a Trimmer* has long been admired as an argument for principled moderation and compromise,[41] but his predilection to await events passively can also be seen as arising out of a confidence that the grand designs of others would likely fail; as he advised William in 1686, "The great thing to be done now, is to do nothing, but wait for the good consequence of their divisions and mistakes."[42]

Daniel Finch, the Earl of Nottingham, was the son of Lord Chancellor Heneage Finch, and in the Commons he, too, had opposed exclusion and the bill to order the Duke of York removed from court. He served as First Lord of the Admiralty from 1680 to 1684, during which time he succeded his father as earl, and served on James's Privy Council until 1687.[43]

Sidney Godolphin was from a Cornish family and, as a page in Charles II's court, became a friend of Sunderland by 1664, when they traveled together to Rome; in 1668, at 23, he was elected to the Commons from a Cornish borough. In 1678, after Danby's fall, he was named a lord of the Treasury, where he served for most of the next 32 years; in 1684 he was elevated to the Lords. "Little Sidney Godolphin was never in the way and never out of the way," summarized one observer early in his career. Ousted from the Treasury in 1685, he was back in in 1687, and was widely respected for his competence and circumspection. A widower from 1678, he was a close friend and confidant of John and Sarah Churchill.[44] Halifax and Nottingham were both out of government in 1688 and in touch with William's agents, but both refused to sign the letter of invitation to William of Orange of June 30. All three, Halifax, Nottingham, and Godolphin, saw themselves as part of a permanent governing class, men who in Halifax's terms were trimmers, keeping the ship of state sailing without listing too far in either direction, who were willing to serve those who had come to the throne by whatever means up to certain limits, but who were not unaware that the wheel of history could revolve. They were not chosen because they were trusted by both James and William; to the contrary, James had reason to mistrust Halifax and Nottingham and kept Godolphin carefully out of his inner circle. William had reason to mistrust them, since they had refused to take the risks on his behalf that Danby, Devonshire, Compton, and Churchill had. But both could recognize them as men of stature and unrashness, steady enough to be reliable bearers of messages, too cautious to advance an agenda of their own.

On November 30, before Halifax, Nottingham, and Godolphin set out, James published his proclamation of a new Parliament and promised a general pardon, security for the Church of England, and early negotiations with William.[45] William was then still at Hindon, a dozen miles west of Salisbury, where he received a message from Feversham asking for passports for the three commissioners.[46] In the meantime, a false proclamation—supposedly issued by William in Sherborne on November 28, but actually written by an extreme Whig named Hugh Speke, a double agent who had been sending reports to James from Exeter—denounced "those execrable Criminals who have justly forfeited their Lives for betraying the Religion, and subverting the Laws of their Native Country" and urged that Catholics found in possession of arms—a category that included many of James's soldiers—be killed. Speke also claimed that Catholic and Irish troops were part of a Jesuit intrigue to massacre Protestants in London.[47] The result was, in J. R. Jones's words, "a nationwide panic . . . remarkably similar to the Grande Peur of July 1789 which pushed France towards revolution."[48] In the countryside people were in terror of rumored Irish troops.[49] The Catholics at James's court, fearing they would be attacked, were already fleeing the kingdom or preparing to do so.

❧

As JAMES'S AUTHORITY was collapsing, William took his time. The matter of the passports took some time to sort out. William advanced to Salisbury by December 4, but took time on the way to examine the Van Dyck paintings at the Earl of Pembroke's Wilton House[50] (the same house where General Dwight Eisenhower did much of the planning for the Normandy invasion of 1944[51]—what could these two cross-Channel invaders have told each other across the centuries?). From Salisbury William moved not east, directly toward London, but north, to Collingbourne Kingston on December 6 and Hungerford on December 7. This was presumably to keep his forces out of reach of any of James's troops; now that the king was on the defensive, it was no time to shed blood needlessly.

Halifax, Nottingham, and Godolphin finally met with William on December 8. They told him that James had summoned a Parliament for January 15 and had proposed that William's army remain

40 miles outside London. William was asked for responses that could achieve these goals.[52] William consulted with his advisers. Tories like Clarendon wanted the elections to go forward; the Tory gentry seemed well in charge of the proceedings. Those Englishmen who had come over with William wanted the writs recalled, because they would need time to influence the results. William rejected this advice, saying, "We may drive away the King; but, perhaps, we may not know how easily to come by a Parliament."[53] His *Declaration* had called for a "free Parliament," and he could not enlist England in the struggle against Louis XIV without one.

But on December 10 he set out stern conditions to James. All Catholics were to be dismissed from office. The proclamations declaring William's followers as rebels must be recalled. James's army was to withdraw from London, and both his army and William's must remain 30 or 40 miles from the city. If the king remained in London when the Parliament met, the prince should be there, too, with an equal number of guards. The Tower and Tilbury, at the chokepoint of the Thames, should be put into the hands of the City of London, and the garrison at Portsmouth should be put into the hands of men William could trust. The English government must pay for William's army until Parliament met.[54] And to Admiral Herbert he sent out that day an order that his ships, though Dutch, should fly the English flag in attacks on French ships.[55] These terms reflected the military reality: William had an army in England plus a navy in the English Channel, and men-at-arms had risen in his support in many parts of the kingdom; James did not trust his army to fight, but William did trust his army and his navy, too — his order to Herbert was an attempt to embroil England, whatever the outcome of these negotiations, in war with France. William was not about to cede to James military control of the capital, and in the circumstances, James's best option was military parity there.

James's one trump card was William's unwillingness to do physical harm to the king, the queen, or their son. England had seen the execution of a king 29 years before, and clearly did not want to see another. William's goal was to enlist England in the war on France, and he would have difficulty doing that as a regicide. James, however, seems not to have been confident that William and his English adversaries would spare his life. It was, after all, his beloved father who had been beheaded. That had happened after he fell into the military control of his enemies and refused to make the concessions they demanded. James did not want the scenario repeated. He was plainly disheartened. "Neuer any Prince took more care of his sea and land men as I have done, & been so very ill repayd by them," he wrote Dartmouth. "If I should go, who can wonder after the treatment I have found?" he said to the loyal Earl of Ailesbury. "My daughter hath deserted me, my army also, and him"—Churchill—"that I raised from nothing, the same, on whom I heaped all favours; and if such betrays me, what can I expect from that I have done so little for? I know not who to speak to or who to trust."[56] A congenital optimist, James had concentrated singlemindedly on his plans to pack Parliament and reshape the army, and paid no attention to the signs of William of Orange's invasion; then, when events shattered his plans, he responded with panicked surrender—and flight.

From the time of his meeting with his Privy Council on November 28, James took steps to send the queen and their baby to France. He surely remembered that during the 1640s his father had sent his mother and then his brother to safety, lest they be captured by his enemies. On November 29 he ordered the Earl of Dover to arrange for the prince to be sent out via Portsmouth. But Dartmouth, commander of the fleet there, refused to allow it, and the baby was returned to London. On December 7, as Halifax, Nottingham, and Godolphin were receiving William's proposals, James authorized the Comte de Lauzun, a French adventurer, to spirit Mary Beatrice and James Edward out of the country.[57] On December 10, James prepared to leave himself. He talked of going the next day to inspect his forces in Uxbridge, northwest of London, but in the meantime entrusted his papers and large sums of money to the ambassador of the Grand Duke of Tuscany. In the evening he received the final report of William's demands from Halifax, Nottingham, and Godolphin. He told his attending peers that he would answer them in the morning. Shortly after midnight he walked down the backstairs of Whitehall Palace, accompanied by two Catholics, Sir Edward Hales (the plaintiff in the collusive suit of *Godden v. Hales*) and Ralph Sheldon. They rowed across the

Thames to Vauxhall, where there were horses waiting, and rode east-ward to find the boat to take them to France.[58]

Forty years and eight months before, in April 1648, the 14-year-old James had crawled out of a window at St. James's Palace, rendezvoused with a royal officer in St. James's Park, and been transported, disguised as a girl, to a Thames River boat and then to a ship that took him to safety in the Netherlands.[59] Now the 55-year-old king, disguised as an ordinary soldier, once again found himself fleeing London, to safety this time in France. What thoughts must have gone through his head about this first escape, and all the things that had happened in the years since.

Before he left Whitehall, James burned most of the writs for the new Parliament. With him down the backstairs of Whitehall, he brought the Great Seal and, on the boat, cast it into the Thames.[60] These were acts of great significance. We may think of official docu-ments as readily fungible; if there is an original somewhere, of an act of Congress or a Supreme Court decision, it is readily replicable, and its validity is not expunged if, by some unhappy accident, the original is consumed by fire or vermin. But in the seventeenth century the docu-ment *was* the law. When Charles II wanted to prove to Parliament that he had revoked his Declaration of Indulgence, he literally ripped the Great Seal off it. And the Great Seal itself, whose wax imprint cer-tified the validity of law, was unique and irreplaceable. Parliament could not be called without a writ, and now James had destroyed the writ; another Parliament could not be called, or an official act of any kind sanctioned, without the Great Seal, and now James had hurled it to the bottom of the Thames. He ordered Feversham to undertake no further hostilities against William's forces.[61] What was the calculation behind James's reckless acts? Presumably he was trying to prevent the formation of a lawful government in his absence, in the hope that he might be called back, or come back with the aid of Louis XIV, and be received again as the one and rightful king.

But James's flight to France also made that unlikely. As king, he had carefully refrained from an alliance with France. Unlike his brother, he had not accepted Louis's money in return for a promise to send an army to fight alongside France. To pay for an army larger than the one he amassed to quell Monmouth's rebellion and kept in existence thereafter, he would have had to recall Parliament. In late 1685 and throughout 1686, that would have meant agreeing to the Tory Parliament's demand that he dismiss Catholic officers. In 1687 and 1688, as he was preparing for new parliamentary elections, an alliance with France—after the revocation of the Edict of Nantes—would have alienated Dissenters and Whigs. His limited treaty with France, establishing a cease-fire in North America, had been trouble enough. In June and July 1688, even as the French were telling him that William was planning an invasion, he turned down Louis's offer of French ships. But now, in his desperate straits, James evidently regarded France as his only safe harbor.[62] Other destinations were unpromising. He obviously could not go to the United Provinces, as he had in 1648; the Spanish Netherlands, where he had stayed in the 1650s, were well within reach of Dutch troops, which garrisoned Spanish forts, and he rejected the Spanish ambassador's suggestion that he go there.[63] In Ireland, where Catholics controlled the government in Dublin, the judiciary, the militia, the commissions of the peace, and the borough corporations, he could count on the support of Tyrconnel's Catholic army.[64] But that army was not large enough to reconquer England, and might not remain in firm control of the island.

So James sent his wife and son to France, and set out to go there himself—where he would be within the power of Louis XIV. That was not likely to enhance his popularity in England. Rather it would detract from the legitimacy which he must have hoped would be his great asset. Louis's France was seen by Englishmen as an absolutist, oppressive, Catholic tyrant, bent on reducing Englishmen to penury and slavery. Moreover, Louis was preoccupied. In December 1688 the main body of his troops was still involved in the siege of Philippsburg, on the middle Rhine. He had also declared war on the United Provinces on November 16/26 in response to William's invasion, but the Dutch were protected by the German troops William had hired, and a campaign against them would have to wait at least until the spring of 1689. The French fleet was in the Mediterranean, and was outnumbered by the combined fleets of England and the Dutch Republic. James, Duke of York, had fled England in April 1648 hoping to return and assert his father's and brother's rights in better times—times that took many years, and unpredictable turns of events, to come. King James II fled England in December 1688 hoping to return and assert his own rights—but he could only hope to do so with the aid of, and in the service of, the King of France.

❧

IN JAMES'S ABSENCE England was suddenly without a government. Tories and Church of England bishops led by the Earls of Rochester and Clarendon and the Bishop of Ely held a meeting at the Guildhall in the City of London on December 11 and sought to promote an early meeting of Parliament, with elections in counties and boroughs where James had not managed to destroy his writs; but they foundered in disagreement.[65]

That evening—the longest night of the year—Londoners set fires in Catholic chapels, and on December 12 rumors circulated that Irish soldiers in James's army were on the rampage. Actually, James's army was dispersing: some soldiers went home, others went over to William's army, some joined the anti-Catholic rioters, and some Irish Catholics roamed the country, heading toward ports where they could get ships for home, seeking food and shelter.[66] On the night of December 12 the rioting and pillage in London were worse. The Spanish ambassador's house was destroyed and the imperial envoy, the representative of the Dutch Republic's key ally, the Holy Roman Empire, denounced the "detestable populace."[67] "The rabble people," John Evelyn wrote in his diary entry for December 13, "demolish all Papists Chapells & several popish Lords & Gent: house, especially that of the Spanish Ambassador, which they pillaged & burnt his Library, &c."[68] The same week there were riots by students and apprentices in Edinburgh, crying, "No Pope, No Papist, No Popish Chancellor, No Melfort, No Father Petres"; the crowds defaced the Catholic chapel at Holyrood House and ransacked the house of the Earl of Perth. Rioting continued around Scotland through January.[69] The hatred and fear of Catholicism and Catholic tyranny burned brightly, and leads one to wonder if James could have governed effectively even with a pliant Parliament.

The anti-Catholic rioting imperiled William's strategy of maintaining an alliance against Louis XIV that included Catholic powers. As Jonathan Israel writes, "The news of anti-Catholic disturbances in England, luridly related in the Dutch newspapers, caused such a sensation, and sense of revulsion, amongst the Catholic courts of Germany that the Dutch resident at the Imperial Diet, at Regensburg, became seriously alarmed and wrote to the States General complaining in particular about a report of English violence which had appeared in the *Haerlemsche Courant.*"[70] But the peers ordered troops to patrol the city and cannon to be set up in St. James's Park, at Charing Cross, and on Piccadilly, and by December 13 order was restored. The Tory lords meeting in Whitehall sought unsuccessfully to affirm James's prerogatives, but the aldermen of the City of London invited William to bring his army to London—which William had already decided to do.[71] But it was a close-run thing: the Lord Mayor, Sir John Chapman, loyal to James, had just died of a stroke, which left the field open for the Recorder, the Whig lawyer Sir George Treby, to propose that the alderman send their invitation.[72]

James's flight opened up new opportunities for William. Before December 11 he was set on negotiating with James and other political figures the terms for a new Parliament, in the hope that he could maneuver it toward an alliance against France. After December 11 he set his sights higher, and his actions all seem designed to force the English to declare him king. With James out of the country, William was in command of the only active military force in England, and any freely elected Parliament would have to deal with him. He was also in control of the navy, whose commander, Lord Dartmouth, pledged his allegiance on December 12.[73] On December 13, William summoned the secretary of war, William Blathwayt, to Windsor to report on troop dispositions and sent Lord Churchill, at the head of the Life Guards, into London on December 14.[74]

Unfortunately for William, James's attempt at escape was foiled. On December 11, he and his companions rode through Kent to the Isle of Sheppey, just east of the estuary of the Thames. As he was preparing to sail, a ship arrived with seamen from Faversham, looking for priests; they recognized Hales and held him and his party. James, disguised in a black wig, was stripped, searched, and deprived of his crucifix; he complained as his captors smoked all night. "For I repent," he said at one point, "that I gave my daughter unto him, for he sought to slay me." In the morning they sailed across the estuary to Faversham, where James was finally recognized. The seamen refused to release James to the lord lieutenant, who happened to arrive, and held him in the mayor's house. On December 13, James had to listen as local gentry read William's *Declaration* and managed to send a letter to the lords at the Guildhall requesting fresh clothes. On December 14 the faithful courtier Ailesbury arrived and the next day James, escorted by his guards, traveled back to London. Encouraged by cheering crowds at Blackheath, he passed through the City and down the Strand on December 16 and was cheered by throngs. That evening at Whitehall Palace he summoned his council and heard mass.[75]

William in the meantime had been advancing toward London. On December 11 he was in Abingdon, on the Thames south of Oxford. He ordered Princess Anne and Bishop Compton to leave Nottingham and join him in Oxford, and ordered Danby to leave York and join his court. In Abingdon he heard of James's flight, and changed his plans to go to Oxford and instead headed toward Windsor, much nearer London. "He was very cheerful, and could not conceal his satisfaction at the King's being gone," Clarendon noted.[76] On December 12 he was in Wallingford, down the river from Abingdon; on December 13 he bypassed Reading and crossed the Chiltern Hills to Henley; on December 14 he was in Windsor. On December 15 he sent an order that James stop short of London and stay in Rochester, but it was not received. The same day James sent the Earl of Feversham to invite William to meet him in London. William was angry that Feversham had dismissed his troops four days before, which led to fears of marauding Irish troops, and had Feversham arrested and sent Zuylestein back with a curt note of refusal: William was determined not to meet with his uncle.[77]

At this point, with William in Windsor and James in London, the purposes of uncle and nephew, father-in-law and son-in-law, king and prince, coincided. Many of the English lords, including the group holding daily meetings under the chairmanship of Archbishop

Sancroft, wanted some kind of negotiated settlement, with James still recognized as king.[78] But William wanted James out of England, and James, afraid of meeting his father's fate, wanted to go. On December 16, William ordered Dartmouth, who had acknowledged him as commander on December 12, to take the fleet back to the Nore. He met with the Duke of Beaufort, the great territorial power in Wales. He snubbed the Earl of Rochester and gave an audience to Irish peers. He met privately with Henry Powle and Sir Robert Howard, veteran House of Commons members who were to take key roles in the Convention Parliament six weeks later.[79]

On December 17 in Windsor, William met with a group of peers of varying views — the Marquis of Halifax, the Earl of Clarendon, Lord Mordaunt, Lord Delamere, and the Earl of Shrewsbury. William said he thought James would not be safe in London, and the peers advised that he be told to stay in Ham House, upriver on the Thames near Richmond Park. Halifax advised that Count Solms give James the order. William said Shrewsbury, Halifax, and Delamere should do so, and that Count Solms should lead the Blue Guards to replace James's soldiers at Whitehall Palace. They went that evening. Solms led the Blue Guards through St. James's Park to Whitehall, and when it was made clear they were willing to fight, the English troops withdrew.[80]

At one o'clock in the morning of December 18, Halifax, Shrewsbury, and Delamere had James awakened and told him that William had ordered him to leave London that morning and go to Ham House. James, after some hesitation, argued he should go to Rochester, where some of his foot guards were stationed. William did not object, and a convoy of barges brought James, guarded by William's troops, down the Thames first to Gravesend and then to Rochester, on the Medway, the broad bay that emptied into the Thames Estuary and the North Sea. For three days he talked with his loyal advisers, who urged him to remain in England. But he told them he feared he would be sent to the Tower and, as he told Ailesbury, "No King ever went out of that place but to his grave." On the night of December 22, furnished with blank passports by his son the Duke of Berwick, he slipped out a back door, which William had ordered to be left unguarded, and boarded a boat that brought him to France on

December 25/January 4. Three days later he saw the queen at the palace at St. Germain-en-Laye, where Louis XIV installed him and treated him with all due ceremony as king.[81]

On December 17, William spent the night at Sion House, across the Thames from Kew. On December 18 he rode in a carriage to London, "to the loud acclamations of a vast number of people of all sorts and ranks, the bells everywhere ringing." Many in the cheering crowds were wearing orange ribbons or waving sticks with oranges stuck on the ends. He entered London through Knightsbridge, along a two-mile route lined with Dutch Blue Guards, but with the English and Scotch regiments of the Dutch army, led by General Hugh Mackay, conspicuously in the lead. He avoided much of the crowd by taking a short cut from Knightsbridge through St. James's Park and entered Whitehall Palace, which James had left just hours before.[82] One of his first acts was to order Lord Churchill to disperse the English, Scottish, and Irish troops from London; the city would be patrolled by the Dutch Blue Guards for the next 10 years.[83] The Dutch stadholder was now the master of England.

Chapter 8

KING WILLIAM

S T. JAMES'S PALACE, London, December 18, 1688. William of
Orange installed himself in St. James's Palace, across St. James's
Park from Whitehall Palace. William disliked pomp and ceremony, and his asthma was aggravated by London's filthy air; St.
James's Palace was then at the edge of the city. On the evening of December 18 he held court. "All the world," wrote John Evelyn in his
diary entry for that day, "go to see the Prince at St. James where there
is a greate Court, there I saw him & severall of my Acquaintance that
come over with him: He is very stately, serious & reserved: the Eng:
souldiers &c. sent out of Towne to distant quarters: not well pleased:
Divers reports & opinions, what all this will end in; Ambition & faction feared."[1] Among those William talked with was the Marquis of
Halifax, who had been one of the three lords James sent to negotiate
with William in November and who had led the meetings of the peers
in the days after James left London on December 11. "The Marquis of
Halifax told the Prince he might be what he pleased himself," according to one account, "for as nobody knew what to do with him, so nobody knew what to do without him."[2]

William may have been the master of England, but he was not, by
hereditary principle, the rightful king. But hereditary principle had
been honored in the breach many times in the history of the English

monarchy. William I became king in 1066 because he was, literally, the Conqueror, though he also asserted a hereditary claim. Henry I was succeeded in 1135 by a nephew, Stephen, rather than by his daughter Matilda. Richard II was ousted in 1399 and replaced by a cousin, Henry IV. The Wars of the Roses of the fifteenth century transferred the crown twice between Henry VI and Edward IV. The hereditary claim of Henry VII to the throne in 1485 was especially risible: his grandfather Owen Tudor had been the stabler of King Henry VI and the lover of his mother, Queen Katherine, not so long before.[3] But since then the hereditary principle had been observed, except for the interregnum of 1649–60, for more than 200 years. By that principle James was the rightful king and James Edward, Prince of Wales, his rightful heir. But James had thrown the Great Seal into the Thames and fled. James Edward was an infant and was in France.

To some, the solution to this problem was to appoint a regent to rule in James's name and, presumably, in the name of his son if he died. Others looked to the next in line under the hereditary principle: Mary, Princess of Orange, who was still in the Netherlands. After her came her sister, Princess Anne, and her husband, Prince William, both of whom were in London. None of these had children living at the time and after them came, inconveniently, the Catholic daughters of Minette, Queen Maria Luisa of Spain (who had no children), and Duchess Anna Maria of Savoy.[4] The hereditary principle did not provide an easy solution to the practical problem of how England should be governed.

The only practical solution was that William should govern. He was in command of the only coherent army in England and in effective command of the navy as well: thus he was the only effective guarantor of civil order at a time when disbanded troops, many of them Irish, were on the loose in England and when the metropolis of London had been swept by riots — and when there was a threat of war with France. The English experiment with republicanism had failed after its only strong leader, Oliver Cromwell, died. The consensus in that age of Thomas Hobbes was that in order to have civic peace, England must have a king. William surely understood this. His wife wrote in her memoir that William had invaded England with the intention of dethroning James and becoming king. He surely knew when he embarked that he could not count on this happening. But after James's flight it was entirely possible. Becoming king was clearly the best way to achieve William's overriding purpose, to bring England into his continental alliance against the France of Louis XIV. But William's *Declaration* had said nothing about his becoming king; it had concentrated instead on the demand for a free parliament, one elected without the kind of overbearing influence of the Crown. So now he set about to secure the election of a free Parliament, with the hope and expectation that Parliament would make him King.

ON DECEMBER 20, William summoned the lords then in London and told them that he would handle military affairs while they took over the civil administration of government and the calling of elections to Parliament.[5] On December 21 the House of Lords met "at the Prince's request" and, since there was no lord chancellor, chose Halifax as Speaker. They met again on Monday, December 23, faced with the news that James had fled to France and that he had left a letter behind saying he would be "within call when the nation's eyes shall be opened," and promised a Parliament that would give tolerance to Dissenters and Catholics.[6] The Lords voted not to seek a copy of the letter; Godolphin said he had read it and that "it would give them no satisfaction."[7] On December 24 they met again. Clarendon proposed an inquiry into the birth of the Prince of Wales, one of the demands in William's *Declaration;* Lord Wharton replied that he "did not expect, at this time of day, to hear anyone mention that child."[8] Lord Paget moved that James's flight was "a demise in law" and said Mary was now queen. But that was not widely accepted, and the Lords voted to ask William to send a circular letter to the counties and boroughs asking them to elect representatives to a Convention—the same form that had been used to bring about the restoration of Charles II in 1660.[9] William said he would not respond to the Lords until he had heard from the Commons.

On December 26 there was a meeting of members of the English House of Commons who had served during Charles II's reign—a category that excluded the large number of mostly Tory MPs elected only in 1685 — and the mayor and the Court of Aldermen of the City of London. This meeting endorsed elections for a Convention, and the circular letters were sent out, at the Commons' prompting not to the sheriffs James had appointed, but to the coroners, on December 27 and 28.[10] Through this period William made a point of being conciliatory and not vengeful. He paid a call on Charles II's widow, Queen Catherine of Braganza, at her quarters in Somerset House and, at her request, released from prison the Earl of Feversham, who had been her chamberlain. He also provided a diplomatic passport to the papal nuncio, that is, ambassador, d'Adda, who had been caught trying to flee in disguise.[11] He was more abrupt with the French ambassador, Barillon, an experienced and skillful political intriguer; on December 21 he ordered him to leave the country within 24 hours.[12]

During the period before the elections, William took care to pacify another threat to his power. On Christmas Day he met with Scottish lords who were in London — the Duke of Hamilton, his sons-in-law the Earl of Dundonald and Lord Murray, and the Earl of Crawford and Lord Drumlanrig — and they offered their "great acknowledgements for his glorious enterprize" and asked him to "take upon him the administration of that kingdome in matters civill and military."[13] This removed the threat of a war between England and Scotland, and on January 7 some 30 Scottish peers and 80 gentry tendered provisional power in their kingdom to William.[14]

Elections took place in January, and the Convention Parliament met on January 22.[15] There were relatively few contested seats — 60 as compared with 79 in 1685 and 106 in 1690 — and many boroughs returned one Whig and one Tory without opposition.[16] Ironically, James's campaign encouraging Dissenters to vote resulted in the election of candidates sympathetic to William, who after all was a Dissenter himself.[17] Seats that had seen furious competition in 1679 and 1681 were quiet in 1689. In the City of London, James had restored the old charter, and four Whigs were elected without opposition.[18] Westminster, with its giant electorate, was noisier, and the son of one Whig candidate threatened to strike one Tory candidate with a cane; two Whigs were returned.[19] Norfolk, solidly Tory as the Whig vote fell in

1685, now was closely contested, and elected a Tory and a Whig.[20] In Essex, the Tory incumbents did not run, and the two Whigs seemed likely to win without opposition. But then a "blustering country justice and a gentleman grazier," John Wroth, who had assisted in the escape of Princess Anne, came forward and demanded a poll; after five days he was ahead in the race for second place, and the Whig in the lead moved successfully to close the poll.[21] Buckinghamshire, the scene of cross-country marches and mounted processions in 1681 and 1685, returned the incumbent Whig Thomas Wharton and a like-minded local landowner without opposition.[22]

William was careful not to be seen influencing the elections. He made no public pronouncements on policy between his *Declaration* and his message to the Convention when it assembled on January 22.[23] While he was silent, news kept coming in of the depradations of the French army overrunning the Palatinate.[24] The 115 Lords elected Halifax Speaker over Danby; the 513 Commons members — 183 of whom had never sat before, and fewer than 100 of whom had first sat in James's Parliament in 1685 — elected Henry Powle, a Whig who had opposed exclusion, over the Tory former Speaker Sir Edward Seymour.[25] There was considerable political balance: 192 members had served in the Oxford Parliament of 1681, while 196 had served in the Tory Parliament of 1685.[26]

In his message to the houses, William dwelt on foreign affairs and the debt owed the United Provinces, and called for speedy action: "Next to the danger of unseasonable divisions among yourselves, nothing can be so fatal as too great delay in your consultations."[27] Powle talked of the necessity of avoiding anarchy in England and threats from Ireland, and emphasized "more particularly the vast Designs of that Turbulent and Aspiring Monarch, not only the open Persecutor of the Protestant Religion, but likewise the sworn Enemy of the English nation."[28] The Commons, with many members not yet seated, then moved to hold off debate until the next Monday, January 28.[29] That motion was advanced by members who hoped that in the intervening week the Lords would vote to recognize James as still king. But the Marquis of Halifax, Speaker of the Lords, persuaded the upper house, over the opposition of the Earls of Nottingham,

Clarendon, and Rochester, to vote to delay its discussion until the Commons had spoken.[30]

On January 28 the Commons met in a committee of the whole chaired by Richard Hampden, a Presbyterian Whig, and considered resolutions. Gilbert Dolben, a Tory, offered a resolution "that king James the second having voluntarily foresaken the government, and abandoned and foresaken the kingdom, it is a voluntary demise in him." The Whig Sir Robert Howard — it was he and Powle with whom William met at Windsor on December 16 — proposed an alternative, "that James II has abdicated the government by breaking the original contract." The difference in wording reflected a difference between the two parties that had sprung up in the Exclusion Crisis. Many Whigs believed that the monarch had something in the nature of a contract with the nation, the theory that John Locke propounded in his *Two Treatises on Government* (but that book, though apparently written in the early 1680s, was not published until November 1689).[31] Tories tended to believe in divine right, and abhorred the idea that the monarchy was elective rather than hereditary. The Whig point of view was articulated and the verb "abdicate" frequently used in the widely circulated pamphlet *A Brief Justification of the Prince of Orange's Descent* by Robert Ferguson, who had fled to the Netherlands with the Earl of Shaftesbury in 1682, had taken part in the Rye House Plot in 1683 and in Monmouth's rebellion in 1685, and had now come over with William's expedition.[32] But there were splits within the old party groupings, and some Tories were ready to accept the word "abdicate" rather than "demise." Other Tories preferred a regency, used traditionally in the case of minor or insane monarchs, but one member replied angrily, "If the question be whether you have power to depose the king, that may tend to calling him back again and then we are all ruined."

The Whig lawyer Sir George Treby summed up the Convention's predicament: "We have found the crown vacant, and are to supply that defect. We found it so, we have not made it so."[33] With few members supporting a regency, agreement was reached without a division on a version of Howard's resolution: "That King James the Second, having endeavoured to subvert the constitution of the Kingdom, by breaking the original contract between the King and the people, and by the advice of Jesuits and other wicked persons having violated the fundamental laws and withdrawn himself out of the kingdom, hath abdicated the government and that the throne is thereby become vacant."[34] Here was a sort of compromise between Tories and Whigs: "breaking the original contract" was a Whig idea; "abdicated the government" was a Tory idea; "the throne is vacant" was a Whig idea.[35] The committee of the whole voted without much dissent to report the measure to the full house and convey it to the Lords that day.[36]

The balance of opinion was different in the House of Lords. Some lords, notably the Earl of Clarendon, favored the recall of James; a scrupulous few, including Archbishop Sancroft, refused to take part in public life while James was not allowed to serve as king.[37] The Earls of Rochester and Nottingham favored a regency; Halifax said that would be a greater change in the constitution than a declaration that the throne was vacant. The question was put to the vote "whether a Regency with the administration of regal power under the style of king James the second during the life of the said king James be the best and safest way to preserve the Protestant religion and the laws of the kingdom." It was defeated by a margin of only 51-48 on January 29, with Halifax and Danby casting decisive nay votes and with Churchill, who had supported a regency, strategically absent.[38] In a private conversation with Halifax on December 30, William, according to Halifax's notes, "[s]aid he was sure of one thing; he would not stay in England if K. James came again. He said with the strongest asseverations that he would go if they went about to make him regent." Halifax evidently kept this communication confidential, but it seems to have led him to leave the side of his many friends who supported a regency.[39] This was the critical vote of the Convention Parliament. Had the Lords persisted in supporting a regency, albeit by a narrow margin, it is hard to see how a compromise could have been reached with the Commons' insistence that the throne was vacant; when the differences between them were reduced to the wording of a resolution declaring the throne vacant, a mutually agreeable formula could be, and was, reached.

But an additional point of dispute arose: Danby and others, mainly Tories, favored making Mary queen in her own right, as the next

Protestant successor, and many regency advocates came over to that view when their own proposal was defeated.[40] On January 30, while considering the Commons' resolution, the Lords voted to change the word "abdicated" to "deserted." It was argued that "abdicated" was a word unknown to English law, and that James had manifestly not made a conscious renunciation of office. In a conference committee, the Commons refused to yield. On January 31 the Lords amended the resolution again, deleting the phrase "that the throne is hereby vacant." An attempt to replace it with the words "the Prince and Princess of Orange should be declared King and Queen" was defeated 52–47. Then the Lords voted 55–41 to drop the declaration that the throne was vacant.[41]

As the Lords divided, the Commons settled one issue and raised another. The issue that was settled was what to do about the claims of the infant Prince of Wales, under the control of James and, more important, Louis XIV. The Convention made no attempt to investigate the circumstances of his birth, as called for in William's *Declaration*. To even the most fervent believer in the hereditary principle, it must have seemed impractical to recognize the claims of an infant who would presumably be raised as a Catholic under the supervision of a hostile King of France, who on his adulthood might claim the throne and who might live for many years (James Edward died in 1766). When the Whig Sir Richard Temple referred to "a pretended Brat beyond the sea, whom you cannot set aside," the Tory Sir Thomas Clarges noted that "James has taken away the child, if it be his, into another kingdom": no one wanted anything to do with the infant prince. On January 29 the House of Commons effectively disposed of the issue by passing a resolution "that it hath been found, by experience, to be inconsistent with the safety and welfare of this Protestant kingdom to be governed by a Popish Prince," and the Lords agreed.[42] This was an assertion of practicality over theory: the Commons invoked no ancient principle, but instead cited "experience."

The issue that was raised by the Commons was the extent of the monarch's powers. On January 29, the day after the Commons passed its resolution declaring the throne vacant, Thomas Wharton moved that the throne be filled by William and Mary. In response, Henry

Carey, Viscount Falkland (a Scottish peerage, which left him eligible to serve in the English House of Commons, to which he was elected as a Tory in 1685 as well as 1689),[43] rose and offered a resolution. In the Convention Parliament he showed himself prepared to accept the transfer of power, but also wanted it limited and called for a Declaration or Rights. "It concerns us to take such care, that, as the Prince of Orange has secured us from Popery, we may secure ourselves from arbitrary government. The Prince's *Declaration* is for a lasting foundation of Government. I would know what our foundation is. Before the question shall but put, who shall be set on the throne, I would consider what powers we ought to give the Crown to satisfy them that sent us hither. We have had a Prince that did dispense with our laws, and I hope we shall never leave that doubtful. The King set up an ecclesiastical court, as he was supreme head of the Church, and acted against law, and made himself head of the charters. Therefore, before you fill the throne, I would have you resolve what power you will give the King and what not."[44]

Was this a Tory plot to delay and possibly prevent William's succession? Perhaps, but Falkland was an active Member of Parliament, and his resolution shrewdly cited William's *Declaration* as its inspiration. Indeed, the second *Declaration* of October 14 had said, "It is plain that there can be no redress nor remedy offered but in parliament by a Declaration of the Rights of the Subjects that have been invaded."[45] It was clear that there was much opposition in the Lords to the installation of William and indeed to the Commons' resolution itself, and a setting out of rights might have been thought likely to make some lords more amenable to declaring William King.[46] Falkland's motion carried, and a committee was set up with Sir George Treby as chairman. By six in the evening the next day, January 30, the 39-member committee produced a document with 23 "Heads of Grievances," including clauses preventing the monarch from curtailing sessions of Parliament, for religious toleration, and for judges to serve on good behavior rather than at the pleasure of the king. These were reported to the Commons on Saturday, February 2.[47]

Pressure to install William as king continued out of doors. On February 2 a petition was organized, with 15,000 signatures and with

10,000 men reportedly ready to deliver it, calling on the Convention to declare William and Mary king and queen.[48] The streets of London, quiet since the rioting of December, were now buzzing. On February 2 the Commons rejected the Lords' amendments and restated their support of their January 28 resolution declaring the throne vacant.[49]

At this point William stepped in. In public he had said little since he opened the Convention Parliament; Dutch troops patrolled the streets of London, but with strict orders to avoid any appearance of coercion. Sometime between February 2 and 5, probably on Sunday, February 3, William held a conference with his supporters in the Lords, including Halifax and Danby, in which he said that he would not serve as regent in any regency, that he would not accept the crown only during the life of his wife, but that he would be willing to see the Crown descend to Anne rather than to any children he might have in a second marriage.[50] If Mary was declared queen, "he could not think of holding any thing by apron strings." If he was not offered the crown, "he would go back to Holland, and meddle no more in their affairs." At another meeting Halifax was told by one of William's Dutch confidants that the prince would not be his wife's "gentleman usher." Gilbert Burnet made it clear that Mary, still in the Netherlands, wished to rule only jointly with her husband, and she so declared in a letter to Danby.[51] As to the rights of Princess Anne, William insisted that he should rule for life, even if Mary died first; and the Churchills secured Anne's agreement to that condition by February 6, when she announced it in a letter carried to the Lords and Commons by Baron Churchill and the Earl of Dorset.[52]

William insisted that he would rule in his own right, and for life, just as he had demanded life tenure as stadholder from the States General in 1672. William in effect gave the Convention a clear choice: make him king or let England get by as it could. There were no good alternatives. Recall of James was unthinkable; Mary, it was clear, would do only William's bidding; the possibility of a regency by the Princess Anne (who turned 24 on February 6) and the Prince of Denmark was unnerving; the experience of a republic was one almost no one wanted to revisit, and in any case the only Cromwell on the scene was William. Ireland was in the hands of a lord deputy loyal to James and a Catholic army ready to fight to restore him; Scotland was in a state of anarchy; war with France seemed sure to come.[53] It was William or chaos.

Still, on February 4 the houses were still in disagreement on the resolution declaring the throne vacant, and the Commons was still considering the Heads of Grievances. On February 4 it adopted a suggestion made by Sir Edward Seymour that it strike from its list policies regarding new legislation; he was "not for making new laws, but declaring old." That meant that the clauses on proroguing and dismissing Parliaments, religious toleration, and judicial tenure were off the table.[54] On February 5 there was a conference between the two houses, at which no agreement was reached on the resolution declaring the throne vacant. In the Commons, Clarges argued for accepting the Lords' wording. "I take the Crown to be hereditary and that king James has 'abdicated' the Crown, and the pretended Prince of Wales being in the power of the French King and the throne vacant, the Crown ought to proceed to the next Protestant successor," Princess Mary. The radical Whig William Harbord pointed out that "the Dutch have sent their best troops to our assistance and the King of France is to rendezvous his army the 10th of March, and we are under unfortunate delays here of settling the government." Lord Wharton proclaimed, "I own driving King James out and I would do it again. Let everyone make his best of it." Sir Robert Howard drove toward a decision: "Where a divided inheritance is the case, all things are not so clear as we should wish; but let us preserve ourselves, which must be our supreme law."

Then came the division, when members trooped out of the chamber and were counted on one side or the other by tellers as they returned. The Commons upheld its rejection of the Lords' amendments by a vote of 282–151—the only major division in the Commons during the controversy.[55] On February 6 there was another conference; again, no agreement. Then the Lords backed down, with, as the Earl of Dartmouth put it, "some Lords being prevailed upon to absent themselves, from an apprehension that if they had insisted it must have ended in a civil war." Halifax was firmly in the chair. "The great argument," wrote Clarendon later, "used by my Lord Halifax (who was at the head of the prevailing faction and drove furiously) was necessity, and that the throne was only made elective *pro hac vice* [meaning 'in this case'] and then reverted to its hereditary channel again."[56] The Lords accepted the Commons' abdication language by a vote variously recorded as 62–47, 64–46, and 65–45: decisive in any case. Then it was moved to offer the crown to William and Mary. Nottingham objected that the monarch's usual title "was king of England, Scotland, Ireland, etc.," but that the English Parliament had no right to confer the crown of Scotland. "Herein," wrote one observer, "Halifax presence of mind (as it was in many other great occurrents this day in this debate) was very serviceable and he offered this expedient, that they might crown the Prince and Princess of Orange King and Queen of England with all the appurtenances thereunto belonging, etc., and afterwards consult with Scotland." The resolution offering the crown to William and Mary passed without a division. The Earl of Clarendon, an opponent, claimed that about 40 peers would have voted against it, but another observer, Roger Morrice, estimated only 25.[57] Clarendon urged the defeated side to secede from the Convention, but the Earl of Nottingham disagreed, saying, "We must support the government as well as we can." Nottingham, who had argued that recognizing William and Mary would violate his oath of allegiance to James, agreed to chair a committee to draw up a new oath that would omit the usual phrase "rightful and lawful": those who could not bring themselves to swear that they ruled de jure could still swear that they ruled de facto.[58]

The Commons, quick to declare the throne vacant, were not so quick to recognize William and Mary — not until they produced what became the Declaration of Rights. On February 7, after a long debate, they deferred action on the proclamation of the monarchs until a declaration could be reported.[59] Sir George Treby reported his draft that day, and debate was "tumultuous" and lasted until "pretty late that night." The house agreed without a division that "no Papist may succeed" to the throne "nor any person that hath made or shall make profession of being a Papist" — a reassertion of the resolution adopted January 29. On February 8 they agreed to join the statement of rights and limitations to the offer of the crown and set out the succession — that William and Mary should rule jointly and that William should have "administration of government," that William should be king for life, to be succeeded by Mary, Anne, and her offspring, and only then any offspring of William by a second marriage.[60] A committee headed by John Somers, the lawyer for the defense in the trial of the seven bishops, "tackt" together into one statement the resolutions the Convention had passed. It quoted the statement in William's second *Declaration* that "the only means for obtaining a full redress and remedy" of grievances was by a "Parliament in a Declaration of Rights of the subject" and it placed those clauses ahead of the offer of the crown.[61] That day Willem van Bentinck told one member of the Commons that William did not want "restrictions and limitations" placed on the crown, but in a meeting the next day Henry Sidney persuaded William to accept them.[62] But William did get the Lords to change the words giving him "administration of the Government" to "sole and full exercise of the regal power."[63] On February 12 both houses voted to place the final version of the Declaration of Rights in the rolls of Parliament and enter it in the Court of Chancery, though technically it was not a law. It was "a compromise document cobbled together to make it possible for Whig and Tory to stand together in league with their new Protestant king. It left it ambiguous whether James's 'abdication' was constituted by his abuses as king or by his flight from the realm."[64] The Lords agreed to meet in Westminster Palace at eight o'clock in the morning of February 13, and invited the Commons to join them in arriving at the Banqueting Hall.[65]

Both houses agreed on Saturday, February 9, to pass an edited and amended version of this declaration, which was done on February 12, and it was read to William and Mary before they were crowned the next day.[66] It was phrased as a declaration of long-standing, traditional rights of Englishmen; but in fact it declared illegal many of James's actions that had colorable claims to being legal.[67] The suspending power was abolished, and the dispensing power limited to occasional cases and abolished "as it hath been assumed and exercised of late."[68] The establishment of "the late courts of commissioners for eccelesiastical causes and all other commissions and courts of like nature are illegal and pernicious."[69] These were powers that James had asserted to be legal (and in the case of the dispensing power had obtained a court decision to that effect) and had effectively exercised.

Advocates of including these clauses in the Declaration of Rights could and did claim that they simply declared the state of existing law, but they effectively reduced the powers of the king and increased the power of Parliament, since they prevented the bypassing of the laws it had passed. Parliaments' powers were asserted: no revenue could be raised or used "by pretence of prerogative without grant of parliament," and "The raising or keeping a standing army within this kingdom in time of peace, unless it be with consent of parliament, is against law." This was a repudiation of James's standing army. The Declaration of Rights asserted "the right and freedom of electing members of the house of commons; and the rights and privileges of parliament and members of parliament, as well in the intervals of parliament as during their sitting." It responded to Charles's and James's practice of ruling during most of the 1680s without a Parliament by asserting that "parliaments ought to sit frequently, and that their frequent sitting be secured"—though how frequently and how it was to be secured, the Declaration did not say.[70] Nonetheless, the demand for a "free Parliament" had been the central tenet of William's *Declaration* and the rallying cry of those who came over: a Parliament elected free from the overbearing interest of the Crown.[71] And William had already shown, by forbearing to influence the elections of January 1689, that he would not attempt, as James had, to manipulate the electoral process to pack Parliament; he did not do so later, and no British monarch since ever has.

The Declaration of Rights has sometimes been described as simply a rearrangement or restatement of the rights of Parliament vis-à-vis the king. But it also guaranteed individual rights. The right to petition the king was asserted, and "prosecutions for such petitioning are illegal." Here was a direct rebuke of James's prosecution of the seven bishops for their petition asking to be allowed to refuse to order the reading of his Declaration of Indulgence. "Excessive bail" and "excessive fines and illegal punishments" were prohibited, "jurors to be duly impanelled and returned and corrupt and false verdicts prevented" and "all grants of fines and forfeitures are illegal and void." Here is a repudiation of James's manipulation of juries and imposition of imprisonment with high bail to keep political opponents out of the way. James had allowed the militia, made up of able-bodied and armed freemen, to wither into disuse, in favor of his standing army, and had disarmed law-abiding subjects. In response, the Declaration of Rights asserted, "It is necessary for the public safety that the subjects which are protestants should provide and keep arms for their common de fence: and that the arms which have been seized and taken from them be restored."[72] After negotiations with the Lords, the wording was changed to "That the Subjects which are Protestants may have arms for their Defence suitable to their conditions and as allowed by Law."[73] The monarch was bound by the Test Act, which meant that any Catholic was barred from the throne: so much not only for James, but for the Prince of Wales. William and Mary were to be king and queen, but "the sole and full exercise of regal power" was reserved to William during his lifetime.[74]

Historians have disagreed on whether the Declaration was a condition on the offer of the crown and a restriction on William's prerogatives as king.[75] To be sure, the Declaration was not a statute, and even after it had been passed as a statute by Parliament and given royal approval as the Bill of Rights in December 1689, it was still subject to repeal by a subsequent Parliament.[76] But the very ambiguity of its status means that it was something in the nature of a limitation on the power of the monarch. Having heard the Declaration read out to him before he was proffered the crown, William would have had to pay a high political price if he violated its terms — and he never did so.[77] Moreover, while the Declaration was described by many advocates as a simple restatement of the traditional rights of Englishmen, it also prohibited practices that James II had employed under claims of right — the dispensing and suspending powers, the maintenance of a standing army, the collection of revenue (if only for a few months) without parliamentary authorization, imposing excessive bail, packing juries. It is hard to disagree with the historian Lois Schwoerer's conclusion that the drafters of the Declaration "wanted to change the kingship as well as the king"[78] — and that they did so, as it turned out, permanently.

※

ON FEBRUARY 13, a rainy Ash Wednesday, at 10:30 in the morning, William and Mary entered Inigo Jones's Banqueting Hall, from which

Charles I had stepped out to the scaffold on which he was beheaded in January 1649 and at which Charles II was received when he returned to London in the Restoration of May 1660.[79] Before them were members of the Convention and close friends of the prince. The Gentleman Usher of the Black Rod led the Speakers of both houses, Halifax and Powle, and other peers across the great hall, under the ceiling paintings of James I that Peter Paul Rubens had painted for Charles I. There they bowed before William and Mary as they sat hand in hand under a canopy of state. The Deputy Clerk of Parliament read the Declaration of Rights that both houses had passed the day before. Then Halifax and Powle advanced with the crown and offered it to the seated William and Mary in the name of both houses as "the representative of the nation." William made a brief speech, first accepting the crown and then acknowledging the Declaration; Mary said nothing.[80] The crowd inside responded with a great shout, echoed by those outside.[81] Trumpeters and heralds went out into the streets in grand procession to proclaim William and Mary king and queen at four places in London.[82] Elaborate bonfires were lit all over London; one of "extraordinary great height in St. James's Square had effigies of the Pope, the Devil and James's Lord Chancellor Jeffreys, all of which were cast into the fire and burned."[83] Printed copies of the proclamation of the new king and queen were distributed throughout England and abroad. William and Mary that afternoon attended a service of thanksgiving, conducted by Bishop Henry Compton, at the Chapel Royal in Whitehall Palace. That evening they attended a party at Whitehall.[84] Among those present was the queen dowager, Catherine of Braganza, the widow of Charles II and a Catholic, whose presence lent an element of continuity to the accession of the new king and queen.[85] Ten days after the offer of the crown, on February 23, the Convention declared itself with the sanction of royal authority a regular Parliament.[86] The King-in-Parliament could proceed to govern England.

William had a rasping cough when he accepted the crown, and Mary, who had not seen him for more than three months when she reached London on February 12, noticed that he had lost weight. John Evelyn describes Mary as "riant & jolly . . . whilst the Pr: her husband has a thoughtful Countenance, & is wonderfull serious & silent, seemes to treat all persons alike gravely."[87] William thought his asthma was aggravated by the filthy air of coal-heated London, and he soon moved out of St. James's Palace, first to Hampton Court Palace,[88] which proved too far away for him to conveniently do business, and then to Kensington, where he purchased Nottingham House from the Earl of Nottingham, and which, as rebuilt and added on to by Sir Christopher Wren, became Kensington Palace.[89] William's health seemed so precarious that Halifax expressed the fear that he would die — he wrote one friend that he thought he "might" outlive the summer — or that he would be assassinated, as his great-grandfathers William the Silent and Henri IV had been.[90]

The 38-year-old prince who showed so little outward emotion must have felt himself under excruciating pressure for the past four months, in which time any number of plausible contingencies could have defeated his enterprise and caused ruin for him and for the United Provinces. But the pressure did not end when he accepted the offer of the crown. He told Halifax shortly afterwards that "he fancied he was like a King in a play."[91] William's chief purpose in coming over was to enlist England in the war against France; for that he needed Parliament to vote revenue. He also needed to establish his authority in his two other kingdoms, Scotland and Ireland. Unbeknownst to him, James left the Palace of St. Germain on February 15, two days after the offer of the crown, to go to Ireland, where Tyrconnel's mostly Catholic army held power.[92]

And there remained issues of government and religion left over from James's reign. James's Declaration of Indulgence created a competition in which different political actors — James, the Tories, William, the Whigs — vied to show their support for religious toleration: a virtuous circle. William, though he had made known through Fagel's letter his support of the Test Act, also declared himself for toleration of all religions. Backers of the Church of England like the Earl of Nottingham insisted they supported toleration of Dissenting worship and the comprehension of Presbyterians and others within the Church of England. The Whigs had long tended to support toleration of Dissenters; indeed when James adopted that policy, many cooperated with him in his campaign to pack Parliament.

William could and did appoint ministers, of varying political backgrounds — Halifax as Lord Privy Seal and Danby (soon to become the Marquis of Carmarthen) as Lord President of the Council (but not Lord Treasurer, which he had been under Charles II and wanted to be again), the Whig Earl of Shrewsbury and the Tory Earl of Nottingham as Secretaries of State.[93] It was a balanced ticket: the longtime Tory Danby and the Whig Shrewsbury had signed the Invitation of the Seven; the sometime Whig Halifax and the Tory Nottingham had not; in the Convention, Halifax and Shrewsbury had pressed for William to be king, Danby for Mary to be queen, and Nottingham had opposed both, but had accepted William as king de facto. But the issues that needed to be settled and the revenue that was needed to wage war could not be produced by the king and his ministers; it had to be voted by Parliament.

Before 1688, Parliament was out of session more often than it was in session. It was an event more than an institution.[94] Charles I had governed for 11 consecutive years without a Parliament, Charles II for four, James II for three. Starting in 1689, Parliament has been in session every year for more than 300 years. This was not because William was enamored of Parliament — he was soon heartily sick of it — but because the struggle against Louis XIV, which had been the primary purpose of his invasion, turned out to be a long war, and only Parliament could raise the money.[95]

On some issues Parliament was helpful to William. On March 1 the Commons quickly passed a bill authorizing him to suspend habeas corpus, so that the government could detain Jacobites, supporters of James.[96] After soldiers at Ipswich, on the coast northeast of London, mutinied on March 15 and began marching to Scotland as supporters of James, Parliament passed the Mutiny Act authorizing the king and his officers to discipline men in the army and navy free from threat of civil suit. But conditions were attached; the Mutiny Act also prohibited the raising of a standing army without parliamentary approval, which was effective for no more than a year, thus requiring Parliament to be summoned every year to renew it.[97] And even with the Mutiny Act, William continued to rely on Dutch rather than English troops in England and, later, Ireland.[98]

In February, William sought legal advice that the revenues Parliament had granted James for life in 1685 were still in force, but Parliament decided that this was not so; James's unauthorized raising of revenues granted to Charles was, after all, one of the Heads of Grievances drawn up by the Convention.[99] Seeking to mollify Parliament, William on March 1 gave up the hereditary revenue from the hearth tax, a source of complaint for many years and characterized by "abuses and oppressions," in the words of the Heads of Grievances.[100] Parliament did vote £420,000 to be raised by a six months' assessment on land on February 28. And it was relatively generous in authorizing extraordinary spending—it voted £600,000 to repay the Dutch for the cost of the expedition on March 16, £714,000 for the reduction of Ireland on March 22, and £1,199,000 for the fleet and summer and winter guards on April 5.[101] But it was less willing to authorize taxes to raise the revenue needed for that spending. On March 11 it voted William the right to collect the revenue granted James for life, but only until June 24.[102]

On religion the Earl of Nottingham, a fervent believer in the Church of England, took the lead. He sponsored a toleration bill to allow public worship by Dissenting Protestants (except those who did not believe in the Trinity), and a comprehension bill to provide for inclusion of Dissenters, principally Presbyterians, within the Church of England. The toleration bill was supported by Tories as well as Whigs.[103] In the Commons, Sir Robert Howard called for allowing Dissenters to be exempted from the Test Act, and thus to be eligible for public office.

On March 16, William, prompted by Richard Hampden, gave a speech calling for office to be opened to all Protestants.[104] This was a departure from his support of the Test Acts in Fagel's letter, and there was a furious reaction from Church of England men. That evening some 150 members of the House of Lords, including Sir Thomas Clarges, Heneage Finch (Nottingham's brother), Sir Robert Sawyer, and Sir Christopher Musgrave, met at the Devil Tavern Club in the City of London, and agreed to oppose any dilution of the Test Acts. Their lead was followed by Tories like Nottingham and Carmarthen and by the Whig Earl of Devonshire.[105] Those in favor of upholding the Church's status seemed to have the majority when the Commons, on March 25 or 26, passed Sir Thomas Clarges's law adding to the coronation oath words binding the monarch to uphold the Church of England "as now established by law" over the alternative "as now or shall be established by law" by a 188–149 margin.[106] As Roger Morrice noted, "The house of commons was stronger by 80 or 100 voices to reform things amiss in the State than in the Church."[107]

If William's sudden opposition to the Test Acts was obnoxious to Tories, his plea on March 25 for a general act of indemnity from prosecution, with exceptions only as "shall seem necessary for the vindication of public justice, the safety of their Majesties, and the settlement and welfare of the nation for the future," was obnoxious to Whigs who had hoped to remove from public life those who had cooperated with James and perhaps even some who had cooperated with Charles.[108]

Nottingham's comprehension act was an attempt to gather in all or almost all Protestants into the Church of England. Dissenting worship had been discouraged since the Restoration and Dissenters had been persecuted, especially from 1681 to 1685. The hope was that this unique Protestant church could accommodate almost all Englishmen in a Protestant faith that would uphold the divine sanction of the king and the civil order — and avoid the discord and civil war that had raged for years within the living memory of most of men active in public life in 1689. But the ouster of James and the installation of William and Mary had, as Tories argued in the Convention, undermined the idea that the monarchy was divinely sanctioned, and the Dissenters who had persevered in their faith despite penalties were not necessarily interested in coming under the cloak of the Church of England. Nor, as it turned out, were Church of England leaders interested in introducing what they regarded as schism into "the very bowels of the Church."[109] On April 1, after the Easter recess, the Commons considered a bill to repeal the Corporation Act, the law overseeing local government and requiring its officers to be members of the Church of England, and the Whigs got a postponement for ten days of an amendment to preserve the Test Act for county and borough office by a margin of only 116–114.[110]

This was a matter of great import: government in Stuart England depended on the participation of local freemen, and James, in his campaign to pack Parliament, had ousted Church of England men for Dissenters and Catholics. The closeness of the vote suggested that the Tory goal of maintaining the Test Act was in some peril. Against that background, the Lords considered Nottingham's comprehension bill on third reading and added an occasional conformity provision, stating that those who took communion in the Church of England just once a year, presumably in order to qualify for office, would not be considered to have met the requirements of the Test Act if they continued otherwise to worship in Dissenting churches.[111] The Commons, considering a much broader comprehension bill sponsored by John Hampden, voted on April 8 to put off debate for ten days. On April 9, William Harbord, a radical Whig who had come over with William and was now postmaster general, rose as the Commons considered the Lords' comprehension bill and stated, presumably with authority, that he "could assure them that his Majesty was altogether of the judgement of the Church of England." He urged the Commons to thank the king for "declaring he would preserve the Church of England as by law established," and request the summoning of a convocation of Church of England bishops and clergy to consider comprehension, which he said "in no way hinders the intended ease for Dissenting Protestant subjects." That evening the Tories at the Devil Tavern Club agreed to accept this proposal, and it was approved by the Commons without division, and by the Lords.[112]

※

IN THE MEANTIME, the Scottish Convention, which met March 16, was reaching the end of its deliberations. This one-house body chose as president the Duke of Hamilton, a supporter of William, over the Earl of Atholl, a supporter of James, by a vote of 95–55; it was firmly controlled by Presbyterians and Whigs, who had no use for either James VII (as James II was known in Scotland) or the bishops of the Church of Scotland. The Scots were in no position to claim, as the English Convention had done, that James had abdicated the kingdom; since James VI of Scotland journeyed from Edinburgh to London in 1603 to become James I of England, no Scottish king except Charles I had set foot in Scotland during his reign (unless one counts Charles II's sojourn there in 1651). On April 4 the Convention resolved that James, "by doing acts contrary to law," had "forefaulted the right to the crown" for himself and his heirs by his "subversione of the protestant religione, and the violation of the lawes and liberties of the Kingdome, inverting all the Ends of Government." This was both a resort to medieval legal language and something closer to a clear assertion of a contract theory of government than the English Convention had made.

On April 11 the Convention offered the crown to William and Mary and passed a Claim of Right outlining the illegal acts of James VII/II and laying down prescriptions for the future in the guise of "vindicating and asserting . . . antient rights and liberties." No Catholic could be king or queen or hold public office; "the fyneing husbands for their wives withdrawing from the church was Contrary to law"; and the "Prelacy"—the bishops of the Church of Scotland—was "a great and insupportable grievance and trouble to this Nation, and contrary to the Inclinationes of the generality of the people . . . and therefor ought to be abolished." The Presbyterians had triumphed over the bishops. Two days later, on April 13, the Scottish convention passed Articles of Grievances abolishing the Lords of the Articles (the committee through which the Crown manipulated Parliament), repealing the 1669 Supremacy Act (giving the Church a monopoly of legal worship) and making the offer of the Crown contingent on William and Mary's acceptance of the Claim of Right and the Articles of Grievances.[113] Soon after, the Scottish Convention, like its English counterpart, made itself a Parliament and decreed that church clergymen "in possession and exercise of their ministrie" as of April 13 would be immune from "any injurie." This ratified the result of the "rabblings"—the forcible ejections by local Scots of their Episcopal ministers from their churches and manses, which had been ongoing since Christmas—and left Jacobite Episcopalians and Cameronian Covenanters outside the Church and the law.[114]

The news of the offer of the crown to William and Mary took longer to reach the American colonies. The first to hear it, thanks to the trade winds, were the Caribbean colonies, where the governors of

Jamaica, Barbados, and the Leeward Islands maintained control from the time the first reports were received in February until they could be confirmed in May.[115] In Boston, Sir Edmund Andros tried to maintain control, but was overthrown April 18 by a coup of townsmen, who captured him and forced the surrender of the royal frigate in the harbor. In the New England colonies, former magistrates under the charter governments assumed power; in New York the local militia under German-born merchant Jacob Leisler ousted the lieutenant governor, Francis Nicholson, in May. In Maryland and Virginia stories circulated of a Catholic plot to incite Indians to kill Protestant settlers; Protestant leaders ousted Lord Baltimore's appointees in Maryland in July.[116]

Governments loyal to William and Mary were thus, in one way or another, installed; the problem of how and by whom the colonies should be governed remained. Decisions were mostly made in Westminster, with a military expedition sent to overthrow Leisler in New York, a revocation of Lord Baltimore's charter, and a charter for Massachusetts worked out in negotiations between the Massachusetts lobbyist Increase Mather and bureaucrat William Blathwayt agreed on in 1691, with a royal governor nominated by the Puritans, provisions for religious toleration, and the franchise extended from church members to all freeholders.[117] The result—"a synthesis between the virtual autonomy of the colonists' founding years and the radical centrism of royal policy in the 1680s"[118]—provided the framework for the governance of the North American colonies, which held about 70,000 people in 1660, 240,000 in 1688, and more than 2 million in the 1770s.[119] Royal governors (with exceptions: William Penn was restored as proprietor in Pennsylvania in 1694[120] and the Lords Baltimore, converted to Protestantism, in Maryland in 1715),[121] elected assemblies, stable land rights, restrictions on navigation and trade, a continuing reliance on decisions made in London that made lobbying there a quintessentially American profession: these were the conditions under which the colonies prospered, even as they faced military threats from the French and Indians to the north and west; and the conditions under which they in time chafed and were prompted to demand independence.[122] "London officials following the Glorious

Revolution," writes historian Jack Greene, "managed to retain, probably even to enhance, the authority of the center in the peripheries of empire by acquiescing in the devolution of considerable power to provincial governments."[123]

The Revolution of 1688–89 was thus a mixed heritage for the North American colonies. As the historian Richard Johnson writes, "The colonists' embrace of the Glorious Revolution cemented their ties to England and English authority. But it also furnished a wholly respectable grounds for defining that relationship in terms that protected local autonomy and limited executive excess." When, in the 1760s, "Parliament tried to implement in America what it had come to claim within England . . . [it ran] full tilt into the now entrenched position of assemblies claiming constitutional parity as fellow legislatures."[124] Or, as Greene writes, "Far from rejecting the results of the Glorious Revolution, the colonists simply assumed that they were entitled to *all* of its benefits."[125] The Glorious Revolution settlement in America turned out to be pregnant with the American Revolution.

THE KING AND queen were crowned in Westminster Abbey on April 13 in formal ceremony — a "foolish" and "popish" ritual, William told a Dutch intimate[126] — and took the coronation oath to preserve the Church of England "as by law established." That same day William made Baron Churchill the Earl of Marlborough.[127]

Parliament continued to attend to unfinished business. The proposal to refer the issue of comprehension to Church of England leaders was presented to William on April 19; he eventually appointed a commission, but, as it turned out, the Church leaders were unwilling to water down their doctrine to allow the admission of those who did not accept its current doctrines, and failed to reach any agreement in sessions in November and December 1689.[128] Meanwhile, the Toleration Act — or, more exactly, "An Act for Exempting Their Majesties' Protestant Subjects Dissenting from the Church of England from the Penalties of Certain Laws"[129] — passed the Lords on April 19,[130] and was accepted by the Commons with minor disagreements on May 17. The Devil Tavern Club group was in accord, and William gave his consent on May 24.[131] The second *Declaration* of October 14 had said, "It is plain that there can be no redress nor remedy offered but in parliament by a Declaration of the Rights of the Subjects that have been invaded."[132] The Toleration Act removed the penalties on trinitarian Dissenters for refraining from worshiping at Church of England services, but did not qualify them for public office. It did leave open the possibility of their qualifying for it by occasional conformity, a loophole (in the view of Church of England advocates) that was closed by the occasional conformity act passed in 1711 in the reign of Queen Anne and then opened again by the repeal of that act in 1718 after the accession of George I.[133] On its face it allowed only a grudging amount of toleration, limited to certain Christians, who were not allowed to hold public office. But by removing penalties, it encouraged the proliferation of Dissenting churches and worship.[134]

This trend was given additional impetus by the attitude of the king. Out of a personal inclination toward religious toleration and out of concern for the sensibilities of his Catholic allies in Europe, William took care to "thwart popular and ecclesiastical opposition to the religious practices of Dissenters and Catholics"; hundreds of Dissenting chapels were licensed, and prosecution of Catholics was minimal.[135] Just as England generally, apart from moments of inflammation like the Popish Plot, was more tolerant in fact than in law before the Revolution of 1688–89, so it was afterwards; the narrow toleration of the law was broadened in practice.

The question remained what to do with the Church of England clergy who refused to recognize the succession of William and Mary on the grounds that they had sworn an oath to uphold King James and that the Church of England required passive obedience to a lawful monarch. Nottingham had sworn an oath to William and Mary as de facto monarchs, but Archbishop Sancroft, among others, adamantly refused to do so. The Lords, consistent with their recognition of William and Mary, voted on March 20 to require the Church clergy to do so by August 1 or be deprived of their benefices and income; the Commons voted on April 5 to similar effect by a margin of 193–138.[136] On April 17, Bishops Compton and Burnet (he had been named Bishop of Salisbury) got the Lords to vote to allow William to waive this requirement, but William and the Commons opposed that, and the Lords on April 24 voted 45–42 to accept the Commons position, with the proviso that the king could pay up to a dozen of the clergy some of their otherwise lost income.[137] William sent a messenger to Sancroft to tell him that he need not move out of Lambeth Palace on August 1.

Such was the religious settlement of the Revolution. The Church of England still had the status of an established church, and its members a monopoly on public office. But Dissenting Protestant worship was tolerated and therefore authorized, and the practice of occasional conformity made it easy for Dissenters to qualify for public office. The project of gathering together all Protestants under the cloak of the Church of England was tacitly abandoned; the Church of England did not want to abandon some of its beliefs to accommodate Dissenters, and Dissenters could gain the privileges of Church membership without difficulty, though with some violence to their consciences.[138] The problem of the nonjurors — the clergy who refused to take the oaths to obey William and Mary — was finessed. Nonjurors like Sancroft would in time die out and, provided the Revolutionary settlement stayed in place, those appointed to fill their places would not be nonjurors.[139] As the historian John Morrill notes, "The limited rights accorded to the few who set up in competition with the Church created a space to be taken advantage of by the many who chose to ignore all organized religion. The collapse of ecclesiastical discipline and the ability of church courts to enforce moral and spiritual norms was far steeper in the decades after 1688 than in the previous period."[140] A little hypocrisy remained on all sides. The Church of England still purported to represent the religion of the nation, but remained open to competition in the spiritual marketplace; the Dissenters could still purport to portray themselves as disadvantaged, but could overcome their disadvantages with little difficulty. As Morrill has argued, "The Toleration Act made fanaticism and persecution *impracticable*."[141]

Of course, Catholics were not included in the Toleration Act. At a time when the Catholic James II and Louis XIV were seen as actively seeking to overthrow the regime, and to declare all who had taken part in the installation of William and Mary as guilty of treason, this was unthinkable. The more so as Catholics were regarded as inherently subversive, willing to take oaths with "mental reservations" that left them unbound to God to fulfill their undertakings, willing to employ any subterfuge to undermine and overthrow the English polity, eager to make Englishmen submit to the persecution so vividly portrayed in *Foxe's Martyrs*. The recent experiences of the Popish Plot and the reign of James II left Englishmen utterly willing to exclude Catholics from the body politic and to leave them to the tender mercies of their countrymen. Which, as it turned out, were mostly tender. Catholics were left, in the reigns of William and Anne as they had been during most of the reigns of Charles and James, able to worship in their own private chapels and to live their lives in peace with their countrymen. They could not hold public office or take their seats in the House of Lords, but they were safe in their property, as much as they were in the Dutch Republic—and much safer than were Protestants in the Kingdom of France.

But even as Parliament agreed on a religious settlement, it could not agree on an indemnity bill. William had called for an act providing indemnity from prosecution with only a few exceptions.[142] But many Whigs wanted their adversaries in the 1680s punished or removed from public life, and in May the Commons agreed on 10 and later 12 categories of offenses, perpetrators of which would be subject to prosecution.[143] But there the issue languished; there was clearly no appetite in the Lords for such a bill.

The religious settlement was followed, posthaste, by success in Scotland, major setbacks in Ireland, and a determination to wage war against Louis XIV. But all of these enterprises depended on revenue— and Parliament was reluctant to supply revenue. On April 26 the Commons passed a poll tax and an authorization of the ordinary revenue up through December 24, £600,000 for civil charges of government and £700,000 for war.[144] An additional poll tax was voted on May 6. But the poll tax was a land tax, with the amount dependent on the value of the land, and the Lords, almost all of them great landowners, insisted on rating their property themselves—a procedure obviously obnoxious to the Commons. On May 10 the Commons voted a tax of one shilling on the pound—5 percent—calculated to be worth

£500,000.[145] But the Lords' insistence on rating themselves killed measure late May.[146] On June 15 the Commons passed one shilling on land, and this time the Lords narrowly rejected an amendment allowing them to rate their property themselves.[147] In June, on the eve of the expiration of revenues, William got an extension for another six months, until December 24.[148] On July 30 the Commons voted customs duties, but for only three years, not for life as James had.[149]

This was an English Parliament determined to keep its Dutch king on a short leash. Granting revenues for life to Charles II and James II, both Whigs and Tories agreed, had been a mistake. Two former Speakers made this clear. "We that have placed the King on the Throne, are those that will keep him in it," said the Tory Sir Edward Seymour. "If you give the crown too little," said the Whig Sir William Williams, "you may add at any time; if once you give too much, you will never have it back again."[150] William became discouraged; in late June he told Halifax that "a king of England who will govern by law as he must do, if he hath conscience, is the worst figure in Christendom — He hath power to destroy the nation and not to protect it."[151] In July he conceded when Parliament sought access to the Privy Council committee records on the course of the military struggle in Ireland.[152] On July 10 he sent a message urging Parliament to finish its money bills and the indemnity and then go into recess.[153]

Parliament responded: on July 12 the Commons and on July 15 the Lords voted to spend £600,000 out of general revenues to reimburse the Dutch for the costs of the invasion that had landed in England seven months before, and on August 20 Parliament went into recess.[154] But on August 5 they also voted the extraordinary sum of £70,000 a year for Princess Anne — a slap at William, whose reluctance to accept it led to a bitter feud between Mary and Anne, two sisters who had seen little of each other since Mary had gone off to live in The Hague 11 years before. It also put Sarah, Countess of Marlborough, and her husband in disfavor with the queen.[155] Anne's delivery of a healthy baby, the Duke of Gloucester, in August 1689 was greeted as a sign that the Protestant succession was assured. But William's popularity was at its ebb. He went to the races at Newmarket and dutifully lost thousands of pounds on the races, but his frosty ceremony and dislike of vibrant court life made him unpopular with courtiers who could remember the days of Charles II. He remarked to Dijkvelt, "I see that I am not made for this people, nor they for me."[156] He dined with his Dutch generals while English noblemen in attendance had to stand by watching until they "were dismissed when the dinner was half over."[157]

When Parliament reassembled on October 19, some leading members proposed a brief prorogation, and William agreed to prorogue it for four days. This had the legal effect of voiding all the previous bills passed by one house but not the other, and so swept the slate clean on the difficult issues — revenue, the Bill of Rights, indemnity, the corporation act — still pending.[158] Since the Declaration of Rights was not a statute, Parliament was determined to pass it into law, and there was general agreement on the terms of the Declaration agreed to so speedily in February. But then there had been pressure to act because of the need to declare William king, and the desire to present him with a Declaration. After February there was delay as the two houses disagreed on provisions, without much in the way of intervention from the king. In May the Lords omitted the section outlawing the royal dispensing power and added the Electress Sophia of Hanover to the line of succession;[159] she was 27th in line of succession in 1688, but after Mary, Anne, and William, she was the next Protestant in line. Sophia was 20 years older than William, the daughter of the long-deceased Frederick Elector Palatine and Elizabeth, the daughter of James I and sister of Charles I; she was married to Ernst August, the Duke of Hanover.[160] William favored naming Sophia (Hanover was a major supplier of military forces to the Dutch Republic),[161] but the Commons rejected both amendments in June.[162] In July the Lords conceded on the dispensing power, but voted 38–29 on July 31 to name Sophia.[163] Now, after the prorogation, there was more amity. The Commons passed the Bill on November 6,[164] and the Lords refrained from naming Sophia and passed an almost identical bill on November 23. On December 10 the Commons accepted minor amendments,[165] and on December 16, William gave his royal consent.

Revenue proved a more difficult issue. On November 2 the Commons voted £2,000,000 in extraordinary supply, or a one-time revenue.[166] But the House was still scouting around for revenue sources, considering such expedients as £500 penalties on those who had taken office under James without complying with the Test Act and a £100,000 levy on England's Jews.[167] On December 11 the Commons passed a two-shilling land tax — a 10 percent levy — and, perhaps as a slap back at the king, called for £50,000 for Princess Anne, which passed a week later.[168] On December 14 the Whigs furiously attacked William's government and on December 18 voted him revenue for only one year, not three as they had proposed earlier in the year, and for which they had voted him customs.[169] Only in January did the Commons and the Lords finally pass the tax measures needed to finance the government.[170]

Alarmed by a resolution proposed in the Lords on January 25, urging him not to go to Ireland, William on January 27 prorogued Parliament until April 2.[171] William was heartily sick of English party politics. The Whigs were unhappy that he had not created a Whig government and that he opposed them on many issues. The Tories were also unhappy with his opposition on many issues and looked with favor on the alternative of Princess Anne, ever loyal to the Church of England. But William, after all his experience with the intricacies of Dutch politics, was willing to endure frustration and rebuff on many issues. What he would not countenance was interference with his determination to make war. When he got the revenue needed, he proceeded to act. He decided that he did not want to face the Convention Parliament again and did not want to wait for another Parliament until April 2. So on February 6 he dissolved Parliament and called for new elections and for the new Parliament to assemble on March 20. On February 8 he told Halifax that he would "first see some of the elections returned" and then might postpone the new Parliament.[172]

William and the Convention Parliament had done much to secure guaranteed liberties and strengthen representative government — with all its messiness, compromises, half-measures, and delays. "After twelve months, then, the Convention parliament received its *quietus,*" writes historian Henry Horwitz:

> In retrospect, it would seem that the first parliament of the new reign had substantial accomplishments to its credit. After all, the

declaration of war against France, the passage of the toleration act, and the enactment of the bill of rights now stand out as milestones in the course of English history. But contemporaries had a different perspective; they were more conscious of the wide gulf between their initial expectations and the parliament's actual achievements. From William's vantage point, the failure to settle the ordinary revenue, to approve an act of indemnity, and to agree upon comprehension were major disappointments. As for the Whigs and their Dissenting friends, their sense of frustration was even keener since they had begun the new reign with such high hopes. Only the Churchmen had any cause for satisfaction; even so, they had not been able to avert a schism among the clergy over the new oaths and most of their parliamentary successes had been defensive in nature.[173]

But now other business awaited, business that would in short time advance anti-hegemonic foreign policy and global capitalism: the business of war.

Chapter 9

WAR

THE KING'S GUARD Chamber, Hampton Court Palace, 1699. As the 1690s went on, and especially after the death of Queen Mary in December 1694, King William III increasingly resided and tended to business at Hampton Court Palace, more than 10 miles from Westminster, and upwind from the filthy coal-smoke-choked air of London that so aggravated William's asthma. The palace was out of reach for most of the courtiers who had swarmed over Charles II's disorderly court and stood attentively at James II's more businesslike sessions. William engaged Sir Christopher Wren, the great architect of the age, to design his apartments at Hampton Court, and today they survive much as he left them, for no later monarch chose to do business there.

Most striking to the visitor is the King's Guard Chamber, just beyond the entrance to the apartments. There the Yeomen of the Guard kept watch over the king and made sure that "no idle, mean or unknown persons" entered his presence. The wood-paneled walls rise more than 20 feet to the ceiling, their bottom half bare, their top half decorated by what at first seem like geometric designs. In the middle are woodcarvings by Grinling Gibbons, Master Carver to the Crown from 1693. On each side are arrayed objects of wood with incised metal, pointing outward from central foci. As a visitor's upward gaze concentrates, it becomes clear that these objects are weapons, more than 3,000 muskets, pistols, bayonets, and swords. They were arranged there in 1699 by William's gunsmith, John Harris, with weapons brought from the Tower of London.

In the Guard Chamber and throughout William's rooms in Hampton Court, artists painted images of Hercules, a symbol of Christian fortitude intended to stress William's martial ardor for the Protestant cause.[1] Hercules had been the symbol of William's great-grandfather Henri IV of France, promulgator of the Edict of Nantes; he and William's other slain great-grandfather, William the Silent, the great leader of the Dutch revolt against the Spanish, had been military leaders who used their prowess to advance religious toleration and domestic peace.[2]

"Who was William?" asks the historian of ideas J. G. A. Pocock. "He was a man who in his life played many roles: prince of Orange, *prince d'Orange,* prince of Nassau, stadholder of most of the seven provinces, captain general of the united Netherlands, king of England and Ireland, king of Scots. In which of these many roles did he perceive himself as acting? He was a reserved man; was he an introspective one? If he had asked himself to state his innermost identity, what would have been his answer?"[3] The answer seems to bristle from the high walls of the King's Guard Chamber: William was a soldier, a man of arms, a general who personally led men into battle, the great captain of the forces that opposed the overweening power of the great hegemonic tyrant of his day, his cousin Louis XIV. However accomplished he had become in his political dealings with the States General and the various States of Holland, and with the House of Commons and the House of Lords in England, or the parliaments of Scotland and Ireland; however shrewd a practitioner of diplomacy he showed himself in making alliances with the Holy Roman Emperor or the representatives of the King of Spain and in hiring mercenary troops in Brandenburg and Hanover and other small states in Germany; however much he had to submit to the "foolish" and "popish" splendors of English royal protocol; however much time and psychic energy he had to invest in these activities, he saw himself primarily as a soldier, whose purposes in life ultimately had to be achieved on the field of battle.

William was a soldier all his adult life. In May 1668, at age 17, he traveled to Bergen-op-Zoom in Zeeland to watch a review of the Dutch army, and he soon sought the post of captain-general of the Republic for life.[4] Six of the seven states backed him by December 1671, but the state of Holland insisted the appointment be for only one year. William initially refused, but, after further negotiations, agreed and was named captain-general and admiral-general for one year. Holland then voted to extend the appointment to life when he turned 22.[5] As captain-general and then stadholder he led the Dutch forces after Louis XIV's army overran five of the seven states of the Republic in 1672, and insisted on the opening of the dikes and the flooding of farmland that prevented Louis from advancing into the states of Holland and Zeeland.[6] William managed to detach England from its alliance with France in 1673, but fought on against the French in battle after battle — at Maastricht and Charleroi in 1672, Naarden in 1673, the Boyne in 1690 (where he defeated James II and his Irish and French army), Namur in 1692, Landan in 1693, Charleroi again in 1693, Huy in 1694, and Namur once more in 1695.[7] Ever since his heroic defense of the Dutch Republic in 1672, writes the historian Tony Claydon, "the prince always strove to get to the battlefield, showing a preference for the front over the ease of his palaces."[8] His biographer Stephen Baxter notes his insistence on "rigid discipline" and his "severity," and points out that he vastly improved the Republic's fighting skills.[9] He was evidently a good judge of military talent: he confirmed Marlborough's appointment as lieutenant general and put him in charge, though nominally under the Duke of Schomberg, of the reconstitution of the English army in February 1689, and in May put him in command of the 8,000-man English army in Flanders.[10]

Members of the English Parliament had every reason to know that they had installed a soldier-king, and William made no secret of his enmity toward the France of Louis XIV. They were bound to share his feelings. "He hath such a mind to France that it would incline one to think, hee tooke England onely in his way," Halifax said.[11] But having given the crown to William, the Convention Parliament had inevitably become his accomplice.

Members knew that Louis had welcomed James to France in January 1689 (it was still December in England) and recognized him as king; they knew that James had landed in Ireland in March, with Louis's support and at the head of Tyrconnel's army; they knew that if James was restored in England, they would be adjudged traitors and might well pay with their lives. France was already at war with the Netherlands and in effect was at war with England in Ireland. So the great issue of going to war with the mightiest power in Europe was surprisingly uncontroversial. On April 15 the Commons took up the issue, and Richard Hampden and Sir Thomas Clarges — the one an heir of the great hero of Parliament in the Civil War, the other a staunch Tory — both called for war. On April 16 the war was agreed to unanimously in the committee of the whole. Delay followed, as the Commons declined to approve the text of a declaration drafted by John Hampden, which inconveniently denounced Louis's bribes of English politicians in the 1670s. Finally on April 25 the Commons presented the petition for war to William.[12]

On May 8, war was declared on France. On May 12 in The Hague, a Grand Alliance was signed between the Dutch Republic and the Holy Roman Emperor; Leopold recognized William as King in June, and called him Majesty: a serious concession, since emperors were not in the habit of endorsing those who ousted kings.[13] In good time, other measures forced by these commitments followed: on August 20 the Commons approved a Lords amendment on a bill cutting off English trade with France; on August 24/September 3 a treaty with the Dutch Republic was signed.[14] England had committed itself to war.

WILLIAM CAME TO England as the head of the largest army to invade the island since the Roman legions. Fortunately, he had not had to fight much there. But the two other kingdoms whose crowns he sought, Scotland and Ireland, were another matter. The Scottish Convention and Parliament had settled the succession and legal and religious issues by the middle of April 1689. But their decisions were not accepted by all. In early April, Viscount Dundee, an anti-Presbyterian,[15] raised an army of 2,000 from the western clans on James's behalf north of the Firth of Forth. They faced the Scottish regiments formerly stationed in the Netherlands and now led by General Hugh Mackay.[16] Mackay pursued Dundee's army into the Highlands through the narrow valley of the Tay and was defeated on July 27 at Killiecrankie. But Dundee was killed in the battle, and his army was subdued by Mackay's at Dunkeld on August 21.[17]

For months thereafter, there were disputes over the constitutional settlement, and William told Halifax, "The Scotchmen by their severall stories distracted his mind more than anything."[18] But William was effectively king of Scotland though he never went there, and the Church of Scotland never again had bishops. The constitutional issues were rendered moot by the Act of Union of 1707, which united England and Scotland into one kingdom but preserved Scottish law and the Presbyterian Kirk, while giving the Scotch seats in the English Parliament.[19]

Opposition to the Protestant monarch still smoldered in the Highlands, and the Highlands would rise in the Jacobite cause when James II's son, the Old Pretender, landed in 1715 and his grandson, the Young Pretender, landed in 1745. But those rebellions were defeated militarily, and Scotland, poor almost to the point of starvation and riven by sectarian religious struggles in the seventeenth century, contributed more than its share to the British Enlightenment in the eighteenth century, the industrial revolution in the eighteenth and nineteenth centuries, and British military forces and colonial settlers and administrators in the nineteenth and twentieth.

Ireland posed greater problems. William initially considered appeasing Tyrconnel, whose mostly Catholic army was the only serious military force on the island; in February 1689 he considered offering Tyrconnel toleration of Catholicism in return for submission.[20] But neither Tyrconnel nor the English Parliament were inclined to agree, and events forced their hands. James left St. Germain on February 15 for Ireland, and Admiral Herbert was unable to stop his French fleet.[21] His arrival, with French arms and advisers, became known in England in mid-March.[22] Protestants fled, and in the far north crowded into the fortresses of Enniskillen and Londonderry, where thirteen apprentice boys refused to allow the Catholic army in the gates in December 1688.[23]

James's arrival blocked any peaceful settlement between William and Tyrconnel. James proceeded to summon an Irish Parliament, the first since 1666, to meet in May 1689. Thanks to Tyrconnel's remodeling of borough charters and purges, almost all of its members were Catholics; there were fewer than a dozen Protestants in the 230-member House of Commons, and only a few Protestant peers and Church of Ireland bishops in the House of Lords. With some reluctance James acceded to a land act that undid the Cromwellian settlement and turned over many lands to Catholics; the Parliament also outlawed those who had fled to England or were fighting for William in the north. But James vetoed a repeal of Poynings' Law, which required acts of the Irish Parliament to be approved by the English Privy Council, and barred the establishment of the Catholic Church; though he was trying to please his Irish followers, he still had an eye on opinion in England.

The actions of the Irish Parliament and Tyrconnel's success in Catholicizing the Irish government naturally antagonized Irish Protestants, especially the Presbyterians in the north.[24] At the same time, Irish Protestants started distinguishing between England's interests and their own. Both Presbyterians and Church of Ireland adherents were, writes the historian D. W. Hayton, "more deeply alienated from each other, more militant in their demands, and more sharply aware of their own separate interests."[25]

For William, Ireland was a sideshow, a diversion from the all-important war raging on the Continent. But he could not ignore James and his French forces. In Westminster, Parliament was seething at the Protestant reverses in Ireland and fearful of the French troops there. On June 1 the Commons, exerting its prerogatives over the executive, investigated the conduct of the government in Ireland.[26] William sent ships, and on July 28 the boom, or barrier, at Lough Foyle was broken and Londonderry, in the far northeast, was relieved. On July 30 the Protestant men of Enniskillen beat the Irish Catholic forces at Newton Butler in the north. By mid-August, William's generals Friedrich Schomberg and Godert de Ginkel and some 7,000 troops landed nearby in County Down. But the Commons were not pleased at the course of the war: in November the House set up two committees headed by Whigs to investigate the conduct of the war in Ireland.[27] Parliament was supporting, pretty generously with declarations and more grudgingly with money, William's wars. But members were demanding superintending powers as well. William, intent on war, was prepared to allow this, and to accede to some of their demands. He wanted to go to the Netherlands in December 1689, but Shrewsbury and Carmarthen insisted that he not do so. Then he planned to go to Ireland, and to fight James's forces there; when the House of Lords threatened to prevent him from doing so, he prorogued and then dissolved Parliament.[28]

Once Parliament was dissolved, William assembled his forces—34,560 foot and 9,300 horse, considerably larger than James's army of 25,000 and, with experienced Dutch and German forces, more experienced and competent. It was the first time in his military career that he entered a campaign with superior numbers.[29] He set out from London on June 4/14, leaving the inexperienced and politically naïve queen in charge. He was cheered by crowds on his three-day march to Chester. After a rough crossing, he landed at Carrickfergus and proceeded to nearby Belfast. Schomberg, previously in charge, had avoided battle with James's forces; William was determined to fight.

On June 19/29 he marched south toward Dublin, past the current border of Northern Ireland and the Irish Republic, and on June 30/July 10 found the Irish and French armies a mile south of the River Boyne and a mile west of the port of Drogheda. William inspected his troops north of the river, in open view of the enemy, and a cannonball grazed his right shoulder blade, tearing away his coat, vest, and shirt. He rose a little in his stirrups and said, "It was as well it came no nearer." After dining, he rode up and down the entire line, waving his hat with his right arm to show it was not injured. The next day, July 1/11, came the battle. Count Meinhard Schomberg, the duke's son, led a diversion on the enemy's flank, and the Dutch Blue Guards crossed the river at the central ford, braved two charges by the enemy's cavalry, and stood their ground. Then William rode across the river with his cavalry to lead the Guards up the hill and capture the enemy's cannons. A few enemy troops got across the river and killed the elderly Duke of Schomberg. But they were wiped out, and the

Irish troops threw away their weapons and fled; only the French re-tired in good order. King James, observing the rout, retired quickly and headed to Dublin, where he went on board the French fleet, head-ing once again to exile.[30]

This was not the end of the Irish campaign, but it was a decisive victory. William marched west and laid siege to Limerick, but the at-tack was broken by Irish troops led by Patrick Sarsfield, and William's army was bogged down by heavy rains. William decided to leave the task of eliminating the Irish army to his generals. He approved Marlborough's proposal that he sail with 4,900 troops to Cork and Kinsale, on the south coast of Ireland, then went overland to Water-ford, from which he sailed to Bristol and reached Kensington Palace September 10, in substantial control of the kingdoms of England, Scotland, and Ireland.

Marlborough sailed from Portsmouth on September 17 and, in a brilliant military action, captured the garrison of Cork on Septem-ber 27 and the town of Kinsale September 28; after a siege, the Irish forces at the New Fort of Kinsale, on high land overlooking the har-bor, surrendered on October 15.[31] That effectively prevented the French from aiding the remaining Irish forces. Marlborough returned to London, and the Dutch general Ginkel, in command of the main forces, took Athlone and Aughrim and laid siege to Limerick in the summer of 1691.[32] At Limerick, Ginkel made a treaty with the remain-ing Irish forces under Patrick Sarsfield. Freedom of worship was guar-anteed to Catholics, they were given some concessions on property rights, and Irish soldiers were allowed to go to France; 12,000 of 15,000 did so, and were known afterwards as the "wild geese."[33]

In 1692, William summoned an Irish Parliament, entirely Protes-tant, but it hectored his lord lieutenant and refused to raise revenues. Lord Capel, appointed lord lieutenant in 1695, cooperated with these critics, and a rash of anti-Catholic legislation followed. All the acts of James's 1689 Parliament were repealed. In 1695 the Parliament or-dered the disarming of Catholics and banned the practice of sending children abroad (for a Catholic education). In 1697 the Catholic bish-ops were banished. The Irish Parliament refused to ratify the Treaty of Limerick, and instead omitted the provision allowing freedom of worship; more confiscations of lands followed, to the point that only 14 percent of land was held by Catholics. Catholics were barred from public office and the professions.[34]

The revolutionary settlement that followed the English triumph in Ireland has been seen as the source of Irish troubles in the succeeding three centuries. As the historian R. F. Foster wrote in the 1980s, "The uniqueness of Irish development from that time to this owes everything to the fundamental and protracted revolution of the seventeenth century."[35] While William's first impulse was to placate Irish Catholics, their alliance with the French meant that William was bound to see Ireland as a possible launching pad for an enemy attack and to regard Irish Catholics, the large majority of the population, as potential aiders and comforters of the enemy—an enemy bent on imposing what the English regarded as popish tyranny on their own island. So William and the English Parliament were content with the Irish Parliament's assertion of Protestant authority and its maintenance of the Cromwellian and Restoration land settlements that had granted the minority Protestants almost all the land in Ireland.[36]

The potential of a French assault on Britain through Ireland remained, and became reality in 1798 when revolutionary France landed an army in Ireland in the aid of Irish rebellion, a rebellion not of Catholics, but one led by Protestants of the landowning class. It resulted in the Act of Union of 1801, which abolished the Irish Parliament and gave Ireland representation in Westminster, but kept in force trade restrictions that helped to hobble the Irish economy and were among the reasons that Ireland, half as populous as England and in some regions almost as prosperous at the turn of the nineteenth century, failed to share in the extraordinary economic growth of Britain over the next hundred years. Instead it suffered the demographic disaster of the potato famine of the 1840s, which, together with mass migration to America and other places, reduced Ireland's population from more than 8 million in 1841 to less than 4 million in 1901.

All of which is to say that the events of 1688–91 constituted just one of many episodes in Irish history that have left an unhappy imprint on that now prosperous and mostly peaceful island. Where those events are remembered most vividly is in the six counties of Northern Ireland. Already by 1688 it was settled by Scots Presbyterians who outnumbered the native Catholics. The Northern Irish Protestants still remember the horrors of the siege of Londonderry and still celebrate with Orange Order marches the glorious victory at the Battle of the Boyne every July 11. Marchers carry banners with pictures of King Billy, remembered as a hero here as he is nowhere else in the world.[37] And at the site of the battle, in the Irish Republic, he is remembered as well; as part of the peace negotiations of the 1990s, the government of the republic agreed to make a living-history memorial at the battle site, and tourists can watch Irish men and women, of whatever religion, dressed in seventeenth-century uniforms, set off seventeenth-century guns and cannons where they were deployed with such decisive effect more than three hundred years ago, and step on the same soil that King William III and King James II trod, where one came within inches of losing his life and the other lost his last remaining kingdom.

THE BOYNE WAS not King William's last battle. After James's flight, he was happy to leave the command there to Marlborough and Ginkel, and he shifted his focus to the war on the Continent. He traveled there for extended periods during the military campaigning season. He was in the Netherlands from January to October 1691, and again from March to September 1692, March to October 1693, May to October 1694, May to October 1695, May to October 1696, April to November 1697. Thus for seven years of his reign William was out of England more than he was in it. Only with the signing of the Treaty of Rijswick in September 1697, ending the war with France, did these military sojourns end. During their course William suffered defeats — at Mons in April 1691, Namur in 1692, Landan and Huy in July 1693, Charleroi in October 1693; endured stalemate — at Steenkirk in August 1692; and won victories — at Huy in September 1694 and, decisively, Namur in August 1695.[38] All this naturally cost huge sums of money. James II's peacetime revenues had amounted to £2,000,000 in 1688, enough to conduct the business of government and maintain a standing army of 40,000 in England. But William and his allies were employing far larger forces abroad, at enormous cost, up to 68,000 troops in Flanders in 1694 (20,000 of them hired mercenaries); by 1697 the English were paying for 75,000 troops and 323 ships with 40,000 men. English remittances to support these troops amounted to £795,000 in 1690, £557,000 in 1691, £788,000 in 1692, £876,000 in 1693, £1,358,000 in 1694, £1,238,000 in 1695, £1,041,000 in 1696, and £706,000 in 1697. From 1694 to 1697 the Crown borrowed another £400,000 abroad.[39] The government's income rose to £5 million by the middle 1690s; expenditure rose from £2 million in James's last year to £8 million in 1696.[40] The customs and excise rates were increased and a new land tax imposed, and the government borrowed as much as £3.3 million in 1696. James's government had employed some 4,000 civil servants; William's employed 12,000.[41] In the course of fighting his wars, William had to — or, more accurately, managed to persuade Parliament to — construct what historian Dale Hoak calls "a tax-collecting British Leviathan — a permanently armed, bureaucratic, imperial monarchy."[42]

He did so with the active cooperation of Parliament. As we have seen, Parliament refused to vote William revenues for life, and declined to extend the customs duties for more than three years. But William patiently waited for Parliament to vote more, urging members to support the war against Louis XIV both to advance "the Protestant interest"and to support the large number of states of Europe, many of them Catholic, which had leagued together to contain the French. Once again William made skillful use of propaganda, from anonymous pamphlets to sermons by sympathetic ministers, arguing that this was a war to protect and advance Protestantism, even while making different points to his allies abroad.[43] The war was widely popular and questioned by few inside or outside Parliament.

⁂

THE TAXES PARLIAMENT voted drew on English experience. The excises had been good revenue producers for Charles II and James II as trade increased; the rates were raised on salt, beer, tobacco, wine, spirits, tea, coaches, and coffee. A land tax had been imposed as long before as the 1640s, and though it may seem strange that a Parliament made up almost entirely of landed gentry and peers would choose to tax the major source of their own wealth, the sting was alleviated by the fact that assessments were controlled by local authorities, which is to say local landed gentlemen, who were left to determine how to achieve the total revenues as determined by the Commons; in time this land tax, at 1 shilling to 4 shillings to the pound, produced a reliable income stream of 39 percent of government income from 1689 to 1700, as compared with 24 percent from the customs and 26 percent from the excise.[44] William left it to Parliament to make these decisions and took the unusual step, as early as June 1689, to invite Parliament to examine government accounts, an invitation that the astonished Commons did not take up until it was renewed four months later. William supported a nine-member Commission on Public Accounts, which, after some legislative manuevering, was finally set up in January 1691. "William," writes Tony Claydon, "should therefore receive much of the credit for establishing the modern annual cycle of parliamentary budget setting, and financial scrutiny."[45]

William's deference to Parliament was surely influenced by his experience of advancing his policies dexterously through the complex political system of the United Provinces, with the difference that he had more support from the City of London than he usually had from the burghers of Amsterdam. If absolutism was the preferred mode of Louis XIV and seemed to be the model for James II, William's experience had come in a small country where people tolerated very high taxation and a huge military establishment because they believed those were necessary means to protect their liberties and because they were put into effect only by vote of representative assemblies.[46]

THE DUTCH EXAMPLE also seems to have been an inspiration to English parliamentarians. As the war went on year after year, it was apparent that revenues were not sufficient to pay for it; borrowing was necessary. England under Charles II and James II had to pay interest of 10 to 15 percent on loans, because of the risk of default, like Charles's Stop of the Exchequer in 1672. The Dutch, with better credit and through the mechanism of the Bank of Amsterdam, were able to borrow at 4 to 6 percent . In 1693, Parliament, drawing on Dutch practice, raised money by paying annuities of 14 percent a year, to be paid by an increase in excises on beer and vinegar.[47] It also authorized a £1-million tontine, in which subscribers could get a return of 10 percent a year if a named person survived until 1700, and then an increasing share of some £70,000 divided among survivors over the next 99 years: this was England's first funded national debt.[48] In March 1694, Parliament authorized a lottery, with 100,000 tickets at the steep price of £10 per ticket (many buyers sold fractional shares); winning tickets would pay at least £1 a year for 16 years and as much as £1,000, all financed by salt and liquor duties.[49]

Others proposed a bank. In January 1692 the House of Commons considered proposals "that a public bank might be established for taking up money" and "for raising a Sum of Money towards the carrying on of the war against France upon a Fund of perpetual Interest."[50] The operations of the Bank of Amsterdam, established in 1609, were well known; other banks had been founded in Barcelona (1609), Middleburg (1616), Hamburg (1619), Delft (1621), Nuremberg (1621), Rotterdam (1635), and Sweden (1656; in 1661 this became the first chartered bank to issue notes).[51] The plan finally adopted is often credited to William Paterson, a Scots-born English London merchant, who first called for raising £1 million for a "yearly rent" (a translation of the Dutch *jaarlike rente*) of £65,000, with £5,000 to pay for administration, but the parliamentary committee rejected his plan out of dislike of the provision allowing the bills to be legal currency.[52]

In April 1694, still seeking means of raising loans (the annuities and lottery were popular, but the tontine brought in less than expected), Paterson and a London merchant, Michael Godfrey, brought forward another proposal for a Bank of England, with the help of Treasury Commissioner (and, from May 1694, Chancellor of the Exchequer) Charles Montagu.[53] The act provided for £140,000 from taxes on shipping and liquor to be used to repay subscribers on a £1,200,000 loan at 8 percent, to pay £4,000 a year in management fees and to service £300,000 of annuities. In effect the Bank of England was given a monopoly of government borrowing, and investors ("subscribers") were guaranteed 8 percent in interest.[54]

The subscription period opened on June 21 and, with the king and queen both quickly subscribing (and John Locke as well)[55] the £1,200,000 was raised by July 2, and on July 27 the bank charter was sealed in Lord Somers's residence (confiscated from a supporter of James) in Lincoln's Inn Fields, and the bank went into business in the headquarters of the Grocers' livery company in the City of London. The bank issued paper £100 notes to the Exchequer and also issued paper notes in amounts from £5 to £100 to depositors, thus creating a form of circulating paper money—an immense boon when England's silver coins were being clipped and the cut-off silver melted down and sold. The bank also advanced cash to the government over and above its original loan, and remitted funds to British forces in Flanders. The Dutch played a key role in the establishment of the bank: Dutch investors were among the initial subscribers and also loaned money to the bank for operations.[56]

"The first measures to create a system of government long-term borrowing were thus marked by haste, carelessness, and episodic failure," writes the historian P. G. M. Dickson.[57] The Treasury bureaucracy was not sophisticated enough to bring forward proposals, which came from London merchants like Paterson and Godfrey, who drew on the example of the Bank of Amsterdam, and Thomas Neale, whose lottery proposal was based on the lottery in Venice.[58] As Dickson notes, "Some valuable lessons had been learned: about the connections between long- and short-term finance, about consultation with the City of London, about the importance of foreign confidence in sterling, about the relative popularity of different kinds of loans. Above all, a national bank had been established which quickly showed that in the quality of management it could challenge comparison with the Bank of Amsterdam, hitherto the cynosure of European eyes. It provided a point of growing importance around which the developing machine of government finance could turn."[59]

In effect, the Bank of England created a bond market, providing safe investment at reliable rates for investors and providing the government with a ready source of funds at low rates.[60] It also systematized over several years the national debt.[61] Over the long run, through the continental and world wars of the 1690s and the long eighteenth century until Waterloo, Britain had a huge financial advantage over much larger and arguably wealthier France, because its government could borrow at much lower rates, thanks to the Bank of England. The bank facilitated that borrowing and provided a ready source of currency, and the representative Parliament, which levied the taxes that provided reliable interest payments: institutions that got their beginnings in the arrangements that Parliament devised to finance the wars of William III.[62]

The creation of the funded national debt and the foundation of the Bank of England left William, unlike his uncles Charles and James, forced to summon Parliament every year in order to raise money for his wars. That in turn gave Parliament the opportunity to put flesh on the bare words of the Heads of Grievances calling for "frequent sitting" of parliaments. In 1693 and 1694 there were moves to bar members from taking office under the Crown on the grounds that it gave the king too much influence in the Commons. These failed, but in December 1694, Parliament passed and forced William to sign the Triennial Act, limiting every Parliament to three years. It still left the king the powers of proroguing and dissolving Parliament, but a king with William's financial needs was not likely to use them much.[63]

Further limits on the monarch were made in the Act of Settlement in 1701. William and Mary had no children, and Mary died of smallpox in December 1694, at age 32; Anne's longest-surviving child, the Duke of Gloucester, died in 1700. Parliament was determined that William and Anne should have a Protestant successor, and the Act of Succession decreed that it should be Sophia, Electress of Hanover, and her heirs. By hereditary principles, Sophia was at the time only the 21st person in line for the throne, but all those ahead of her were Catholics. The Act of Settlement also required that the monarch be a communicating member of the Church of England, and it added two provisions suggested by the Heads of Grievances: that judges should hold office on good behavior after William's and Anne's reigns (William and Anne in fact never removed a judge, as Charles and James had often done); and that royal pardons could not be a defense to impeachment in the House of Commons.[64] The king still had substantial powers — he could conduct foreign policy, command the army and navy, choose his ministers and their subordinates, limit sessions of Parliament. But he did not have absolute power. Absolutism still seemed on the march in France and in many kingdoms and principalities in Europe. But not in England. A monarch who, like William and Anne and most of their successors, was determined to tip the balance of power against a hegemonic tyrant that threatened to dominate Europe and the world had, of necessity, to depend on cooperation from Parliament.

All these developments had lasting importance. This military revolution and financial revolution created, J. G. A. Pocock writes, a *novus ordo seclorum,* "which formed no part of the intentions of the community of political actors in 1688–89 and took a number of years to emerge."[65] This new order was created in order to carry on the war that William had invaded England to involve her in. In the process, William and Parliament created England's first modern bureaucratic state and, in creating the Bank of England, created the financial institution that was not only "an engine of public credit enabling the British to generate sufficient cash during the next century to defeat a far richer French adversary,"[66] but also fostered the growth of the private sector economy and provided unprecedented scope for entrepreneurship. Parliament gained de facto control of the royal army and navy, and control of the purse, even as the private sector gained permanent influence over the state through the bond market.[67] These were all vital preconditions for the extraordinary growth of the British economy over the next centuries and for Britain's emergence as a great power in the world.

For it was William III who made England for the first time a world power. The Tudors and Stuarts tended, with varied success, to the affairs of their island kingdoms. Only occasionally did they intervene in European wars, and then only with small numbers of troops and usually with dismal results. Their one lunge toward world power was the expansion of the navy, started by Charles I and financed by his resented ship money in the 1630s, expanded by Cromwell in the 1650s, then carried on by James, Duke of York, the Earl of Sandwich, and the civil servant Samuel Pepys in the 1660s and after. This was what the politicians of the eighteenth century would call a blue-water policy: defend English merchants on the sea and interpose the Royal Navy in the Channel against any invaders.

William had a different strategy, a strategy of opposing the hegemonic tyrant of his time who threatened to dominate all Europe and whose power spread over much of the world. More than anyone else, William engineered the alliance that opposed Louis in 1689 and the years after, and his conduct of his invasion of England enabled him to bring England smoothly into its ranks. His England would be not just an island power, but a continental and a world power. And so it turned out to be.

Chapter 10

REVOLUTIONARY REVERBERATIONS

THE REVOLUTION OF 1688–89 has long been called an English revolution, and recent British historians have taken pains to describe it as a British revolution, which took place in different ways and with different consequences in Scotland and Ireland than in England. But this Revolution was even wider in its origins and impact. The Revolution of 1688–89 turned out to have, and today still has, reverberations that sweep around the world.

The Glorious Revolution would not have occurred without the actions of the English King James II, but the driving force behind it, the prime mover, was the stadholder William, Prince of Orange. William was a Dutchman through and through, but he was also a statesman with a continental strategy and colonial interests, and a man who, as J. G. A. Pocock reminds us, was "prince of Orange, *prince d'Orange,* prince of Nassau, stadholder of most of the seven provinces, captain general of the united Netherlands, king of England and Ireland, king of Scots."[1] He kept his eye on all of Europe, and beyond. He would never have left the Netherlands in 1688 had not the King of Poland defeated the Turks at the gates of Vienna five years before and the Holy Roman Emperor's forces conquered the Hungarian plain by 1687, leaving them free to tie down Louis XIV in 1688: the catastrophe for Islam at one end of Europe was a necessary condition for the triumph of Protestantism in the British Isles.

The Revolutionary settlement worked out by William III and Parliament transformed England and Britain in many ways, and made it a very different country than it would have been had James II remained on the throne and if he had been succeeded on his death in 1701 by James Edward.[2] (James Edward lived on until 1766, and had he been king, his reign would have been longer than Queen Victoria's.) James might have gotten a Parliament that would agree to repeal the Test Acts and the penal laws, and with an adequate revenue, he would not have had to summon another Parliament except in the unlikely event he decided to go to war against France. The funded debt and the Bank of England would not have come into being, at least not in the way they did. Though James had long taken a serious interest in promoting trade and in the North American colonies, he wanted them governed his way, by direct royal authority and, if possible, without representative assemblies.

To be sure, even after William III was installed as King, the success of his Revolution was still contingent. Just as his successful invasion was, in Pocock's words, "far more improbable, and far less foreseeable, than any of the alternative scenarios,"[3] so it was very far from inevitable that the Revolutionary settlement would stay in place. William III was unpopular for most of his reign, and far from secure. The Duke of Berwick organized an assassination plot against him that came near to succeeding in February 1696; William's reaction when told that the assassins had planned to shoot him in his carriage was characteristically cool, and characteristically stated in French: *"Les pauvres glaces de mon carosse auroient esté bien maltraittés"* (the poor windows of my carriage would have been very badly treated).[4] In 1697, after the Peace of Rijswick, Parliament forced him to reduce his standing army,[5] and in 1701 some of his ministers were, briefly and ineffectively, impeached.[6] His death in March 1702 was not followed by widespread mourning. But he had already persuaded the English to join the alliance against Louis XIV in what became the War of Spanish Succession, a conflict in which Britain's leading diplomat and its most astonishingly successful general was John Churchill, by then Duke of Marlborough.[7]

Even so, Jacobitism—the belief that James and then his son

should be on the throne—had many followers in England for many years thereafter. Linda Colley argues persuasively that Tories had many more supporters than did Whigs in the elections during the reign of Queen Anne,[8] and many Tories schemed in the last years of Anne's life to have her followed by James Edward rather than by George Ludwig of Hanover. The Jacobite rebellions of 1715 and 1745, the first led by James Edward and the second by his son, long remembered as Bonnie Prince Charlie, came closer to success than is generally realized. Those rebellions had more supporters than were willing to come forward after their failures. The historian J. C. D. Clark has argued that Samuel Johnson, the literary critic and lexicographer and an obdurate Tory, may have been a supporter of the '45 rebellion and gone into hiding during it; there is no evidence of his whereabouts at the time.[9] The restoration of the Stuarts remained a lively possibility, and one sought by many in Britain, for more than 50 years after the coronation of William III and Mary II.[10]

⁂

BUT THE REVOLUTIONARY settlement did endure. It changed England from a nation in which representative government was threatened to one where it was ingrained, from a nation in which liberties were based on tradition to one where they were based in part on positive law, from a nation where the place of religion was a matter of continued political dispute and even armed struggle to one where it became settled in a way that generally respected individual choice, from a nation that mostly kept apart from the wars of continental Europe to one that saw its duty as maintaining a balance of power there and around the world. These were momentous changes—momentous not just for England and Britain, but for the American colonies and later the United States and the entire world. It was the English and British example of representative government that inspired the Founding Fathers of the United States of America and was copied, with minor variations, in British colonies, many of which have become major nations—Canada, Australia, New Zealand, India. This improbable revolution did much to shape the world in which we live today.

First, and most visibly, the Revolution of 1688–89 perpetuated and strengthened representative government in England, Scotland, and Ireland, and in the North American colonies as well. By the 1680s representative assemblies seemed to be relics of a feudal past in most of Europe, set aside by absolutist monarchs, allowed sometimes to maintain a formal existence without the capacity to exert power like the Roman Senate after Augustus. That trend, toward absolutism and away from representative assemblies, seemed to be operating in England and the colonies through most of the 1680s as well.[11] The repeated dissolution of Parliament by Charles II and James II was just part of a program of absolutism. James "did attempt to make royal authority in England absolute," W. A. Speck writes, through "the growth of the army, the rigging of the judiciary, the professionalization of the major institutions of the state, and the attack on local autonomy"—processes begun during Charles II's reign and carried on during most of James's.[12] William's *Declaration* was a pledge to reverse this process, and its principal demand was for a "free parliament," one in which the members of the House of Commons were chosen without the guiding hand of the king. William was taking a resolute stand against the trend to downgrade representative assemblies in England and throughout Europe.

William's detractors past and present may scoff that he did so only to get England to fight France. But the important facts are that he did so and that his successors felt obliged to follow his example. His experience in the Netherlands taught him that to achieve his goals he must be seen to comply with national and local custom and precedent, and with the various representative assemblies of the Dutch Republic. Just as he waited in the Netherlands to be offered the offices of captain-general and stadholder, so in England he carefully and ostentatiously abstained from influencing the elections for the Convention Parliament. He let the Commons and the Lords deliberate—until, in a meeting so private that its date remains uncertain, he jogged them into reaching the decision he desired. He understood that he could not lead England into war except by governing through Parliament, as distasteful and frustrating as he found that to be. His invasion and his acceptance by the English made war with France inevitable, even welcome, to the English. But his need for revenue to wage that war forced him and his successors to rely on annual parliaments.[13] Parliament has met every year since 1689.

And so the Revolution of 1688–89 was a giant step forward for representative government. William not only depended on Parliament to provide revenue; he also accepted and on occasion welcomed its investigations into the administration of government. He accepted grudgingly the Triennial Act, which required parliamentary elections every three years; it was replaced by the Septennial Act in 1716, requiring elections only every seven years. Neither William nor any of his successors as monarch attempted to influence elections to the House of Commons quite as directly as Charles II and James II did. By the time of Queen Victoria, it had been established that a government must fall, even against the monarch's wishes, if it could not command a majority in the House of Commons. Thus, Britain's representative government, greatly strengthened by the Revolution of 1688–89, eventually became a representative democracy.

Our founding fathers' deliberate creation of a representative government, which quickly became a representative democracy, also owes much to the Revolution of 1688–89. That Revolution reversed James II's policy of eliminating many independent representative assemblies and subjecting them to royal control.[14] In New England and New York and New Jersey he imposed a Dominion of New England that eliminated the colonial representative assemblies, and in the colonies farther south — Maryland, Virginia, Carolina — he sought to strengthen royal control. After the Revolution of 1688–89 most colonies still had royal governors, but they all had independent representative assemblies. The Revolutionary settlement established the cockpit of colonial politics, of royal governors in tension with or opposition to representative assemblies — the institutional setting from which the American Revolution would arise. In contrast, the Spanish colonies in Latin America never had representative assemblies — one reason, historian J. H. Elliott argues, that they were slow to gain independence and had difficulty setting stable and workable governments afterward.[15]

The Revolutionary settlement also provided a template for the colonial rebels. Its guarantees of representative government and individual rights to Englishmen were taken by the colonials as promises to them — promises that they came to believe had been broken. "The executive branches of government," writes the historian Bernard Bailyn, describing the pamphlet literature in the years that led to the American Revolution, "held, and used, powers that in England had been stripped from the crown in the settlement that had followed the Glorious Revolution."[16] The Revolutionary settlement was seen as guaranteeing parliamentary sovereignty, which is to say representative government.[17] Thus the Massachusetts lawyer James Otis wrote that the Glorious Revolution created "that happy establishment which Great Britain has since enjoyed."[18] Boston minister Jonathan Mayhew charged that George III's ministers, "not improbably in the interests of the houses of Bourbon and the Pretender [Charles Edward]," was trying to reverse the consequences of the Revolution.[19] Challenged by a parishioner, Mayhew defended a sermon as being "composed in a high strain of liberty, tho' I humbly conceive not higher than is warranted by the principles of the Glorious Revolution."[20] Pennsylvanians howled when the Crown vetoed a law passed by their assembly establishing life tenure for judges, established in England by the final law of the Revolutionary settlement, the Act of Settlement of 1701.[21] "Most of the ideas and beliefs that shaped the American Revolutionary mind," Bailyn concludes, "can be found in the voluminous writings of the Exclusion Crisis and in the literature of the Glorious Revolution that in effect brought that upheaval to a peaceful conclusion."[22]

Americans were thus not rebelling against the Revolutionary settlement. They were seeking to preserve in their own states what they believed the Revolution of 1688–89 had established.

THE REVOLUTION OF 1688–89 turned out to be a bold step forward also for guaranteed liberties. The right to bear arms asserted in the Bill of Rights was very different from the obligation to bear arms asserted earlier in the seventeenth century. The obligation to bear arms was part of a duty of the subject to support the king and his government. The right to bear arms was a way for the freeman to protect his property and his liberty. The wording of the Bill of Rights was carried over almost exactly by George Mason in his Declaration of Rights in Virginia in 1776 and was the inspiration for the wording of the Second Amendment, adopted by the First Congress and ratified by the states in 1790.[23]

Other provisions of the 1689 Bill of Rights were inspirations for the 1791 American Bill of Rights: the Third Amendment provision banning the quartering of troops, the Fourth Amendment ban on unreasonable searches and seizures, the Fifth Amendment protection against self-incrimination, the Sixth Amendment right to jury trial and its guarantee that indictments could only issue from grand juries (remember that a grand jury had famously refused to indict the Earl of Shaftesbury in 1682), the Eighth Amendment prohibition of cruel and unusual punishments.[24] The 1689 Bill of Rights was from our point of view a limited and grudging document: nothing about freedom of religion, freedom of expression, freedom of the press. It did not prohibit the king from appointing judges or removing them at pleasure, as Charles II and James II had done; but the Act of Succession of 1701 did prohibit monarchs after 1714 from doing so, and William and Anne never did.[25] Yet as an affirmative statement of individual rights, however limited, the Bill of Rights broke new ground, ground that would be extended in the New World.

❧

The Revolutionary settlement was also a step forward for religious liberty. To our eyes the Toleration Act seems a very limited advance. Old laws against Catholics remained in force, and public office was limited to members of the Church of England. Dissenting worship, by believers in the Trinity, was allowed but disfavored. The extent of legal religious toleration in William III's kingdom of England was less than in stadholder William III's United Provinces of the Netherlands. But the Toleration Act, combined with the rejection of comprehension by the divines of the Church of England (allowing a wider range of beliefs in the established Church), encouraged widespread Protestant worship in many forms. In other words, by not letting Presbyterians and Dissenters in the Church, but tolerating their worship outside the Church, the result was several Protestant denominations.

Anglicanism, rather than achieving the religious monopoly its leaders had sought through most of the seventeenth century, found itself open to competition in a spiritual marketplace. Membership in Dissenting churches no longer carried civil penalties, and public office was even left open to Dissenters who took the trouble to qualify by the simple means of occasional conformity. Enthusiasts for the Church of England responded by passing the occasional conformity law during Anne's reign, which gave the Established Church a tighter grip on the population and a more preferred place in public life; it was repealed three years into the reign of her successor George I.[26]

The effect of the Toleration Act, writes Diarmaid MacCulloch, the preeminent chronicler of the Reformation in our time, was a step toward allowing Christians of different denominations to live together in the same nation and a rejection of the idea that the Church of England should have a monopoly of worship in the land. This was very different from the Calvinist domination of Protestantism in the Netherlands or the monopoly the established Lutheran churches held in Scandinavia. The result was that "several different faces of British Protestantism were each destined to give rise to worldwide families of Churches. Moreover, the centre of gravity in these bodies other than Anglicanism was destined to move from the Atlantic Isles to the western seaboard of the ocean, to the new English-speaking colonies of America."[27]

Religious competition and pluralism flowered most in the North American colonies, where Dissenting churches were established in Massachusetts, Connecticut, and New Hampshire. Anglicanism was established only weakly in New York, Maryland, Virginia, and Carolina (though in Virginia the established Anglican church was able to enforce some measure of uniformity) and a melange of churches and sects thrived in colonies with no religious establishments—Rhode Island, Pennsylvania, Delaware, and New Jersey. Methodism, a new evangelical movement that arose within the Established Church in England, became a separate denomination, and the fastest growing one in the young American republic.[28] In practice, toleration reigned.[29] All this stood in stark contrast to the enforced religious uniformity of France and most of the German states—and very much closer to the regime of tolerance in William of Orange's Netherlands.

THE REVOLUTION OF 1688–89 also had profound economic reverberations. In 1650, Amsterdam was the world's leading center of finance and trade, but a century later London was, in the words of P. G. M. Dickson, "the leading world centre of foreign trade, dealings in jewels and gold, provision of insurance cover, and the flotation of public loans."[30] The Revolution—or, rather, the financial innovations that followed the Revolution—accounted for much of the change.

It is true that some factors were already in play before 1688; London was already a strong rival of Amsterdam. And it was not part of William of Orange's purpose in invading to displace Amsterdam in favor of London. Still, William might have been ambivalent on that point. Amsterdam had long been the chief source of opposition to his plans in the Dutch Republic, and was only enlisted in support of his expedition to England at the last minute—and was only disposed to help because of French protectionism and threats of war. The merchants of London, in contrast, tended to welcome his invasion.

And it was the merchants of London, working with members of Parliament, who devised the financial expedients needed to finance William's war with France. The creation of the national debt in 1693, regularized later by the sinking fund, and of the Bank of England in 1694 gave London and England financial institutions that closely resembled those of Amsterdam and the Dutch Republic. Those institutions had enabled the Dutch to punch above their weight in war and diplomacy in the seventeenth century, and the Bank of England did the same for England and Britain in the eighteenth.[31] As J. H. Plumb writes, "The Recoinage [of 1696], the foundation of the Bank, and above all the establishment of the Sinking Fund, gave a strength to England's financial system unmatched by any other European country except Holland—a fact rapidly appreciated by the Dutch who invested heavily in both the Bank and the Funds."[32] Or, as P. G. M. Dickson writes, "The newly aggressive and dynamic English monarchy became, in effect, an eighteenth-century version of the seventeenth-century Dutch Republic, with its powerful fleet, numerous army, extended credit, and sophisticated indirect taxation."[33]

The financial arrangements put in place after the Revolution increased the political leverage of London's financial community, which in turn helped to create something like a religious balance of power. If Parliament was made up primarily of landed nobles and gentry, almost all members of the Church of England, the financial community of London was made up of merchants and tradesmen, a large percentage of them Dissenting Protestants; by one account, Dissenters made up 36 percent of colonial merchants, 43 percent of Bank of England directors, 30 percent of United East India Company directors, and between 11 and 18 percent of subscribers to new financial and trading companies in the 1690s.[34] And it was merchants and businessmen more than rural gentry who invested in the national debt. The landed and Anglican interests may have had a monopoly of formal political power in Westminster, but in order to finance the state they had to pay heed — and certainly could not afford to oppress — the mercantile and Dissenting interests so busy two or three miles down the Thames in the City of London.

The national debt gave Englishmen a readily liquid financial security in which they could invest and disinvest, and accumulate capital that could be and was put to other uses — to the creation of insurance offices, partnership banks, trading companies, and, in time, agricultural improvements and industrial factories.[35] "Delay in the emergence of the City as a financial centre," writes Dickson, "would, like failure to hold existing overseas markets and win new ones, have put back England's industrialization, and thus changed the course of European history."[36] "The great British Empire, the most flourishing and opulent country in the world," exulted Daniel Defoe in the early eighteenth century: "no clothes can be made to fit a growing child."[37]

Nowhere in the English-speaking world was the growth more exuberant than in the North American colonies, whose population quintupled between 1675 and 1740.[38] James II had long been interested in the North American and Caribbean colonies. Had he remained king after 1688, he undoubtedly would have encouraged the economic development and exploitation of the colonies, and they might have developed economically as they did in the eighteenth century, but certainly not politically. James had been abolishing representative assemblies and consolidating the northern colonies, with a view toward making them impervious to French conquest. Also, the Stuart regime most likely would not have waged continuous wars with France in North America, as the English governments after 1689 did. They would probably have left France solidly in possession of Quebec and with a network of fur traders and Indian agents in the Great Lakes basin and the Mississippi Valley. The North American colonies might not have been threatened by war, but they would have had no trans-Appalachian hinterland in which to expand, nor might they have been allowed to trade as widely in the Caribbean and Europe as they did. By the 1740s, some historians argue, the North American colonies were the home of the most affluent people, on average, in the world. That affluence increased after the success of the American Revolution and the adoption of the Constitution. The new United States of America became a prosperous and innovative commercial republic in large part because Alexander Hamilton consciously followed the example of William III's Parliament and got Congress to establish a funded national debt and the first Bank of the United States.[39]

THE FINAL AND most momentous reverberations of the Revolution of 1688–89 were in foreign policy. William came to England determined to yoke the three island kingdoms to *la cause commune,* opposing the hegemonic and tyrannical power of Louis XIV's France. The success of the Revolution of 1688–89 enabled him to do just that. This was an entirely new foreign policy for England. From the end of the Wars of the Roses in the 1470s until 1688, English monarchs concentrated on extending their power in Wales, Ireland, and Scotland, by administrative absorption, conquest, and dynastic liaisons, and remained aloof from Continental conflicts. They were "less active in European wars, less important certainly in the calculations of continental rulers, for the most part reacting to, and on the defensive about, events abroad."[40]

The English acceptance of William as king unavoidably plunged the kingdom into war with France. For William, in his position as stadholder of the Netherlands, opposition to a hegemonic European power, especially France, came naturally. Louis's attack on the Netherlands in 1672 was clearly a threat not just to the interests of the Dutch Republic, but to its existence. William of Orange came to power that year at age 21, fully aware of that threat, and defeating France remained his central purpose for the rest of his life. He worked unflaggingly to enlist in that cause the merchants of Amsterdam, the princes of Germany, the rulers of Spain, and the kingdom of England.

But the English and the Dutch were not in the same position. England, with 5 million people, was not as heavily outnumbered, and its island position off the coast of Europe left it more protected against French attacks — though Ireland, with its smaller population and Catholic majority, was more vulnerable. Charles II and James II had not regarded France as a threat.

But other Englishmen did. The revocation of the Edict of Nantes in 1685 and the prosecution of the *guerre de commerce* in the late 1680s caused many more Englishmen to see France as a threat whose power needed to be restrained. In 1689, English pamphleteers wrote of the need to maintain a balance of power in Europe. A pamphlet titled *A View of the True Interests of the Several States since the Accession of their Present Majesties to the Imperial Crown of Great Britain* stated a theme that eventually became a commonplace: "It is a Maxim of True Policy that whensoever any Prince is exalted too high, and becomes formidable to his Neighbours, the other Princes ought to enter into a League together, to pull him down, or at least hinder him from growing greater."[41] As the historian John Rule writes, "Thus 1688 is not only momentous in the personal life of William of Orange and in the national life of England, but in the international life of Europe, for it marks the birth of a theory and practice of a power balance that has lasted until today."[42]

Maintaining that balance of power and opposing hegemonic tyrants on the continent of Europe became the dominant foreign policy of England and Britain and, in time, of the United States to the present day. The tradition was firmly established in the two decades immediately after the Revolution, through the rule of King William III and, under his successor Queen Anne, by the Duke of Marlborough, John Churchill.

William initially relied primarily on Dutch generals to prosecute his war against France and, after a series of naval and land reverses, won a decisive military victory at Namur in 1695 and negotiated the Treaty of Rijswick with Louis in 1697. That proved only a pause in a long struggle. King Charles I of Spain, long expected to die, finally did so in November 1700, and Louis XIV promptly claimed the Kingdom of Spain, with its extensive holdings in Italy and the Netherlands, the Americas and the Philippines, for his grandson Philip, Duke of Anjou. There followed the War of Spanish Succession (1702–13), undertaken by William and, after his death in 1702, carried on by Queen Anne. William in his last years had shown his favor to Marlborough, and Anne entrusted to him the direction of her armies in Germany and the Netherlands and the conduct of diplomatic and financial negotiations with her European allies. Marlborough won a series of dazzling victories and was only relieved of command in 1711 after the explosive breakup of the long and intimate relationship between his wife and the queen.[43] But the pattern had been set. Despite opposition from some members of Parliament, who wanted Britain to rely on its navy for safety and to avoid wars on the Continent, the belief that Britain must maintain a balance of power against a hegemonic and tyrannical power in Europe became deeply ingrained.

So Britain continued to follow, with some gaps and exceptions, an anti-hegemonic foreign policy in the eighteenth, nineteenth, and twentieth centuries. There were wars against monarchical France in 1739–48, 1754–63, and 1775–83, and against revolutionary and Napoleonic France in 1793–1802 and 1803–15. These were worldwide struggles, with fighting in Europe and on the oceans, in North America and the Caribbean and India. The war of 1754–63 started with the rout of General Braddock's army in western Pennsylvania, with the retreat to safety led by a young Virginia colonel named George Washington. The organizer of victory in London was William Pitt, who urged a strategy of attack on all fronts and solid support of the beleaguered King of Prussia Frederick II. The result was a rousing British victory and the surrender of French Canada.[44] But postwar British policies led to protests and then to revolution in the North American colonies: British defeat, and the emergence of another

English-speaking nation that in time would take Britain's place as the leader in combating hegemonic powers.

Britain's leader in the struggle against revolutionary and Napoleonic France was Pitt's son, William Pitt the Younger, prime minister at 24 and for most of the rest of his life. Pitt the Younger, like William III, fought on despite setbacks on the battlefield and at home. He died in January 1806, a month after Britain's decisive naval victory at Trafalgar, and he left behind as a testament the blueprint Britain persuaded the Continental powers to follow for a long generation after Napoleon's defeat, an alliance of great powers to resist revolution and preserve the peace of Europe and the world. It was a testament that helped to guide British leaders through the rest of the nineteenth century and into the twentieth, a time when several European countries — Britain, France, Russia, Austria-Hungary, Prussia, and then Germany — were undeniable great powers, and Britain served for the most part as the arbiter of peace between them.[45] Prime Minister Lord Palmerston (an Irish peer, and thus a member of the House of Commons) said that Britain had no permanent allies, only permanent interests.[46]

Prime Minister Benjamin Disraeli was the great peacemaker at the Congress of Berlin in 1878; "Der alte Jude, das ist der Mann," as Otto von Bismarck said. Disraeli's foreign minister[47] and his successor as prime minister, the third Marquis of Salisbury,[48] saw his mission as preventing the great powers from stumbling into a general war that he, surveying the brief course of the Franco-Prussian war of 1870–71 and the longer and more horrifying course of the American Civil War of 1861–65, saw could be disastrous for Western civilization.

Salisbury was successful; his Liberal Party successors were not. The great powers stumbled into war in August 1914, eleven years after his death, and the reverberations of that conflict still ring harshly in our ears. Britain, after initial reluctance, went to war against Imperial Germany in 1914 and against Nazi Germany in 1939. The United States, which had avoided wars with European powers from 1815 to 1898, entered World War I in 1917 and World War II in 1941 on Britain's side. The hegemonic power was twice, the second time conclusively, defeated. Winston Churchill, the biographer of his ancestor the first Duke of Marlborough, was First Lord of the Admiralty and munitions minister during World War I; Franklin Roosevelt, cousin and nephew by marriage of former President Theodore Roosevelt, and like him a descendant of the Dutch settlers of Nieuw Amsterdam, was assistant secretary of the navy. In 1940, Franklin Roosevelt, by then in his second term as President of the United States, started a private correspondence with Churchill, by then once again First Lord of the Admiralty. They were agreed in their purposes and their attitudes.

Like John Churchill and William III, 262 years before when they met at the Binnenhof, Winston Churchill and Franklin Roosevelt were united in their belief that the great hegemonic power of Europe must be defeated. When the Germans threatened to invade England in the summer of 1940, Roosevelt speeded arms and aid to Britain. After Pearl Harbor, the United States joined the war and in 1945 the hegemonic powers of Nazi Germany and Imperial Japan were utterly defeated. In the late 1940s the United States, with Britain at its side, embarked on the long Cold War to contain the hegemonic power of the Soviet Union. Victory came with the fall of the Berlin Wall in 1989 and the end of the Soviet Union in 1991. Then, after September 11, 2001, the United States, with Britain among many others on its side, found itself at war with Islamofascist terrorists, believers in a totalitarian ideology seeking weapons of mass destruction and determined to inflict terrible damage on the democratic and tolerant West.

What kind of world would there be if Britain and then the United States had not gotten into the habit of opposing tyrannical hegemonic powers? The question is unanswerable. But it does seem clear that it would have been a world with vastly more potential for expansion of the reach of Louis XIV and Louis XV, the revolutionary Jacobins and the Emperor Napoleon, Kaiser Wilhelm II and the Führer Adolf Hitler, Josef Stalin and his Communist heirs, the terrorists of Osama bin Laden and the mullahs of Iran. Of course we cannot say that Britain or the United States would have declined to oppose such hegemonic powers if James II had remained on the throne and William of Orange had remained in the Netherlands. But we do know that the shift of England and Britain from a policy of isolation and noninvolvement to a policy of active opposition to tyrants and hegemons occurred at one moment, as the result of one highly improbable event, the Revolution of 1688–89.

And as the result of the actions of one highly unlikely and not well remembered individual, William, Prince of Orange. "What William of Orange and John Churchill severally did is still enough to take your breath away if you think about it," writes J. G. A. Pocock.[49] And while the decisiveness of Churchill's role in the Revolution can be debated — he did not bring large numbers of troops over to William, and the extent of the conspiracy to desert the king, which he seems to have headed, is not entirely known — there can be no question that the indispensable actor, the man who made the Revolution turn, was William of Orange. Pocock calls him "a revolutionary actor in the history of the British monarchy" and compares him to Machiavelli's Prince: a *principe nuovo* in the Netherlands, in England, in Scotland, in Ireland.[50] Contemporaries seem to have had the same idea; Pocock notes that "[t]he Venetian ambassador to London in 1693–94 described William in explicitly Machiavellian terms."[51] This hook-nosed and asthmatic man, an orphan in his childhood who lived in the custody of his political enemies as an adolescent, became a leader of impassive self-control, punctilious in his devotion to his work and courageous in his willingness to risk all in battle, straightforward in his purposes, but flexible and adaptable and devious in his methods. He was one of the first European princes who saw the need to enlist public opinion on his side and stealthily flooded England with propaganda that helped to detach England from the war against the Netherlands in 1673 and to attach England to his expedition, and thus to his war against France, in 1688–89.

"He was never a great commander," writes Winston Churchill, who goes on to describe him in terms reminiscent of Machiavelli's description of the *principe nuovo*. "It was in the sphere of politics that his inspiration lay. Perhaps he has never been surpassed in the sagacity, patience, and discretion of his statecraft. The combinations he made, the difficulties he surmounted, the adroitness with which he used the time factor, or played upon the weakness of others, the unerring sense of proportion and power of assigning to objectives their true priorities, all mark him for the highest fame."[52] William III and the improbable Revolution of 1688–89 were indispensable in bringing into being the world we live in today. His daring and determination and perseverance should be an inspiration to any who are inclined to weariness and flagging resolve in trying times.

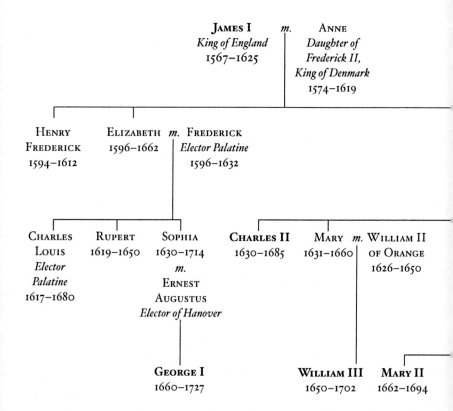

JAMES I *m.* ANNE
King of England | Daughter of
1567–1625 | Frederick II,
King of Denmark
1574–1619

HENRY | ELIZABETH *m.* FREDERICK
FREDERICK | 1596–1662 | Elector Palatine
1594–1612 | 1596–1632

CHARLES | RUPERT | SOPHIA | CHARLES II | MARY *m.* WILLIAM II
LOUIS | 1619–1650 | 1630–1714 | 1630–1685 | 1631–1660 | OF ORANGE
Elector | | *m.* | | 1626–1650
Palatine | | ERNEST
1617–1680 | | AUGUSTUS
Elector of Hanover

GEORGE I | WILLIAM III | MARY II
1660–1727 | 1650–1702 | 1662–1694

Royal Family Tree

HENRI IV
King of France
1553–1610

CHARLES I *m.* **HENRIETTA**   **LOUIS XIII**
1600–1649   **MARIA**   1601–1643
         1609–1669

JAMES II   **HENRIETTA** *m.* **PHILIPPE**   **LOUIS**
1633–1701   **ANNE**   *Duke of*   **XIV**
m.   *m.*   "**MINETTE**"   *Orleans*   1638–1715
ANNE HYDE   **MARY**   1644–1670   1640–1701
Daughter of Earl   *Daughter of*
of Clarendon   *Duke of Modena*

ANNE   **JAMES FRANCIS** *m.* **MARY CLEMENTINA**
1665–1714   **EDWARD**   *Granddaughter of*
m.   1688–1766   *John III,*
PRINCE GEORGE   *King of Poland*
OF DENMARK   1702–1735
Son of Frederick III,
King of Denmark
1653–1708

CHARLES   **HENRY**
EDWARD   *Cardinal of York*
1720–1788   1725–1807

Cast of Non-royal Characters

BATH, EARL OF. CHARLES GRANVILLE (1628–1701). Tory leader in south-west England.

BERWICK, DUKE OF. JAMES FITZJAMES (1670–1734). Illegitimate son of James II and Arabella Churchill. Soldier. Fought for France in 1690s and later.

BUCKINGHAM, DUKE OF. GEORGE VILLIERS (1628–1687). Mercurial figure who was a childhood friend of Charles II and James II.

BURNET, GILBERT (1643–1715). Scottish-born minister of the Church of England and historian. Moved to the Netherlands in 1687 and accompanied William III on his invasion of England.

CARSTARES, WILLIAM (1649–1715). Scottish minister and adviser to William III.

CHURCHILL, ARABELLA (1648–1730). Sister of John Churchill, mistress of James II and mother of four of his illegitimate children, including the Duke of Berwick.

CHURCHILL, GEORGE (1654–1710). Brother of John Churchill and navy officer. MP, 1685–1710. Leading admiral in the navy, 1702–1708.

CHURCHILL, JOHN (1650–1722). Page to James, Duke of York, 1664–1667. Army officer, 1667–1711. MP, March 1679. Created Baron Churchill in Scotland 1682, Baron Churchill in England 1685, Earl of Marlborough 1689, Duke of Marlborough 1702–1722.

CHURCHILL, SARAH JENNINGS (1660–1744). Married John Churchill in 1678. Intimate friend of Queen Anne, 1683–1708.

CHURCHILL, WINSTON (1620–1688). Father of Arabella Churchill and John Churchill. MP, 1661–1679, 1685–1688.

CLARENDON, FIRST EARL OF. EDWARD HYDE (1609–1674). Adviser to Charles II in exile and his chief minister 1660–1667.

CLARENDON, SECOND EARL OF. HENRY HYDE (1638–1709). MP, 1660–1674. Second Earl of Clarendon from 1674. Tory.

CLEVELAND, DUCHESS OF. BARBARA PALMER CASTLEMAINE (1640–1709). Mistress of Charles II, mother of his illegitimate son the Duke of Grafton.

COMPTON, HENRY (1632–1713). Tutor to Princess Anne and Bishop of London. Opponent of James II.

DANBY, EARL OF. THOMAS OSBORNE (1632–1712). Chief minister of Charles II, 1673–1678. Pro-Anglican and anti-French. Supported invasion of William III. Created Marquis of Carmarthen 1689, Duke of Leeds 1694.

DARTMOUTH, BARON. GEORGE LEGGE (1647–1691). Navy officer promoted by James II, tried to stop invasion of William III but later came over to his side.

EVELYN, JOHN (1620–1706). Landowner, writer, diarist, and founder of the Royal Society. Anglican and critical of James II.

GODOLPHIN, SIDNEY (1645–1712). MP, 1668–1684, House of Lords, 1684–1712, Treasury official, 1679–1696, 1700–1701, 1702–1710.

GRAFTON, DUKE OF. HENRY FITZROY (1663–1690). Illegitimate son of James II and the Duchess of Cleveland. Army officer; with John Churchill, deserted James II and went over to William III. Killed in battle in Ireland.

HALIFAX, MARQUIS OF. GEORGE SAVILE (1633–1695). Writer and politician. Known as "the trimmer," he tried to take a cautious middle course, opposing Charles II, supporting James II on exclusion, refusing to sign the invitation to William III to invade England, but also declining to support James, then supporting William strongly after James's flight. Leading minister to James and William during each one's first year as king.

HERBERT, ADMIRAL ARTHUR (1648–1716). Navy officer and MP, 1685–1689. Protégé of James II, but was admiral in the fleet of William III in the invasion. Created Earl of Torrington 1689.

LOCKE, JOHN (1632–1704). Physician, philosopher, and political adviser to the Earl of Shaftesbury. Fled to the Netherlands in 1683, returned to England after William III's invasion.

LOWTHER, SIR JOHN (1642–1706). Large landowner, MP, from Cumberland in northwest England 1665–1696, memoirist. Tory under Charles II and James II, Whig under William III.

MONMOUTH, DUKE OF. JAMES SCOTT (1649–1685). Oldest illegitimate son of Charles II. Executed after leading an unsuccessful rebellion in 1685.

MONCK, CHRISTOPHER (1653–1688). Son of General George Monck, elected MP from Devon in 1667 at age 13, apparently the youngest man ever to serve in the House of Commons. Lost his seat in 1670 when his father died and he became the second Duke of Albemarle.

MONCK, GENERAL GEORGE (1608–1670). General in Oliver Cromwell's army who marched from Scotland into England in 1660 and brought about the Restoration of Charles II. Created Duke of Albemarle 1660.

NOTTINGHAM, EARL OF. DANIEL FINCH (1647–1730). MP, 1673–1682. On his father's death he became the second Earl of Nottingham from 1682. Tory, opposed declaring William "rightful and lawful" king, but accepted him as king nonetheless.

ROCHESTER, EARL OF. LAURENCE HYDE (1642–1711). Son of the first Earl of Clarendon and thus brother-in-law to James II. MP, 1660–1681. Created Viscount Hyde 1681, Earl of Rochester 1682. Tory.

RUSSELL, ADMIRAL EDWARD (1652–1727). Navy officer from Whig family. Sent on a mission to William III in April 1688 to persuade him to invade England.

RUSSELL, LORD WILLIAM (1639–1683). MP, 1660–1683. Whig. Beheaded for his role in the Rye House Plot of 1683.

SANCROFT, WILLIAM (1616–1693). Archbishop of Canterbury, 1677–1693. Protested James II's measures and prosecuted with six other bishops. Opposed recognizing William III as king.

SCHOMBERG, DUKE OF. FREDERIC-ARMAND DE SCHOMBERG (1615–1690). German soldier. General in French army 1665–1685. A Protestant, he left France after the revocation of the Edict of Nantes in 1685. Entered the army of Brandenburg in 1685, then joined William III's invasion of England in 1688. Killed at the Battle of the Boyne.

SEYMOUR, SIR EDWARD (1633–1708). Tory MP from the West Country, 1661–1708. Supported William III's invasion after his landing.

SHAFTESBURY, EARL OF. ANTHONY ASHLEY COOPER (1621–1683). Dorset landowner. MP, 1640 and 1653–1661. Supported Charles I, then Cromwell, then the restoration of Charles II in the Civil War. Created Baron Ashley 1661, Earl of Shaftesbury 1672. Chancellor of the Exchequer 1661–1672; Lord Chancellor 1672–1674. Investor in many enterprises and Proprietor of the Carolina colony. Leading Whig from 1673, led Whigs during the Exclusion Crisis. Fled to the Netherlands in 1682.

SIDNEY, HENRY (1641–1704). Soldier, MP, 1679–1681, 1689–1690. Ambassador to the Netherlands 1679–1681. Agent of William III in 1688, seeking signatures for the invitation to invade England.

SUNDERLAND, EARL OF. ROBERT SPENCER (1641–1702). Inherited the title at age two. Served as minister at various times to Charles II, James II, and William III. Changed policies and alliances many times; changed religion twice.

Dutch

BENTINCK, WILLEM VAN (1649–1709). Boyhood friend and longtime adviser to William III. Created Earl of Portland 1689.

DIJKVELT, EVERAARD VAN WEEDE, HEER VAN (1626–1702). Envoy and confidant of William III.

FAGEL, GASPAR VAN (1634–1688). Grand Pensionary of Holland 1672–1688. Ally of William III.

ZUYLESTEIN, FREDERIK VAN NASSAU (1608–1672). Tutor of William III and illegitimate son of William's grandfather.

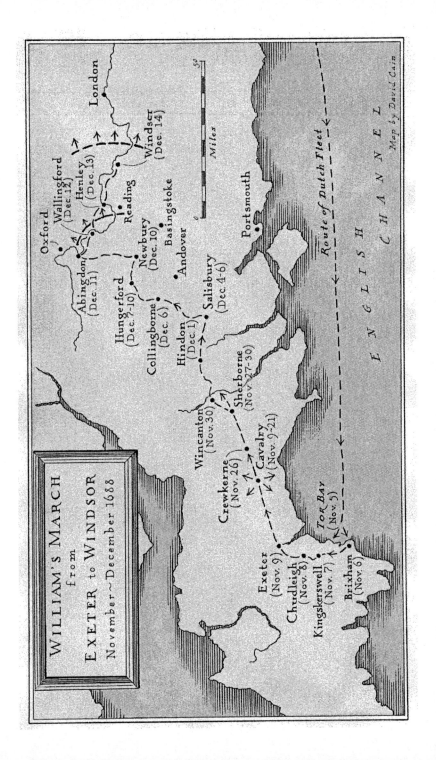

WILLIAM'S MARCH from EXETER to WINDSOR November~December 1688

London

Windsor (Dec. 14)

Henley (Dec. 13)

Wallingford (Dec. 12)

Oxford

Reading

Newbury (Dec. 10)

Basingstoke

Andover

Abingdon (Dec. 11)

Hungerford (Dec. 7–10)

Collingborne (Dec. 6)

Hindon (Dec. 1)

Salisbury (Dec. 4–6)

Portsmouth

Sherborne (Nov. 27–30)

Wincanton (Nov. 30)

Crewkerne (Nov. 26)

Cavalry (Nov. 9–21)

Exeter (Nov. 9)

Chudleigh (Nov. 8)

Kingskerswell (Nov. 7)

Tor Bay (Nov. 5)

Brixham (Nov. 6)

Route of Dutch Fleet

E N G L I S H   C H A N N E L

Miles

Map by David Cain

APPENDIX

Selections from the Invitation to the Prince of Orange, June 30, 1688

The following invitation was sent to the Prince of Orange by:
- *Charles Talbot, Earl of Shrewsbury (i.e. 25)*
- *William Cavendish, Earl of Devonshire (i.e. 24)*
- *Thomas Osborne, Earl of Danby (i.e. 27)*
- *Richard Lumley, Lord Lumley (i.e. 29)*
- *Henry Compton, Bishop of London (i.e. 31)*
- *Edward Russell (i.e. 35)*
- *Henry Sidney (i.e. 33)*

We have great satisfaction to find by 35 [i.e. Russell] and since by Monsieur Zuylestein that Your Highness is so ready and willing to give us such assistance as they have related to us. We have great reason to believe we shall be every day in a worse condition than we are, and less able to defend ourselves, and therefore we do earnestly wish we might be so happy as to find a remedy before it be too late for us to contribute to our own deliverance. But although these be our wishes, yet we will by no means put Your Highness into any expectations which might misguide your own councils in this matter; so that the best advice we can give is to inform Your Highness truly both of the state of things here at this time and of the difficulties which appear to us.

As to the first, the people are so generally dissatisfied with the present conduct of the government in relation to their religion, liberties and properties (all which have been greatly invaded), and they are in such expectation of their prospects being daily worse, that Your Highness may be assured there are nineteen parts of twenty of the people throughout the kingdom who are desirous of a change and who, we believe, would willingly contribute to it, if they had such a protection to countenance their rising as would secure them from being destroyed before they could get to be in a posture to defend themselves. It is no less certain that much the greatest part of the nobility and gentry are as much dissatisfied, although it is not safe to speak to many of them beforehand; and there is no doubt but that some of the most considerable of them would venture themselves with Your Highness at your first landing, whose interests would be able to draw great numbers to them whenever they could protect them and the raising and drawing of men together. And if such a strength could be landed as were able to defend itself and them till they could be got together into some order, we make no question but that strength would quickly be increased to a number double to the army here, although their army should all remain firm to them; whereas we do upon very good grounds believe that their army then would be very much divided among themselves, many of the officers being so discontented that they continue in their service only for a subsistence (besides that some of their minds are known already), and very many of the common soldiers do daily show such an aversion to the popish religion that there is the greatest probability imaginable of great numbers of deserters which could come from them should there be such an occasion; and amongst the seamen it is almost certain there is not one in ten who would do them any service in such a war.

Besides all this, we do much doubt whether the present state of things will not yet be much changed to the worse before another year, by a great alteration which will probably be made both in the officers and soldiers of the army, and by such other changes as are not only to be expected from a packed parliament, but what the meeting of any parliament (in our present circumstances) may produce against those who will be looked upon as principal obstructers of their proceedings there, it being taken for granted that if things cannot then be carried to their wishes in a parliamentary way other measures will be put in execution by more violent means; and although such proceedings will then heighten the discontents, yet such courses will probably be taken at that time as will prevent all possible means of relieving ourselves.

These considerations make us of the opinion that this is a season in which we may more probably contribute to our own safeties than hereafter (although we must own to Your Highness there are some judgments differing from ours in this particular), insomuch that if the circumstances stand so with Your Highness that you believe you can get here time enough, in a condition to give assistances this year sufficient for a relief under these circumstances which have been now represented, we who subscribe this will not fail to attend Your Highness upon your landing and to do all that lies in our power to prepare others to be in as much readiness as such an action is capable of, where there is so much danger in communicating an affair of such a nature till it be near the time of its being made public. But, as we have already told Your Highness, we must also lay our difficulties before Your Highness, which are chiefly that we know not what alarm your preparations for this expedition may give, or what notice it will be necessary for you to give the States beforehand, by either of which means their intelligence or suspicions here may be such as may cause us to be secured before your landing. And we must presume to inform Your Highness that your compliment upon the birth of the child (which not one in a thousand here believes to be the Queen's) hath done you some injury, the false imposing of that upon the princess and the nation being not only an infinite exasperation of people's minds here, but being certainly one of the chief causes upon which the declaration of your entering the kingdom in a hostile manner must be founded on your part, although many other reasons are to be given on ours.

If upon a due consideration of all these circumstances Your Highness shall think fit to adventure upon the attempt, or at least to make such preparations for it as are necessary (which we wish you may), there must be no more time lost in letting us know your resolution concerning it, and in what time we may depend that all the preparations will be ready, as also whether Your Highness does believe the preparations can be so managed as not to give them warning here, both to make them increase their force and to secure those they shall suspect would join with you. We need not say anything about ammunition, artillery, mortar pieces, spare arms, etc., because if you think fit to put anything in execution you will provide enough of these kinds, and will take care to bring some good engineers with you; and we have desired Mr. H[erbert] to consult you about all such matters, to whom we have communicated our thoughts in many particulars too tedious to have been written, and about which no certain resolutions can be taken till we have heard again from Your Highness.

Declaration of the Prince of Orange, October 10, 1688

PROTESTANT RELIGION AND LIBERTY

Loco sigilli.
Je maintiendray.

The Declaration of His Highness William Henry, by the Grace of God, Prince of Orange, etc., of the reasons inducing him to appear in arms in the Kingdom of England, and for preserving the Protestant religion, and for restoring the laws and liberties of England, Scotland, and Ireland.

It is both certain and evident to all men, that the public peace and happiness of any state or kingdom cannot be preserved where the law, liberties, and customs, established by the lawful authority in it, are openly transgressed and annulled; more especially, where the alteration of religion is endeavoured, and that a religion, which is contrary to law, is endeavoured to be introduced; upon which those who are most immediately concerned in it are indispensably bound to endeavour to preserve and maintain the established laws, liberties, and customs, and above all the religion and worship of God that is established among them, and to take such an effectual care, that the inhabitants of the said state or kingdom may neither be deprived of their religion, nor of their civil rights; which is so much the more necessary, being the greatness and security both of kings, royal families, and of all such as are in authority, as well as the happiness of their subjects and people, depend in a most especial manner upon the exact observations and maintenance of these their laws, liberties, and customs.

Upon these grounds it is that we cannot any longer forbear to declare that, to our great regret, we see that those counsellors, who have now the chief credit with the King, have overturned the religion, laws, and liberties of these Realms, and subjected them in all things relating to their consciences, liberties, and properties to arbitrary government, and that not only by secret and indirect ways, but in an open and undisguised manner.

Those evil counsellors, for the advancing and colouring this with some plausible pretexts, did invent and set on foot the King's dispensing power, by virtue of which they pretend that, according to law, he can suspend and dispense with the execution of laws, that have been enacted by the authority of the King and Parliament for the security and happiness of the subjects, and so have rendered those laws of no effect; though there is nothing more certain than that as no laws can be made, but by the joint concurrence of King and Parliament, so likewise laws, so enacted, which secure the public peace and safety of the nation, and the lives and liberties of every subject in it, cannot be repealed or suspended but by the same authority.

For though the King may pardon the punishment that a transgressor has incurred, and to which he is condemned, as in the cases of treason and felony, yet it cannot be with any colour of reason inferred from thence, that the King can entirely suspend the execution of those laws relating to treason or felony; unless it is pretended that he is clothed with a despotic and arbitrary power, and that the lives, liberties, honours, and estates of the subjects depend wholly on his goodwill and pleasure, and are entirely subject to him, which must infallibly follow on the King's having a power to suspend the execution of the laws and to dispense with them.

Those evil counsellors, in order to the giving some credit to this execrable maxim, have so conducted the matter, that they have obtained sentence from the judges, declaring that this dispensing power is a right belonging to the Crown, as if it were in the power of the twelve judges to offer up the laws, rights, and liberties of the whole nation to the King, to be disposed of by him arbitrarily and at his pleasure, and expressly contrary to laws enacted for the security of the subjects. In order to the obtaining this judgement, these evil counsellors did beforehand examine secretly the opinion of the judges, and procured such of them, as could not in conscience concur in so pernicious a sentence, to be turned out, and others to be substituted in their room, till by the changes which were made in the courts of judicature they at last obtained that judgment. And they have raised some to those trusts who have made open profession of the popish religion, though those are by law rendered incapable of such employments.

It is also manifest and notorious, that as His Majesty was, upon his coming to the Crown, received and acknowledged by all the subjects of England, Scotland, and Ireland, as their King, without the least opposition, though he then made open profession of the popish religion, so he did then promise, and solemnly swear at his coronation, that he would maintain his subjects in the free enjoyment of their laws and liberties, and, in particular, that he would maintain the Church of England as it was established by law. It is likewise certain, that there hath been at diverse and sundry times several laws enacted for the preservation of those rights, and liberties, and of the Protestant religion; and among other securities it has been enacted, that all persons whatsoever that are advanced to any ecclesiastical dignity, or bear office in either University, and all others that should be put into any employment, civil or military, should declare that they were not papists, but were of the Protestant religion, and that by their taking the Oaths of Allegiance and Supremacy and the Test, yet those evil counsellors have in effect annulled and abolished all those laws, both with relation to ecclesiastical and civil employments.

In order to ecclesiastical dignities and offices, they have not only without any colour of law, but against most expressive laws to the contrary, set up a commission of a certain number of persons, to whom they have committed the cognizance and direction of all ecclesiastical matters; in which commission there hath been, and still is, one of His Majesty's Ministers of State who makes now public profession of the popish religion, and, at the time of his first professing of it, declared that for a great while before he had believed that to be the only true religion. By all which the deplorable state to which the Protestant religion is reduced is apparent, since the affairs of the Church of England are now put into the hands of persons, who have accepted of a commission that is manifestly illegal, and who have executed it contrary to all law; and that now one of their chief members has abjured the Protestant religion and declared himself a papist, by which he is become incapable of holding any public employment.

The said commissioners have hitherto given such proof of their submission to the directions given them, that there is no reason to doubt, but they will still continue to promote all such designs as will be most agreeable to them; and those evil counsellors take care to raise none to any ecclesiastical dignities, but persons who have no zeal for the Protestant religion, and that hide now their unconcernedness for it under the specious pretence of moderation.

The said commissioners have suspended the Bishop of London, only because he refused to obey an order that was sent him to suspend a worthy divine, without so much as citing him before him to make his own defence, or observing the common form of process. They have turned out a President chosen by the Fellows of Magdalen College, and afterwards all the Fellows, without so much as citing them before any court that could take legal cognizance of that affair, or obtaining any sentence against them by a competent judge. And the only reason that was given for their turning them out was their refusing to choose for their President a person that was recommended to them by the instigation of those evil counsellors, though the right of a free election belonged undoubtedly to them. But they were turned out of their freeholds, contrary to law, and to that express provision of *Magna Carta,* that no man shall lose his life, or goods, but by the law of the land. And now those evil counsellors have put the said College wholly into the hands of papists, though, as it is abovesaid, they are incapable of all such employments, both by the law of the land and the statutes of the College.

The Commissioners have also cited before them all the Chancellors and Archdeacons of England, requiring them to certify to them the names of all such clergymen, as have read the King's *Declaration for Liberty of Conscience,* and of such as have not read it, without considering that the reading of it was not enjoined the clergy by the Bishops, who are their ordinaries.

The illegality and incompetency of the said Court of Ecclesiastical Commissioners was so notoriously known, and it did so evidently appear that it tended to the subversion of the Protestant religion, that the most reverend Father in God, William, Archbishop of Canterbury, Primate and Metropolitan of All England, seeing that it was raised for no other end, but to oppress such persons as were of eminent virtue, learning, and piety, refused to sit or to concur in it.

And though there are many express laws against all churches and chapels for the exercise of the popish religion, and also against all monasteries and convents, and, more particularly against the Order of the Jesuits, yet those evil counsellors have procured orders for the building of several churches and chapels for the exercise of that religion. They have also procured diverse monasteries to be erected, and, in contempt of the law, they have not only set up several colleges of Jesuits in diverse places, for the corrupting of youth, but have raised up one of the order to be a Privy Counsellor and Minister of State. By all which they do evidently shew that they are restrained by no rules of law whatsoever, but that they have subjected the honours and estates of the subjects and the established religion to a despotic power and arbitrary government: in all which they are served and seconded by these Ecclesiastical Commissioners.

They have also followed the same method in relation to civil affairs, for they have procured orders to examine all Lords Lieutenants, Deputy

Lieutenants, Sheriffs, Justices of the Peace, and all others that were in any public employment, if they would concur with the King in the repeal of the Test and penal laws; and all such, whose conscience did not suffer them to comply with their designs, were turned out, and others put in their places, who, they believed, would be more compliant to them in their designs of defeating the intent and execution of those laws, which have been made with so much care and caution for the security of the Protestant religion. And in many of these places they have put professed papists, though the law has disabled them, and warranted the subjects not to have any regard to their orders.

They have also invaded the privileges and seized on the charters of most of those towns, that have a right to be represented by their burgesses in Parliament, and have procured surrenders to be made by them, by which the magistrates in them have delivered up all their rights and privileges to be disposed of at the pleasure of these evil counsellors, who have thereupon caused new magistrates in those towns, such as they can most entirely confide in; and in many of them they have popish magistrates, notwithstanding the incapacities under which the law has put them.

And whereas no nation whatsoever can subsist without the administration of good and impartial justice, upon which men's lives, liberties, honours, and estates do depend, those evil counsellors have subjected these to an arbitrary and despotic power. In the most important affairs they have endeavoured to discover beforehand the opinions of the judges, and have turned out such as they have found would not conform themselves to their intentions, and have put others in their places, of whom they were more assured, without any regard to their abilities. And they have not stuck to raise even professed papists to the courts of judicature, notwithstanding their incapacity by law, and that no regard is due to any sentences flowing from them.

They have carried this so far, as to deprive such judges, who, in the common administration of justice, showed that they were governed by their consciences, and not by the directions which the others gave them. By which it is apparent that they design to render themselves the absolute masters of the lives, honours, and estates of the subjects, of what rank or dignity soever they may be, and that without having any regard either to the equity of the cause, or to the consciences of the judges, whom they will have to submit in all things to their own will and pleasure: hoping by such means to intimidate those who are yet in employment, as also such others as they shall think fit to put in the room of those whom they have turned out; and to make them see what they must look for, if they should at any time act in the least contrary to their good liking, and that no failings of that kind are pardoned in any persons whatsoever. A great deal of blood has been shed in many parts of the Kingdom by judges governed by those evil counsellors, against all the rules and forms of law, without so much as suffering the persons that were accused to plead in their own defence.

They have also, by putting the administration of justice into the hands of papists, brought all the matters of civil justice unto great uncertainties, with how much exactness and justice soever that these sentences may have been given: for, since the laws of the land do not only exclude papists from all places of judicature, but have put them under an incapacity, none are bound to acknowledge or obey their judgments, and all sentences given by them are null and void of themselves; so that all such persons, as have been cast in trials before such popish judges, may justly look on their pretended sentences as having no more force and efficacy, than the sentences of any private and unauthorized person whatsoever; so deplorable is the case of the subjects, who are obliged to answer such judges, that must in all things stick to the rules which are set them by those evil counsellors, who, as they raised them up to such employments, so can turn them out at pleasure; and who can never be esteemed lawful judges, so that all their sentences are in the construction of the law of no force or efficacy.

They have likewise disposed of all military employments in the same manner, for though the laws have not only excluded papists from all such employments, but have, in particular, provided that they should be disarmed, yet they in contempt of these laws have not only armed the papists, but have likewise raised them up to the greatest military trusts, both by sea and land, and that strangers as well as natives, and Irish as well as English; that so, by that means having rendered themselves masters both of the affairs of the Church, of the government of the nation, and of the course of justice, and subjected them all to a despotic and arbitrary power, they might be in a capacity to maintain and execute their wicked designs by the assistance of the Army, and thereby to enslave the nation.

The dismal effects of this subversion of the established religion, laws, and liberties in England appear more evidently to us by what we see done in Ireland, where the whole government is put in the hands of papists, and where the Protestant inhabitants are under the daily fears of what may be justly apprehended from the arbitrary power which is set up there; which has made great numbers of them leave that Kingdom, and abandon their estates in it, remembering well that cruel and bloody massacre which fell out in that island in the year 1641.

Those evil counsellors have also prevailed with the King to declare in Scotland that he is clothed with absolute power, and that all the subjects are bound to obey him without reserve, upon which he has assumed an arbitrary power, both over the religion and laws of that Kingdom; from all which it is apparent what is to be looked for in England, as soon as matters are duly prepared for it.

Those great and insufferable oppressions, and the open contempt of all law, together with the apprehensions of the sad consequences that must certainly follow upon it, have put the subjects under great and just fears, and have made them look after such lawful remedies as have been allowed of in all nations, yet all has been without effect. And these evil counsellors have endeavoured to make all men apprehend the loss of their lives, liberties, honours, and estates, if they should go about to preserve themselves from this oppression by petitions, representations, or other means authorized by law. Thus did they proceed with the Archbishop of Canterbury, and the other bishops, who, having offered a most humble *petition* to the King in terms full of respect, and not exceeding the number limited by law, in which they set forth in short the reasons for which they could not obey that order, which by the instigation of those evil counsellors was sent them, requiring them to appoint their clergy to read in their churches the *Declaration for Liberty of Conscience,* were sent to prison, and afterwards brought to a trial, as if they had been guilty of some enormous crime. They were not only obliged to defend themselves in that pursuit, but to appear before professed papists, who had not taken the Test, and, by consequence, were men whose interest led them to condemn them; and the judges who gave their opinions in their favours were thereupon turned out.

And yet it cannot be pretended that any kings, how great soever their power has been, and how arbitrary and despotic soever they have been in the exercise of it, have ever reckoned it a crime for their subjects to come in all submission and respect, and in a due number, not exceeding the limits of the law, and to represent to them the reasons that made it impossible for them to obey their orders. Those evil counsellors have also treated a Peer of the Realm as a criminal, only because he said that the subjects were not bound to obey the orders of a popish justice of the peace, although it is evident that they being by law rendered incapable of all such trusts, no regard is due to their orders; this being the security which the people have by law for their lives, liberties, and estates, that they are not to be sub-jected to the arbitrary proceedings of papists, that are, contrary to law, put into any employments, civil or military.

Both we ourselves, and our dearest and most entirely beloved consort, the Princess, have endeavoured to signify, in terms full of respect to the King, the deep and just regret which all these proceedings have given us; and, in compliance with His Majesty's desires, signified unto us, we de-clared both by word of mouth to his envoy, and in writing, what our thoughts were touching the repealing of the Test and penal laws, which we did in such a manner, that we hoped we had proposed an expedient, by which the peace of these Kingdoms, and an happy agreement amongst the subjects of all persuasions, might have been settled. But those evil counsel-lors have put such ill constructions on those our good intentions, that they have endeavoured to alienate the King more and more from us, as if we had designed to disturb the quiet and happiness of this Kingdom.

The last and great remedy for all these evils is the calling of a Parlia-ment for securing the nation against the evil practices of the wicked coun-sellors, but this could not be yet compassed, nor can it be easily brought about; for these men apprehending that a lawful Parliament, being once assembled, they would be brought to an account for all their open viola-tions of law, and for their plots and conspiracies against Protestants, be-tween those of the Church of England and the dissenters: the design being laid to engage Protestants, that are equally concerned to preserve them-selves from popish oppression, into mutual quarellings, that so, by these, some advantages might be given them to bring about their designs, and that both in the election of the Members of Parliament, and afterwards in the Parliament itself. For they see well that, if all Protestants could enter into a mutual good understanding, one with another, and concur together in the preserving of their religion, it would not be possible for them to compass their wicked ends.

They have also required all persons in the several counties of England, that either were in any employment, or were in any considerable esteem, to declare beforehand that they would concur in the repeal of the Test and penal laws; and that they would give their voices in the elections to Parlia-ment only for such as would concur in it. Such as would not thus pre-engage themselves were turned out of all employments, and others, who entered into those engagements, were put in their places, many of them

being papists; and contrary to the charters and privileges of those boroughs, that have a right to send burgesses to Parliament, they have ordered
such regulations to be made, as they thought fit and necessary for assuring
themselves of all the members that are to be chosen by those corporations.
And by this means they hope to avoid that punishment which they have
deserved, though it is apparent that all acts made by popish magistrates are
null and void of themselves, so that no Parliament can be lawful for which
the elections and returns are made by popish sheriffs and mayors of towns;
and, therefore, as long as the authority and magistracy is in such hands, it is
not possible to have any lawful Parliament.

And though according to the ancient constitution of the English government and immemorial custom, all elections of Parliament men ought
to be made with an entire liberty, without any sort of force, or requiring
the electors to choose such persons as shall be named unto them, and the
persons, thus freely elected, ought to give their opinions freely upon all
matters that are brought before them, having the good of the nation ever
before their eyes, and following in all things the dictates of their conscience; yet now the people of England cannot expect a remedy from a free
Parliament, legally called and chosen, but perhaps they may see one called,
in which all elections will be carried by fraud or force, and which will be
composed of such persons, of whom those evil counsellors hold themselves well assured, in which all things will be carried on according to their
direction and interest, without any regard to the good or happiness of the
nation. Which may appear evidently from this, that the same persons tried
the members of the last Parliament, to gain them to consent to the repeal
of the Test and penal laws, and procured that Parliament to be dissolved
when they found that they could not, neither by promises, or threatenings,
prevail with the members to comply with their wicked designs.

But, to crown all, there are great and violent presumptions inducing us
to believe that those evil counsellors, in order to their carrying on their
ill designs, and to the gaining to themselves more time for effecting the
same, for the encouraging of their accomplices, and for the discouraging
all good subjects, have published that the Queen hath brought for[th] a
son: though there have appeared, both during the Queen's pretended bigness, and in the manner in which the birth was managed, so many just and
visible grounds of suspicion, that not only we ourselves, but all the good
subjects of these Kingdoms, do vehemently suspect that the pretended
Prince of Wales was not born by the Queen. And it is notoriously known

to all the world, that many both doubted of the Queen's bigness, and of the birth of the child, and yet there was not any one thing done to satisfy them, or put an end to their doubts.

And since our dearest and most entirely beloved consort, the Princess, and likewise we ourself, have so great an interest in this matter, and such a right, as all the world knows, to the succession of the Crown; since also the English did in the year 1672, when the States General of the United Provinces were invaded in a most unjust war, use their utmost endeavours to put an end to that war, and that in opposition to those who were then in government, and, by their so doing, they ran the hazard of losing both the favour of the Court and their employments; and since the English nation has ever testified a most particular affection and esteem, both to our dearest consort, the Princess, and to ourself, we cannot excuse ourself from espousing their interest in a matter of so high consequence, and from contributing all that lies in us for the maintaining both the Protestant religion and the laws and liberties of these Kingdoms, and for the securing to them the continual employment of all their rights; to the doing of which we are most earnestly solicited by a great many lords, both spiritual and temporal, and by many gentlemen and other subjects of all ranks.

Therefore it is, that we have thought fit to go over into England, and to carry over with us a force sufficient, by the blessing of God, to defend us from the violence of these evil counsellors. And we, being desirous that our intentions in this matter be rightly understood, have for this end prepared this Declaration, in which as we have hitherto given a true account of the reasons inducing us to it, so we now think fit to declare, that this our expedition is intended for no other design, but to have a free and lawful Parliament assembled, as soon as possible; and that, in order to this, all the late charters by which the election of burgesses is limited, contrary to the ancient custom, shall be considered as null and of no force; and likewise all magistrates, who have been unjustly turned out, shall forthwith re-assume their former employments, as well as the boroughs of England shall return again to their ancient prescriptions and charters; and, more particularly, that the charter of the ancient and famous City of London shall again be in force; and that the writs for the Members of Parliament shall be addressed to the proper officers, according to custom; that also none be suffered to choose, or to be chosen, Members of Parliament, but such as are qualified by law; and that the Members of Parliament being thus lawfully chosen, they shall meet and sit in full freedom, that so the two Houses may concur in the preparing [of] such laws, as they upon free and full debate shall judge necessary and convenient, both for confirming and executing the law concerning the Test, and such other laws as are necessary for the securing and maintenance of the Protestant religion; as likewise for making such laws as may establish a good assurance between the Church of England and the Protestant dissenters, as also for the covering and securing of all such, who will live peaceably under the government as becomes good subjects, from all persecution upon the account of their religion, even papists themselves not excepted, and for the doing of all things, which the two Houses of Parliament shall find necessary for the peace, honour, and safety of the nation, so that there may be no more danger of the nation's falling at any time hereafter under arbitrary government. To this Parliament we will also refer the enquiry into the birth of the pretended Prince of Wales, and of all things relating to it, and to the right of succession.

And we, for our part, will concur in everything that may procure the peace and happiness of the nation, which a free and lawful Parliament shall determine, since we have nothing before our eyes, in this our undertaking, but the preservation of the Protestant religion, the covering of all men from persecution for the[ir] consciences, and the securing to the whole nation the free enjoyment of all their laws, rights, and liberties, under a just and legal government.

This is the design that we have proposed to ourselves in appearing upon this occasion in arms, in the conduct of which we will keep the forces under our command under all the strictness of martial discipline, and take especial care, that the people of the countries through which we must march shall not suffer by their means: and as soon as the state of the nation will admit of it, we promise that we will send back all those foreign forces that we have brought along with us.

We do, therefore, hope that all people will judge rightly of us, and approve of these our proceedings; but we chiefly rely on the blessing of God for the success of this our undertaking, in which we place our whole and only confidence.

We do in the last place invite and require all persons whatsoever, all the Peers of the Realm, both Spiritual and Temporal, all Lords Lieutenants, Deputy Lieutenants, and all gentlemen, citizens, and other commons of all ranks to come and assist us, in order to the executing of this our design against all such as shall endeavour to oppose us; that so we may prevent all those miseries, which must needs follow upon the nation's being kept under arbitrary government and slavery, and that all the violences and disorders, which have overturned the whole constitution of the English government, may be fully redressed in a free and legal Parliament.

And we do likewise resolve, that, as soon as the nation is brought to a state of quiet, we will take care that a Parliament shall be called in Scotland for restoring the ancient constitution of that Kingdom, and for bringing the matters of religion to such a settlement, that the people may live easy and happy, and for putting an end to all the unjust violences that have been in a course of so many years committed there.

We will also study to bring the Kingdom of Ireland to such a state, that the settlement there may be religiously observed, and that the Protestant and British interest there may be secured. And we will endeavour by all possible means to procure such an establishment in all the three Kingdoms, that they may all live in a happy union and correspondence together; and that the Protestant religion, and the peace, honour, and happiness of these nations may be established upon lasting foundations.

Given under our hand and seal, at our Court in The Hague, the 10th day of October in the year 1688.

William Henry, Prince of Orange
By His Highness's special command,
C. Huygens

Additional Declaration of the Prince of Orange, October 24, 1688

After we had prepared and printed this our *Declaration,* we have understood that the subverters of the religion and laws of these Kingdoms, hearing of our preparations to assist the people against them, have begun to retract some of the arbitrary and despotic powers that they have assumed and vacate some of their unjust judgments and decrees. The sense of their guilt and the distrust of their force have induced them to offer unto the City of London some seeming relief from their great oppressions, hoping thereby to deceive the people and divert them from demanding a secure re-establishment of their religion and their laws under the shelter of our arms. They do also give out that we intend to conquer and enslave the nation, and therefore it is that we have thought fit to add a few words to our Declaration.

We are confident that no person can have so hard thoughts of us as to imagine that we have any other design in this undertaking than to procure a settlement of the religion and of the liberties and properties of the subjects upon so sure a foundation, that there may be no danger of the nation's relapsing into the like miseries at any time hereafter. And as the forces we have brought along with us are utterly disproportioned to that wicked design of conquering the nation, if we were capable of intending it, so the great numbers of the principal nobility and gentry that are men of eminent quality and estates, are persons of known integrity and zeal, both for the religion and gover[n]ment of England, many of them being also distinguished by their constant fidelity to the Crown, who do both accompany us in this expedition, and have earnestly solicited us to it, will deliver us from all such malicious insinuations; for it is not to be imagined that either those who have invited us or those who are already come to assist us can join in a wicked attempt of conquest, to make void their own lawful titles to their honours, estates, and interests.

We are also confident that all men see how little weight there is to be laid on all promises and engagements that can now be made, since there can be so little regard had in times past to the most solemn promises, and as that imperfect redress, that is now offered, is a plain confession of those violations of the government that we have set forth, so the [defectiveness] of it is no less apparent, for they lay down nothing which they may not take up at pleasure, and they reserve entire, and not so much as mention, their claims and pretences to an arbitrary and despotic power, which has been the root of all their oppression, and of the total subversion of the government. And it is plain that there can be no redress, nor remedy offered, but in Parliament by a declaration of the rights of the subject that have been invaded, and not by any pretended acts of grace to which the extremity of their affairs has driven them. Therefore it is that we have thought fit to declare that we will refer all to a free assembly of the nation in a lawful Parliament.

Given under our hand and seal, at our Court in The Hague, the 24th day of October in the year 1688.

William Henry, Prince of Orange
By His Highness's [special] command,
C. Huygens

Act Declaring the Rights and Liberties of the Subject, and Settling the Succession of the Crown, December 16, 1689

Whereas the Lords Spiritual and Temporal and Commons assembled at Westminster, lawfully, fully, and freely representing all the estates of the people of this realm, did upon the thirteenth day of February in the year of our Lord one thousand six hundred eighty-eight present unto their Majesties, then called and known by the names and style of William and Mary, Prince and Princess of Orange, being present in their proper persons, a certain declaration in writing made by the said Lords and Commons in the words following, viz.:

Whereas the late King James the Second, by the assistance of divers evil counsellors, judges, and ministers employed by him, did endeavour to subvert and extirpate the Protestant religion and the laws and liberties of this kingdom;

1. By assuming and exercising a power of dispensing with and suspending of laws and the execution of laws without consent of Parliament;

2. By committing and prosecuting divers worthy prelates for humbly petitioning to be excused from concurring to the said assumed power;

3. By issuing and causing to be executed a commission under the great seal for erecting a court called The Court of Commissioners for Ecclesiastical Causes;

4. By levying money for and to the use of the Crown by pretence of prerogative for other time and in other manner than the same was granted by Parliament;

5. By raising and keeping a standing army within this kingdom in time of peace without consent of Parliament, and quartering soldiers contrary to law;

6. By causing several good subjects being Protestants to be disarmed at the same time when papists were both armed and employed contrary to law;

7. By violating the freedom of election of members to serve in Parliament;

8. By prosecutions in the Court of King's Bench for matters and causes

cognizable only in Parliament, and by divers other arbitrary and illegal courses;

9. And whereas of late years, partial, corrupt, and unqualified persons have been returned and served on juries in trials, and particularly divers jurors in trials for high treason which were not freeholders;

10. And excessive bail has been required of persons committed in criminal cases to elude the benefit of the laws made for the liberty of the subjects;

11. And excessive fines have been imposed; and illegal and cruel punishments inflicted;

12. And several grants and promises made of fines and forfeitures before any conviction or judgment against the persons upon whom the same were to be levied;

All which are utterly and directly contrary to the known laws and statutes and freedom of this realm;

And whereas the said late King James the Second having abdicated the government and the throne being thereby vacant, His Highness the Prince of Orange (whom it has pleased Almighty God to make the glorious instrument of delivering this kingdom from popery and arbitrary power) did (by the advice of the Lords Spiritual and Temporal and divers principal persons of the Commons) cause letters to be written to the Lords Spiritual and Temporal, being Protestants, and other letters to the several counties, cities, universities, boroughs, and cinque ports, for the choosing of such persons to represent them as were of right to be sent to Parliament, to meet and sit at Westminster upon the two and twentieth day of January in this year one thousand six hundred eighty and eight, in order to such an establishment as that their religion, laws, and liberties might not again be in danger of being subverted, upon which letters elections having been accordingly made;

And thereupon the said Lords Spiritual and Temporal, and Commons, pursuant to their respective letters and elections, being now assembled in a full and free representative of this nation, taking into their most serious consideration the best means for attaining the ends aforesaid, do in the first place (as their ancestors in like case have usually done) for the vindicating and asserting their ancient rights and liberties declare

1. That the pretended power of suspending the laws or the execution of laws by regal authority without consent of Parliament is illegal;

2. That the pretended power of dispensing with laws or the execution of laws by regal authority, as it has been assumed and exercised of late, is illegal;

3. That the commission for erecting the late Court of Commissioners for Ecclesiastical Causes, and all other commissions and courts of like nature, are illegal and pernicious;

4. That levying money for or to the use of the Crown by pretence of prerogative, without grant of Parliament, for longer time, or in other manner than the same is or shall be granted, is illegal;

5. That it is the right of the subjects to petition the King, and all commitments and prosecutions for such petitioning are illegal;

6. That the raising or keeping a standing army within the kingdom in time of peace, unless it be with consent of Parliament, is against law;

7. That the subjects which are Protestants may have arms for their defence suitable to their conditions and as allowed by law;

8. That election of members of Parliament ought to be free;

9. That the freedom of speech and debates or proceedings in Parliament ought not to be impeached or questioned in any court or place out of Parliament;

10. That excessive bail ought not to be required, nor excessive fines imposed, nor cruel and unusual punishments inflicted;

11. That jurors ought to be duly impanelled and returned, and jurors which pass upon men in trials for high treason ought to be freeholders;

12. That all grants and promises of fines and forfeitures of particular persons before conviction are illegal and void;

13. And that for redress of all grievances, and for the amending, strengthening and preserving of the laws, Parliaments ought to be held frequently.

And they do claim, demand and insist upon all and singular the premises as their undoubted rights and liberties, and that no declarations, judgments, doings or proceedings to the prejudice of the people in any of the said premises ought in any wise to be drawn hereafter into consequence or example.

To which demand of their rights they are particularly encouraged by the declaration of His Highness the Prince of Orange as being the only means for obtaining a full redress and remedy therein.

Having therefore an entire confidence that His said Highness the

Prince of Orange will perfect the deliverance so far advanced by him, and will still preserve them from the violation of their rights which they have here asserted, and from all other attempts upon their religion, rights and liberties:

II. The said Lords Spiritual and Temporal, and Commons, assembled at Westminster, do resolve that William and Mary, Prince and Princess of Orange, be and be declared King and Queen of England, France and Ireland and the dominions thereunto belonging, to hold the crown and royal dignity of the said kingdoms and dominions to them, the said prince and princess, during their lives and the life of the survivor to them, and that the sole and full exercise of the regal power be only in and executed by the said Prince of Orange in the names of the said prince and princess during their joint lives, and after their deceases the said crown and royal dignity of the same kingdoms and dominions to be to the heirs of the body of the said princess, and for default of such issue to the Princess Anne of Denmark and the heirs of her body, and for default of such issue to the heirs of the body of the said Prince of Orange. And the Lords Spiritual and Temporal, and Commons, do pray the said prince and princess to accept the same accordingly.

III. And that the oaths hereafter mentioned be taken by all persons of whom the oaths have allegiance and supremacy might be required by law, instead of them; and that the said oaths of allegiance and supremacy be abrogated.

I, A.B., do sincerely promise and swear that I will be faithful and bear true allegiance to their Majesties King William and Queen Mary. So help me God.

I, A.B., do swear that I do from my heart abhor, detest and abjure as impious and heretical this damnable doctrine and position, that princes excommunicated or deprived by the Pope or any authority of the see of Rome may be deposed or murdered by their subjects or any other whatsoever. And I do declare that no foreign prince, person, prelate, state or potentate hath or ought to have any jurisdiction, power, superiority, pre-eminence or authority, ecclesiastical or spiritual, within this realm. So help me God.

IV. Upon which their said Majesties did accept the crown and royal dignity of the kingdoms of England, France and Ireland, and the dominions thereunto belonging, according to the resolution and desire of the said Lords and Commons contained in the said declaration.

V. And thereupon their Majesties were pleased that the said Lords Spiritual and Temporal, and Commons, being the two Houses of Parliament, should continue to sit, and with their Majesties' royal concurrence make effectual provision for the settlement of the religion, laws and liberties of this kingdom, so that the same for the future might not be in danger again of being subverted, to which the said Lords Spiritual and Temporal, and Commons did agree, and proceed to act accordingly.

VI. Now in pursuance of the premises the said Lords Spiritual and Temporal, and Commons, in Parliament assembled, for the ratifying, confirming and establishing the said declaration and the articles, clauses, matters and things therein contained by the force of law made in due form by authority of Parliament, do pray that it may be declared and enacted that all and singular the rights and liberties asserted and claimed in the said declaration are the true, ancient, and indubitable rights and liberties of the people of this kingdom, and so shall be esteemed, allowed, adjudged, deemed and taken to be, and that all and every the particulars aforesaid shall be firmly and strictly holden and observed as they are expressed in the said declaration, and all officers and ministers whatsoever shall serve their Majesties and their successors according to the same in all time to come.

VII. And the said Lords Spiritual and Temporal, and Commons, seriously considering how it has pleased Almighty God in his marvelous providence and merciful goodness to this nation to provide and preserve their said Majesties' royal persons most happily to reign over us upon the throne of their ancestors, for which they render unto him from the bottom of their hearts their humblest thanks and praises, do truly, firmly, assuredly, and in the sincerity of their hearts think, and do hereby recognize, acknowledge and declare, that King James the Second having abdicated the government, and their Majesties having accepted the crown and royal dignity as aforesaid, their said Majesties did become, were, are, and of right ought to be by the laws of this realm our sovereign liege lord and lady, King and Queen of England, France and Ireland, and the dominions thereunto belonging, in and to whose princely persons the royal state, crown and dignity of the said realms with all honours, styles, titles, regalities, prerogatives, powers, jurisdictions and authorities to the same belonging and appertaining are most fully, rightfully and entirely invested and incorporated, united and annexed.

VIII. And for preventing all questions and divisions in this realm by reason of any pretended titles to the crown, and for preserving a certainty in the succession thereof, in and upon which the unity, peace, tranquility and safety of this nation does under God wholly consist and depend, the said Lords Spiritual and Temporal, and Commons, do beseech their Majesties that it may be enacted, established and declared, that the crown and regal government of the said kingdoms and dominions, with all and singular the premises thereunto belonging and appertaining, shall be and continue to their said Majesties and the survivor of them during their lives and the life of the survivor of them, and that the entire, perfect and full exercise of the regal power and government be only in and executed by His Majesty in the names of both their Majesties during their joint lives; and after their deceases the said crown and premises shall be and remain to the heirs of the body of Her Majesty, and for default of such issue to Her Royal Highness the Princess Anne of Denmark and the heirs of the body of His said Majesty; and thereunto the said Lords Spiritual and Temporal, and Commons, do in the name of all the people aforesaid most humbly and faithfully submit themselves, their heirs and posterities for ever, and do faithfully promise that they will stand to, maintain, and defend their said Majesties, and also the limitation and succession of the crown herein specified and contained, to the utmost of their powers with their lives and estates against all persons whatsoever that shall attempt anything to the contrary.

IX. And whereas it hath been found by experience that it is inconsistent with the safety and welfare of this Protestant kingdom to be governed by a popish prince, or by any king or queen marrying a papist, the said Lords Spiritual and Temporal, and Commons, do further pray that it may be enacted, that all and every person and persons that is, are or shall be reconciled to or shall hold communion with the See or Church of Rome, or shall profess the popish religion, or shall marry a papist, shall be excluded and be for ever incapable to inherit, possess, or enjoy the crown and government of this realm and Ireland and the dominions thereunto belonging or any part of the same, or to have, use, or exercise any regal power, authority or jurisdiction within the same; and in all and every such case or cases the people of these realms shall be and are hereby absolved of their allegiance; and the said crown and government shall from time to time descend to and be enjoyed by such person or persons being Protestants as should have inherited and enjoyed the same in case the said person or persons so reconciled, holding communion or professing or marrying as aforesaid were naturally dead.

X. And that every king and queen of this realm who at any time hereafter shall come to and succeed in the imperial crown of this kingdom shall on the first day of the meeting of the first Parliament next after his or her coming to the crown, sitting in his or her throne in the House of Peers in the presence of the Lords and Commons therein assembled, or at his or her coronation before such person or persons who shall administer the coronation oath to him or her at the time of his or her taking the said oath (which shall first happen), make, subscribe, and audibly repeat the declaration mentioned in the statute made in the thirtieth year of the reign of King Charles the Second entitled, "An Act for the more effectual preserving the king's person and government by disabling papists from sitting in either House of Parliament". But if it shall happen that such king or queen upon his or her succession to the crown of this realm shall be under the age of twelve years, then every such king or queen shall make, subscribe and audibly repeat the same declaration at his or her coronation or the first day of the meeting of the first Parliament as aforesaid which shall first happen after such king or queen shall have attained the said age of twelve years.

XI. All which their Majesties are contented and pleased shall be declared, enacted and established by authority of this present Parliament, and shall stand, remain, and be the law of this realm for ever; and the same are by their said Majesties, by and with the advice and consent of the Lords Spiritual and Temporal, and Commons, in Parliament assembled and by the authority of the same, declared, enacted, and established accordingly.

XII. And be it further declared and enacted by the authority aforesaid, that from and after this present session of Parliament no dispensation by *non obstante* of or to any statute or any part thereof shall be allowed, but that the same shall be held void and of no effect, except a dispensation be allowed of in such statute, and except in such cases as shall be specially provided for by one or more bill or bills to be passed during this present session of Parliament.

XIII. Provided that no charter or grant or pardon granted before the three and twentieth day of October in the year of our Lord one thousand six hundred eighty-nine shall be any ways impeached or invalidated by this act, but that the same shall be and remain of the same force and effect in law and no other than as if this act had never been made.

Notes

Chapter 1. The Improbable Revolution

1. E.g., J. R. Jones, *The Revolution of 1688 in England* (New York: Norton, 1972), 7.
2. Tim Harris, *Revolution: The Great Crisis of the English Monarchy 1685–1720* (London: Penguin, 2006), 34–35.
3. J. R. Western, *Monarchy and Revolution: The English State in the 1680s* (London: Macmillan, 1972), 1.
4. W. A. Speck, *Reluctant Revolutionaries: Englishmen and the Revolution of 1688* (Oxford: Oxford University Press, 1989), 71.
5. J. G. A. Pocock, " 'Wicked and Turbulent Though It Was': The Restoration Era in Perspective," in Howard Nenner, ed., *Politics and the Political Imagination in Later Stuart Britain: Essays Presented to Lois Green Schwoerer* (Rochester: University of Rochester Press, 1997), 11.
6. Paul Rahe, *Republics Ancient and Modern: Classical Republicanism and the American Revolution* (Chapel Hill: University of North Carolina Press, 1990), 523.
7. Pocock, " 'Wicked and Turbulent,' " 11.
8. John Carswell, *The Descent on England: A Study of the English Revolution and Its European Background* (New York: John Day, 1969), 184.
9. Diarmaid MacCulloch, *The Reformation* (New York: Penguin, 2003), 199–204, 255–58.
10. Ibid., 522–31.
11. Jonathan Scott, *England's Troubles: Seventeenth-Century English Political Instability in European Context* (Cambridge, England: Cambridge University Press, 2000), 29–30. "In 1590 around half of the European land-mass was under the control of Protestant governments and/or Protestant culture: in 1690 the figure was only around a fifth." Also Diarmaid MacCulloch, *The Reformation* (New York: Penguin, 2005), 669; see pp. 669–71 for more detail.
12. K. H. D. Haley, *Politics in the Reign of Charles II* (Oxford: Basil Blackwell, 1985), 61.
13. J. H. Plumb, *The Growth of Political Stability in England 1675–1725* (Harmondsworth: Peregrine, 1969), 16.

14. Diarmaid MacCulloch, *The Reformation* (New York: Penguin, 2005), 669; see pp. 669–71 for more detail. Also see Scott, *England's Troubles*, 58, 80–84.

15. The contemporary architect Gregory King estimated the population of England and Wales in 1688 as 5,318,000. David Ogg, *England in the Reigns of James II and William III* (Oxford: Oxford University Press, 1984), 30–31. W. A. Speck cites E. A. Wrigley and R. Schofield, *The Population History of England, 1541–1871* (Cambridge: Cambridge University Press, 1981, 1989), 208–98, which gives an estimate of 4,864,762 for 1686, down from a peak of 5,281,347 in 1656. W. A. Speck, *Reluctant Revolutionaries: Englishmen and the Revolution of 1688* (Oxford: Oxford University Press, 1989), 189. These estimates for this period thus all hover around 5 million.

16. Speck, *Reluctant Revolutionaries,* 201–4.

17. These figures are extrapolated from Colin McEvedy, *Atlas of World Population History* (New York: Facts on File, 1978).

18. Jonathan Israel, *The Dutch Republic: Its Rise, Greatness and Fall 1477–1806* (Oxford: Oxford University Press, 1995), 797.

19. MacCulloch, *The Reformation,* 670–71.

20. F. L. Carsten, "Introduction," in F. L. Carsten, ed., *The New Cambridge Modern History,* vol. 5 (Cambridge: Cambridge University Press, 1961), 11–12; Barry Coward, *The Stuart Age: England 1603–1714* (London: Pearson, 2003), 333.

21. Jonathan Israel, "General Introduction," in Jonathan Israel, ed., *The Anglo-Dutch Moment* (Cambridge: Cambridge University Press, 1993), 37–38.

22. Scott, *England's Troubles,* 80–84.

23. Cartsen, *The New Cambridge Modern History,* vol. 5, 17–18.

Chapter 2. The Catholic Duke

1. Simon Thurley, *Lost Buildings of Britain* (London: Viking Penguin, 2004), 7.; Robert Latham and William Matthews, eds., *The Diary of Samuel Pepys,* vol. 10, Companion (Berkeley and Los Angeles: University of California Press, 2000), 477.

2. Marion Grew, *William Bentinck and William (Prince of Orange)* (Port Washington, NY: Kennikat Press, 1971), 24.

3. J. H. Plumb, *The Growth of Political Stability in England 1675–1725* (Harmondsworth: Peregrine, 1969), 27.

4. Ibid., 477–84.

5. Thurley, *Lost Buildings,* 17.

6. This was the second year in a row that James had failed to take communion at Easter. He continued attending Easter services at the king's chapel until 1676. K. H. D. Haley, *Politics in the Reign of Charles II* (Oxford: Basil Blackwell, 1985), 52.

7. John Kenyon, *The Popish Plot* (London: Phoenix Press, 2000), 37.

8. Antonia Fraser, *Royal Charles: Charles II and the Restoration* (New York:

Knopf, 1979), 447–69, 290; Ronald Hutton, *Charles II, King of England, Scotland, and Ireland* (Oxford: Clarendon Press, 1989), 296.

9. Fraser, *Royal Charles,* 468.

10. Hutton, *Charles II,* 301.

11. John Miller, *James II: A Study in Kingship* (London: Methuen, 1989), 57.

12. J. P. Kenyon, *Robert Spencer, Earl of Sutherland 1641–1702* (London: Longmans, Green, 1958), 30.

13. David Ogg, *England in the Reigns of James II and William III* (Oxford: Oxford University Press, 1984), 221.

14. Encyclopedia Britannica, 11th ed., vol. 28 (New York: Encyclopedia Britannica, 1911), 674.

15. Hutton, *Charles II,* 1–14; John Miller, *James II: A Study in Kingship* (London: Methuen, 1978), 1–6.

16. H. C. Foxcroft, *A Character of the Trimmer, Being a Short Life of the First Marquis of Halifax* (Cambridge: Cambridge University Press, 1946), 69n.

17. Hutton, *Charles II,* 39–44.

18. G. A. Pocock, " 'Wicked and Turbulent Though It Was': The Restoration Era in Perspective," in Howard Nenner, ed., *Politics and the Political Imagination in Later Stuart Britain: Essays Presented to Lois Green Schwoerer* (Rochester, NY: University of Rochester Press, 1997), 15. "Hyde was fairly sure that the king was pushed toward Calvinism by his mother, who wanted to use it as an instrument to break up any Anglican restoration and bring about a Catholic regime in England. In light of what was to happen in the 1670s and 1680s, this was not at all a paranoid fantasy. Henrietta Maria did have something, though it needs to be established what, to do with the lazy Catholic leanings of her son Charles and the militant devotion of her son James."

19. K. H. D. Haley, *Charles II* (London: Historical Association, 1966), 8.

20. Tim Harris, *Politics Under the Later Stuarts* (London: Longman, 1993), 54–56.

21. Hutton, *Charles II,* 49–69.

22. K. H. D. Haley, *Politics in the Reign of Charles II* (Oxford: Basil Blackwell, 1985), 11.

23. Joseph Alsop, *The Rare Art Traditions* (New York: Harper & Row, 1982), 162. This sale is the subject of Jerry Brotton, *The Sale of the Late King's Goods: Charles I and His Art Collection* (London: Macmillan, 2006).

24. Hutton, *Charles II,* 75; W. A. Speck, *Reluctant Revolutionaries: Englishmen and the Revolution of 1688* (Oxford: Oxford University Press, 1989), 122–23.

25. Diarmaid MacCulloch, *The Reformation* (New York: Penguin, 1965), 529.

26. Mark Kishlansky, *A Monarchy Transformed* (London: Penguin Press, 1996), 218.

27. Scott, *England's Troubles,* 47, citing Charles Carlton, *Going to the Wars: The Experience of the British Civil Wars 1638–1651* (London: Routledge, 1992).

28. Thomas Hobbes, *Leviathan,* edited by Richard Turke (Cambridge: Cambridge University Press, 1991), 88, 89.

29. Harris, *Politics Under the Later Stuarts,* 32; Gordon Schochet, "The Act of Toleration and the Failure of Comprehension: Persecution, Nonconformity, and Religious Indifference," in Dale Hoak and Mordechai Feingold, eds., *The World of William and Mary* (Stanford: Stanford University Press, 1996), 174.

30. Kishlansky, *A Monarchy Transformed,* 218–22.

31. Tim Harris, *London Crowds in the Reign of Charles II: Propaganda and Politics from the Restoration Until the Exclusion Crisis* (Cambridge: Cambridge University Press, 1987), 38.

32. Harris, *Politics Under the Later Stuarts,* 26–33.

33. Plumb, *The Growth of Political Stability in England,* 28.

34. Haley, *Charles II,* 12.

35. Harris, *Politics Under the Later Stuarts,* 34–35.

36. John J. Miller, *James II* 42–44.

37. Speck, *Reluctant Revolutionaries,* 29–30; Gordon Schochet, "Toleration and Comprehension," 176.

38. Gordon Schochet, "Toleration and Comprehension," 176–77.

39. Speck, *Reluctant Revolutionaries,* 26–29, 73; Schochet, "Toleration and Comprehension," 176.

40. Schochet, "Toleration and Comprehension," 177.

41. Speck, *Reluctant Revolutionaries,* 206–7; Kishlansky, *A Monarchy Transformed,* 222–36.

42. Schochet, "Toleration and Comprehension," 177–78.

43. Kishlansky, *A Monarchy Transformed,* 292.

44. Charles Carlton, *Royal Mistresses* (London: Routledge, 1990), 75.

45. Haley, *Charles II,* 10.

46. Hutton, *Charles II,* 158–60; Miller, *James II,* 48.

47. Hutton, *Charles II,* 7.

48. Miller, *James II,* 44–47.

49. Ibid., 70.

50. Quoted in Miller, *James II,* 50.

51. Russell Shorto, *The Island at the Center of the World* (New York: Doubleday, 2004), 288–300.

52. Giles Milton, *Nathaniel's Nutmeg* (New York: Farrar, Straus and Giroux, 1999), 362–64.

53. Miller, *James II,* 50–53.

54. Speck, *Reluctant Revolutionaries,* 123.

55. Haley, *Politics in the Reign of Charles II,* 61–62; John Spurr, *England in the 1670s: "The Masquerading Age"* (Oxford: Blackwell, 2000), 42.

56. Spurr, *England in the 1670s,* 42.

57. Miller, *James II,* 57.

58. Hutton, *Charles II,* 159.

59. Spurr, *England in the 1670s,* 9–10.

60. Ibid., 11–13.

61. Carlton, *Royal Mistresses,* 71.

62. Hutton, *Charles II,* 291–92.

63. Spurr, *England in the 1670s*, 28–29; Speck, *Reluctant Revolutionaries*, 31–32.
64. Schochet, "Toleration and Comprehension," 175.
65. Hutton, *Charles II*, 297–98.
66. Ibid., 300–302; John J. Miller, *Charles II* (London: Weidenfeld and Nicolson, 1991), 202–5; Fraser, *Royal Charles*, 317.
67. Fraser, *Royal Charles*, 469.
68. William Bray, ed., *The Diary of John Evelyn*, vol. 2 (London: J. M. Dent, 1907), 86.
69. Stephen Saunders Webb, *1676: The End of American Independence* (New York: Knopf, 1984), 113.
70. Henry Ball to Joseph Williamson, in Williamson (no publication information), vol. 1, p. 24, quoted in Spurr, *England in the 1670s*, 42.
71. Miller, *James II*, 71–73.
72. Ibid., 68.
73. For an exhaustive treatment of the subject, see Arthur Marotti, *Religious Idolatory and Cultural Fantasy: Catholic and Anti-Catholic Discourses in Early Modern England* (Notre Dame, IN: University of Notre Dame Press, 2005).
74. Quoted in J. P. Kenyon, *The Popish Plot* (London: Heineman, 1972), 1.
75. Scott, *England's Troubles*, 54–55.
76. Speck, *Reluctant Revolutionaries*, 168. See also Tim Harris, *London Crowds in the Reign of Charles II*, 111.
77. Kenyon, *The Popish Plot*, 8–11, quotation at p. 10; J. R. Jones, *The Revolution of 1688 in England* (New York: Norton, 1972), 75–79.
78. Speck, *Reluctant Revolutionaries*, 170–71.
79. Kenyon, *The Popish Plot*, 3–5.
80. Kenyon, *The Popish Plot*, 5–9; Spurr, *England in the 1670s*, 22, 42–43, 61, 232–33; John Carswell, *The Descent on England* (New York: John Day, 1969), 65.
81. Bray, *The Diary of John Evelyn*, vol. 2, p. 92.

Chapter 3. Young Revolutionaries

1. Simon Schama, *The Embarrassment of Riches: An Interpretation of Dutch Culture in the Golden Age* (New York: Knopf, 1987), 226–27.
2. Encyclopedia Britannica, 11th ed., vol. 12 (New York: Encyclopedia Britannica, 1910), 817–18.
3. Jonathan Israel, *The Dutch Republic: Its Rise, Greatness, and Fall, 1477–1806* (Oxford: Clarendon Press, 1995), 292.
4. Winston Churchill, *Marlborough, His Life and Times*, vol. 1 (London: Harrap, 1947), 135n.
5. Israel, *The Dutch Republic*, 607.
6. K. H. D. Haley, *The Dutch in the Seventeenth Century* (London: Thames and Hudson, 1972), 91–93.
7. John Carswell, *The Descent on England* (New York: John Day, 1969), 11.
8. Haley, *The Dutch in the Seventeenth Century*, 29.
9. Israel, *The Dutch Republic*, 611; Haley, *The Dutch in the Seventeenth Century*,

13–30; Michael North, *Art and Commerce in the Dutch Golden Age* (New Haven: Yale University Press, 1997), 22–27, 31–38.

10. Israel, *The Dutch Republic*, 611–12; North, Art and Commerce, 27–31; Haley, *The Dutch in the Seventeenth Century*, 43–45; Russell Shorto, *The Island at the Center of the World* (New York: Doubleday, 2004), 291.

11. Haley, *The Dutch in the Seventeenth Century*, 22.

12. Ibid., 38–43.

13. Ibid., 41.

14. Israel, *The Dutch Republic*, 621, table 30.

15. Schama, *The Embarrassment of Riches*, 8.

16. Israel, *The Dutch Republic*, 450.

17. Haley, *The Dutch in the Seventeenth Century*, 67.

18. North, *Art and Commerce*, 20–21.

19. Haley, *The Dutch in the Seventeenth Century*, 63.

20. See Jonathan Israel, *The Dutch Republic*, 286, table 8. From 1587 to 1792 the state of Holland was required to provide 57 to 64 percent of the financing of the Generality. Also see Carswell, *The Descent on England*, 9–11.

21. Stephen Baxter, *William III and the Defense of European Liberty 1650–1702* (New York: Harcourt Brace, 1966), 181.

22. Schama, *The Embarrassment of Riches*, 64–67; Israel, *The Dutch Republic*, 125–28; Haley, *The Dutch in the Seventeenth Century*, 69–71.

23. Haley, *The Dutch in the Seventeenth Century*, 69. Here the New Style dates are used for all events in the Netherlands, since almost all the key events occurred in Holland.

24. Haley, *The Dutch in the Seventeenth Century*, 71.

25. Schama, *The Embarrassment of Riches*, 65.

26. Haley, *The Dutch in the Seventeenth Century*, pp. 92–99.

27. Ibid., 83, 111–13.

28. Stephen B. Baxter, *William III and the Defense of European Liberty 1650–1702* (New York: Harcourt, Brace & World, 1966), 10, 29.

29. Jonathan Israel, "General Introduction," in Jonathan Israel, ed., *The Anglo-Dutch Moment* (Cambridge: Cambridge University Press, 1991) , pp. 39–40; Carswell, *The Descent on England*, 12, quotation from Israel is on 39.

30. Quoted in Haley, *The Dutch in the Seventeenth Century*, 196.

31. Ibid., 72–74.

32. Ibid., 73–74.

33. Carswell, *The Descent on Europe*, 11.

34. In 1682, according to David Kaiser, *Politics and War: European Conflict from Philip II to Hitler* (Cambridge, MA: Harvard University Press, 1990), 168. In 1672, according to the Encyclopaedia Britannica, 11th ed., vol. 20 (New York: Encyclopaedia Britannica, 1911), 146. In 1681, according to Baxter, *William III*, 184. Louis also seized Orange in 1660, but returned it to the young Prince in 1665. (Baxter, *William III*, 32–36.) Carswell, in *The Descent on England*, writes that Louis pulled down the fortifications of Orange in

1660 and seized all its revenues during William's minority (p. 32), that it was returned to William by the Treaty of Nijmegen in 1678 and he ordered the fortifications rebuilt (p. 47), but that Louis declared its status as an independent principality abolished in 1681 (p. 36), and his dragoons seized it in 1682 and tore down the fortifications (p. 47).

35. Tony Claydon, *William III* (London: Pearson, 2002), 10. Most of these properties were inherited by the eleven–year-old William of Nassau, later known as William the Silent, in 1544 after the death during a siege of his first cousin René of Nassau-Chalons. Encyclopaedia Britannica, vol. 20, p. 146; Geoffrey Parker, *The Dutch Revolt* (Harmondsworth: Penguin, 1979), 50–51.

36. Baxter, *William III*, 16.

37. Claydon, *William III*, 9–15; Israel, *The Dutch Republic*, 604–9, 700–713, 717–38, 748–58, 774–85, 791–92.

38. Baxter, *William III*, 36–37.

39. Marjorie Bowen, *William III and the Revolution of 1648 & Gustavus Adolphus* (Neerlandia, Alberta: Inheritance, 1988), 32.

40. Marion Grew, *William Bentinck and William III (Prince of Orange): The Life of Bentinck Earl of Portland from the Welbeck Correspondence* (Port Washington, NY: Kennikat Press, 1971), 4–5.

41. Baxter, William III, 51.

42. H. C. Foxcroft, *The Character of a Trimmer* (Cambridge: Cambridge University Press, 1946), 175.

43. Israel, *The Dutch Republic.*

44. Baxter, *William III*, 52.

45. John Miller, *James II: A Study in Kingship* (London: Methuen, 1978), 85.

46. Foxcroft, *The Character of a Trimmer,* 175; Claydon, *William III*, 20.

47. Carswell, *The Descent on England,* 20–21, 25, 39–40, 85.

48. Baxter, *William III,* 40–41.

49. Ibid., 48–49.

50. Claydon, *William III,* 15–18; Israel, *The Dutch Republic,* 785–95.

51. The others were the Archbishops of Mainz and Trier, the Duke of Bavaria, the Duke of Saxony, the Elector Palatine, and the Margrave of Brandenburg. The King of Bohemia (a title by now hereditary in the House of Hapsburg), though technically an elector, "did not exercise his electoral dignity." That meant from 1648 to 1685 the electors included five Catholics and three Protestants. In 1685, however, the electorate of the Palatinate fell to a Catholic, in 1692 Leopold I made the Duke of Hanover an elector, and in 1697 the Duke of Saxony became a Catholic. Thus by 1697 the electors included seven Catholics and two Protestants (Brandenburg and Hanover). F. L. Carsten, "The Empire After the Thirty Years War," in F. L. Carsten, ed., *The New Cambridge Modern History,* vol. 5, pp. 444–45.

52. Stephen Baxter, *William III,* 70–78.

53. Quoted in Bowen, *William III and the Revolution of 1648,* 42–43.

54. Carswell, *The Descent on England,* 27. In an apparent typographical error, Carswell introduces this act as occurring in "the critical summer of 1673, when William was swept to power over the constitutional dykes the republicans had built to contain the House of Orange," but then he writes that the letter was published "five days before the de Witts were butchered by the mob," which happened in 1672.

55. Israel, *The Dutch Republic,* 798–806; Baxter, *William III,* 80–85; Claydon, *William III,* 18–20.

56. Baxter, *William III,* 83.

57. K. H. D. Haley, *William of Orange and the English Opposition 1672–4* (Oxford: Oxford University Press, 1953), 88–111; Baxter, *William III,* 109; J. R. Western, *Monarchy and Revolution: The English State in the 1680s* (London: Macmillan, 1985), 245.

58. Haley, *William of Orange,* 220–21.

59. Israel, *The Dutch Republic,* 807–13; Baxter, *William III,* 100; Claydon, *William III,* 20–21.

60. Baxter, *William III,* 161; Carswell, *The Descent on England,* 36, and map on p. 4.

61. Carswell, *The Descent on England,* 37.

62. Ibid., 21–22.

63. Israel, "General Introduction," 17.

64. Baxter, *William III,* 125; Grew, *William Bentinck and William III,* 32–33.

65. K. H. D. Haley, *Politics in the Reign of Charles II* (Oxford: Basil Blackwell, 1985), 65–66.

66. Grew, *William Bentinck and William III,* 34–43.

67. Haley, *Politics in the Reign of Charles II,* 66.

68. Baxter, *William III,* 223–24.

69. Miller, *James II,* 85; Grew, *William Bentinck and William III,* 44–46.

70. Grew, *William Bentinck and William III,* 46.

71. Winston Churchill, *The Duke of Marlborough: His Life and Times,* vol. 1 (London: Harrap, 1947), 135.

72. Ibid.

73. J. R. Jones, *Marlborough* (Cambridge: Cambridge University Press, 1993), 11.

74. Churchill, *Marlborough,* 24–28.

75. Ibid., 44–45, 46–48.

76. Ibid., 46–47.

77. Jones, *Marlborough,* 10–16; Stephen Saunders Webb, *Lord Churchill's Coup* (New York: Knopf, 1995), 19–25; Churchill, *Marlborough,* 30–50; quotations from pp. 50, 31–32.

78. Quoted in John Hussey, *Marlborough: Hero of Blenheim* (London: Weidenfeld & Nicolson, 2004), 26.

79. Jones, *Marlborough,* 16–20; Churchill, *Marlborough,* 51–64, 79–93; Webb, *Lord Churchill's Coup,* 25–36; quotation at p. 34.

80. Webb, *Lord Churchill's Coup,* 40–42.

81. Churchill, *Marlborough,* 107–32.

82. Ophelia Field, *Sarah Churchill Duchess of Marlborough* (New York: St. Martin's Press, 2002), 23–24.

83. Grew, *William Bentinck and William III*, 48.

84. Israel, *The Dutch Republic*, 824.

85. Webb, *Lord Churchill's Coup*, 43–44.

86. Jones, *Marlborough*, 19–20. He maintains the negotiations were a sham because Charles II never meant to go to war. The Dutch and French signed the treaty July 31, which would have been counted as July 21 in England. J. R. Jones, *Country and Court: England 1658–1714* (Cambridge, MA: Harvard University Press, 1978), 194; Webb, *Lord Churchill's Coup*, 44–45.

87. Webb, *Lord Churchill's Coup*, 44, quoting Viscount Wolsey, *The Life of John Churchill Duke of Marlborough to the Accession of Queen Anne*, 4th ed., vol. 1 (London: 1894), 204–5, 211.

88. Churchill, *Marlborough*, 135.

89. Baxter, *William III*, 150.

90. Webb, *Lord Churchill's Coup*, 113.

91. Ibid., 46.

92. Another view comes from William's biographer, who states that William "disliked" Churchill "personally," perhaps because he "had secured his position by less than honorable means." Baxter, *William III*, 150.

93. Bowen, *William III*, 38.

CHAPTER 4. EXCLUSION POLITICS

1. Guy de la Bedoyere, ed., *The Diary of John Evelyn* (Woodbridge, England: Boydell Press, 1995), 226.

2. Tim Harris, *Politics Under the Later Stuarts* (London: Longman, 1993), 54.

3. Bedoyere, *The Diary of John Evelyn*, 225.

4. Ibid.

5. John Kenyon, *The Popish Plot* (London: Phoenix Press, 2000), 52–97; John Spurr, *England in the 1670s: "This Masquerading Age"* (Oxford: Blackwell, 2000), 260–64.

6. Kenyon, *The Popish Plot*, 84–87.

7. Ibid., 65, 73, 74.

8. Ibid., 68, 77; John Miller, *James II: A Study in Kingship* (London: Methuen, 1989), 87.

9. Kenyon, *The Popish Plot*, 99–101.

10. Stephen Saunders Webb, *1676: The End of American Independence* (New York: Knopf, 1984), 179.

11. Ibid., 333, 337–40, 396–98; quotation at p. 398.

12. Ibid., 211–13, 192–93, 409–16; quotation at p. 410.

13. J. G. A. Pocock, "'Wicked and Turbulent Though It Was': The Restoration Era in Perspective," in Howard Nenner, ed., *Politics and the Political Imagination in Later Stuart Britain: Essays Presented to Lois Green Schwoerer* (Rochester, NY: University of Rochester Press, 1997), 13.

14. W. A. Speck, *Reluctant Revolutionaries: Englishmen and the Revolution of 1688* (Oxford: Oxford University Press, 1689), 32.

15. Kenyon, *The Popish Plot*, 97–106.

16. Ibid., 106–37, 150–63. Quotation at pp. 127–28.

17. Bedoyere, *The Diary of John Evelyn,* 226.

18. K. H. D. Haley, *The First Earle of Shaftesbury* (Oxford: Oxford University Press, 1968), 457.

19. Spurr, *England in the 1670s,* 268–69; Basil Duke Henning, *The House of Commons 1660–1690,* vol. 2 (London: Secker & Warburg, 1983), 87–89.

20. Mark Kishlansky, *Parliamentary Selection: Social and Political Choice in Early Modern England* (Cambridge: Cambridge University Press, 1986), 12.

21. Ibid., 16. On this issue generally, see pp. 12–18.

22. Ibid., 18–21.

23. Ibid., 19.

24. Ibid., 138–39.

25. Ibid., 140 and n.12.

26. Henning, *The House of Commons,* vol. 1, 455–57, 468.

27. Kishlansky, *Parliamentary Selection,* 139–54.

28. Ibid., 150–58.

29. Ibid., 183–87.

30. Calculated from the numbers presented in Henning, *The House of Commons,* 107–10.

31. K. H. D. Haley, *Politics in the Reign of Charles II* (Oxford: Basil Blackwell, 1985), 28; Harris, *Politics Under the Later Stuarts,* 18. J. H. Plumb gives a figure of 200,000. Plumb, *The Growth of Political Stability in England,* 40–41. Speck, *Reluctant Revolutionaries,* 247: "Sawyer, moreover, was right to assess the electorate at about 25 percent of adult males." Mark Knights provides similar figures. "The number voting in 1715 amounted to at least 250,000, almost 20 percent of the adult male population—a higher percentage than *after* the 1832 Reform Act." Mark Knights, *Representation and Misrepresentation in Later Stuart Britain* (Oxford: Oxford University Press, 2005), 12.

32. Henning, *The House of Commons,* 106.

33. Linda Colley, *Britons: Forging the Nation 1707–1837* (London: Yale University Press), 346.

34. Henning, *The House of Commons,* 85–87. By my count, Parliament was out of session for 244 of the 357 months from April 1660 to January 1690: December 1660–May 1661, May 1662–February 1663, July 1663–March 1664, May–November 1664, March–October 1665, November 1665–September 1666, February–October 1667, March–October 1669, December 1669–February 1670, April 1671–February 1673, November 1673–January 1674, February 1674–April 1675, June–October 1675, November 1675–February 1677, July–October 1678, December 1678–March 1679, May 1679–October 1680, January–March 1681, March 1681–May 1685, November 1685–January 1689.

35. Harris, *Politics Under the Later Stuarts,* 6, 81–82. "Parties as such did not really come into being until after the Popish Plot," 6.

36. Kishlansky, *Parliamentary Selection,* 190–91.

37. Miller, *James II*, 89–91; Winston Churchill, *Marlborough, His Life and Times*, vol. 1 (London: Harras, 1947), 139–40.

38. J. R. Jones, *The First Whigs: The Politics of the Exclusion Crisis 1678–1683* (Oxford: Oxford University Press, 1961), 36.

39. Ibid., 36–42; Plumb, *The Growth of Political Stability*, 15–16, 31–32.

40. Ibid., 32.

41. Haley, *The First Earl of Shaftesbury*, 500.

42. Ibid.; Jones, *The First Whigs*, 48–49.

43. Jones, *The First Whigs*, 17.

44. Encyclopaedia Britannica, 11th ed., vol. 24 (New York: Encyclopaedia Britannica, 1911), 760–63; J. P. Ferris, in Henning, *The House of Commons*, 121–24. Quotations at pp. 762, 123.

45. Haley, *The First Earl of Shaftesbury*, 440.

46. Ibid., 7–497, 734–46.

47. Maurice Cranston, *John Locke, A Biography* (London: Longmans, Green, 1957), 93–99; Haley, *The First Earl of Shaftesbury*, 202–06; Paul Rahe, *Republics Ancient and Modern: Classical Republicanism and the American Revolution* (Chapel Hill: University of North Carolina Press, 1990), 447–50a.

48. Quoted in Cranston, *John Locke*, 104.

49. Jones, *The First Whigs*, 48–49.

50. Haley, *The First Earl of Shaftesbury*, 500.

51. Ibid., 505–10.

52. Jones, *The First Whigs*, 61–62; Haley, *The First Earl of Shaftesbury*, 513–14.

53. Jones, *The First Whigs*, 56.

54. Quoted in Haley, *The First Earl of Shaftesbury*, 518.

55. Ibid., 519–27.

56. John Miller, *Charles II* (London: Weidenfeld and Nicolson, 1991), 72.

57. Haley, *Politics in the Reign of Charles II*, 41–44.

58. K. H. D. Haley, *William of Orange and the English Opposition 1672–4* (Oxford: Oxford University Press, 1953), 88–111.

59. Haley, *The First Earl of Shaftesbury*, 414.

60. Mark Knights, *Representation and Misrepresentation in Later Stuart Britain: Partisanship and Political Culture* (Oxford: Oxford University Press, 2005), 7.

61. Quoted in Jonathan Scott, *England's Troubles: Seventeenth-Century English Political Stability in European Context* (Cambridge: Cambridge University Press, 2000), 51.

62. Mark Knights, *Politics and Opinion in Crisis, 1678–81* (Cambridge: Cambridge University Press, 1994), 360. See Plumb, *The Growth of Political Stability*, 15–16: "Neither monarch nor minister was able to create a system of control by which the social, economic, and political life of the nation could be given coherence and order."

63. Tim Harris, *London Crowds in the Reign of Charles II: Propaganda and Politics from the Restoration Until the Exclusion Crisis* (Cambridge: Cambridge University Press, 1987), 98.

64. Scott, *England's Troubles*, 85.

65. See the map in Hugh Clout, ed., *The Times London History Atlas* (London: HarperCollins, 1991), 64–65.
66. Spurr, *England in the 1670s,* 165.
67. Haley, *Politics in the Reign of Charles II,* 41; Antony Clayton, *London's Coffee Houses: A Stimulating Story* (London: Historical Publications, 2003), 10–19.
68. Spurr, *England in the 1670s,* 165–78; Knights, *Representation and Misrepresentation,* 17–18.
69. Harris, *Politics Under the Later Stuarts,* 84; cf. Harris, *London Crowds,* 100.
70. Liza Picard, *Restoration London: Engaging Anecdotes and Tantalizing Trivia from the Most Magnificent and Renowned City in Europe* (New York: Post Road Press, HarperCollins, 2000), 209.
71. Maureen Waller, *1700: Scenes from London Life* (New York: Four Walls Eight Windows, 2000), 196.
72. Spurr, *England in the 1670s,* 148–49.
73. Ibid., 34.
74. Ibid., 44.
75. Ibid., 79, 176–77.
76. Harris, *London Crowds,* 99.
77. Spurr, *England in the 1670s,* 175–76.
78. Waller, *1700,* 200–201.
79. Kenyon, *The Popish Plot,* 207. See also pp. 211, 272.
80. Jones, *The First Whigs,*. 60.
81. Ibid., 73.
82. Haley, *Politics in the Reign of Charles II,* 38.
83. Cf. Haley, *Charles II,* 11–12.
84. The argument that there were effective Court and Country parties in the years from 1673 to 1678 is effectively refuted in Harris, *Politics Under the Later Stuarts,* 61–65.
85. Harris, *Politics Under the Later Stuarts,* 8; Speck, *Reluctant Revolutionaries,* 32–33; http://www.hfac.uh.edu/gbrown/philosophers/leibniz/BritannicaPages/WhigTory/WhigTory.html.
86. Jones, *The First Whigs,* 82.
87. Haley, *Politics in the Reign of Charles II,* 45.
88. Jones, *The First Whigs,* 92–93.
89. Knights, *Politics and Opinion in Crisis,* 367.
90. Knights, *Representation and Misrepresentation,* 24.
91. Jones, *The First Whigs,* 93–94.
92. Scott, *England's Troubles,* 183.
93. Jones, *The First Whigs,* 95.
94. Haley, *The First Earl of Shaftesbury,* 552–53.
95. Jones, *The First Whigs,* 95.
96. Kishlansky, *Parliamentary Selection,* 174.
97. Ibid., 182.
98. Jones, *The First Whigs,* 97; Henning, *The House of Commons,* 322.

99. Henning, *The House of Commons,* vol. 1, p. 229; Kishlansky, *Parliamentary Selection,* 183.

100. Henning, *The House of Commons,* vol. 1, p. 2, vol. 3, pp. 73–74.

101. Kishlansky, *Parliamentary Selection,* 183; Jones, *The First Whigs,* 99–100.

102. Henning, *The House of Commons,* vol. 1, p. 313.

103. Ibid., 316; Kishlansky, *Parliamentary Selection,* 173, 190.

104. Kenyon, *The Popish Plot,* 192–201.

105. Bedoyere, *The Diary of John Evelyn,* 228.

106. Haley, *The First Earl of Shaftesbury,* 545.

107. Stephen Saunders Webb, *Lord Churchill's Coup* (New York: Knopf, 1995), 50.

108. Haley, *The First Earl of Shaftesbury,* 545–46.

109. Webb, *Lord Churchill's Coup,* 50–51.

110. Haley, *The First Earl of Shaftesbury,* 546–49.

111. Speck, *Reluctant Revolutionaries,* 34; Harris, *London Crowds,* 103–6; Scott, *England's Troubles,* 191.

112. Bedoyere, *The Diary of John Evelyn,* 231.

113. That hereditary line, as it has turned out, continues to this day; the male line of succession runs straight from the king's bastard son to the ninth Duke of Buccleuch, one of the largest landowners in Europe and owner of the only painting by Leonardo da Vinci in private hands, which was stolen in 2003 and at this writing has not been recovered. Encyclopaedia Britannica, 11th ed., vol. 18 (New York: Encyclopaedia Britannica Co., 1911), 727; Simon Winchester, *Their Noble Lordships* (New York: Random House, 1992), 82–92. On the Leonardo, see http://news.bbc.co.uk/2/hi/uk_news/scotland3185441.stm and http://news.scotsman.com/topics.cfm?tid=976.

114. Jones, *The First Whigs,* 159.

115. Ibid., 112–17.

116. Ibid., 117.

117. Harris, *Politics Under the Later Stuarts,* 106–7.

118. Jones, *The First Whigs,* 117–23.

119. Henning, *The House of Commons,* vol. 1, p. 86.

120. Scott, *England's Troubles,* 192, 195; Jones, *The First Whigs,* 126–27.

121. Jones, *The First Whigs,* 124–26.

122. Knights, *Politics and Opinion in Crisis,* 63.

123. Jones, *The First Whigs,* 129–30.

124. Baxter, *William III,* 163–70.

125. J. P. Kenyon, *Robert Spencer, Earl of Sutherland, 1641–1702* (London: Longmans, Green, 1958), 63.

126. Jones, *The First Whigs,* 130–33; Baxter, *William III,* 170–71.

127. Scott, *England's Troubles,* 196.

128. Jones, *The First Whigs,* 133–39.

129. Henning, *The House of Commons,* vol. 2, 396–97.

130. H. R. Foxcroft, *A Character of the Trimmer, Being a Short Life of the First Marquis of Halifax* (Cambridge: Cambridge University Press, 1946), 18. The

astonishing Miss Foxcroft had written an earlier book on Halifax, published in 1897.

131. Ibid., 21.

132. Ibid., 35–49, 53–61.

133. Ibid., 63.

134. Ibid., 66–67.

135. Ibid., 115–19.

136. Andrew Swatland, *The House of Lords in the Reign of Charles II* (Cambridge: Cambridge University Press, 1996), 256–59.

137. Jones, *The First Whigs,* 140–41.

138. Ibid., 141–47.

139. Ibid., 155; Gordon Schochet, "The Act of Toleration and the Failure of Comprehension: Persecution, Nonconformity, and Religious Indifference," in Dale Hoak and Mordechai Feingold, eds., *The World of William and Mary* (Stanford, CA: Stanford University Press, 1996), 176.

140. Henning, *The House of Commons*, vol. 2, 238.

141. Jones, *The First Whigs,* 166–67

142. Ibid., 159–60.

143. Ibid., 160.

144. Quoted in Harris, *Politics Under the Later Stuarts,* 99.

145. Jones, *The First Whigs,* 160–72.

146. Henning, ed., *The House of Commons,* vol. 1, pp. 228–29.

147. Ibid., 135–36.

148. Jones, *The First Whigs,* 162–63.

149. Ibid., 164–65.

150. Ibid., 166–70.

151. Ibid., 172–73.

152. Speck, *Reluctant Revolutionaries,* 36.

153. Bedoyere, *The Diary of John Evelyn,* 244.

154. Jones, *The First Whigs,* 178–80.

155. Antonia Fraser, *Royal Charles: Charles II and the Restoration* (New York: Knopf, 1979), 400–06.

156. Harris, *Politics Under the Later Stuarts,* 96.

157. Ibid., 97.

158. Plumb, *The Growth of Political Stability in England,* 29.

159. Miller, *Charles II,* 342–43.

160. Jones, *The First Whigs,* 194–96.

161. Marion Grew, *William Bentinck and William III (Prince of Orange), The Life of Bentinck Earl of Portland from the Welbeck Correspondence* (Port Washington, NY: Kennikat Press, 1971), 65.

162. P. G. M. Dickson, *The Financial Revolution in England: A Study in the Development of Public Credit* (London: Macmillan, 1967), 55.

163. Jones, *The First Whigs,* 189–94.

164. Ibid., 198.

165. Harris, *Politics Under the Later Stuarts,* 107.

166. Jones, *The First Whigs,* 198–206; Scott, *England's Troubles,* 192.

167. Fraser, *Charles II*, 424.

168. Jones, *The First Whigs*, 206–10; Kishlansky, *A Monarchy Transformed*, 260–61.

169. Speck, *Reluctant Revolutionaries*, 39.

170. Miller, *James II*, 112–13.

171. Harris, *Politics Under the Later Stuarts*, 123; Speck, *Reluctant Revolutionaries*, 39–40.

172. Miller, *Charles II*, 366–68.

173. Cranston, *John Locke*, 229–30.

174. Peter Laslett, "Introduction," in Peter Laslett, ed., John Locke, *Two Treatises on Government* (Cambridge: Cambridge University Press, 1988), 12, 45–66; Ashcraft, *Revolutionary Politics*, 82–83, 86–87, 183–84; Rahe, *Republics Ancient and Modern*, 491. Laslett notes, p. 45, that Locke arrived in London from the Netherlands on February 11, 1689, one day before the completion of the Declaration of Right, and that there is no evidence he had anything to do with the latter. Laslett believes that the Second Treatise was written in 1679–80 and the First Treatise in 1680 and perhaps 1681; Ashcraft believes that the First Treatise was written in 1680–81 and the Second Treatise in 1681–82. Laslett, pp. 123–26. Thus Laslett believes that the entire book, or almost all of it (he acknowledges that Locke added some small bits in 1689), was written during the Exclusion Crisis, while Ashcraft believes that much of it was written after the dissolution of the Oxford Parliament and at a time when Shaftesbury was planning the revolution that became the foiled Rye House Plot. Quote is from Paul Rahe, personal communication.

175. Rahe, *Republics Ancient and Modern*, 480.

176. Scott, *England's Troubles*, 203–4.

177. Miller, *Charles II*, 275–76; Fraser, *Charles II*, 427–28.

178. Grew, *William Bentinck and William III*, 67–75.

179. Webb, *Lord Churchill's Coup*, 70.

180. Churchill, *Marlborough*, vol. 1, 168–70.

181. Baxter, *William III*, 187–88.

182. Tim Harris, *Restoration: Charles II and His Kingdoms 1660–1685* (London: Allen Lane, 2005), 416–17.

183. Ibid., 419.

184. Webb, *Lord Churchill's Coup*, pp. 53–57.

185. Speck, *Reluctant Revolutionaries*, pp. 14–16.

186. Webb, *Lord Churchill's Coup*, 56–57.

187. Ibid., 60–61.

188. Miller, *James II*, 105–10.

189. Webb, *Lord Churchill's Coup*, 63–65.

190. Harris, *Politics Under the Later Stuarts*, 109.

191. Speck, *Reluctant Revolutionaries*, 172–73.

192. Miller, *James II*, 113–18.

193. Webb, *Lord Churchill's Coup*, 61–62.

194. Ibid., 65–66.

195. Ibid., 61–62; Richard Johnson, "The Revolution of 1688–9 in the American

Colonies," in Jonathan Israel, ed., *The Anglo-Dutch Moment* (Cambridge: Cambridge University Press, 1991), 219–20.

196. Haley, *Politics in the Reign of Charles II,* 38.

CHAPTER 5. KING JAMES

1.   John Miller, *Charles II* (London: Weidenfeld and Nicolson, 1991), 381–82.

2.   Guy de la Bedoyere, ed., *The Diary of John Evelyn* (Woodbridge: Boydell Press, 1995), 275.

3.   John Childs, *The Army, James II and the Glorious Revolution* (Manchester, England: Manchester University Press, 1980), 1–2.

4.   Stephen Saunders Webb, *Lord Churchill's Coup* (New York: Knopf, 1995), 83.

5.   Marion Grew, *William Bentinck and William III (Prince of Orange) The Life of William Bentinck Earl of Portland from the Welbeck Correspondence* (Port Washington, NY: Kennikat Press, 1971), 82–84.

6.   Tim Harris, *Restoration: Charles II and His Kingdoms 1660–1685* (London: Allen Lane, 2005), 413.

7.   David Ogg, *England in the Reigns of James II and William III* (Oxford: Oxford University Press, 1984), 166–67. The favorite text of the advocates of passive obedience was Romans XIII.1: "Let every soul be subject unto the higher powers. For there is no power but God: the powers that be are ordained of God. Whosoever resisteth the power, resisteth the ordinance of God: and they that resist shall receive to themselves damnation." John Carswell, *The Descent of England* (New York: John Day, 1969), 69.

8.   J. R. Jones, *Marlborough* (Cambridge: Cambridge University Press, 1993), 21–24; Webb, *Lord Churchill's Coup,* 83–85.

9.   W. A. Speck, *Reluctant Revolutionaries: Englishmen and the Revolution of 1648* (Oxford: Oxford University Press, 1989), 43.

10. Speck, *Reluctant Revolutionaries,* 125.

11. John Miller, *James II* (London: Methuen, 1989), 120–23.

12. David Green, *Sarah Duchess of Marlborough* (New York: Scribner's, 1967), 44; Lisa Jardine, *On a Grander Scale: The Outstanding Life of Christopher Wren* (New York: HarperCollins, 2002), 348–49, 369.

13. Bedoyere, *The Diary of John Evelyn,* 277.

14. Miller, *James II,* 123.

15. Ibid., 126–27.

16. Speck, *Reluctant Revolutionaries,* 44–46.

17. Mark Kishlansky, *Parliamentary Selection: Social and Political Choice in Early Modern England* (Cambridge: Cambridge University Press, 1986), 148.

18. Basil Duke Henning, *The House of Commons 1660–1690,* vol. 1 (London: Secker & Warburg, 1983), 26–27. Also, 53 percent of the Commons members in this Parliament served only in this Parliament, again the highest percentage during this period.

19. Henning, *The House of Commons* , vol. 1, 310–17.
20. Ibid., 322.
21. Ibid., 229.
22. Ibid., 136–37.
23. Ibid., 11–13.
24. Speck, *Reluctant Revolutionaries,* 47, 158–59.
25. Miller, *James II,* 136.
26. Ibid., 137.
27. Stephen Baxter, *William III and the Defense of European Liberty 1650–1702* (New York: Harcourt Brace, 1966), 196–201; Miller, *James II,* 117; Grew, *William Bentinck and William III,* 82–85.
28. Miller, *James II,* 138–39; Baxter, *William III,* 204.
29. Carswell, *The Descent on England,* 51–52.
30. Miller, *James II,* 139–40; Baxter, *William III,* 204; Carswell, *The Descent on England,* 52–53.
31. Miller, *James II,* 140.
32. Tim Harris, "The Scots and the Revolution of 1688–89," in Howard Nenner, ed., *Politics and the Political Imagination in Later Stuart England* (Rochester, NY: University of Rochester Press, 1997), 100.
33. Joyce Malcolm, *To Keep and Bear Arms: The Origins of an Anglo-American Right* (Cambridge: Harvard University Press, 1994), 4.
34. Malcolm, *To Keep and Bear Arms,* 100–101.
35. John Hussey, *Marlborough: Hero of Blenheim* (London: Weidenfeld & Nicolson, 2004), 26; Webb, *Lord Churchill's Coup,* 91–92.
36. J. G. A. Pocock, "Standing Army and Public Credit: The Institutions of Leviathan," in Dale Hoak and Mordechai Feingold, eds., *The World of William and Mary* (Stanford, CA: Stanford University Press, 1996), 93.
37. Winston Churchill, *Marlborough His Life and Times,* vol. 1 (London: Harrap, 1947), 185–97; Webb, *Lord Churchill's Coup,* 85–88, 90–96.
38. Churchill, *Marlborough,* vol. 1, pp. 198–200; Miller, *James II,* 141–42; Webb, *Lord Churchill's Coup,* 97. Webb, contra other historians, writes that Churchill was present during the Bloody Assizes.
39. Childs, *The Army, James II and the Glorious Revolution,* xvii.
40. Ibid., 7–8.
41. Malcolm, *To Keep and Bear Arms,* 101–02.
42. Harris, *The Scots and the Revolution of 1688–89,* 100.
43. Carswell, *The Descent on England,* 6–7.
44. Ibid., 43.
45. Baxter, *William III,* 207–8; Pierre Goubert, *The Course of French History* (London: Routledge, 1991), 132–33.
46. Bedoyere, *The Diary of John Evelyn,* 295.
47. Miller, *James II,* 143–45; Baxter, *William III,* 209; J. R. Jones, *The Revolution of 1688 in England* (New York: Norton, 1972), 61–65.
48. Harris, *The Scots and the Revolution of 1688–89,* 100.

49. J. R. Jones, *The Revolution of 1688 in England* (New York: Norton, 1972), 111–13.

50. Malcolm, *To Keep and Bear Arms,* 101–2.

51. Miller, *James II,* 146–47; Speck, *Reluctant Revolutionaries,* 56–62; Churchill, *Marlborough,* vol. 1, 202–3.

52. Jones, *The Revolution of 1688,* 79–83, 91–97.

53. Harris, *The Scots and the Revolution of 1688–89,* 100–01.

54. Miller, *James II,* 213.

55. Malcolm, *To Keep and Bear Arms,* 96–98.

56. Miller, *James II,* 216–17; Speck, *Reluctant Revolutionaries,* 14.

57. Richard Johnson, "The Revolution of 1688–9 in the American Colonies," in Jonathan Israel, ed., *The Anglo-Dutch Moment* (Cambridge: Cambridge University Press, 1991), 219–22.

58. Johnson, "The Revolution of 1688–9," 219–22; Stephen Saunders Webb, *1676: The End of American Independence* (New York: Knopf, 1984), 410–16.

59. J. P. Kenyon, *Robert Spencer, Earl of Sunderland 1641–1702* (London: Longman, Green, 1958), 1–7; Ogg, *England in the Reigns of James II and William III,* 192–93.

60. Kenyon, *Sunderland,* 8.

61. Ibid., 83.

62. Ibid., 7–20.

63. Ibid., 73.

64. Ibid., 80.

65. Ibid., 87; Churchill, *Marlborough,* vol. 1, p. 168, vol. 2, pp. 674–76; Webb, *Lord Churchill's Coup,* 70.

66. Baxter, *William III,* 187–88.

67. Churchill, *Marlborough,* vol. 1, 166–71.

68. Green, *Sarah Duchess of Marlborough,* 46–47.

69. Jones, *Marlborough,* 28–29.

70. Webb, *Lord Churchill's Coup,* 70–72.

71. Kenyon, *Sunderland,* 111–44.

72. Ibid., 84.

73. Miller, *James II,* p. 124. See also Ogg, *England in the Reigns of James II and William III,* 193–94: "From long experience the secretary [Sunderland] knew that James was a fool; but it is unlikely that he tried deliberately to ruin his royal master, because he perceived that in this matter James would need no help: and it was a matter of indifference to him which master he cheated. So he decided to make the best of both worlds. On the one hand, he retained his place by pandering to the king, and pretending to favour his religious policy; on the other hand, he ingratiated himself secretly with the Prince of Orange. The greatest exponent in his century of what is now called 'double crossing,' he impressed James by an appearance of intellectual brilliance — indeed the Stuarts were very susceptible to such flashy creatures — while other men, equally uncritical, were fascinated by

Sunderland's assurance, his quickness, his bluster, his vehemently expressed contempt for better men, characteristics which they mistook for ability. He must have known that James's policy was suicidal; but he remained the sycophant in office, because he so desperately needed the money."

74. Churchill, *Marlborough*, vol. 1, pp. 241–42.
75. Miller, *James II*, 128, 150.
76. Ibid., 149–50.
77. Carswell, *The Descent on England*, 73.
78. Harris, *The Scots and the Revolution of 1688–89*, 102.
79. Ogg, *England in the Reigns of James II and William III*, 168.
80. Miller, *James II*, 155–58.
81. J. R. Jones, "James II's Revolution: Royal Policies, 1686–92," in Jonathan Israel, ed., *The Anglo-Dutch Moment* (Cambridge: Cambridge University Press, 1993), 52–53.
82. Webb, *Lord Churchill's Coup*, caption to illustrations between 112–13.
83. Miller, *James II*, 152–55; Ogg, *England in the Reigns of James II and William III*, 179–80; Jones, *The Revolution of 1688*, 68–74.
84. Kenyon, *Sunderland*, 137–39, 155–57, 166.
85. Speck, *Reluctant Revolutionaries*, 64.
86. Ibid., 64–65.
87. Webb, *Lord Churchill's Coup*, 127.
88. Churchill, *Marlborough*, vol. 1, p. 204.
89. Ogg, *England in the Reigns of James II and William III*, 169; Malcolm, *To Keep and Bear Arms*, 107.
90. Harris, *The Scots and the Revolution of 1688–89*, 102–3; Carswell, *The Descent on England*, 87; Bruce Lenman, "The Poverty of Political Theory in the Scottish Revolution of 1688–1690," in Lois G. Schwoerer, *The Revolution of 1688–89: Changing Perspectives* (Cambridge: Cambridge University Press, 1992), 247. Lenman gives the date of the "proclamation of toleration" as February 12/22; others give it as March.
91. Speck, *Reluctant Revolutionaries*, 16–17.
92. Harris, *The Scots and the Revolution of 1688–89*, 103–4.
93. Lenman, *The Poverty of Political Theory*, 247.
94. Jones, "James II's Revolution," 54–56. But William's biographer says that at this time the prospect of the succession of Anna Maria or her older sister, Marie-Louise, the Queen of Spain, "was too remote for serious consideration" (Baxter, *William III*, 218). It was obvious at the time that Marie-Louise and her sickly husband, Carlos II, would produce no heir. What would have been the dynastic consequences of a Savoy succession? They are imponderable and recede into the realm of counterfactual history. Anna Maria's surviving son, Carlo Emmanuele III, succeeded to the throne of Savoy, as did his son and thee of his grandsons, all of whom had no legitimate heirs and the last of whom died in 1831. The English evidently assumed the succession would go through Anna Maria's eldest daughter, Louisa

Maria. But in 1702 she married Philip, Duke of Anjou, the son of the Dauphin of France, whom Louis XIV had recognized in 1700 as King Philip V of Spain. The dispute about that throne was the subject of the War of Spanish Succession, waged from 1701 to 1713, which resulted in Philip's holding the Spanish throne. Louisa Maria died in 1714, leaving a son who would be King Ferdinand VI of Spain from 1746 to 1759, when he died without legitimate heirs; the throne of Spain then passed to the son of Philip V by his second wife. But of course if Louisa Maria had been recognized as an heir to the British throne, she would never have married Philip. Her succession was mooted by the Bill of Rights of 1689 and the Act of Succession of 1701, both of which forbade the succession of a Catholic heir. See the genealogical tables in Israel, *The Anglo-Dutch Moment*, 368, and William Langer, *Encyclopedia of World History* (Boston: Houghton Mifflin, 1956), 449, 456.

95. Jones, "James II's Revolution," 56.

96. Jones, *The Revolution of 1688*, 98–100; Speck, *Reluctant Revolutionaries*, 66–67.

97. Churchill, *Marlborough*, vol. 1, p. 206.

98. Kenyon, *Sunderland*, 152–53.

99. Miller, *James II*, 164–66; Jones, *The Revolution of 1688*, 104–5.

100. Ogg, *England in the Reigns of James II and William III*, 180–81.

101. Speck, *Reluctant Revolutionaries*, 175–77.

102. Ibid., 174–75.

103. Ibid., 171.

104. Grew, *William Bentinck and William III*, 85–89. Bentinck was dispatched July 14 N.S., two days before the Battle of Sedgmoor, which was fought July 6 O.S.

105. Miller, *James II*, 158–59; Kenyon, *Sunderland*, 150.

106. Baxter, *William III*, 214–15.

107. Miller, *James II*, 159–60; J. R. Western, *Monarchy and Revolution: The English State in the 1680s* (London: Macmillan, 1985), 239. His royal status was important to William: "Even as a boy he always used the royal 'we.'" Ibid., 243 n.

108. Churchill, as governor of the Hudson's Bay Company, opposed the treaty and protested to the king in February 1687 that French aggressions were continuing on company outposts (including Fort Churchill on Hudson's Bay); James granted the company letters of marque and reprisal authorizing them to attack French ships.

109. Miller, *James II*, 160–61; Western, *Monarchy and Revolution*, 246; Jonathan Israel, *The Dutch Republic: Its Rise, Greatness, and Fall, 1477–1806* (Oxford: Oxford University Press, 1995), 843.

110. Miller, *James II*, 159; Baxter, *William III*, 216, 220–21; Western, *Monarchy and Revolution*, 250. Miller and Baxter say the appointment was made in July, Western says October.

111. Baxter, *William III*, 217.

112. Quoted in Baxter, *William III*, 217

113. Ibid., 217; Webb, *Lord Churchill's Coup*, 124.

114. Carswell, *The Descent on England*, 83, quoting Bishop Gilbert Burnet.

115. Baxter, *William III*, 216.

116. Ibid., 218: Western, *Monarchy and Revolution*, 248–49.

117. Baxter, *William III*, 259.

118. Kenyon, *Sunderland*, 151, 157.

119. Carswell, *The Descent on England*, 93–94.

120. Ogg, *England in the Reigns of James II and William III*, 196–97; Carswell, *The Descent on England*, 94–95.

121. Baxter, *William III*, 219–20.

122. Churchill, *Marlborough*, vol. 1, p. 213; Webb, *Lord Churchill's Coup*, 125–26.

123. Churchill, *Marlborough*, vol. 1, p. 211; Webb, *Lord Churchill's Coup*, 124–25.

124. Baxter, *William III*, 219.

125. Miller, *James II*, 169–71; Kenyon, *Sunderland*, 153–54; Jones, *The Revolution of 1688 in England*, 119–21.

126. Jones, *The Revolution of 1688*, 128–75.

127. Jones, *The Revolution of 1688*, 129. "Indeed James had to appropriate the electoral techniques and propaganda methods that Shaftesbury had developed and used against him during the Exclusion Crisis," p. 138. See also p. 144: James's agents' "techniques closely resembled those which had been developed and used by Shaftesbury, the architect of the first Whig party and the first organizer of systematic parliamentary opposition to the crown in the country as well as at Westminster." Some of James's agents had worked for Shaftesbury; like Shaftesbury, he had a single objective, ignored other issues, and relied increasingly on propaganda and organization (pp. 138, 151–52).

128. Jones, *The Revolution of 1688 in England*, 11–12.

129. Ibid., 145; Speck, *Reluctant Revolutionaries*, 158–62.

130. Jones, *The Revolution of 1688*, 129–30.

131. Ibid., 133, 135.

132. Kenyon, *Sunderland*, 161–62; Jones, *The Revolution of 1688 in England*, 132.

133. Malcolm, *To Keep and Bear Arms*, 103.

134. Ibid., 105–6.

135. Jones, *The Revolution of 1688*, 132–33.

136. Ibid., 134–35.

137. Ibid., 137–38.

138. Jones, "James II's Revolution," 61–62.

139. Bedoyere, *The Diary of John Evelyn*, 304.

140. Kenyon, *Sunderland*, 155–57.

141. Baxter, *William III*, 220.

142. Kenyon, *Sunderland*, 165.

143. Gordon Schochet, "The Act of Toleration and the Failure of Comprehension: Persecution, Nonconformity, and Religious Indifference," in Dale

Hoak and Mordechai Feingold, eds., *The World of William and Mary* (Stanford: Stanford University Press, 1996), 179; Ogg, *England in the Reigns of James II and William III,* 181; Jones, *The Revolution of 1688,* 117–18.

144. Jones, *The Revolution of 1688,* 109–13; Speck, *Reluctant Revolutionaries,* 184–85.

145. Miller, *James II,* 171–75.

146. Kenyon, *Sunderland,* 141–44.

147. Ibid., 162–63.

148. Carswell, *The Descent on England,* 99–100.

149. Miller, *James II,* 216–19; Jones, *The Revolution of 1688,* 113–14.

150. Baxter, *William III,* 218; Kenyon, *Sutherland,* 150.

151. Speck, *Reluctant Revolutionaries,* 13.

152. Carswell, *The Descent on England,* 101–02.

153. Ibid., Baxter, *William III,* 221.

154. Kenyon, *Sunderland,* 167; Webb, *Lord Churchill's Coup,* 129.

155. Encylcopaedia Britannica, 11th ed, vol. 17 (New York: Encyclopaedia Britannica, 1911), 826.

156. http://www.nndb.com/people/553/000093274/.

157. Kenyon, *Sunderland,* 168.

158. Miller, *James II,* 180–81.

CHAPTER 6. DUTCH INVASION

1. Pierre Goubert, *Louis XIV and Twenty Million Frenchmen* (New York: Vintage, 1972), 173–74.

2. Winston Churchill, *Marlborough,* vol. 1 (London: Harrap, 1947), 228–29.

3. Ted Morgan, ed., *The Age of Magnificence: Memoirs of the Court of Louis XIV: Duc de Saint-Simon* (New York: Paragon House, 1990), 142, 160–66.

4. Ibid., 150, 155. Historian John Rule notes the resemblance between Louis XIV and William of Orange. "Their very resemblance may have made them strangers. Both were deeply religious, although Louis's sister-in-law called the king's faith that of a babe in the nursery. Each was concerned with the salvation of his soul and each believed in Providence. For William, Providence was a predestined 'high and sacred destiny,' and for Louis it was a fulfillment of God's plan for his anointed servant. Both had a taste for personal and military *gloire,* though Voltaire says William made war like a soldier and Louis like a king. Both were intensely loyal and generous to ministers and servants who had won their trust. Both were masters at masking emotion: of course, there were those who said William had none. Both were followers of Machiavelli, exponents of *raison d'état.* Both were noted builders, gardeners, and hunters. And both were precise, hard-working rulers, princely bureaucrats." John Rule, "France Caught Between Two Balances: The Dilemma of 1688," in Lois Schwoerer, ed., *The Revolution of 1688–1689: Changing Perspectives* (Cambridge: Cambridge University Press, 1992), 46.

5. John B. Wolf, *Louis XIV* (London: Gollancz, 1968), 435–46; Rule, "France Caught Between Two Balances," 43–45.

6. The others were the Archbishops of Mainz and Trier, the Duke of Bavaria, the Duke of Saxony, the Elector Palatine, and the Margrave of Brandenburg. The King of Bohemia (a title by now hereditary in the House of Hapsburg), though technically an elector, "did not exercise his electoral dignity." That meant from 1648 to 1685 the electors included five Catholics and three Protestants. In 1685, however, the electorate of the Palatinate fell to a Catholic, in 1692 Leopold I made the Duke of Hanover an elector, and in 1697 the Duke of Saxony became a Catholic. Thus by 1697 the electors included seven Catholics and two Protestants (Brandenburg and Hanover). F. L. Carsten, "The Empire After the Thirty Years War," in F. L. Carsten, ed., *The New Cambridge Modern History*, vol. 5 (Cambridge: Cambridge University Press, 1961), 444–45.

7. Wolf, *Louis XIV*, 432–35; Stephen Baxter, *William III and the Defense of European Liberty 1650–1702* (New York: Harcourt Brace, 1966), 222–23; Rule, "France Caught Between Two Balances," 43.

8. John Carswell, *The Descent on England* (New York: John Day, 1969), 12–13; Rule, "France Caught Between Two Balances," 39.

9. Carswell, *The Descent on England*, 53–54; Rule, "France Caught Between Two Balances," 39.

10. Carswell, *The Descent on England*, 76.

11. Rule, "France Caught Between Two Balances," 39.

12. Carswell, *The Descent on England*, 77–78.

13. Ibid., 54–55.

14. Rule, "France Caught Between Two Balances," 39–40.

15. Carswell, *The Descent on England*, 79–80.

16. J. R. Western, *Monarchy and Revolution: The English State in the 1680s* (London: Macmillan, 1985), 246; Baxter, *William III*, 222–23; Wolf, *Louis XIV*, 441, 444; Carswell, *The Descent on England*, 13–14, 44–45.

17. Jones, *The Revolution of 1688 in England* (New York: Norton, 1972), 267; Wolf, *Louis XIV*, 441–44.

18. Jones, *The Revolution of 1688 in England*, 254, 268.

19. Western, *Monarchy and Revolution*, 244–45.

20. Baxter, *William III*, 230.

21. Jones, *The Revolution of 1688 in England*, 209–12.

22. Ibid., 222–24.

23. Carswell, *The Descent on England*, 131–32.

24. Quoted in ibid., 132–33.

25. Ibid., 83–84.

26. Ibid., 96–98, 100, 103–4, 107.

27. Ibid., 103.

28. David Ogg, *England in the Reigns of James II and William III* (Oxford: Oxford University Press, 1984), 197; Western, *Monarchy and Revolution*, 249; Jones, *The Revolution of 1688 in England*, 211, 226–27; Speck, *Reluctant Revolutionaries*, 217. Speck notes that the letter was dated November 4, before the rumors of Mary Beatrice's pregnancy were known in either London or The Hague, but of course by November 15 they were known in both places. Was

the letter drafted after the pregnancy became known? I have not been able to determine the answer.

29. Marion Grew, *William Bentinck and William III (William of Orange) The Life of William Bentinck Earl of Portland from the Welbeck Correspondence* (Port Washington, NY: Kannikat Press, 1971), 102.

30. Carswell, *The Descent on England,* 107–9.

31. Ibid., 109–10; Western, *Monarchy and Revolution,* 249; Ogg, *England in the Reigns of James II and William III,* 197; Grew, *William Bentinck and William III,* 102–3; Jones, *The Revolution of 1688 in England,* 227.

32. Speck, *Reluctant Revolutionaries,* 218.

33. Foxcroft, *A Character of the Trimmer,* 281. Cf. Jones, *The Revolution of 1688 in England,* 190: "All his actions after 1688 demonstrate the fact that for William England was always a means, not an end in itself. The ultimate purpose was the containment of France, the reduction of the power which enabled Louis to dominate his neighbours."

34. Baxter, *William III,* 229.

35. Jones, *The Revolution of 1688 in England,* 191–97; Baxter, *William III,* 209–12; Jonathan Israel, *The Dutch Republic: Its Rise, Greatness, and Fall* (Oxford: Oxford University Press, 1995), 842–47; Jonathan Israel, "The Dutch Role in the Glorious Revolution," in Jonathan Israel, ed., *The Anglo-Dutch Moment* (Cambridge: Cambridge University Press, 1993), 114–16.

36. Jones, *The Revolution of 1688 in England,* 176–81; Carswell, *The Descent on England,* 105–07, 110–16.

37. Jones, *The Revolution of 1688 in England,* 133.

38. Ibid., 255–57.

39. Ibid., 257–61.

40. Kenyon, *Sunderland,* 168, 169.

41. Churchill, *Marlborough,* vol. 1, p. 221.

42. J. R. Jones, *Marlborough* (Cambridge: Cambridge University Press, 1993), 29.

43. Churchill, *Marlborough,* vol. 1, p. 217.

44. Ibid., 215. The date of September appears on p. 221. A slightly different version is given in Stephen Saunders Webb, *Lord Churchill's Coup* (New York: Knopf, 1995), 128–29.

45. Churchill, *Marlborough,* vol. 1, pp. 217–18.

46. Ibid., 236–37.

47. Jones, *Marlborough,* 30.

48. John Childs, *The Army, James II, and the Glorious Revolution* (Manchester, England: Manchester University Press, 1980), 141.

49. Childs, *The Army, James II, and the Glorious Revolution,* 144.

50. Webb, *Lord Churchill's Coup,* 124–30; quotation on p. 125. Webb writes on p. 130: "A few days later, at the outset of the new-style year of 1688, convinced that the crisis of both their church and their careers was at hand, emboldened by the unanimous refusal of the Anglican ruling class to accept the king's measures, Churchill and other leaders pledged to the Protestant

succession approached Prince William. The prince must reassure them, even publicly declare, that he would claim the throne and that, as king, he would preserve the Protestant ascendancy as protected by law. Otherwise they and other Anglican soldiers and statesmen could not remain in office without conforming to the king's religion and politics." But I have not found references in other sources to any such approach, and Webb's footnotes cite letters to William written by other English figures in May and July—five and seven months later. Moreover, as Webb points out, p. 131, Churchill's preferred supplanters of James would have been Anne and her husband Prince George, not Mary and her husband Prince William. "Reliance on the dangerous abilities, absolutist instincts, and professional army of Prince William could be reduced, if not avoided altogether, if only Prince George would fight to bring Princess Anne immediately to the throne. In his September 1688 proclamation issued to justify his invasion, William made no claim whatever to the throne and said he came instead to obtain 'a free parliament.' "

51. Webb, *Lord Churchill's Coup,* 131–33.
52. Speck, *Reluctant Revolutionaries,* 129–31.
53. Miller, *James II,* 162.
54. Ibid., 184; Baxter, *William III,* 221; Western, *Monarchy and Revolution,* 250.
55. Edward Gregg, *Queen Anne* (New Haven: Yale University Press, 2001), 54; Baxter, *William III,* 226.
56. Basil Duke Henning, ed., *The House of Commons 1660–1690,* vol. 3 (London; Secker & Warburg, 1983), 185–88.
57. Western, *Monarchy and Revolution,* 251.
58. Henning, *The House of Commons 1660–1690,* vol. 3, pp. 359–61.
59. Ibid., 526–28, quotation on p. 528.
60. Jones, *The Revolution of 1688 in England,* 181.
61. Henning, *The House of Commons 1660–1690,* vol. 3., pp. 433–35, quotation on p. 434. John writes that Sidney was commander of the Anglo-Dutch brigade in 1685 and that William declined James's request to replace him with his ambassador Bevil Skelton, but this appears to be in error. Carswell, *The Descent on England,* 52.
62. Encyclopaedia Britannica, 11th ed., vol. 24 (New York: Encyclopaedia Britannica, 1911), 1016–17; Ogg, *England in the Reigns of James II and William III,* 196–97; Carswell, *The Descent on England,* 99; quotation from Carswell.
63. Tim Harris, "The Scots and the Revolution of 1688–89," in Howard Nennen, ed., *Politics and the Political Imagination in Later Stuart Britain* (Rochester: University of Rochester Press, 1997), 104–5.
64. Baxter, *William III,* 225.
65. Ibid., 231. Others believe that William's fear that the English would set up a republic was exaggerated, but concede that it was real. Jones, *The Revolution of 1688 in England,* 235.
66. Western, *Monarchy and Revolution,* 252.

67. Miller, *James II*, 185. William's biographer Stephen Baxter, in his pungent prose, espies another motive. William, he writes, "could see another reason for intervention. That was that James had already destroyed the English monarchy, and that the only way of saving anything out of the wreckage was to take direct action. For two generations the Stuarts had indulged in the most fatuous misgovernment, and had done so largely at the expense of the House of Orange. Once before, Charles I had dragged the House of Orange down with him into ruin; what might be the consequence of the fall of James II? William had every reason to intervene for the protection of his own position as Prince; and it is clear that he more than half thought himself the head of the Stuarts as well. One might argue that James's first marriage had been morganatic. Or one might argue that James, as a Catholic, was disqualified from being King of England. This did not become the law until 1689, but it had been the deep-felt belief of the Whig party for a decade. And whichever theory William used to justify himself, there was always the demonstrable fact that James had misgoverned and that he had destroyed the monarchy." Baxter, *William III*, 227.

68. Baxter, *William III*, 224–25.

69. Carswell, *The Descent on England*, 53–54, 76, 79–80; Baxter, *William III*, 233.

70. Baxter, *William III*, 225.

71. Jones, *The Revolution of 1688 in England*, 133.

72. Miller, *James II*, 182.

73. J. G. A. Pocock, "Standing Army and Public Credit: The Institutions of Leviathan," in Dale Hoak and Mordechai Feingold, eds., *The World of William and Mary* (Stanford, CA: Stanford University Press, 1996), 93. "Mark Goldie has reminded us that, when these [James's pro-Catholic] policies grew to be more than Protestant Englishmen could support, they were effectively derailed by the doctrine of passive resistance in the Church of England as practiced by the bishops, the clergy, and the justices of the peace." Pocock cites Mark Goldie, "The Anglican Revolution of 1688," in R. A. Beddard, ed., *The Revolution of 1688: The Andrew Browning Lectures, 1988* (Oxford: Oxford University Press, 1990).

74. Miller, *James II*, 185; Ogg, *England in the Reigns of James II and William III*, 198; Jones, *The Revolution of 1688 in England*, 122–24; Carswell, *The Descent on England*, 133–40.

75. Carswell, *The Descent on England*, 139.

76. Ibid., 140.

77. Miller, *James II*, 185–87: Kenyon, *Sunderland*, 195–96; Speck, *Reluctant Revolutionaries*, 222–24.

78. Beyodere, *The Diary of John Evelyn*, 310.

79. Webb, *Lord Churchill's Coup*, 134.

80. Ibid., 135.

81. Baxter, *William III*, 225, 233.

82. Jones, *The Revolution of 1688 in England*, 253.

83. Kenyon, *Sunderland,* 203–4; Miller, *James II,* 190–91; Jones, *The Revolution of 1688 in England,* 255–58; Carswell, *The Descent on England,* 142. Kenyon and Carswell say 15 ships, Miller 16.

84. Kenyon, *Sunderland,* 197.

85. Bedoyere, *The Diary of John Evelyn,* 210.

86. Gregg, *Queen Anne,* 53–58. Quotation on p. 58.

87. Carswell, *The Descent on England,* 144–45.

88. Webb, *Lord Churchill's Coup,* 137.

89. Miller, *James II,* 187; Ogg, *England in the Reigns of James II and William III,* 198–200; Jones, *The Revolution of 1688 in England,* 124–27. Kenyon, *Sunderland,* 199–200; Carswell, *The Descent on England,* 146–50.

90. Bedoyere, *The Diary of John Evelyn,* 311.

91. Miller, *James II,* 187; Kenyon, *Sunderland,* 199–200.

92. Churchill, *Marlborough,* vol. 1, p. 238. A slightly different version is in Webb, *Lord Churchill's Coup,* 135.

93. Miller, *James II,* 188.

94. Kenyon, *Sunderland,* 200.

95. Miller, *James II,* 188–89.

96. Jones, *The Revolution of 1688 in England,* 238–40.

97. Ibid., 240–41.

98. Speck, *Reluctant Revolutionaries,* 220 ("[T]hey were hardly household names, and even Macaulay's omniscient schoolboys might well have had difficulty identifying them all"); Kenyon, *The Nobility in the Revolution of 1688,* p. 9 (they were "neither considerable nor representative").

99. Jones, *The Revolution of 1688 in England,* 243–44.

100. Bedoyere, *The Diary of John Evelyn,* 286.

101. Miller, *James II,* 187; Ogg, *England in the Reigns of James II and William III,* 202; Churchill, *Marlborough,* vol. 1, p. 242; Carswell, *The Descent on England,* 150; Speck, *Reluctant Revolutionaries,* 192; Henning, *The House of Commons 1660–1690,* vol. 2, p. 39.

102. Joyce Malcolm, *To Keep and Bear Arms* (Cambridge: Harvard University Press, 1994), 101–2.

103. J. R. Jones, "James II's Revolution: Royal Policies, 1686–92," in Israel, *The Anglo-Dutch Moment,* 63.

104. John Summerson, *Georgian London* (New Haven: Yale University Press, 2003), 12–16.

105. Childs, *The Army, James II, and the Glorious Revolution,* 158.

106. Ibid., 154–56, quotation on p. 156; Webb, *Lord Churchill's Coup,* 133.

107. Webb, *Lord Churchill's Coup,* 132–33.

108. Childs, *The Army, James II, and the Glorious Revolution,* 156–57, quotation on p. 157; Webb, *Lord Churchill's Coup,* 132.

109. Childs, *The Army, James II, and the Glorious Revolution,* 159–62.

110. Ibid., 162.

111. Ibid., 51–53; Webb, *Lord Churchill's Coup,* pp. 137–39.

112. Jones, *The Revolution of 1688 in England*, p. 229.

113. Webb, *Lord Churchill's Coup*, 131: "The two ex-Tangerines [Kirke and Trelawney] and Churchill, joined by Grafton of the foot guards and the young duke of Ormonde (representative of the Anglo-Irish officers and one of the first to reject King James's three questions), began to recruit candidates for the impending coup. Churchill's own troop of the Life Guards would follow him anywhere, and he counted on the backing of the Huguenot refugees in Dover's supposedly Catholic corps. As the Life Guards' executive officer, Lord Churchill could at least confuse and subvert the rest of the royal bodyguard. At the head of the [Prince of] Denmark connection, Churchill spoke for lord Cornbury and the rest of Churchill's old regiment, the Royals. Churchill also represented another of his former subordinates, a fellow Tangier veteran, Thomas Langston, now the executive officer of Princess Anne's cavalry (succeeding Sir Edmund Andros). Of course, he could count on [his brother] Charles Churchill, now colonel of the Buffs (succeeding Oglethorpe). Lord Churchill was also in daily touch with nets of Protestant professional officers in such new units as the 15th."

114. Churchill, *Marlborough*, vol. 1, p. 240. The spelling here is as in the facsimile printed opposite p. 240.

115. Churchill, *Marlborough*, vol. 1, p. 240.

116. Jones, *The Revolution of 1688 in England*, 145–46.

117. Ibid., 133, 146–50.

118. Jones, "James II's Revolution," 50–51, 63; Jones, *The Revolution of 1688 in England*, 145.

119. Jones, *The Revolution of 1688 in England*, 140.

120. Ibid., 133.

121. Ibid., 150. For more fascinating detail, see pp. 152–75.

122. Ibid., 151, 172–74.

123. Ibid., 160–61.

124. For some evidence on this point, see Speck, *Reluctant Revolutionaries*, 129–35.

125. Jones, "James II's Revolution," 62–63.

126. Henning, *The House of Commons 1660–1690*, vol. 1, pp. 308–17.

127. Jones, *The Revolution of 1688 in England*, 164.

128. Ibid., 165–66.

129. Ibid., 166.

130. On the Lords, see Speck, *Reluctant Revolutionaries*, 129.

131. Ibid., 161, 162. Speck goes on: "Moreover, as we have seen, there was still plenty of scope for exploiting the powers of the Crown under the later Stuarts. Both Charles II and James sought to take advantage of these. From this point of view the 1680s are all of a piece throughout. The growth of the army, the rigging of the judiciary, the professionalization of the major institutions of the state, and the attack on local autonomy all began in Charles II's reign. James merely continued a move towards absolutism

which his brother had begun. Indeed there is some evidence that he instituted it before his brother died, and that the driving force behind the throne in the early 1680s was the Duke of York."

132. Bedoyere, *The Diary of John Evelyn*, 311.

133. Kenyon, *Sunderland*, 168.

134. Speck, *Reluctant Revolutionaries*, 76.

135. Wolf, *Louis XIV*, 441–42.

136. Ibid., 443–44.

137. Rule, "France Caught Between Two Balances," 49.

138. Carswell, *The Descent on England*, 155–56.

139. Wolf, *Louis XIV*, 446. The conclusion is similar to that of the French historian Pierre Goubert: "These surprising aggressions resulted from calculations that were not entirely absurd. Louis XIV and Louvois wanted to act quickly. They thought that the partners in the coalition would quarrel among themselves, that the Emperor would be occupied with the war against the Turks (whom he crushed, reconquering Buda and Belgrade), and that William of Orange would get himself entangled in Holland or in England. It so happened, however, that each of these calculations was mistaken. With the exception of insignificant neutrals such as Portugal, Denmark, and Switzerland, all of Europe was arrayed against Louis, and these enemies were led by the tenacious William of Orange." Pierre Goubert, *The Course of French History* (London: Routledge, 1991), 137–38. See also Goubert, *Louis XIV and Twenty Million Frenchmen*, 169–72; Speck, *Reluctant Revolutionaries*, 76–77; and Rule, "France Caught Between Two Balances," 49.

140. Grew, *William Bentinck and William III*, 112.

141. Carswell, *The Descent on England*, 156–60.

142. Baxter, *William III*, 231–32.

143. Israel, "The Dutch Role in the Glorious Revolution," 114–16.

144. Baxter, *William III*, 233.

145. Israel, "The Dutch Role in the Glorious Revolution," 109; Miller, *James II*, 192.

146. Israel, "The Dutch Role in the Glorious Revolution," 116; Western, *Monarchy and Revolution*, 254–55; Jones, *The Revolution of 1688 in England*, 257–58. See also Jonathan Israel, *The Dutch Republic: Its Rise, Greatness and Fall 1477–1806* (Oxford: Oxford University Press, 1995), 844–50.

147. Miller, *James II*, 193–94.

148. Ibid., 194–95; Jones, *The Revolution of 1688 in England*, 259–62.

149. Baxter, *William III*, 235.

150. Wolf, *Louis XIV*, 444–45.

151. Israel, "The Dutch Role in the Glorious Revolution," 118.

152. Ibid.

153. Wolf, *Louis XIV*, 444–45.

154. Baxter, *William III*, 235.

155. Israel, "The Dutch Role in the Glorious Revolution," 119.

156. Ibid., 119–20. Quotation on p. 120.

157. Ibid., 120.

158. Baxter, *William III,* 236–37.

159. Miller, *James II,* 195; Kenyon, *Sunderland,* 215; Speck, *Reluctant Revolutionaries,* 81. J. R. Jones says the relevant dispatches were sent on September 20/30 and September 21/October 1. Jones, *The Revolution of 1688 in England,* 258. Speck writes that two dispatches were sent, September 18 and 21.

160. Carswell, *The Descent on England,* 165; Speck, *Reluctant Revolutionaries,* 81.

161. Harris, *The Scots and the Revolution of 1688–89,* 105.

162. Bedoyere, *The Diary of John Evelyn,* 313.

163. Jones, *The Revolution of 1688 in England,* 133, 159, 263; Miller, *James II,* 197–98.

164. Kenyon, *Sunderland,* 215.

165. Miller, *James II,* 197–98; Kenyon, *Sunderland,* 215–18.

166. Webb, *Lord Churchill's Coup,* 140.

167. Jones, *The Revolution of 1688 in England,* 263; Ogg, *England in the Reigns of Charles II and James II,* 204–05.

168. Israel, "The Dutch Role in the Glorious Revolution," 106.

169. Dale Hoak, "The Anglo-Dutch Revolution of 1688–89," in Dale Hoak and Mordechai Feingold, eds., *The World of William and Mary* (Stanford, CA: Stanford University Press, 1996), 16–17. Hoak continues: "In scale, organization, financing, and sheer firepower — this includes the pieces of artillery actually put ashore — it dwarfed the forces of the fabled Spanish Armada. In 1588, Philip II threw 131 ships and 25,000 men against Elizabeth's England. In 1688, William launched 463 vessels and 40,000 soldiers and mariners against James II. The flotilla inlcuded 49 great men-of-war (with an average of 45 guns each) and hundreds of flutes and transports conveying tens of thousands of tons of munitions and stores — boots, bread, coats, and carbines for a landing force of 21,000 men; harnesses, saddles, fodder, and hay for 5,000 horses (1,000 of which suffocated on the storm-tossed, abortive first crossing and had to be replaced); thousands of barrels of brandy, water, and beer; four tons of tobacco; and among the instruments of an extended authority, dies for casting William's own coins. The Dutch armada also carried the essential components of William's propaganda machine — a mobile printing press, printers, and copy-writers." See also Jonathan Scott, *England's Troubles: Seventeenth-Century English Political Instability in European Context* (Cambridge: Cambridge University Press, 2000), 215: "This armada was by far the greatest operation ever mounted in Atlantic waters."

170. Carswell, *The Descent on England,* 11.

171. Jonathan Israel, "General Introduction," in Jonathan Israel, ed., *The Anglo-Dutch Moment,* 12–18; Speck, *Reluctant Revolutionaries,* 74–75. Speck writes that the *Declaration* was "issued from the Hague on 20 September" O.S.; Israel says it was "of 30 September/10 October 1688." The full title is in Tony Claydon, *William III and the Godly Revolution* (Cambridge: Cambridge University Press, 1996), 24, n.1.

172. Carswell, *The Descent on England,* 179–80.
173. Israel, *The Dutch Republic,* 850.
174. Israel, "The Dutch Role in the Glorious Revolution," 120–23; Eveline Cruickshanks, *The Glorious Revolution* (London: Macmillan, 2000), 27; Ogg, *England in the Reigns of Charles II and James II,* 202; Jones, *The Revolution of 1688 in England,* 247–49; Claydon, *William III and the Godly Revolution,* 24–28.
175. Miller, *James II,* 199.
176. Israel, "The Dutch Role in the Glorious Revolution," 123.
177. Ibid., 122–24.
178. Baxter, *William III,* 233–34.
179. Israel, "The Dutch Role in the Glorious Revolution," 121.
180. Cruickshanks, *The Glorious Revolution,* 23–24.
181. E.g., Webb, *Lord Churchill's Coup,* 141: "The odds against the Dutch were almost two to one."
182. Israel, "The Dutch Role in the Glorious Revolution," 106 (emphasis in the original). For a similar calculation, see Hoak, "The Anglo-Dutch Revolution of 1688–89," 17.
183. Carswell, *The Descent on England,* 123–25.
184. Jones, *The Revolution of 1688 in England,* 133, 263–64; Miller, *James II,* 198; Western, *Monarchy and Revolution,* 269–70.
185. Kenyon, *Sunderland,* 220.
186. Jones, *The Revolution of 1688 in England,* 266.
187. Harris, *The Scots and the Revolution,* 105.
188. Speck, *Reluctant Revolutionaries,* 194.
189. Ibid., 83–84.
190. Bedoyere, *The Diary of John Evelyn,* 314.
191. Webb, *Lord Churchill's Coup,* 140.
192. Jones, *The Revolution of 1688 in England,* 133.
193. Ibid., 231–32.
194. Speck, *Reluctant Revolutionaries,* 83.
195. Jones, *The Revolution of 1688 in England,* 231–34; Carswell, *The Descent on England,* 167–68; Churchill, *Marlborough,* vol. 1, p, 257.
196. Israel, "General Introduction," in Jonathan Israel, ed., *The Anglo-Dutch Moment,* 39.
197. Baxter, *William III,* 239–40.
198. The course of William's voyage can be seen on the map in Carswell, *The Descent on England,* 164.
199. Jones, *The Revolution of 1688 in England,* 287–90; J. R. Western, *Monarchy and Revolution: The English State in the 1680s* (London: Macmillan, 1972), 263.

Chapter 7. The Civil War that Did Not Happen

1. Jones, *The Revolution of 1688 in England* (New York: Norton, 1972), 287–91; John Carswell, *The Descent on England: A Study of the English Revolution of 1688 and Its Background* (New York: John Day, 1969), 183–84. William's advance can be followed on the map in Carswell, p. 186.

2. Carswell, *The Descent on England,* 185.

3. Lois Schwoerer, "The Glorious Revolution as Spectacle: A New Perspective," in Stephen Baxter, ed., *England's Rise to Greatness, 1660–1763* (Berkeley and Los Angeles: University of California Press, 1983), 132–33.

4. Encyclopaedia Britannica, 11th ed., vol. 10 (New York: Encyclopaedia Britannica Co., 1911), 65–66; W. A. Speck, *Reluctant Revolutionaries: Englishmen and the Revolution of 1688* (Oxford: Oxford University Press, 1989), 202.

5. Mark Knights, *Representation and Misrepresentation in Later Stuart Britain* (Oxford: Oxford University Press, 2005), 22.

6. Jones, *The Revolution of 1688 in England,* 160–63, describes the rivalry of Seymour and Bath.

7. Basil Duke Henning, ed., *The House of Commons 1660–1690,* vol. 1 (London: Secker & Warburg, 1983), 197–201. Quotation at p. 200. Speck, *Reluctant Revolutionaries,* 209.

8. Jones, *The Revolution of 1688 in England,* 294.

9. Ibid., 294.

10. J. P. Kenyon, *The Nobility in the Revolution of 1688* (Hull: Hull University Press, 1963), cited in Speck, *Reluctant Revolutionaries,* 7.

11. J. R. Western, *Monarchy and Revolution: The English State in the 1680s* (London: Macmillan, 1972), 270–71; Carswell, *The Descent on England,* 188–89.

12. Joyce Malcolm, *To Keep and Bear Arms: The Origins of an Anglo-American Right* (Cambridge, MA: Harvard University Press, 1994), 111.

13. Western, *Monarchy and Revolution,* 272–73.

14. J. P. Kenyon, *Robert Spencer Earl of Sunderland 1641–1702* (London: Longmans Green, 1958), 222–27.

15. John Miller, *James II* (London: Methuen, 1989), 200–201; Jones, *The Revolution of 1688 in England,* 290–93.

16. Miller, *James II,* 201.

17. Carswell, *The Descent on England,* 189–90, 192–93; Western, *Monarchy and Revolution,* 274; Stephen Saunders Webb, *Lord Churchill's Coup* (New York: Knopf, 1995), 143–44. Webb dates Cornbury's going over on November 13.

18. Henning, *The House of Commons 1660–1690,* vol. 3, pp. 411–20. Quotations on pp. 418, 420. Jones, *The Revolution of 1688 in England,* 295–96; Speck, *Reluctant Revolutionaries,* 230–32.

19. Jones, *The Revolution of 1688 in England,* 295–96; Speck, *Reluctant Revolutionaries,* 192; Webb, *Lord Churchill's Coup,* 150–52.

20. Carswell, *The Descent on England,* 194.

21. Miller, *James II,* 201–03; Jones, *The Revolution of 1688 in England,* 296–97.

22. Carswell, *The Descent on England,* 193; Western, *Monarchy and Revolution,* 274–76.

23. Carswell, *The Descent on England,* 196.

24. Speck, *Reluctant Revolutionaries,* 87.

25. Webb, *Lord Churchill's Coup,* 146.

26. Miller, *James II,* 202–3; Jones, *The Revolution of 1688 in England,* 297–98.

27. Miller, *James II*, 202.
28. Edward Gregg, *Queen Anne* (New Haven: Yale University Press, 2001), 65, 64.
29. Winston Churchill, *Marlborough His Life and Times*, vol. 1 (London: Harrap, 1947), 258–63; Carswell, *The Descent on England*, 197–98.
30. Churchill, *Marlborough*, 263. The whole letter is on pp. 263–64.
31. Ibid., 263 n.1.
32. Webb, *Lord Churchill's Coup*, 17.
33. Jones, *The Revolution of 1688 in England*, 297–98; Western, *Monarchy and Revolution*, 276–78; Speck, *Reluctant Revolutionaries*, 87, 228. Speck gives the date of the seizure of Nottingham as November 20, Jones as November 21.
34. Jones, *The Revolution of 1688 in England*, 298–99.
35. Gregg, *Queen Anne*, 63–64.
36. Carswell, *The Descent on England*, 197–98.
37. Gregg, *Queen Anne*, 65–66. Quotation on p. 66. Churchill, *Marlborough*, vol. 1, pp. 266–68; Speck, *Reluctant Revolutionaries*, 229; Webb, *Lord Churchill's Coup*, 148–49.
38. Gregg, *Queen Anne*, 66; Speck, *Reluctant Revolutionaries*, p. 81.
39. Western, *Monarchy and Revolution*, 280–83; H. C. Foxcroft, *A Character of the Trimmer* (Cambridge: Cambridge University Press, 1946), 257–61.
40. Bedoyere, *The Diary of John Evelyn*, 316.
41. Foxcroft, *A Character of the Trimmer*, 205–09. Foxcroft praises him for suggesting "the possibility of a *via media* between the extremes of bravado and subservience," 208.
42. Jones, *The Revolution of 1688 in England*, 242–45. Quotation on p. 244.
43. Henning, *The House of Commons 1660–1690*, vol. 2, pp. 312–15.
44. Ibid., 405–6.
45. Jones, *The Revolution of 1688 in England*, 300.
46. Ibid., 303.
47. Carswell, *The Descent on England*, 201–2; Jones, *The Revolution of 1688 in England*, 301–2. Quotation on p. 302.
48. Jones, *The Revolution of 1688 in England*, 301.
49. Western, *Monarchy and Revolution*, 304–5; Speck, *Reluctant Revolutionaries*, 233–35.
50. Stephen Baxter, *William III* (New York: Harcourt Brace, 1966), 241.
51. http://www.likesbooks.com/uktripday7.html.
52. Miller, *James II*, 205.
53. Jones, *The Revolution of 1688 in England*, 304; Speck, *Reluctant Revolutionaries*, 88.
54. Baxter, *William III*, 241; Jones, *The Revolution of 1688 in England*, 304–5; Miller, *James II*, 205; Foxcroft, *A Character of the Trimmer*, 262.
55. Jones, *The Revolution of 1688 in England*, 310.
56. Webb, *Lord Churchill's Coup*, 158–59.
57. Jones, *The Revolution of 1688 in England*, 305; Miller, *James II*, 205; Western, *Monarchy and Revolution*, 285–87. Miller says that James sent them out the

night of December 9, after receiving the first reports from Halifax, Nottingham, and Godolphin of their meeting with William.

58. Miller, *James II*, 205; Jones, *The Revolution of 1688 in England*, 305.

59. Hutton, *Charles II*, 1–14; Miller, *James II*, 1–6.

60. Jones, *The Revolution of 1688 in England*, 305; Carswell, *The Descent on England*, 205.

61. Miller, *James II*, 206.

62. Carswell, *The Descent on England*, 206: "It was only two years since he had exclaimed with such passion against the idea of being a vassal of France. Now he was passing into the mechanical grip of Louis."

63. Western, *Monarchy and Revolution*, 279.

64. D. W. Hayton, "The Williamite Revolution in Ireland, 1688–91," in Jonathan Israel, ed., *The Anglo-Dutch Moment* (Cambridge: Cambridge University Press, 1991), 192.

65. Jones, *The Revolution of 1688 in England*, 308–9; Miller, *James II*, 206.

66. Miller, *James II*, 206.

67. Ibid.

68. Bedoyere, *The Diary of John Evelyn*, 316.

69. Tim Harris, "The Scots and the Revolution of 1688–89," in Howard Nennen, ed., *Politics and Political Imagination in Late Stuart England* (Rochester, NY: University of Rochester Press, 1997), 106–7.

70. Jonathan Israel, "General Introduction," in Israel, *The Anglo-Dutch Moment*, 37.

71. Miller, *James II*, 206; Baxter, *William III*, 245.

72. Jonathan Scott, *England's Troubles: Seventeenth-Century English Political Instability in European Context* (Cambridge: Cambridge University Press, 2000), 220.

73. Baxter, *William III*, 242.

74. Webb, *Lord Churchill's Coup*, 162–63.

75. Miller, *James II*, 206–8; Baxter, *William III*, 242, 245. Quotation from Baxter, p. 242.

76. Western, *Monarchy and Revolution*, 292.

77. Carswell, *The Descent on England*, 210–11; Western, *Monarchy and Revolution*, 292–93.

78. Carswell, *The Descent on England*, 211–12.

79. Ibid., 212; Western, *Monarchy and Revolution*, 290–91, 293.

80. Carswell, *The Descent on England*, 213–14; Foxcroft, *A Character of the Trimmer*, 267–68; Western, *Monarchy and Revolution*, 296–97.

81. Miller, *James II*, 208–9; Carswell, *The Descent on England*, 214; Baxter, *William III*, 243–46; Foxcroft, *A Character of the Trimmer*, 266–70; Jones, *The Revolution of 1688 in England*, 309.

82. Baxter, *William III*, 248; Israel, "General Introduction," 1–3.

83. Webb, *Lord Churchill's Coup*, 164–65, 172–73.

CHAPTER 8. KING WILLIAM

1. Guy de la Bedoyere, ed., *The Diary of John Evelyn* (Woodbridge, England: Boydell Press, 1995), 316.

2. H. C. Foxcroft, *The Character of a Trimmer* (Cambridge: Cambridge University Press, 1946), 270.

3. John Morrill, "The Sensible Revolution," in Jonathan Israel, ed., *The Anglo-Dutch Moment* (Cambridge: Cambridge University Press, 2003), 82–83: "The legitimate line had been broken at almost half the accessions between 1066 and 1685, and several 'usurpers' were further removed from the natural line of succession than was William III from James II. Neither was there anything in the fact that a living monarch was superseded by a rival following a coup. The period 1327–1485 saw more irregular than regular transmissions of the kingly office, with kings regnant being deposed on no less than seven occasions." See also Jonathan Scott, *England's Troubles: Seventeenth-Century English Political Instability in European Context* (Cambridge: Cambridge University Press, 2000), 74; Paul Murray Kendall, *Richard the Third* (New York: Norton, 1956), 184–86.

4. See the genealogical table in Israel, *The Anglo-Dutch Moment*, 368–69. Ranking twenty-seventh in line for the throne was Georg Ludwig, Duke of Hanover, who succeeded Queen Anne as George I in 1714.

5. Stephen Baxter, *William III and the Defense of European Liberty, 1650–1702* (New York: Harcourt Brace 1966), 246; Foxcroft, *The Character of a Trimmer,* p. 270.

6. J. R. Western, *Monarchy and Revolution: The English State in the 1680s* (London: Macmillan, 1985), 298–99.

7. Ibid., 298–99; John Carswell, *The Descent on England* (New York: John Day, 1969), 217.

8. Western, *Monarchy and Revolution,* 300.

9. J. R. Jones, *The Revolution of 1688 in England* (New York: Norton, 1972), 311; Western, *Monarchy and Revolution,* 300; Foxcroft, *The Character of a Trimmer,* 271; Carswell, *The Descent on England* (New York: John Day, 1969), 217.

10. Carswell, *The Descent on England,* 217–18.

11. Ibid., 216; Encyclopaedia Britannica, 11th ed., vol. 5 (New York: Encyclopaedia Britannica Co., 1911) 531.

12. Carswell, *The Descent on England,* 218.

13. Tim Harris, "The Scots and the Revolution of 1688–89," in Howard Nennen, ed., *Politics and the Political Imagination in Late Stuart Britain* (Rochester: University of Rochester Press, 1997), 105–6.

14. Ian Cowan, "Church and State Reformed? The Revolution of 1688–89 in Scotland," in Jonathan Israel, ed., *The Anglo-Dutch Moment* (Cambridge: Cambridge University Press, 2003), 163–64; Baxter, *William III,* 252.

15. Jones, *The Revolution of 1688 in England,* 312.

16. W. A. Speck, *Reluctant Revolutionaries* (Oxford: Oxford University Press, 1989), 93–94.

17. Carswell, *The Descent on England,* 218–19; Western, *Monarchy and Revolution,* 305–6.

18. Basil Duke Henning, *The House of Commons 1660–1690,* vol. 1 (London: Secker & Warburg, 1983), 314–15.

19. Ibid., 317.

20. Ibid., 319–22.

21. Ibid., 230.

22. Ibid., vol. 1, pp. 135–39, vol. 2, pp. 221–22. 718–23.

23. Carswell, *The Descent on England,* 221.

24. Ibid., 216–17.

25. Speck, *Reluctant Revolutionaries,* 94; Carswell, *The Descent on England,* 221–22.

26. Western, *Monarchy and Revolution,* 306.

27. Speck, *Reluctant Revolutionaries,* 95; Carswell, *The Descent on England,* 222–23.

28. Carswell, *The Descent on England,* 222–23. Quotation on p. 223.

29. Speck, *Reluctant Revolutionaries,* 95; Henning, *The House of Commons 1660–1690,* vol. 2, pp. 74–81.

30. Speck, *Reluctant Revolutionaries,* 95–96.

31. Dale Hoak, "The Anglo-Dutch Revolution of 1688–89," in Dale Hoak and Mordechai Feingold, eds., *The World of William and Mary* (Stanford, CA: Stanford University Press, 1996), 2; Speck, *Reluctant Revolutionaries,* 96–97; J. G. A. Pocock, *Virtue, Commerce, and History* (Cambridge: Cambridge University Press, 1985), 217; Peter Laslett, Introduction to Peter Laslett, ed., *John Locke, Two Treatises on Government* (Cambridge: Cambridge University Press, 2003), 12.

32. Melinda Zook, "Violence, Martyrdom, and Radical Politics: Rethinking the Glorious Revolution," in Howard Nenner, ed., *Politics and the Political Imagination in Later Stuart Britain: Essays Presented to Lois Green Schwoerer* (Rochester: University of Rochester Press, 1997), 77, 80, 89–91; Bruce Lenman, "The Poverty of Political Theory in the Scottish Revolution of 1688–1690," in Lois Schwoerer, *The Revolution of 1688–89: Changing Perspectives* (Cambridge: Cambridge University Press, 1992), 256–57.

33. Speck, *Reluctant Revolutionaries,* 96–98; Carswell, *The Descent on England,* 223; Western, *Monarchy and Revolution,* 307.

34. Morrill, "The Sensible Revolution," 93, n.69.

35. Ibid.; quoting George Macaulay Trevelyan, *The English Revolution, 1688–1689* (Oxford: Oxford University Press, 1938), 146.

36. Speck, *Reluctant Revolutionaries,* 98.

37. Jones, *The Revolution of 1688 in England,* 313; Speck, *Reluctant Revolutionaries,* 99–100.

38. Speck, *Reluctant Revolutionaries,* 100; Western, *Monarchy and Revolution,* 309–10; Winston Churchill, *Marlborough His Life and Times,* vol. 1 (London: Harrap, 1934), 276.

39. Foxcroft, *A Character of the Trimmer,* 272, 274; Western, *Monarchy and Revolution,* 302.

40. Baxter, *William III,* 247; Jones, *The Revolution of 1688 in England,* 313–15.

41. Speck, *Reluctant Revolutionaries,* 100–2; Western, *Monarchy and Revolution,* 311.

42. Speck, *Reluctant Revolutionaries,* 102–03.

43. Falkland, after a lucrative marriage, had purchased from Sir Edward Seymour the office of Treasurer of the Navy for £15,000 in 1681, at age 25, and had prospered further from his share in a syndicate led by Christopher Monck, second Duke of Albemarle, to recover a Spanish treasure ship. See John Evelyn's diary entry for June 12, 1687. Bedoyere, *The Diary of John Evelyn,* 306.

44. Speck, *Reluctant Revolutionaries,* 104–6; Lois Schwoerer, "The Glorious Revolution as Spectacle: A New Perspective," in Stephen Baxter, ed., *England's Rise to Greatness, 1660–1763* (Berkeley and Los Angeles: University of California Press, 1983), 122–24; Henning, ed., *The House of Commons 1660–1690,* vol. 2, pp. 16–17.

45. Speck, *Reluctant Revolutionaries,* 106.

46. Cf. the analysis in Speck, *Reluctant Revolutionaries,* 105–7.

47. Ibid., 107; Schwoerer, "The Glorious Revolution as Spectacle," 122–24.

48. Referred to in Schwoerer, "The Glorious Revolution as Spectacle," 116.

49. Jones, *The Revolution of 1688 in England,* 316.

50. Carswell, *The Descent on England,* 224; Western, *Monarchy and Revolution,* 314–15.

51. Speck, *Reluctant Revolutionaries,* 108; Foxcroft, *A Character of the Trimmer,* 275; Western, *Monarchy and Revolution,* 314–15. Foxcroft dates the meeting of William with Halifax, Danby, and Shrewsbury as February 5; Speck and Western say it was probably February 3.

52. Western, *Monarchy and Revolution,* 315; Henry Horwitz, *Revolution Politicks: The Career of Daniel Finch, Second Earl of Nottingham* (Cambridge: Cambridge University Press, 1968), 79–80; Churchill, *Marlborough,* vol. 1, p. 276; Webb, *Lord Churchill's Coup,* 174–75.

53. Morrill, "The Sensible Revolution," 84–85.

54. Speck, *Reluctant Revolutionaries,* 108.

55. Ibid., 103–4; Western, *Monarchy and Revolution,* 311–12.

56. Foxcroft, *A Character of the Trimmer,* 276; Western, *Monarchy and Revolution,* 311–12.

57. Jones, *The Revolution of 1688 in England,* 316; Speck, *Reluctant Revolutionaries,* 108–10; Carswell, *The Descent on England,* 225; Foxcroft, *A Character of the Trimmer,* 276; Western, *Monarchy and Revolution,* 315. Jones has the vote as 62–47, Speck 64–46, Foxcroft 65–45; Western says the motion passed "by a majority of at least 15."

58. Speck, *Reluctant Revolutionaries,* 109–10; Western, *Monarchy and Revolution,* 315–16.

59. Schwoerer, "The Glorious Revolution as Spectacle," 122–24.

60. Speck, *Reluctant Revolutionaries,* 110–13; Western, *Monarchy and Revolution,* 316–17; Schwoerer, "The Glorious Revolution as Spectacle," 125–26.

61. Ibid., 126–28.

62. Ibid., 128–30.

63. Speck, *Reluctant Revolutionaries,* 113.

64. Paul Rahe, *Republics Ancient and Modern: Classical Republicanism and the American Revolution* (Chapel Hill: University of North Carolina Press, 1990), 525.

65. Schwoerer, "The Glorious Revolution as Spectacle," 130–31.

66. Jones, *The Revolution of 1688 in England*, 316; Morrill, "The Sensible Revolution," 84; Schwoerer, "The Glorious Revolution as Spectacle," 111.

67. Speck, *Reluctant Revolutionaries*, 140–57.

68. Lois Schwoerer, "The Bill of Rights, 1689, Revisited," in Dale Hoak and Mordechai Feingold, eds., *The World of William and Mary: Anglo-Dutch Perspectives on the Revolution of 1688–89* (Stanford, CA: Stanford University Press, 1996), 47; Speck, *Reluctant Revolutionaries*, 141–42, 148–52. On the limiting of the dispensing power, see Stephen Baxter, *William III*, 256.

69. Western, *Monarchy and Revolution*, 331; Speck, *Reluctant Revolutionaries*, 143–45; Schwoerer, "The Bill of Rights, 1689, Revisited," 47.

70. Speck, *Reluctant Revolutionaries*, 145–46, 153–56; Schwoerer, "The Bill of Rights, 1689, Revisited," 47; Western, *Monarchy and Revolution*, 331–32.

71. Speck, *Reluctant Revolutionaries*, 245–47.

72. Joyce Malcolm, *To Keep and Bear Arms: The Origins of an Anglo-American Right* (Cambridge, MA: Harvard University Press, 1994), 115–18; Speck, *Reluctant Revolutionaries*, 147–48; Schwoerer, "The Bill of Rights, 1689, Revisited," 47–48; Western, *Monarchy and Revolution*, 331–32.

73. Malcolm, *To Keep and Bear Arms*, 118–21.

74. Schwoerer, "The Bill of Rights, 1689, Revisited," 48; Western, *Monarchy and Revolution*, 330–33; Jones, *The Revolution of 1688 in England*, 318–19; Morrill, *The Sensible Revolution*, 79.

75. Schwoerer, "The Glorious Revolution as Spectacle," 127: "Recently these questions have been raised by scholars, three of whom (Pinkham, Frankle, and Nenner) concluded that the Declaration was not a condition and two (Carter and Horwitz) that it was." Schwoerer concludes that the men who endorsed the Declaration did want it to be a condition and a restriction: "They wanted to change the kingship as well as the king," pp. 127–28. She writes to similar effect elsewhere; e.g., "The Bill of Rights, 1689, Revisited," 44. Dale Hoak seems to argue that the Declaration of Rights was, in William Sacheverell's words, not "a new limitation of the Crown, but what of right is ours by law," and states that William explicitly declared that it was not a condition for the offer of the crown. But he concedes that the abolition of the dispensing power "circumscribed royal action" and that the requirement that Parliament authorize any standing army "boldly checked one of the king's most important prerogatives" and "signaled a seismic shift in the relations of Crown and Parliament." Hoak, *The Anglo-Dutch Revolution of 1688–89*, 4–6.

76. The issues are discussed and the academic opinion on the issue summarized in Morrill, "*The Sensible Revolution*," 89–91. See Lois Schwoerer, *The Declaration of Rights* (Baltimore: Johns Hopkins Press, 1981).

77. Cf. Speck, *Reluctant Revolutionaries*, 164–65. "While the letter of the law might not have changed greatly, the whole attitude of and towards government altered drastically."

78. See endnote 61.

79. Schwoerer, "The Glorious Revolution as Spectacle," 131–32.

80. Ibid., 133–34.

81. Ibid., 120–22.

82. Carswell, *The Descent on England*, 225–26; Schwoerer, "The Glorious Revolution as Spectacle," 109.

83. Ibid., 116–17.

84. Ibid., 132–33.

85. Stephen Baxter, "William III as Hercules: The Political Implications of Court Culture," in Lois Schwoerer, ed., *The Revolution of 1688–1689: Changing Perspectives* (Cambridge: Cambridge University Press, 1992), 101–2.

86. Western, *Monarchy and Revolution*, 317; Henry Horwitz, *Parliament, Policy and Politics in the Reign of William III* (Manchester: Manchester University Press, 1977), 14, 16.

87. Bedoyere, *The Diary of John Evelyn*, 320.

88. http://www.historicroyalpalaces.org/history/default.asp?sectID=4&id=4.

89. http://www.historicroyalpalaces.org/history/default.asp?sectID=3&id=3.

90. Foxcroft, *A Character of the Trimmer*, 283–84. Quotation on p. 284.

91. Ibid., 279.

92. Horwitz, *Parliament, Policy and Politics*, 17.

93. B. W. Hill, *The Growth of Parliamentary Parties* (London: Allen & Unwin, 1976), 35–36.

94. The phrase is W. A. Speck's. See Speck, *Reluctant Revolutionaries*, 246.

95. Ibid., 164.

96. Horwitz, *Parliament, Policy and Politics*, 21; Morrill, "The Sensible Revolution," 94.

97. Speck, *Reluctant Revolutionaries*, 163–64. Speck notes that the Act lapsed for several days in 1689 and 1690, for nearly three months in 1692, and for almost three years from 1698 to 1701. But such lapses are, as we know, typical of parliamentary politics, and were signs more of the executive's dependence on the legislature than of his dominance over it.

98. Baxter, *William III*, 250–51.

99. Horwitz, *Parliament, Policy and Politics*, 26.

100. Ibid., 27; Hill, *The Growth of Parliamentary Parties*, 38.

101. Horwitz, *Parliament, Policy and Politics*, 27.

102. Hill, *The Growth of Parliamentary Parties*, 38.

103. Morrill, "The Sensible Revolution," 96–97.

104. Horwitz, *Parliament, Policy and Politics*, 22; Hill, *The Growth of Parliamentary Parties*, 38–39.

105. Horwitz, *Parliament, Policy and Politics*, 22; Hill, *The Growth of Parliamentary Parties*, 38–39.

106. Horwitz, *Parliament, Policy and Politics*, 22; Hill, *The Growth of Parliamentary Parties*, 39. Horwitz says March 25, Hill says March 26.

107. Speck, *Reluctant Revolutionaries*, 186.

108. Horwitz, *Parliament, Policy and Politics*, 23, 29.

109. Hoak, "The Anglo-Dutch Revolution of 1688–89," 9.

110. Horwitz, *Parliament, Policy and Politics*, 24–25.

111. Ibid., 24.

112. Ibid., 25.

113. Harris, "The Scots and the Revolution of 1688–89," 108–12; Cowan, "Church and State Reformed?" 163–66; Morrill, "The Sensible Revolution," 99.

114. Harris, *The Scots and the Revolution of 1688–89*, 107–8.

115. Richard Johnson, "The Revolution of 1688–9 in the American Colonies," in Jonathan Israel, ed., *The Anglo-Dutch Moment* (Cambridge: Cambridge University Press, 1991), 221.

116. Ibid., 221–29.

117. Ibid., 229–34.

118. Ibid., 234. Cf. Jack Greene, "The Glorious Revolution and the British Empire 1688–1783," in Lois Schwoerer, ed., *The Revolution of 1688–89: Changing Perspectives* (Cambridge: Cambridge University Press, 1992), 262: "A broad interpretive framework seems to be gaining considerable scholarly support. According to this framework, an extraordinary devolution of authority outward to the new colonial peripheries during the first half of the seventeenth century was followed by a gradual resumption of that authority between the Restoration and the middle decades of the eighteenth century as a result of several related developments: the imposition of the Navigation Acts; the royalization of many private colonies; the establishment of successful patronage networks running between the metropolis and the colonies; the expansion of the royal bureaucracy; growing colonial dependence upon the metropolis for defense; and what one scholar has referred to as 'the gradual and grudging adjustment [on the part of the colonists] to imperial and monarchical rule.'" Greene argues that "this line of interpretation" has "been carried vastly too far."

119. Carswell, *The Descent on England*, 16.

120. Greene, "The Glorious Revolution and the British Empire," 265.

121. Johnson, "The Revolution of 1688–9 in the American Colonies," 232.

122. Ibid., 234–40.

123. Greene, "The Glorious Revolution and the British Empire," 268.

124. Johnson, "The Revolution of 1688–9 in the American Colonies," 238.

125. Greene, "The Glorious Revolution and the British Empire," 270.

126. Hoak, "The Anglo-Dutch Revolution of 1688–89," 10.

127. Churchill, *Marlborough*, vol. 1, pp. 276–77.

128. Horwitz, *Parliament, Policy and Politics*, 39–40; Gordon Schochet, "The Act of Toleration and the Failure of Comprehension: Persecution, Nonconformity, and Religious Indifference," in Dale Hoak and Mordechai Feingold, eds., *The World of William and Mary* (Stanford: Stanford University Press, 1996), 181–86.

129. Schochet, "Toleration and Comprehension," 166.

130. Horwitz, *Parliament, Policy and Politics,* 28.
131. Jones, *The Revolution of 1688 in England,* 319–20; Morrill, "The Sensible Revolution," Horwitz, *Parliament, Policy and Politics,* 29; Schochet, "Toleration and Comprehension," 180–81.
132. Speck, *Reluctant Revolutionaries,* 106.
133. William Langer, *An Encyclopedia of World History* (Boston: Houghton Mifflin, 1952), 432, 434.
134. Schochet, "Toleration and Comprehension," 180, 186–87.
135. Hoak, "The Anglo-Dutch Revolution of 1688–89," 11.
136. Horwitz, *Parliament, Policy and Politics,* 23–25.
137. Ibid., 26.
138. Hill, *The Growth of Parliamentary Parties,* 39–40.
139. Horwitz, *Parliament, Policy and Politics,* 21–22; Hill, *The Growth of Parliamentary Parties,* 39.
140. Morrill, "The Sensible Revolution," 96.
141. Ibid., 98.
142. Horwitz, *Parliament, Policy and Politics,* 23, 29.
143. Ibid., 30.
144. Ibid., 27.
145. Ibid., 28.
146. Ibid., 30.
147. Ibid., 32.
148. Hill, *The Growth of Parliamentary Parties,* 40.
149. Horwitz, *Parliament, Policy and Politics,* 35.
150. Quoted in Henry Roseveare, *The Financial Revolution 1660–1760* (London: Longman, 1991), 32.
151. Horwitz, *Parliament, Policy and Politics,* 33.
152. Ibid., 34.
153. Ibid., 33.
154. Ibid., p. 35.
155. Churchill, *Marlborough,* vol. 1, pp. 282–84; Webb, *Lord Churchill's Coup,* 230–31.
156. Baxter, *William III,* 255.
157. Churchill, *Marlborough,* vol. 1, p. 302.
158. Horwitz, *Parliament, Policy and Politics,* 36.
159. Ibid., p. 30.
160. See the genealogical table in Israel, *The Anglo-Dutch Moment,* 368–69.
161. Baxter, *William III,* p. 251.
162. Horwitz, *Parliament, Policy and Politics,* 32.
163. Ibid., 34.
164. Ibid., 36.
165. Ibid., 37.
166. Ibid., 37.
167. Ibid., 39.

168. Ibid., 40.

169. Hill, *The Growth of Parliamentary Parties*, 42.

170. Horwitz, *Parliament, Policy and Politics*, 42–43.

171. Ibid., 43.

172. Ibid., 43.

173. Ibid., 44.

CHAPTER 9. WAR

1. Tony Claydon, *William III* (London: Pearson, 2002), 139.

2. Stephen Baxter, "William III as Hercules: The Political Implications of Court Culture," in Lois Schwoerer, ed., *The Revolution of 1688–1689: Changing Perspectives* (Cambridge: Cambridge University Press, 1992), 97–100.

3. J. G. A. Pocock, "Standing Army and Public Credit: The Institutions of Leviathan," in Dale Hoak and Mordechai Feingold, eds., *The World of William and Mary* (Stanford: Stanford University Press, 1996), 88–89.

4. Stephen Baxter, *William III and the Defense of European Liberty 1650–1702* (New York: Harcourt Brace, 1966), 48–49.

5. Claydon, *William III*, 15–18; Jonathan Israel, *The Dutch Republic: Its Rise, Greatness, and Fall, 1477–1806* (Oxford: Clarendon Press, 1995), 785–95.

6. Baxter, *William III*, 70–85.

7. Claydon, *William III*, xv–xix.

8. Ibid., 20.

9. Baxter, *William III*, 93.

10. Winston Churchill, *Marlborough His Life and Times*, vol. 1 (London: Harrap, 1937), 276–78; Stephen Saunders Webb, *Lord Churchill's Coup* (New York: Knopf, 1995), 176–81.

11. H. C. Foxcroft, *A Character of the Trimmer* (Cambridge: Cambridge University Press, 1946), 281. Cf. J. R. Jones, *The Revolution of 1688 in England* (New York: Norton, 1972), 190: "All his actions after 1688 demonstrate the fact that for William England was always a means, not an end in itself. The ultimate purpose was the containment of France, the reduction of the power which enabled Louis to dominate his neighbours."

12. Henry Horwitz, *Parliament, Policy and Politics in the Reign of William III* (Manchester, England: Manchester University Press, 1977), 27.

13. Baxter, *William III*, 252.

14. Horwitz, *Parliament, Policy and Politics*, 35; Foxcroft, *A Character of the Trimmer*, 281.

15. Tim Harris, "The Scots and the Revolution of 1688–89," in Howard Nennen, ed., *Politics and Political Imagination in Late Stuart Britain* (Rochester: University of Rochester Press, 1997), 103.

16. Baxter, *William III*, 252.

17. Baxter, *William III*, 253; Ian Cowan, "Church and State Reformed? The Revolution of 1688–89 in Scotland," in Jonathan Israel, ed., *The Anglo-Dutch Movement* (Cambridge: Cambridge University Press, 2003), 165.

18. John Carswell, *The Descent on England: A Study of the English Revolution and Its*

European Background (New York: John Day, 1969), 220–21; Cowan, "Church and State Reformed?" 166–74.

19. Harris, *The Scots and the Revolution of 1688–89*, 117.

20. Carswell, *The Descent on England*, 220.

21. B. W. Hill, *The Growth of Parliamentary Parties* (London: Allen & Unwin, 1976), 40.

22. Horwitz, *Parliament, Policy and Politics*, 17, 20.

23. Baxter, *William III*, 253–55; R. F. Foster, *Modern Ireland 1600–1972* (London: Penguin, 1988), 141.

24. D. W. Hayton, "The Williamite Revolution in Ireland, 1688–91," in Jonathan Israel, ed., *The Anglo-Dutch Moment* (Cambridge: Cambridge University Press, 1991), 189, 196–99; Foster, *Modern Ireland 1600–1972*, 140, 144–46.

25. Hayton, "The Williamite Revolution in Ireland," 199–202.

26. Horwitz, *Parliament, Policy and Politics*, 31.

27. Foster, *Modern Ireland*, 146–47; Horwitz, *Parliament, Policy and Politics*, 38.

28. Baxter, *William III*, 256–57.

29. Ibid., 262–63.

30. Ibid., 262–66; Webb, *Lord Churchill's Coup*, 236–37.

31. Churchill, *Marlborough*, vol. 1, pp. 287–94; Webb, *Lord Churchill's Coup*, 239–44.

32. Foster, *Modern Ireland*, 149–50; Baxter, *William III*, 266–69.

33. Foster, *Modern Ireland*, 150–52; Hayton, "The Williamite Revolution," 206–8.

34. Foster, *Modern Ireland*, 159–60; Hayton, "The Williamite Revolution," 208–11.

35. Foster, *Modern Ireland*, 163.

36. Karl Bottigheimer, "The Glorious Revolution and Ireland," in Lois Schwoerer, ed., *The Revolution of 1688–1689: Changing Perspectives* (Cambridge: Cambridge University Press, 1992), 239–40.

37. Ibid., 242–43.

38. Claydon, *William III*, xviii–xxi.

39. From the table on p. 65 in D. W. Jones, "Defending the Revolution: The Economics, Logistics, and Finance of England's War Effort, 1688–1712," in Dale Hoak and Mordechai Feingold, eds., *The World of William and Mary* (Stanford: Stanford University Press, 1996), 59–66. The final three digits have been reduced to zeroes in the interest of clarity. Claydon, *William III*, 126; Henry Roseveare, *The Financial Revolution 1660–1760* (London: Longman, 1991), 33. Roseveare places the size of the army as "up to 90,000." Cf. the figures in table 2.1 in John Brewer, *The Sinews of Power: War, Money and the English State, 1688–1783* (New York: Knopf, 1989), 30, which show an average authorized strength of 76,404 in the army and 40,262 in the navy from 1689 to 1697.

40. Claydon, *William III*, 125–26.

41. Ibid., 126.

42. Dale Hoak, "The Anglo-Dutch Revolution of 1688–89," in Dale Hoak and

Mordechai Feingold, eds., *The World of William and Mary* (Stanford, CA: Stanford University Press, 1996), 13.

43. Tony Claydon, *William III and the Godly Revolution* (Cambridge: Cambridge University Press, 1976), 134–47.

44. Roseveare, *The Financial Revolution 1660–1760*, 34.

45. Claydon, *William III*, 126–55. Quotation on p. 147.

46. Claydon, *William III*, 154–55. "Unlike his predecessors, he had had a continental career that taught him to see through the paradox of royal power and the state. He knew that if the rulers gave up some of their control over finance and the military, they could have been more than compensated by a vast increase in the size and capability of the machine they still headed [p. 155]."

47. Claydon, *William III*, 128–29; P. G. Dickson, *The Financial Revolution in England: A Study in the Development of Public Credit 1688–1756* (London: Macmillan, 1967), 53–54.

48. Dickson, *The Financial Revolution in England*, 52–54.

49. Roseveare, *The Financial Revolution 1660–1760*, 35; Dickson, *The Financial Revolution in England*, 54.

50. Dickson, *The Financial Revolution in England*, 50–51.

51. http://www.ex.ac.uk/-RDavies/arian/amser/chrono7.html.

52. Dickson, *The Financial Revolution in England*, 51.

53. Eveline Cruickshanks et al., eds., *The House of Commons 1690–1715*, vol. 4 (Cambridge: Cambridge University Press, 2002), 856–57; Dickson, *The Financial Revolution in England*, 54–55.

54. Dickson, *The Financial Revolution in England*, 55; Niall Ferguson, *The Cash Nexus: Money and Power in the Modern World 1700–2000* (London: Penguin, 2001), 114–15.

55. Paul Rahe, *Republics Ancient and Modern: Classical Republicanism and the American Revolution* (Chapel Hill: University of North Carolina Press, 1990), 517.

56. Dickson, *The Financial Revolution in England*, 55–56; Roseveare, *The Financial Revolution 1660–1760*, 36–38.

57. Dickson, *The Financial Revolution in England*, 57. See also Brewer, *The Sinews of Power*, 149–51.

58. Dickson, *The Financial Revolution in England*, 52.

59. Ibid., 58.

60. Ferguson, *The Cash Nexus*, 114–16. John Brewer acknowledges "the central contribution of borrowing to the survival and subsequent expansion of the English state," but also notes that "an effective tax system, providing the government with a substantial and *regular* income, was a necessary condition of the new credit mechanism which, as we shall see, revolutionized eighteenth-century public finance." Brewer, *The Sinews of Power*, 88, 89.

61. Brewer, *The Sinews of Power*, 154.

62. Ferguson, *The Cash Nexus*, 180. "The key difference between France and Britain in the eighteenth century, then, was not a matter of economic resources. France had more. Rather, it was a matter of institutions. Britain

had the superior revenue-collecting system, the Excise. After the Glorious Revolution, Britain also had representative government, which not only tended to make budgets transparent, but also—more importantly—reduced the likelihood of default, since the bondholders who had invested in the National Debt were among the interests best represented in Parliament. The National Debt itself was largely funded (long-term) and transparently managed (especially after the advent of the consol). And the Bank of England—which again had no French analogue—also guaranteed the convertibility of the currency into gold (save in extreme emergency), reducing if not eliminating the risk of default through inflation. It was these restrictions which enabled Britain to sustain a much larger debt/GDP ratio than France because they ensured that the interest Britain paid on her debt was substantially less than France could pay on hers. If one seeks a fiscal explanation for Britain's ultimate triumph over France in their global contest, it lies here." See also Brewer, *The Sinews of Power,* 133–34.

63. Horwitz, *Parliament, Policy and Politics,* 199–200; Tim Harris, *Revolution: The Great Crisis of the English Monarchy, 1685–1720* (London: Penguin, 2006), 492–93.

64. Harris, *Revolution,* 493. On the hereditary succession, I have relied on the table in Israel, *The Anglo-Dutch Moment,* 368–69.

65. Pocock, "Standing Army and Public Credit," 87.

66. Hoak, "The Anglo-Dutch Revolution of 1688–89," 12–13. Hoak also writes (p. 14), "This, the Dutch military occupation of London in 1688–89 signaled more than a dramatic turn in the dynastic affairs of Orange and Stuart. By harnessing England to his anti-French war machine, William of Orange forced English politicians to build the greatest military-commercial engine the world had yet seen."

67. Ibid; Brewer, *The Sinews of Power,* 151–53.

Chapter 10. Revolutionary Reverberations

1. J. G. A. Pocock, "Standing Army and Public Credit: The Institutions of Leviathan," in Dale Hoak and Mordechai Feingold, eds., *The World of William and Mary* (Stanford: Stanford University Press, 1996), 88–89.

2. James Edward's older son, Charles Edward, lived until 1788, but left no legitimate heirs. His second son, Henry, Cardinal of York, lived until 1807, but again there were, unsurprisingly given his vocation, no legitimate heirs.

3. J. G. A. Pocock, "The Fourth English Civil War: Dissolution, Desertion, and Alternative Histories in the Glorious Revolution," in Lois Schwoerer, ed., *The Revolution of 1688–1689: Changing Perspectives* (Cambridge: Cambridge University Press, 1992), 61.

4. Stephen Baxter, *William III and the Defense of European Liberty 1650–1702* (New York: Harcourt Brace, 1966), 336–37.

5. Ibid., 359–64.

6.　Ibid., 386–87.

7.　Ibid., 395–98; Winston Churchill, *Marlborough His Life and Times,* vol. 1 (London: Harrap, 1937), 487–990; vol. 2, pp. 24–872.

8.　Linda Colley, *In Defiance of Oligarchy: The Tory Party 1714–60* (Cambridge: Cambridge University Press, 1982), 17.

9.　J. C. D. Clark, *Samuel Johnson: Literature, Religion and English Cultural Politics from the Restoration to Romanticism* (Cambridge: Cambridge University Press, 1994), 168–76.

10.　Paul Rahe, *Republics Ancient and Modern: Classical Republicanism and the American Revolution* (Chapel Hill: University of North Carolina Press, 1990), 523–24.

11.　As is still the case between when the prime minister advises the queen to dissolve Parliament at the beginning of the six-week official campaign period in Britain; MPs are no longer MPs, but simply the "Labour candidate" or "Conservative candidate," as they are careful to introduce themselves while campaigning. Members of the House of Lords remain lords, and ministers remain in office, but the House of Commons ceases to exist.

12.　W. A. Speck, *Reluctant Revolutionaries: Englishmen and the Revolution of 1688* (Oxford: Oxford University Press, 1989), 162: "What was defeated in both countries [the Dutch Republic and England] was an apparently more modern and efficient system of government, based on a professional bureaucracy, centralization and the subordination of all classes to the sovereign. Instead anomalies were perpetuated; municipal and provincial autonomy, representative institutions that were used by sectional interests and foreign powers for their own purposes. In the localities and at the centre, government was directed by amateurs, although governmental functions were becoming more complex and onerous. The experts were used as subordinates. They functioned under the amateurs, who retained overall control, whereas in France, Scandinavia and the Empire the trend was in the opposite direction. In the seventeenth-century United Provinces, as in eighteenth-century England, an army could not be dispensed with, but it was feared as a possible political menace and was often deliberately allowed to run down for this reason. Foreign policy became subject to a constant tug of war between those who believed it should concentrate on furthering economic interests and those (Frederick Henry, William II, William III, George I and George II) who were suspected of trying to follow an unnecessarily aggressive and essentially personal or dynastic policy." See also J. R. Jones, *The Revolution of 1688 in England* (New York: Norton, 1972), 16–17.

13.　Western, *Monarchy and Revolution,* 3.

14.　Stephen Saunders Webb, *1676: The End of American Independence* (New York: Knopf, 1984), 413–16.

15.　Webb, *1676,* 414: "The institutional expressions of political revolution and American independence in 1676 — the association of taxation with representation; the introduction of general elections and popular participation at every level of the extant government; revolutionary rule by committees . . .

and its legacy to the American Revolution of 1776." J. H. Elliott, *Empires of the Atlantic World: Britain and Spain in America, 1492–1830* (New Haven: Yale University Press, 2006), 375, 387, 398, 407, 411.

16. Bernard Bailyn, *The Ideological Origins of the American Revolution* (Cambridge: Harvard University Press, 1967), 52.

17. Ibid., 200–201.

18. Ibid., 81.

19. Ibid., 123.

20. Bernard Bailyn, *Faces of Revolution: Personalities and Themes in the Struggle for American Independence* (New York: Knopf, 1990), 129.

21. Bailyn, *Ideological Origins*, 105–6.

22. Ibid., 204.

23. Joyce Malcolm, *To Keep and Bear Arms* (Cambridge: Harvard University Press, 1994).

24. Dale Hoak, "The Anglo-Dutch Revolution of 1688–89," in Dale Hoak and Mordechai Feingold, eds., *The World of William and Mary* (Stanford: Stanford University Press, 1996), 3: "The first ten amendments to the Constitution — that inventive distillate of Lockean natural-right theory and traditions of common law — bear the direct impact of Mason's Declaration of Rights of 1776, a document carrying over verbatim sections of the English Bill of Rights."

25. Speck, *Reluctant Revolutionaries*, 164–65.

26. William Langer, *An Encyclopedia of World History* (Boston: Houghton Mifflin, 1952), 432, 434.

27. Diarmaid MacCulloch, *The Reformation* (New York: Penguin, 2005), 532–33.

28. Walter McDougall, *Freedom Just Around the Corner: A New American History, 1585–1828* (New York: HarperCollins, 2004), 323–25.

29. Richard Hofstadter, *America at 1750: A Social Portrait* (New York: Random House Vintage, 1973), 198–204; Bailyn, *Faces of the Revolution*, 182–83.

30. P. G. M. Dickson, *The Financial Revolution in England: A Study in the Development of Public Credit 1688–1756* (Aldershot: Gregg Revivals, 1993), 7.

31. John Brewer, *The Sinews of Power: War, Money and the English State, 1688–1783* (New York: Knopf, 1989), 27; Niall Ferguson, *The Cash Nexus: Money and Power in the Modern World 1700–2000* (London: Penguin, 2001), 17. Rahe, *Republics Ancient and Modern*, 521–22.

32. J. H. Plumb, *The Growth of Political Stability in England 1675–1735* (London: Penguin, 1969), 152.

33. P. G. M. Dickson, *The Financial Revolution in England: A Study in the Development of Public Credit* (London: Macmillan, 1967)

34. Ibid., xxii.

35. Ibid., 7–12.

36. Ibid., 11–12.

37. Roy Porter, *English Society in the Eighteenth Century* (London: Penguin, 1990), 186.

38. Linda Colley, *Britons*, 70.

39. Ron Chernow, *Alexander Hamilton* (New York: Penguin, 2004), 295–306, 319–31, 344–55.

40. John Morrill, "The Sensible Revolution," in Jonathan Israel, ed., *The Anglo-Dutch Moment* (Cambridge: Cambridge University Press, 2003), 100.

41. John C. Rule, "France Caught Between Two Balances: The Dilemma of 1688," in Lois Schwoerer, ed., *The Revolution of 1688–1689: Changing Perspectives* (Cambridge: Cambridge University Press, 1992), 38.

42. Ibid., 50–51.

43. Churchill, *Marlborough*, vol. 1, pp. 424–990; vol. 2, pp. 1–938.

44. Fred Anderson, *Crucible of War: The Seven Years' War and the Fate of the British Empire in North America, 1754–1766* (New York: Knopf, 2000).

45. Henry Kissinger, *Diplomacy* (New York: Simon & Schuster, 1994), 56–77.

46. Ibid., 96–97.

47. Ibid., 154–56.

48. Andrew Roberts, *Salisbury: Victorian Titan* (London: Weidenfeld & Nicolson, 1999).

49. J. G. A. Pocock, " 'Wicked and Turbulent Though It Was': The Restoration Era in Perspective," in Howard Nenner, ed., *Politics and the Political Imagination in Later Stuart Britain: Essays Presented to Lois Green Schwoerer* (Rochester, NY: University of Rochester Press, 1997), 11.

50. J. G. A. Pocock, *Virtue, Commerce, and History* (Cambridge: Cambridge University Press, 1985), 230; Pocock, "Standing Army and Public Credit," 88–89.

51. Ibid., 283, n. 3, citing *Eluggero Pii, Immagini dell'Inghilterra politica nella cultura del primo settecento* (Florence, 1984), 31.

52. Churchill, *Marlborough*, vol. 1, p. 301.

Acknowledgments

In 1985 or 1986, I set about writing a narrative history of American politics from 1930 to 1988. Since I had never written a narrative book before, I decided to read some of the great narrative history. I splurged and paid $125 for a five-volume set of Thomas Babington Macaulay's *The History of England from the Accession of James II*, published in New York in 1849. In long winter evenings I pored through Macaulay's lush prose. I had trouble keeping all the characters straight; Macaulay assumed that his readers would begin his volume with a detailed knowledge of the period, which I lacked. I have been interested in the Revolution of 1688–89 ever since. In 1989, in my first year at *U.S. News & World Report*, when the magazine was running a several-page story on the 200th anniversary of the French Revolution, I volunteered to write a one-page addendum on the 300th anniversary of the Glorious Revolution. In response I got a note of thanks from my friend Daniel Patrick Moynihan. His encouragement helped keep the Revolution of 1688–89 in my mind and inspired me to read more about it over the years. My appetite was particularly whetted by Mark Kishlansky's fine narrative *A Monarchy Transformed: Britain 1603–1714*. And so in 2004, when I decided I wanted my next book to reach farther back in history, I decided to go back three centuries and write what has become this book.

And to make it a book for readers who, as I quickly discovered when I mentioned the subject to friends and relatives, have almost no idea what the Revolution of 1688–89 was or how much difference it has made to the world. Even former history majors had to be reminded that it involved the ouster of King James II and the installation of King William III and Queen Mary II, and that it turned out to be a significant step forward for representative government, guaranteed liberties, global competition, and a foreign policy of opposing hegemonic tyrannies.

I am grateful for the encouragement and assistance of my agents, Lynn Chu and Glen Hartley, and of my editors at Crown, Jed Donahue and Mary Choteborsky. I am also grateful for the forebearance of my editors at *U.S. News & World Report,* especially Brian Duffy and Brian Kelly. I benefited from initial guidance from Timothy Dickinson and from Paul Rahe of the University of Tulsa, the latter of whom was kind enough to read the first draft of the manuscript and to make valuable suggestions. I benefited as well from reading widely in the works of both professional historians and of some amateurs who have added to the knowledge of this period and these events in recent years. Of particular help were several collections of essays gathered in response to the 300th anniversary of the Revolution; many writers of history time their books for historic anniversaries, but there is something to be said for waiting a decade or so and then profiting from the work of others.

I should add that most of these works, much like Macaulay's, contemplate that the reader will be British and will come to the work with a considerable knowledge of the subject already; many are clearly written for professional historians specializing in the period. I have assumed that an American reader will come to the book with almost no knowledge of the period, but may be curious to learn more about a series of events, some of them very improbable indeed, which did so much to shape the future of Britain and of America and the world as well. The Revolution of 1688–89 — our first revolution, as I have called it — shaped the polity in which our Founders made their Revolution and established the United States. Many Americans in recent years have been reading the splendid volumes on our Founders written by both academic and popular historians. This book is an attempt to introduce them to the men — and women — who created the framework in which the Founders lived and did their work.

Index

About the Author

MICHAEL BARONE is a Senior Writer at *U.S. News & World Report* and is a contributor to Fox News Channel. He is the principal coauthor of *The Almanac of American Politics,* published every two years since 1971. He is also the author of *Our Country: The Shaping of America from Roosevelt to Reagan* (1990), *The New Americans: How the Melting Pot Can Work Again* (2001), and *Hard America, Soft America: Competition and the Battle for America's Future* (2004). He grew up in Detroit and Birmingham, Michigan, and is a graduate of Harvard College and Yale Law School. He lives in Washington, D.C.

Also by Michael Barone

A Tale of Two Americas

In this groundbreaking book, Michael Barone reveals how the divide between "Hard America"—defined by competition and accountability—and "Soft America"—in which no one loses and everyone gets a gold star—explains the state of our society from our economy to our schools to the military to the government and beyond.

HARD AMERICA, SOFT AMERICA
Competition vs. Coddling and the Battle for the Nation's Future
$12.00 paper (Canada: $17.00)
978-1-4000-5324-7